Illustrations
for Biblical Preaching

Illustrations for Biblical Preaching

Edited by
Michael P. Green

Foreword by
Haddon W. Robinson

BAKER BOOK HOUSE

Grand Rapids, Michigan 49516

Library of Congress Cataloging-in-Publication Data

Illustrations for Biblical preaching.

    Rev. ed. of: The expositor's illustration
file and index to the revised edition.
      includes index.
      1. Homiletical illustrations.   I. Green,
Michael P.   II. Expositor's illustration
file and index to the revised edition.
BV4225.2.I44   1989   251'.08   88-35077
ISBN 0-8010-3819-7

Contents

5

Foreword

It's a dangerous mission to preach to a king. It's even more dangerous to preach to a king nursing a guilty conscience. It is most dangerous to preach to a king with a guilty conscience who has already murdered a man as a cover-up for his sin. When Nathan, a prophet, confronted David, his king, about adultery, he thought about the dynamics of the situation—and he told David a story. Actually, the story itself was the sermon. Like the sword in the umbrella, it had a sharp point. And David, with all his defenses up, could not avoid its penetration.

When preachers stand up in the pulpit, they face audiences with their guard up. A few in the congregation wait eagerly for the sermon to begin. Most wait eagerly for the sermon to conclude. Like Nathan before them, the preachers have to smash through barricades erected by indifference, confusion, comfort and guilt. Preachers must turn ears into eyes and free listeners to think with pictures in their heads.

Appropriate illustrations do that. They do everything a sermon must do to communicate—explain, prove or apply a truth. Effective preachers stalk and store illustrations to tell the truth in fresh ways.

The anecdotes, quotes, poems and observations in this book are the best on the market today. I recommend them highly to students at Denver Seminary, and I am delighted to endorse them to biblical preachers who know the power of the phrase "let me illustrate."

Haddon W. Robinson
President, Denver Seminary

Preface

When Henry Ford first began the mass marketing of his famous Model A automobiles, they were well known for coming in any color you wanted—so long as it was black. Of course, we all know that any automobile manufacturer who offered cars only in black today would be out of business by tomorrow. Color does not make for a better designed or more reliable car, but it does make for a more interesting one. Good biblical preaching or teaching is built on God's Word. Sermon illustrations are like color on a car. Although they are no substitute for careful study and exposition of the text, they do make its presentation more interesting. In addition, like a flashing red light in your rear-view mirror, they can arrest attention. And they can ignite a response as quickly as a lightning bolt in a drought-stricken land. Such, I hope, are the illustrations in this volume. They have been carefully selected, developed, and edited for use by pastors, para-church workers, Bible-study leaders, and others who preach or teach the Word of God.

Acknowledgments

From thousands of illustrations submitted to the Pastoral Ministries Department of Dallas Theological Seminary by aspiring preachers was drawn much of the raw material from which this collection of illustrations has been fashioned. Although their work has been extensively revised, edited, and supplemented, it is with gratefulness that we acknowledge the work of hundreds of students and their professors, especially Dr. Haddon W. Robinson, Dr. Duane Litfin, and Dr. John Reed.

Many of the illustrations contained herein were first published in a card-file format as The Expositor's Illustration File in 1982 and in a revised edition published in 1985. The current work is a major revision of the 1985 edition.

Where the original source for an illustration could be determined with reasonable certainty, credit is given. Sermon illustrations are most remarkable creatures that pop up time and time again in numerous variant forms over generations of preachers. To those whose work has not been properly credited, forgiveness is requested.

Finally, acknowledgment must be given to our Lord and Savior and to those in his church who repeatedly encouraged me to persevere in the development of this resource book. Our desire is that it may be a useful tool for those servants of Christ who labor to teach others the Word of God so that they may love him and keep his commandments.

PART ONE

Topical Illustrations

Abiding

One year the peaches were especially abundant. The fruit was big and juicy, and it was one of the best crops in memory. While harvesting the crop, a picker noticed a limb that had fallen from a tree. Its fruit was rotten and shriveled. Because the limb was detached from the tree, it was no longer producing the good fruit that it should. The same is true of the Christian who ceases to abide in Christ—he ceases to produce good fruit.[1]

Abortion

In 1944, a forty-one-year-old woman sought an abortion from her doctor. He firmly refused, asserting that abortion was just not right, morally, ethically, or legally. The woman later gave birth to a baby boy and named him James Robison. This unwanted child grew up to become a well-known evangelist. God has a plan for every human life, even those who are not wanted.[2]

Ballad of the Unborn

My shining feet will never run on early morning lawn;
   my feet were crushed before they had a chance to greet the dawn.
My fingers now will never stretch to touch the winning tape;
   my race was done before I learned the smallest steps to take.
My growing height will never be recorded on the wall;
   my growth was stopped when I was still unseen, and very small.
My lips and tongue will never taste the good fruits of the earth;
   for I myself was judged to be a fruit of little worth.
My eyes will never scan the sky for my high-flying kite;
   for when still blind, destroyed were they in the black womb of night.
I'll never stand upon a hill, Spring's winds in my hair;
   aborted winds of thought closed in on Motherhood's despair.
I'll never walk the shores of life or know the tides of time;

for I was coming but unloved, and that my only crime.
Nameless am I, a grain of sand, one of the countless dead;
but the deed that made me ashen grey floats on seas of red.

Fay Clayton[3]

Accidents

When a cowboy applied for health insurance, the agent routinely asked if he had had any accidents during the previous year. The cowboy replied, "No. But I was bitten by a rattlesnake, and a horse kicked me in the ribs. That laid me up for a while." The agent said, "Weren't those accidents?" "No," replied the cowboy, "They did it on purpose."

The cowboy realized that there are no such things as "accidents." How much more so should the Christian who understands the sovereignty of God have the same attitude.[4]

Adoption

A new mother stayed with her parents for several days after the birth of her first child. One afternoon she remarked to her mother that it was surprising the baby had dark hair, since both her husband and she were fair. The grandmother said, "Well, your daddy has black hair." To which the daughter replied, "But, Mama, that doesn't matter, because I'm adopted." With an embarrassed smile, that mother said the most wonderful words her daughter had ever heard: "I always forget."

All Christians are adopted children of God who are accepted by God with the same unconditional love that this mother had for her daughter.[5]

In 1952 a probation officer in New York City tried to find an organization that would assist in the adoption of a twelve-year-old boy. Although the child had a religious background, none of the major denominations would assist in his adoption. Said the officer later, "His case had been reported to me because he had been truant. I tried for a year to find an agency that would care for this needy youngster. Neither Catholic, Protestant, nor Jewish institutions would take him because he came from a denomination they did not recognize. I could do nothing constructive for him."

If the principles of Christian love had prevailed in the Bronx in 1952, perhaps a good home could have been found for that young, mixed-up lad. In fact, providing a better environment in which to grow up might have changed history. For, you see, the boy was Lee Harvey Oswald.[6]

Adultery

Returning from Sunday school, where the Ten Commandments had been the topic of the day, a young boy asked his father, "Daddy, what does it mean when it says, 'Thou shalt not commit agriculture'?" There was hardly a beat between the question and the father's reply: "Son, that just means that you're not supposed to plow the other man's field," an answer satisfactory to both of them.[7]

Adversity

In his book *Mere Christianity*, C. S. Lewis likened God's use of adversity to walking a dog. If the dog gets its leash wrapped around a pole and tries to continue running forward, he will only tighten the leash more. Both the dog and the owner are after the same end, forward motion, but the owner must resist the dog by pulling him opposite the direction he wants to go. The master, sharing the same intention, but understanding better than the dog where he really wants to go, takes an action precisely opposite to that of the dog's will. It is in this way that God uses adversity.[8]

Advice

"A wise man seeks much counsel . . . a fool listens to all of it" (Larry Burkett).[9]

A man was on the practice golf course when the club pro brought another man out for a lesson. The pro watched the fellow swing several times and started making suggestions for improvement, but each time the pupil interrupted with his own version of what was wrong and how to correct it. After a few minutes of this interference, the pro began nodding his head in agreement. At the end of the lesson, the student paid the pro, congratulated him on his expertise as a teacher, and left in an obviously pleased frame of mind.

The observer was so astonished by the performance that he asked,

"Why did you go along with him?" "Son," the old pro said with a grin, as he carefully pocketed his fee, "I learned long ago that it's a waste of time to sell answers to a man who wants to buy echoes."[10]

Affection, Child's Need of

Salimbene, a thirteenth-century historian, wrote this about the attempt of King Frederick II to raise children without maternal affection: "He wanted to find out what kind of speech children would have when they grew up if they spoke to no one beforehand. So he bade foster mothers and nurses to suckle the children, to bathe and wash them but in no way to prattle with them, or to speak to them, for he wanted to learn whether they would speak the Hebrew language, which was the oldest, or Greek, or Latin, or Arabic, or perhaps the language of their parents, of whom they had been born. But he labored in vain, because the children all died. For they could not live without the petting and joyful faces and loving words of their foster mothers." (Cited in Gary Collins, *Fractured Personalities*, [Carol Stream, Ill.: Creation House] pp. 35–36.)

Age

Esteem age and you will always have life to look forward to. Esteem youth and you proclaim your own obsolescence.[12]

Agnosticism

G. K. Chesterton once said that it is often supposed that when people stop believing in God, they believe in nothing. Alas, it is worse than that. When they stop believing in God, they believe in *anything*.[13]

Angels

The Rev. John G. Paton, a missionary in the New Hebrides Islands, told a story involving the protective care of angels. Hostile natives surrounded his mission headquarters one night, intent on burning out the Patons and killing them. John Paton and his wife prayed all during that terror-filled night that God would deliver them. When daylight came they were amazed to see the attackers unaccountably leave.

A year later, the chief of the tribe was converted to Christ, and Paton, remembering what had happened, asked the chief what had kept him and his men from burning down the house and killing them. The chief replied in surprise, "Who were all those men you had there with you?" The missionary answered, "There were no men there; just my wife and I." The chief argued that they had seen many men standing guard—hundreds of big men in shining garments with drawn swords in their hands. They seemed to circle the mission station, so the natives were afraid to attack. Only then did the Rev. Paton realize that God had sent his angels to protect them (cited in Billy Graham, *Angels: God's Secret Agents* [Waco, Texas: Word Books, 1986] p. 3).[14]

Anger   5|16|93

A boy once asked, "Dad, how do wars begin?"

"Well, take the First World War," said his father. "That got started when Germany invaded Belgium."

Immediately his wife interrupted him: "Tell the boy the truth. It began because somebody was murdered." The husband drew himself up with an air of superiority and snapped back, "Are *you* answering the question, or am I?" Turning her back upon him in a huff, the wife walked out of the room and slammed the door as hard as she could.

When the dishes stopped rattling in the cupboard, an uneasy silence followed, broken at length by the son when he said, "Daddy, you don't have to tell me any more; I know now!"[15]

"As long as anger lives, she continues to be the fruitful mother of many unhappy children" (St. John Climacus, *Climax*).[16]

Anger, Effect of

"When I repress my emotions, my stomach keeps score" (John Powell).[17]

"Of the seven deadly sins, anger is possibly the most fun. To lick your wounds, to smack your lips over grievances long past, to roll over your tongue the prospect of bitter confrontations still to come, to savor to the last toothsome morsel both the pain you are given and the pain you are giving back; in many ways it is a feast fit for a king. The chief drawback is that what you are wolfing down is yourself. The skeleton at the feast is you" (Frederick Buechner, *Wishful Thinking: A Theological ABC* [New York: Harper & Row, 1973]).[18]

19

Anger is often more harmful than the injury that caused it. The story is told of the time when Leonardo da Vinci was working on his painting "The Last Supper" and became angry with a certain man. Losing his temper, he lashed the other fellow with bitter words. Returning to his canvas, Leonardo attempted to work on the face of Jesus but was so upset he could not compose himself for the painstaking work. Finally he put down his tools and sought out the subject of his wrath and asked his forgiveness. The man accepted his apology and Leonardo was able to return to his workshop and finish painting the face of Jesus.[19]

Anger, Righteous

"A man that does not know how to be angry does not know how to be good. A man that does not know how to be shaken to his heart's core with indignation over things evil is either a fungus or a wicked man" (H. W. Beecher).[20]

Anger, Uncontrolled

Alexander the Great was one of the few men in history who seemed to deserve his descriptive title. He was energetic, versatile, and intelligent. Although hatred was not generally part of his nature, several times in his life he was tragically defeated by anger. The story is told of one of these occasions, when a dear friend of Alexander, a general in his army, became intoxicated and began to ridicule the emperor in front of his men. Blinded by anger and quick as lightning, Alexander snatched a spear from the hand of a soldier and hurled it at his friend. Although he had only intended to scare the drunken general, his aim was true and the spear took the life of his childhood friend.

Deep remorse followed his anger. Overcome with guilt, Alexander attempted to take his own life with the same spear, but he was stopped by his men. For days he lay sick, calling for his friend and chiding himself as a murderer.

Alexander the Great conquered many cities and vanquished many countries, but he had failed miserably to control his own spirit.[21]

Anger Without Sin

Anyone can become angry. That is easy. But to be angry with the right person, to the right degree, at the right time, and in the right way—that is not easy.[22]

Antichrist

A few years ago, when inflation was overwhelming the average worker, Arthur Garcia, 43, who supported a wife and five children on a $19,000 wage as a worker in U.S. Steel's South Chicago mill said: "You really want to revolt, but what can you do? I keep waiting for a miracle—for some guy who isn't born yet—and when he comes, we'll follow him like he was John the Baptist" (From "Inflation: Who Is Hurt Worst?" *Time*, January 15, 1979).[23]

Antinomy

J. I. Packer uses the following illustration of the antinomy of divine sovereignty and human responsibility: "Modern physics faces an antinomy, in this sense, in its study of light. There is cogent evidence to show that light consists of waves, and equally cogent evidence to show that it consists of particles. It is not apparent how light can be both waves and particles, but the evidence is there, and so neither view can be ruled out in favor of the other. Neither, however, can be reduced to the other or explained in terms of the other; the two seemingly incompatible positions must be held together, and both must be treated as true. Such a necessity scandalizes our tidy minds, no doubt, but there is no help for it if we are to be loyal to the facts" (J. I. Packer, *Evangelism and the Sovereignty of God* [Downers Grove, Ill.: Inter-Varsity, 1961] p. 19).[24]

Anxiety

Victor Hugo said, "Have courage for the great sorrows of life and patience for the small ones. And when you have finished your daily task, go to sleep in peace. God is awake!"[25]

A doctor had to give a painful shot to a four-year-old girl. When she learned what the doctor was about to do, her face showed her anxiety and her body tensed. As the doctor picked up what looked to the little girl to be a needle large enough to kill an elephant, she turned her eyes to her father, who then took her hand and fixed his eyes on hers. An expression of confidence and calmness came on her face. She knew she was not alone and found comfort, not in her father's spoken answer, but in his presence with her in her time of trial.[26]

Apathy Toward Evangelism

One Sunday, a minister began his sermon in this way: "I'd like to make three points today. First, there are millions of people around the world who are going to hell. Second, most of us sitting here today do not give a damn about it." After a lengthy pause he continued: "My third point is that you are more concerned that I, your pastor, said the word *damn* than you are about the millions of people going to hell."[27]

Apathy Toward God

I looked upon a farm one day,
   that once I used to own;
   the barn had fallen to the ground,
   the fields were overgrown.
The house in which my children grew,
   where we had lived for years . . .
   I turned to see it broken down,
   and brushed aside the tears.
I looked upon my soul one day to find it too had grown,
   with thorns and nettles everywhere,
   the seeds neglect had sown.
The years had passed
   while I had cared for things of lesser worth.

The things of heaven I let go
   while minding things of earth.
To Christ I turned with bitter tears and cried,
   "O Lord, forgive!"
I have not much time left for Thee,
   not many years to live.
The wasted years forever gone,
   the days I can't recall.
If I could live those days again,
   I'd make Him Lord of all.[28]

Apologetics, Limits of

Voltaire is reported to have said, "If a miracle occurred in the market place of Paris and in the presence of two thousand men, I would rather disbelieve my own eyes than the two thousand."

Facts alone, irrespective of how well they are presented, will never bring a man to Christ.[29]

Apology

Do you know what is the best way to have the last word in an argument?
Apologize![30]

Apostasy

You can tell the sheep are in trouble when the shepherd starts speaking kindly of the wolf![31]

There was a pastor of a very well-known Bible church, one that taught the Word of God. Today he is a denier of the deity of Jesus Christ. He is a professor at USC, one who does everything he can to turn young people away from Christianity. He also falls into the category of an apostate, somebody who knows the truth, has all the information about the truth, and willfully turns his back on the truth for his own pursuit. (Cited by John MacArthur, *Sermon on Jude 8–13*).[32]

Apostasy, Development of

A story is told of a man who, resisting the cost of oats he fed his mule, decided to gradually substitute sawdust in its diet. Everything went fine for a while—but by the time the mule was satisfied with sawdust, he died.
The same is true spiritually. The changeover from truth to error is sometimes a slow process, and the people don't always know the difference. But, before you know it, they are dead.[33]

Apostate

One writer said of apostates, "One is reminded by way of contrast with the Lord, whom these men deny. He is the rock of our salvation; they are hidden rocks, threatening shipwreck to the faith. He comes with clouds to refresh his people forever; they are clouds that do not even bring temporary blessing. He is the tree of life; they are trees dead. He leads beside still waters; they are like the restless troubled sea. He is the bright and morning star heralding the coming day; they are wandering stars presaging a night of eternal darkness."[34]

23

Appearances

In the opening scenes of the musical *Camelot*, we see King Arthur standing in a field dressed in the clothes of a common peasant. To look at him you would have no idea he was king. In fact, when Guinevere first met Arthur, she didn't have a clue that he was king over all Camelot. Arthur was, in fact, king, but his outward appearance gave no evidence of this fact.[35]

Approval

A young man once studied violin under a world-renowned master. Eventually the time came for the student's first recital. Following each selection, despite the cheers of the crowd, the performer seemed dissatisfied. Even after the last number, with the shouts louder than ever, the talented violinist stood watching an old man in the balcony. Finally the elderly one smiled and nodded in approval. Immediately the young man relaxed and beamed with happiness. You see, the man in the balcony was his teacher, and thus the applause of the crowd had meant nothing to him until he had first won the hearty approval of his master.[36]

Astrology, Refutation of

Martin Luther said to P. Melanchthon, when the latter showed him the nativity of Cicero from the stars: "Esau and Jacob were born of the same father and mother, at the same time, and under the same planets, but their nature was wholly different. You would persuade me that astrology is a true science!" (Cited by Schaff, *History of the Christian Church* [Grand Rapids: Wm. Eerdmans, 1960], vol. 6, p. 470.)[37]

Atheism

God has clearly revealed his existence to men. Suppose a student were to write on a physics exam that he did not believe in atoms because he could not see them. Would not the professor be justified in failing him? The existence of atoms is clearly undeniable on the basis of their recognized effects. Everyone familiar with Hiroshima knows that atoms exist; they are known from their effect. Likewise, men are responsible to acknowledge God and his eternal power by the effects that are clearly revealed in the Creation.[38]

At the end of the Bob Harrington/Madalyn O'Hair debates, the *Wittenburg Door* interviewed them both. After summing up what she had to say about Harrington, O'Hair summed up what she believed about Christianity: "Christianity is intolerant, anti-democratic, anti-sexual, and anti-life. It is anti-woman, and I cannot stand that. It is anti-everything that is good and human and decent and kind and love-filled and understanding. I used to have an intellectual hatred for Christianity. I think that is broadening now. I am 'enjoying' hating the whole thing."[39]

"If I thought there was an omnipotent God who looked down on battles and deaths and all the waste and horror of this war—able to prevent these things—doing them to amuse Himself, I would spit in His empty face" (H. G. Wells, *Mr. Britling Sees It Through*, 1916 [Salem, N.H.: Merrimack Pub. Cir., 1985 repr.]).[40]

Atheism, Dilemma of

The atheist's dilemma is that when he feels very grateful and wants to give thanks, he has no one to give it to.[41]

Atheism, Response to

The best reply to an atheist is to give him a good dinner and ask him if he believes there is a chef who prepared it.[42]

Atheism's Oversimplification

". . . atheism turns out to be too simple. If the whole universe has no meaning, we should have never found out that it has no meaning: Just as, if there were no light in the universe and therefore no creatures with eyes, we should never know it was dark. 'Dark' would be without meaning" (C. S. Lewis, *Mere Christianity* [New York: Macmillan, 1986], p. 46).[43]

Atonement, Extent of

To say that Christ redeemed men at the cross but did not also purchase for them the ability to believe would be like a man promising to give a thousand dollars to a blind man upon condition that he will open his eyes and see—which he knows full well the blind man cannot do.[44]

Atonement, Governmental View of

In a certain community in England, someone had been stealing sheep. The forces of the law were unable to apprehend the thief. A certain farmer was brought before the judge and accused of being the thief, but he established his innocence of any connection with the offense, beyond the shadow of a doubt. Thereupon the judge said, "You are an innocent man, but someone has been stealing sheep. I must show to this community what the law would do to a sheep thief." Then the judge committed the innocent man to a period of incarceration, "to uphold public justice." But what justice! (Cited by James O. Buswell, *Systematic Theology of the Christian Religion* [Grand Rapids: Zondervan, 1963].)[45]

Authority

The captain on the bridge of a large naval vessel saw a light ahead on a collision course. He signaled, "Alter your course ten degrees south." The reply came back, "Alter your course ten degrees north."

The captain then signaled, "Alter your course ten degrees south. I am a captain." The reply: "Alter your course 10 degrees north. I am a seaman third-class."

The furious captain signaled, "Alter your course ten degrees south. I am a battleship." The reply: "Alter your course ten degrees north. I am a lighthouse."[46]

Authority, Submission to

A little boy finally sat down after first resisting his parents' command to do so. He said to his parents, "I'm sitting down on the outside, but I'm standing up on the inside."[47]

Bachelorhood

Mr. Justice McCardie of the British High Court (himself a bachelor) said, "A bachelor is a man who looks before he leaps and, having looked, he does not leap."[48]

Baptism

A minister was seeking to explain the significance of baptism to a new convert. He was gesturing as he talked and noticed that as he was using his hand its shadow fell on the ground. So he said to the convert,

"Do you see the shadow of my hand on the sand? Now this is just a shadow. The hand is the real thing. And when you came to Jesus, when you believed in Jesus, that was the real baptism. You were joined to him, and what happened to him also happened to you. Jesus was alive, then he died and was buried, and then he rose from the dead. That is what happened to you when you believed in him." He pointed to the shadow on the sand and said, "When you go down in the water and are raised up again, that is a picture of what has already happened." Water baptism is a picture, a symbol to teach us what happened to us when we believed in the Lord Jesus.[49]

Baptism is like a wedding ring: they both symbolize transactions. A wedding ring symbolizes marriage, just as baptism symbolizes salvation. Wearing a wedding ring does not make you married any more than being baptized makes you saved. To extend the parallel, if a person, especially a woman, does not wear a wedding ring you can almost always assume that the person is not married.

So it was in New Testament times. If a person was not baptized, you could probably assume that he or she was not a believer. On this we must be clear: baptism is a symbol of salvation and *only* a symbol. But, like a wedding ring, it is such an effective symbol that it should never be taken for granted.[50]

Bible

In the midst of the enlightenment, when deism was spreading rapidly, Voltaire proclaimed that within twenty-five years the Bible would be forgotten and Christianity would be a thing of the past. Forty years after his death in 1778, the Bible and other Christian literature were being printed in what had once been Voltaire's very own home![51]

Bible, Application of

There is a story of a frontier settlement in the West whose people were engaged in the lumbering business. The town wanted a church, so they built one and called a minister. The preacher was well received until one day he happened to see some of his parishioners clawing onto the bank some logs that had been floating down the river from another village upstream. Each log was marked with the owner's stamp on one end. To his great distress the pastor saw his members pulling in the logs and sawing off the end where the telltale stamp appeared.

The next Sunday he prepared a forceful sermon on the text "Thou shalt not steal." At the close of the service, his people lined up and congratulated him: "Wonderful message, mighty fine preaching." However, as the preacher watched the river that week he saw his parishioners continuing to steal logs. This bothered him a great deal. So he went home and worked on a sermon for the following week. The topic was "Thou shalt not cut off the end of thy neighbor's logs." When he got through, the church membership ran him out of town.[51]

The hardest person to put under the correction of God's Word is yourself.[52]

Bible, Authority of

Trying to destroy or defend the Word of God is like having two men push with toothpicks on opposite sides of the Rock of Gibraltar. While one is trying to push it over with his toothpick, the other is trying to hold it up with his. The rock is going to stay firm regardless of what either man does![53]

The authority of Scripture is so rooted in and closely linked to the authority of Jesus Christ that the two are indivisible. To attempt to distinguish them is like asking which blade of a pair of scissors is more important, or which leg of a pair of pants is more necessary. We know Christ through the Bible, and we understand the Bible through the knowledge of Christ and the Spirit he sent.[54]

Bible, Context in

There is a story of two lawyers on opposing sides of a case. During the trial, one thought he would make a great impression on the jury by quoting from the Bible. So he said, concerning his opponent's client, "We have it on the highest authority that 'All that a man has will he give for his skin.' "

The other lawyer knew the Bible better. He said, "I am very much impressed by the fact that my distinguished colleague here regards as the highest authority the one who said, 'All that a man has will he give for his skin.' You will find that this saying comes from the Book of Job and the one who utters it is the devil. And that is who he regards as the highest authority!"[55]

On a Christmas card the following verse was cited: "They exchanged gifts and made merry... (Rev. 11:10)." The context of the verse, which describes anything but what it appeared to mean on the Christmas greeting, is rejoicing over the death of God's two witnesses at the hand of the beast.[56]

Bible, Effect of Reading

A young believer was discouraged in his attempts to read and remember the Bible. He said, "It's no use. No matter how much I read, I always forget what I have just read."

A wise pastor replied "Take heart. When you pour water over a sieve, no matter how much you pour, you don't collect much. But at least you end up with a clean sieve."[57]

Some seem to expect the Word of God to hit them like a jolt of adrenaline each time they read or study it. Although the "jolt" may hit us periodically, the benefits of the Word of God act more like vitamins. People who regularly take vitamins do so because of their long-term benefits, not because every time they swallow one of the pills, they feel new strength surging through their bodies. They have developed a habit of consistently taking vitamins because they have been told that, in the long haul, vitamin supplements are going to have a beneficial effect on their physical health, resistance to disease, and general well-being.

The same is true of reading the Bible. At times it will have a sudden and intense impact on us. However, the real value lies in the cumulative effects that long-term exposure to God's Word will bring to our lives.[58]

The story has been told of a South Sea Islander who proudly displayed his Bible to a G.I. during World War II. "We've outgrown that sort of thing," the soldier said. The native smiled back, "It's a good thing *we* haven't. If it weren't for this book, you'd have been a meal by now!"[59]

According to C. H. Spurgeon, "A Bible which is falling apart usually belongs to someone who isn't!" The key to victory is "It is written."[60]

Bible, Hatred of

It is told that many years ago, while on a visit to England, a wealthy businessman was fascinated by a powerful microscope. Looking through its lens to study crystals and the petals of flowers, he was amazed at their beauty and detail. He decided to purchase a microscope and take it back home. He thoroughly enjoyed using it until one day he examined some food he was planning to eat for dinner. Much to his dismay, he discovered that tiny living creatures were crawling in it. Since he was especially fond of this particular food, he wondered what to do. Finally, he concluded that there was only one way out of his dilemma—he would destroy the instrument that caused him to discover the distasteful fact. So he smashed the microscope to pieces!

"How foolish!" you say. But many people do the same thing with the Word of God. They hate it and would like to get rid of it because it reveals their evil nature.[61]

Bible, Knowledge of

There is a story about a New England teacher who quizzed a group of college-bound high-school juniors and seniors on the Bible. The quiz preceded a "Bible as Literature" class he planned to teach at Newton High School in Massachusetts, generally considered one of the better public schools in the nation. Among the most unusual answers from his students were: "Sodom and Gomorrah were lovers" and "Jezebel was Ahab's donkey."

Other students thought that the four horsemen appeared "on the Acropolis," that the New Testament Gospels were written by Matthew, Mark, "Luther," and John, that Eve was created "from an apple," and that Jesus was "baptized by Moses." The answer that took the misinformation prize was given by a fellow who was academically in the top 5 percent of the graduating class. The question: "What was Golgotha?" The answer: "Golgotha was the name of the giant who slew the apostle David."[62]

Bible, "Problem" Passages in

Mark Twain once said: "Most people are bothered by those passages of Scripture which they cannot understand; but as for me, I have always noticed that the passages in Scripture which trouble me most are those which I do understand."[63]

Bible, Study of

Have you ever seen a straight river? Canals are straight, but all rivers seem to be crooked. We call it "meandering." Why are rivers crooked?

Because the natural tendency of a river is to take the easiest way around any obstacle. So rivers are always crooked, and they always run downhill.

Some people are like rivers. They are too lazy and immature to put forth much effort into walking with God. For them it's easier to watch T.V. than to pray and easier to read their newspaper than their Bible.[64]

The only way to keep a broken vessel full is by keeping the faucet turned on.[65]

Consider the difference between a strong and a weak cup of tea. The same ingredients—water and tea—are used for both. The difference is that the strong cup of tea results from the tea leaves' immersion in the water longer, allowing the water more time to get into the tea and the tea into the water. The longer the steeping process, the stronger the cup of tea.

In the same way, the length of time we spend in God's Word determines how deeply we get into it and it gets into us. Just like the tea, the longer we are in the Word, the "stronger" we become.[66]

The Bible is so deep that theologians can never touch the bottom, yet so shallow that babes cannot drown.[67]

There are only two ways you can study the Bible:

1. Studying it with your mind made up.
2. Studying it to let it make up your mind.[68]

There is a basic difference between an explorer and a tourist. The tourist travels quickly, stopping only to observe the highly noticeable or publicized points of interest. The explorer, on the other hand, takes his time to search out all that he can find.

Too many of us read the Bible like a tourist and then complain that our devotional times are fruitless. It is necessary that we take time to explore the Bible. Notable nooks and crannies will appear as we get beneath the surface.[69]

31

A U.S. Army officer told of the contrast in his pupils during two different eras of teaching at the artillery training school at Fort Sill, Oklahoma. In 1958–60 the attitude was so lax that the instructors had a problem getting the men to stay awake to listen. During the 1965–67 classes, however, the men, hearing the same basic lectures, were alert and took copious notes. The reason: these men knew that in less than six weeks they would be facing the enemy in Vietnam.

One reason that Bible study seems to be irrelevant to many Christians is that they have no interaction with non-Christians, no vital ministry to growing believers, and no personal and internal struggle for godliness, all of which are factors that bring the truths of the Bible to apply to life.[70]

There is a story about a teenage boy who was deeply interested in scientific subjects, especially astronomy. So his father bought him a very expensive telescope. Since the young fellow had studied the principles of optics, he found the instrument to be most intriguing. He took it apart, examined the lenses, and made detailed calculations on the distance of its point of focus. The youth became so absorbed in gaining a technical knowledge of the telescope itself that he never got around to looking at the stars. He knew a lot about that fine instrument, but he missed seeing the wonders of the heavens.

As Christians, to know all the facts and figures contained in the Bible is not the end for which God has given us this Book. The purpose is that we might see God and know him.[71]

The story is told of a small fishing village where, for many years, a flock of sea gulls fed on the scraps the fishermen left. All was fine and good for the sea gulls until eventually the fishing became poor and the villagers moved down the coast to a location where fish were plentiful. The sea gulls did not follow the fishermen and—because they had lived off the scraps of the fishermen and had never learned to feed themselves—the entire flock of birds died.

Believers who feed only on what others teach them are like these foolish sea gulls.[72]

Mortimer J. Adler, in How to Read a Book, has observed that the one time people read for all they are worth is when they are in love and are reading a love letter. They read every word three ways. They read between the lines and in the margins. They read the whole in terms of the parts, and each part in terms of the whole. They grow sensitive to context and ambiguity, to insinuation and implication. They perceive the color of words, the order of phrases, and the weight of sentences. They may even take the punctuation into account. Then, if never before or after, they read carefully and in depth.

So should believers read the "love letter" that the Eternal Lover of our souls has given to us so that we may better know him and his purposes.[73]

"Don't keep forever on the public road, going only where others have gone. Leave the beaten track occasionally and drive into the woods. You will be certain to see something you have never seen before. It will be a little thing, but do not ignore it. Follow it up, explore all around. One discovery will lead to another and, before you know it, you will have something worth thinking about" (attributed to Alexander Graham Bell).[74]

In an interview, Billy Graham was asked this question: "If you had to live your life over again, what would you do differently?"

His answer: "One of my great regrets is that I have not studied enough. I wish I had studied more and preached less. People have pressured me into speaking to groups when I should have been studying and preparing. Donald Barnhouse said that if he knew the Lord was coming in three years, he would spend two of them studying and one preaching. I'm trying to make it up" (*Christianity Today*, September 12, 1977, p. 19).[75]

A story is told of a devout father whose son was studying for the ministry. The son decided to go to Europe for an advanced degree, and the father worried that his simple faith would be spoiled by sophisticated, unbelieving professors. "Don't let them take Jonah away from you," he admonished, figuring the swallowed-by-a-great-fish story might be the first part of the Bible to go.

Two years later when the son returned, the father asked, "Do you still have Jonah in your Bible?"

The son laughed. "Jonah! That story isn't even in *your* Bible!"

The father replied, "It certainly is! What do you mean?"

Again the son laughed and insisted, "It's not in your Bible. Go ahead, show it to me."

The old man fumbled through his Bible, looking for the Book of

Jonah, but he couldn't find it. At last he checked the table of contents for the proper page. When he turned there, he discovered the three pages comprising Jonah had been carefully cut from his Bible.

"I did it before I went away," said the son. "What's the difference whether I lose the Book of Jonah through studying under non-believers or *you* lose it through neglect?"[76]

In one of his *Just-So Stories*, Rudyard Kipling pulled together all of the interrogative pronouns of the English language in a bit of poetic doggerel, and these probing pronouns will open up any subject thoroughly:

> I keep six honest serving men
> (They taught me all I knew);
> Their names are What and Why and When
> And How and Where and Who.[77]

Bible, Translation of

The story is told of four ministers discussing the pros and cons of various Bible translations and paraphrases. Eventually each stated which version, in his opinion, is the best. The first minister said he used the *King James* because the Old English style is beautiful and produces the most reverent picture of the Holy Scriptures. The second said he preferred the *New American Standard Bible* because he felt it comes nearer to the original Greek and Hebrew texts. The third minister said his favorite was the paraphrased *Living Bible* because his congregation was young, and it related to them in a practical way.

All three men waited while the fourth minister sat silently. Finally he said, "I guess when it comes to translations and paraphrased editions of the Bible, I like my Dad's translation best. He put the Word of God into practice every day. It was the most convincing translation I've ever seen."[78]

Bible, Value of

The Bible is as necessary to our safe passage through this lifetime as oxygen is to sustain life.[79]

Karen's mother was startled to find her five-year-old going through a new Bible storybook and circling the word *God* wherever it appeared on the page. Stifling her first reaction to reprimand the child for defacing a book, she quietly asked, "Why are you doing that?" Karen's matter-of-fact answer was: "So that I will know where to find God when I want him."

Wouldn't it be nice to have her confidence that all we had to do was open a storybook and find God waiting for us? The truth is, we do have such a Book—the Bible.[80]

A. C. Gabaeline rates J. N. Darby as one of the great teachers of the Word of God. Dr. Darby for many years lived among the rustic country people of Ireland—preaching the gospel to these farm families and living at their modest level.

One day an infidel who was very well-known in those times challenged Darby, saying, "You claim that all Scripture is profitable. What possible earthly value could a verse like 1 Timothy 4:13 have—'The cloke that I left at Troas with Carpus, when thou comest, bring with thee, and the books, but especially the parchments'?" To which Darby replied, "Do you know that when I left my ecclesiastical position to come here to live among these very simple persons, it was that very verse that kept me from selling my own theological library? Make no mistake about it," said Darby, "all Scripture is inspired of God and all of it is profitable!"[81]

"I believe the Bible is the best gift that God has ever given to man. All the good from the Savior of the world is communicated to us through this Book. I have been driven many times to my knees by the overwhelming conviction that I had nowhere else to go" (Attributed to Abraham Lincoln).[82]

The following lines are attributed to Martin Luther:

> The Bible is alive, it speaks to me.
> It has feet, it runs after me.
> It has hands, it lays hold of me.[83]

"When home is ruled according to God's Word, angels might be asked to stay with us, and they would not find themselves out of their element" (attributed to C. H. Spurgeon).[84]

35

John Wesley once wrote: "I am a creature of a day, passing through life as an arrow through the air. I am a spirit, coming from God, and returning to God; just hovering over the great gulf; a few months hence I am no more seen; I drop into an unchangeable eternity! I want to know one thing—the way to heaven . . . God Himself has condescended to teach the way. He hath written it down in a book. O give me that Book! At any price, give me the book of God!"[85]

Andrew Young, former U.S. Ambassador to the United Nations, urged the graduating class of the University of Maryland's Eastern Shore campus to "get a Bible" and read a chapter a day. "It won't hurt you at all," he said in his commencement address, "and it will give you more illumination and purpose in life. It's better to invest fifteen dollars in a Bible now than twenty-five dollars an hour for a psychiatrist later."[86]

Blasphemy

"Operationally, God is beginning to resemble not a ruler, but the last fading smile of a cosmic Cheshire cat," wrote Julian Huxley. He also wrote, "For my own part, the sense of spiritual relief that comes from rejecting the idea of God as a supernatural being is enormous" (*Religion Without Revelation* [Westport, Conn.: Greenwood, 1979]).[87]

Blessings

When you think about the blessings of God, remember one child's description of an elevator: "I got into this little room and the upstairs came down."[88]

Carnality, Deliverance from

The story is told of Handley Page, a pioneer in aviation, who once landed in an isolated area during his travels. Unknown to him, a rat got aboard the plane there. On the next leg of the flight, Page heard the sickening sound of gnawing. Suspecting it was a rodent, his heart began to pound as he visualized the serious damage that could be done to the fragile mechanisms that controlled his plane and the difficulty of repairs because of the lack of skilled labor and materials in the area.

What could he do? He remembered hearing that a rat cannot survive at high altitudes, so he pulled back on the stick. The airplane climbed higher and higher until Page found it difficult to breathe. He listened intently and finally sighed with relief. The gnawing had stopped. When he arrived at his destination, he found the rat lying dead behind the cockpit!

Oftentimes we, God's children, are plagued by sin that gnaws at our life simply because we are living at too low a spiritual level. To see sin defeated in our lives requires that we move up—away from the world—to a higher level where the things of this world cannot survive.[89]

Change

Mutability
We are as clouds that veil the midnight moon;
How restlessly they speed, and gleam and quiver,
Streaking the darkness radiantly!—yet soon
Night closes round, and they are lost forever:

Or like forgotten lyres, whose dissonant strings
Give various response to each varying blast,
To whose frail frame no second motion brings
One mood or modulation like the last.

We rest—A dream has power to poison sleep;
We rise—One wandering thought pollutes the day;
We feel, conceive or reason, laugh or weep;
Embrace fond woe, or cast our cares away:

It is the same!—For, be it joy or sorrow,
The path of its departure still is free:
Man's yesterday may ne'er be like his morrow;
Nought may endure but mutability.

Percy Bysshe Shelley[90]

Change, Resistance to

At one time the Duke of Cambridge is reported to have said, "Any change at any time for any reason is to be deplored." That sounds like the old saying "Come weal, come woe, my status is quo," an attitude that can be deadly in a church, when overdone.[91]

January 31, 1829

President Jackson,
The canal system of this country is being threatened by the spread of a

new form of transportation known as railroads. The federal government must preserve the canals for the following reasons.

One, if boats are supplanted by railroads, serious unemployment will result. Captains, cooks, drivers, hostlers, repairmen and lock tenders will be left without means of livelihood, not to mention the numerous farmers now employed in growing hay for horses.

Two, boat builders would suffer and towline, whip, and harness makers would be left destitute.

Three, canal boats are absolutely essential to the defense of the United States. In the event of the expected trouble with England, the Erie Canal would be the only means by which we could ever move the supplies so vital to waging modern war.

As you may well know, Mr. President, railroad carriages are pulled at the enormous speed of 15 miles per hour by engines which, in addition to endangering life and limb of passengers, roar and snort their way through the countryside, setting fire to crops, scaring the livestock and frightening women and children. The Almighty certainly never intended that people should travel at such breakneck speed.

Sincerely Yours,
Martin Van Buren
Governor of New York

Often our early resistance to change seems rather foolish when viewed from a slightly different perspective. (The letter above was cited in "No Growth," *The American Spectator*, Jan. 1984.)[92]

Character

> If we sow a thought, we reap an act;
> If we sow an act, we reap a habit;
> If we sow a habit, we reap character;
> If we sow character, we reap a destiny.[93]

A middle-aged business executive approached the front entrance of the office building in which he worked. A young feminist came up at the same moment, so he stepped back and held the door open for her to pass on through. She looked at him and said with annoyance, "Don't hold the door for me just because I'm a lady."

To her surprise, he looked right back and replied, "I'm not. I'm holding it open because I'm a gentleman."

Likewise, we as Christians must always act toward others on the basis of what we are in Christ Jesus, and not on the basis of what they may or may not be.[94]

Your ideal is what you wish you were.
Your reputation is what people say you are.
Your character is what you are.[95]

Character, Exposure of

Robert Louis Stevenson told the story of a veiled Muhammadan prophet who was a great teacher and light among the people. He wore the veil, he said, because his countenance was so glorious that none could bear the sight of his face. But eventually the veil decayed and fell away, revealing nothing but an ugly old man. Stevenson stressed that "however high the truths the preacher taught, and however skillfully he might excuse the blemishes of character, the time comes when the veil falls away, and a man is seen by people as he really is. It is seen whether beneath the veil is the ugly fact of unmortified egotism or the transfigured glory of Christlike character." (Cited by J. Oswald Sanders, *Spiritual Leadership* [Chicago: Moody Press, 1974], p. 144).[96]

Character, Test of

You can judge a man pretty well by whether—if given a choice—he would ask for a light burden or a strong back.[97]

Character, Value of

"Fame is a vapor, popularity is an accident, and money takes wings. The only thing that endures is character" (attributed to O. J. Simpson, former professional football player).[98]

"Traveling on a train from Perth to Edinburgh, all of a sudden we came to a dead stop because a very small screw in one of the engines had been broken, and when we started again we were obliged to crawl along with one piston rod at work instead of two. Only a small screw was gone. If that had been right the train would have rushed along its iron road, but the absence of that insignificant piece of iron disarranged the whole. The analogy is perfect; a man in all other respects fitted to be useful may by some small defect be exceedingly hindered, or even rendered utterly useless in the ministry" (C. H. Spurgeon, *Lectures to My Students* [Grand Rapids: Zondervan, 1980], p. 1954).[99]

Cheating

The Baltimore Orioles of 1894–96 was the best team that baseball had seen up to that time, and also the craftiest. One of Baltimore's favorite tricks was to plant a few extra baseballs in strategic spots in the tall outfield grass. Any balls hit into that area that looked as if they would go for extra bases were miraculously held to singles.

One day, however, an opposing batter drove a ball to left-center field, where one of those balls had been hidden. The left fielder picked up the hidden ball and threw it in. The center fielder, not seeing what his team-mate did, picked up the hit ball and threw it in. The umpire, seeing two balls coming into second base, called time and then awarded the game to the visiting team by forfeit. (Cited in John Thorn, *The National Pastime* [Cooperstown, N.Y.: Soc. Am. Baseball Res., 1984], pp. 23–24.)[100]

Child-rearing

We live in a time of social decay, expansion of evil in the world, and worsening trends. Have we therefore reached a point where we should call it quits on having a family? No, absolutely not!

Remember history's lessons. Pharaoh was throwing Hebrew babies into the Nile River when Moses was born. The finest of Israel's youth were led into captivity to serve a pagan and evil empire in Daniel's day. Herod was murdering male children after God's own Son was born. The past has been even darker than today. God is still perfectly capable of giving us children who will develop into mature adults.[101]

Every one who raises a child has times of intense frustration over the task. There are days when it seems as if the child will never learn, never respond correctly, never get things right. Perhaps it would raise your patience threshold to try to write with your left hand—and then remember that a child is *all* "left hand" while he or she is learning.[102]

Pouring concrete is hard work. A solid base must be prepared before anything else is done. Then, when the concrete is poured, it must be shaped before it sets, because once set up, change is only possible if preceded by removal of what has already been laid down. If done correctly, a well-poured footing will last far beyond the original owner's lifetime. If done incorrectly, the evidence will appear soon enough as a crumbling surface, structural cracks, and a shift in walls and floors.

Raising children is like pouring concrete. Before a baby arrives, a couple should prepare a solid base in their marriage and share a readiness for parenting. After the child arrives, the first few years can be likened to the time before the concrete sets up. By our presence (more than presents), by careful and thoughtful attention to the thousands of details and tens of thousands of repetitions required, by unfailing prayer and careful instruction in the things of the Lord, we parents attempt to set a mold that will last a lifetime and more—into eternity.[103]

An unknown author has written these powerful thoughts, expressing the influence for good or evil that our lives exert on others. While they refer to parents in particular, they also apply to Christians in general. After reading each statement, ask yourself, "Are people learning this from me?"

If a child lives with criticism, he learns to condemn.

If a child lives with hostility, he learns to fight.

If a child lives with fear, he learns to be apprehensive.

If a child lives with pity, he learns to feel sorry for himself.

If a child lives with jealousy, he learns to feel guilty.

If a child lives with encouragement, he learns to be self-confident.

If a child lives with tolerance, he learns to be patient.

If a child lives with praise, he learns to be appreciative.

If a child lives with acceptance, he learns to love.

If a child lives with approval, he learns to like himself.

If a child lives with recognition, he learns to have a goal.

If a child lives with fairness, he learns what justice is.

If a child lives with honesty, he learns what truth is.

If a child lives with sincerity, he learns to have faith in himself and those around him.

If a child lives with love, he learns that the world is a wonderful place to live in.[104]

The New Jersey Commissioner of Corrections gave the following comment on the "Scared Straight" program and related television documentary: "[Parents] want it to be successful. They want to . . . overcome sixteen years of neglect at home by letting their kids spend two hours with convicts." (Cited by Charles Colson, *Jubilee Prison Fellowship Newsletter*, 3:5 [July 1978], p. 3.)[105]

As young Johnny reached for the ringing phone one Saturday, his dad sighed through his teeth: "If it's the guy from the office, tell him I'm not home." That evening the family went out for dinner. Before leaving the restaurant, Johnny's mother looked at the check and mentioned that the waitress had undercharged them. "That's their tough luck," mumbled the father. On the way home, they joked about the box that dad had bought for the dashboard of the car. He called it the "fuzz buster" and bragged that it had already paid for itself when considering the speeding tickets he might otherwise have received.

Later that night, as Johnny finished his Sunday-school lesson, he thought what a good Saturday it had been. How much better than last weekend—when his father had grounded him for cheating on his arithmetic test.[106]

The following article appeared in a local newspaper as an "Open Letter to My Parents":

> I am your child. You have brought me into this world and raised me to what I am today. If I am not what I should be, please do not be too harsh with me, for I am your product, and by my actions I advertise the quality standard of home. Do not point at one of my playmates as an example of how I should behave, for by doing so you are admitting that they are doing a better job than you.
>
> You say that you love me, and yet it has been years since you put your arms about me at bedtime and with tears in your eyes asked your heavenly Father to watch over me as I slept. You seem to be more interested in my school grades than in the condition of my eternal soul. You give me the impression that it is better to be popular than to be pure; better to be attractive on the outside than to have that "inner beauty" that comes to one who loves the Lord.
>
> So the next time you feel like throwing up your hands and saying, "I just can't do a thing with you," please remember you have had the opportunity to influence me since I was born, and that the Bible says, "Train up a child in the way he should go, and when he is old he will not depart from it" (Prov. 22:6).[107]

Former President Theodore Roosevelt is reported to have said: "It is exceedingly interesting and attractive to be a successful businessman, or railroad man, or a farmer, or a successful lawyer or doctor, or a writer, or a President. . . . But for unflagging interest and enjoyment, a household of children, if things go reasonably well, certainly makes all other forms of success and achievement lose their importance by comparison."[108]

Socrates said to the people of Athens: "Why do you turn and scrape every stone to gather wealth and take so little care of your children to whom one day you must relinquish all?"[109]

Anyone with a small child must feel as Cardinal Wolsey felt about Henry VIII: "Be well advised and assured what you put in his head, for ye shall never pull it out again."[110]

Child-rearing, Discipline and

After a session with his parents, a little boy taped to his parents' door a note that read: "Dear parents, Be nice to your children and they will be nice to you. Love, God."[111]

When the Duke of Windsor was asked what impressed him most in America, he replied, "the way American parents obey their children."[112]

The headline to one "Dear Abby" column read, "Mom spares the rod and earns child's contempt." The letter read:

Dear Abby,
   My problem is my mother. She's too lenient! After she gets angry and punishes me, she often will apologize. Why should she, when I had the punishment coming?

Mixed-Up in Cleveland

Abby replied,

Dear Mixed-Up:
   Your mother (like many others) fears you will love her less because she has punished you. (She's wrong.) No child has ever resented punishment he knew he had coming. Discipline is "proof" of love, . . . Children "know" this. I wish more parents did.[113]

Susanna Wesley, mother of Charles and John Wesley, is perhaps the classic illustration of one who pursued discipline early in a child's life. She believed the assertive self-will of a child must be broken at a young age by the parent. One of her rules in her "plan of education" was:

"When turned a year old (and some before), they were taught to fear the rod and to cry softly, by which means they escaped abundance of correction which they might otherwise have had. . . .

In order to form the minds of children, the first thing to be done is to conquer their will." (Cited by Rebecca Lamar Harmon, *Susanna, Mother of the Wesleys* [Nashville, Tenn.: Abingdon, 1968], pp. 58–59.)[114]

Child-rearing, Expectations of

Psychologists have discovered that children respond according to how they are treated. In a scientific experiment, a particular teacher was told that half of her students were exceptional, while the others were average. After a year, the students she was told were superior had improved a full grade beyond the other half (those she was told were only average). The interesting factor was that all the students were exactly equal intellectually. The two groups were different only in the teacher's mind and her treatment of them. The results were obvious and inevitable. Those she thought were exceptional *became* exceptional, and those she thought were average *became* average.[115]

Child-rearing, Humor in

"You know," said the father of five while busily cleaning up the toys in the yard, "since I've been married, I've learned the meaning of those words in the Bible, 'When I became a man, I put away childish things.' "[116]

Children and Evangelism

Some would gather money
    Along the path of life;
Some would gather roses
    And rest from worldly strife.
But I would gather children
    From among the thorns of sin;
I would seek a golden curl
    And a freckled, toothless grin.
For money cannot enter
    In that land of endless day,

And the roses that are gathered
Soon will wilt along the way.
But, oh, the laughing children,
As I cross the Sunset Sea;
As the gates swing wide to Heaven,
I can take them in with me!

Billie Crawford[117]

The great evangelist D. L. Moody was once asked, "How many converts did you have last night?" He answered, "Two and one-half."
"You mean two adults and a child?"
"No," he replied. "Two children and one adult."
A child converted is an entire life converted.[118]

Children and Parents

The following appeared in *Home Living*, May 1980: My child, what can I give you?

I should like to give you everything so that you lack for nothing, not even one single desire, but I know that for want of many things I have come to be satisfied with what I have and to think of others and their needs.

I should like to give you a life full of fun and games, but I know that because of many "chores" and responsibilities of my youth, I have learned to be responsible.

I should like to protect you from all the errors of your youth, but I know that because of my failures, I have learned to make better decisions.

I should like to give you a profession of wealth or importance, but I realize that man is truly happy only when he fulfills the purpose for which God has created him. What then, my child, can I give you that would be of any real value?

I give you my love, which means that I accept you, without reservations, just as you are and will be.

I give you my personal presence in order that you will have the security you need during your childhood.

I give you my ears, in the sense that I will never be too busy to listen to you—sometimes never uttering even one word.

I give you opportunities to work so that you might learn to do it without shame and come to enjoy the satisfaction of work well done.

I give you my counsel only when it is necessary or you ask for it so that you might avoid some of the mistakes I have made.

45

I give you my consolation when you have failed or feel discouraged, but I will not always protect you from the consequences of your sins.

I give you instructions in the way of the Lord so that when you are old, you will never depart from it.

I give you my daily prayers that the Lord will keep you and guide you in such a way that you, my child, will be a man or woman who will serve and glorify our Heavenly Father.

This I give you with all my love.

Your Mother,
Lydia Lightner[119]

Hudson Taylor, the famous missionary to China, was once in the U.S.A. on furlough on his birthday. His five-year-old daughter, Maria, couldn't afford to buy a gift, so she made one. Beaming, she brought him a small piece of wood with a peg stuck in the middle, topped with half a cockle shell. Since Taylor did not recognize the nature of the gift and did not want to grieve her, he took her on his knee and began probing for clues. Finally, Maria exclaimed, "Why Daddy! Don't you know? It's a 'ship'! I thought you would like best for your birthday a ship to take you back to China!"[120]

Children and Play

Understanding the workings of the atomic bomb is child's play compared to understanding child's play.[121]

Children's Perspective

In teaching your child, never overlook the obvious. Remember, they view life differently than you. One teacher told the following story:

Some third-graders were studying a unit on patriotism. After a discussion about how France had given us the Statue of Liberty, the teacher asked how many of her pupils had seen the statue. Several children raised their hands. Anticipating a chance to be dramatic and to recite "Give me your tired, your poor . . ." the teacher asked if anyone knew what was written on the base of the statue. There was silence. Then one youngster raised her hand and said, "Made in France?"[122]

Choices

A child stood gazing at a freshly opened box of chocolate candies—lips pressed together, concentrating fully upon the decision at hand. The rule was "Only one, no more than one, but any one you want." Should it be the biggest one, or would the small round one be the favorite peppermint cream? Then again, the long one might last longer. Which to choose? And how to decide?

Perhaps a child's decisions seem trivial to us as adults. Oh, we recognize that they are important to the child, but we have a broader perspective. That is the question in making choices, isn't it? To have an eternal perspective on life and its decisions is to know how to choose.[123]

Christ, Divinity of

The following observation is attributed to Napoleon Bonaparte: "I marvel that whereas the ambitious dreams of myself, Caesar, Alexander, should have vanished into thin air, a Judean peasant, Jesus, should be able to stretch His hands across the destinies of men and nations.

"I know men; and I tell you that Jesus Christ is no mere man. Between him and every other person in the world there is no possible term of comparison. Alexander, Caesar, Charlemagne, and I myself have found empires; but upon what do these creations of our genius depend? Upon force. Jesus alone founded his empire upon love; and to this very day millions would die for Him."[124]

"He went about saying to people, 'I forgive your sins.' Now it is quite natural for a man to forgive something you do to *him*. Thus if somebody cheats *me* out of five pounds it is quite possible and reasonable for me to say, 'Well, I forgive him, we will say no more about it.' What on earth would you say if somebody had done *you* out of five pounds and *I* said, 'That is all right, I forgive him'?" (C. S. Lewis, *God in the Dock* [Grand Rapids: Wm. Eerdmans, 1970], Hooper, Walter, ed., p. 157).[125]

"A man who was merely a man and said the sort of things Jesus said wouldn't be a great moral teacher. He'd either be a lunatic—on the level with a man who says he's a poached egg—or else he'd be the devil of hell. You must make your choice. Either this man was, and is, the Son of God, or else a madman or something worse" (C. S. Lewis, *Mere Christianity* [New York: The Macmillan Co., 1952], pp. 40–41).[126]

47

"A Savior not quite God is like a bridge broken at the further end" (Bishop Moule).[127]

Christ, Incarnation of

A man was shown a red glass bottle and asked what he thought was in the bottle. He replied in succession, "Wine? Brandy? Whiskey?" When told it was full of milk, he could not believe it until he saw the milk poured out. What he hadn't known, of course, was that the bottle was made of red glass, and its redness hid the color of the milk it contained.

So it was and is with the Lord's humanity. Men saw him tired, hungry, suffering, weeping, and thought he was only man. He was made in the likeness of men, yet he ever is God over all, blessed forever.[128]

Dogs are man's best friends, so let's assume that the dogs in your town have developed a problem that has them in deep distress and that only you can provide the help they need.

If it would help all the dogs to become more like men, would you be willing to become a dog? Would you put down your human nature, family, job, hobbies, and all else and choose—instead of intimate communion with your beloved—the poor substitute of looking into the beloved's face and wagging your tail, unable to smile or speak?

When Christ became a man through the incarnation, he voluntarily limited what to him was the most precious thing in the world: unhampered, unhindered communion with the Father.[129]

The story is told of Shah Abbis, a Persian monarch who loved his people very much. To know and understand them better, he would mingle with his subjects in various disguises. One day he went as a poor man to the public baths and in a tiny cellar sat beside the fireman who tended the furnace. When it was mealtime the monarch shared his coarse food and talked to his lonely subject as a friend. Again and again he visited and the man grew to love him. One day the Shah told him he was the monarch, expecting the man to ask some gift from him. But the fireman sat gazing at his ruler with love and wonder and at last spoke, "You left your palace and your glory to sit with me in this dark place, to eat of my coarse food, to care whether my heart is glad or sorry. On others you may bestow rich presents, but to me you have given yourself, and it only remains for me to pray that you never withdraw the gift of your friendship."

This beautiful story reminds us that Christ, whose birth we celebrate at Christmas, left the glories of heaven in order to share himself with us. That gift of his love and friendship will never be withdrawn from us. He chose to be your friend and mine forever.[130]

Christ, Lordship of

If Christ as Lord is the center of our lives, the circumference will take care of itself.[131]

One thing a carpenter learns quickly is how to drive nails. He hammers hundreds of nails a day, and that's a lot of practice! The most important thing in hammering nails is to keep your eye on the nail, not on the thumb that's holding the nail. That is because you will always hit what you watch!

If Christ is your "spiritual" nail, what are the "thumbs" you keep hitting?[132]

The story has been told of a farmer who was trying to teach his son how to plow a straight furrow. After the horse had been hitched up and everything was ready, he told the boy to keep an eye on some object at the other end of the field and aim straight toward it. "Do you see that cow lying down over there?" he asked. "Keep your eye on her and plow straight ahead."

The boy started plowing and the farmer went about his chores. When he returned a little later to see what progress had been made, he was shocked to find, instead of a straight row, something that looked more like a question mark. The boy had obeyed his instruction. The trouble was, the cow had moved!

Jesus is an object that will not move. He is the foundation of our faith, the faithful Rock who never moves, never changes in his love for believers. We can be sure that if we set our eyes on him, our path will be straight![133]

Christ, Return of

The New Testament writers speak of Christ's returning "soon" or "quickly," with the apparent expectation that he might return in the writers' own lifetimes. Liberals have long tried to make this a point against the Bible's infallibility. However, the meaning of returning "soon" is that it would happen "at any moment." It is like my phone-answering machine. The message informs the caller that I am away from my desk but will return "soon." I use the same message whether I expect to be gone two minutes or two weeks—for the very simple reason that I want to encourage the person without revealing exactly how long I will be gone![134]

The Lord told us not only to wait for him but to watch for him, and he has pronounced a special blessing on those who watch. The difference between waiting and watching is illustrated in a story told of a Scotch fishing village.

After days at sea, the skipper of a fishing boat was bringing his craft back home. As the boat neared the shore, the men gazed eagerly toward the dock, where a group of their loved ones were waiting. The skipper, looking through his glass, identified some of the women, saying, "I see Bill's Mary, and there is Tom's Margaret, and David's Anne." One man was very anxious because his wife was not there. He left the boat with a heavy heart and pressed his steps up the hill, where he saw a light in his cottage.

As he opened the door, his wife ran to meet him, saying, "I have been waiting for you!"

He replied with a proper rebuke, "Yes, but the other men's wives were *watching* for them."[135]

When a scheduled jet from New York comes toward Dallas/Fort Worth Airport, the controller knows all the details of the flight pattern. He knows exactly where it will be at various stages in the flight, when it departed, and when it will arrive. On the other hand, a young lady whose fiancé is on the flight knows only the approximate time of arrival, but she is still overjoyed at the prospect of his coming! I'd rather know very little about Christ's coming and have a heart full of anxious anticipation than know many of the details about his return and be indifferent. Of course, it might be better to have both, but the important issue is a joyful heart that is waiting in hope.[136]

Mexican jails are not known for their tidiness or orderliness. Shortly after having taken office, the then President of Mexico, Luis Echeverria, decided to do something about this. Without giving any advance notice, he chose to visit the jails at midnight. He found guards away from their posts, prisoners not taken care of, and other discrepancies between the expectations and reality. He proceeded to fire people and clean up the system.

We never know when our Lord may come. Let us not be lax in our responsibilities so that the Lord finds us lacking.[137]

Christ, Sufficiency of

Can you imagine the number of words it took to write a thirty-volume set of the *Encyclopaedia Britannica*? It must be an awesome number, but an even more amazing thing is that only twenty-six different letters were used. The authors did not have to go outside of the alphabet to assemble that massive collection of knowledge. It provided for them everything they needed for this one task.

Jesus Christ called himself the Alpha and Omega, and we do not have to go outside of him for *anything* that we need. He is God's "everything"—for all situations.[138]

Christ, Union with

The phrase "in Christ" is a statement that describes our union with Christ. Perhaps this relationship can be illustrated by the air that is in us, and yet we are also in the air. So, too, is Christ in us and we in him.[139]

Christian, Definition of

The Bible uses many terms to describe Christians. They are called Christians, children, children of God, children of light, children of the day, children of obedience, believers, friends, brothers, sheep, saints, soldiers, witnesses, stewards, fellow citizens, lights in the world, elect of God, ambassadors, ministers, servants, disciples, heirs, joint-heirs, branches, members of the body, living stones, epistles, temples, beloved, followers, overcomers, victors, conquerors, and so forth. All of these terms are loaded with meaning, so it would take a composite of all of them to define what a Christian really is.[140]

Christian Life, Attitude in

"Do little things as if they were great, because of the majesty of the Lord Jesus Christ, who dwells in thee; and do great things as if they were little and easy, because of His omnipotence" (attributed to Blaise Pascal).[141]

Christian Life, Change in

In a children's church service, a seminary student spoke on the Christian's walk. He presented his message in the first person, or—more accurately expressed—"the first butterfly." His dramatic monologue incorporated the following guise: two large antennas with sensors attached to the ends, halved eggshells for his nose and eyes, a bright orange suit, and beautifully knitted wings. He proceeded to tell his story as a butterfly who was describing his former state and lifestyle as a caterpillar. Obviously, he could no longer live as a caterpillar, since his state had been drastically changed.

The message was pointedly driven home. Just as he could no longer live as a caterpillar once he had become a butterfly, so we can no longer live as unbelievers once we have become believers.[142]

Soon after a family moved into their new house, it began to show the effects of their slipshod lifestyle. The yard was littered with trash. The lawn withered for lack of care, and, even when replanted, died out again. To enter this house was to enter a shambles. It never was clean or in order.

Another family eventually bought the house and moved in. They painted the house, cleaned up the yard, and replanted the lawn. The results were completely different. What had happened? There was a dramatic improvement in the appearance of the house because there was a change in those who lived in that house.

In the same way, it is impossible that there not be a change in a person's life once he or she becomes a Christian—because there is a perfect new resident within: the Holy Spirit.[143]

Christian Life, Daily Walk

It is time to call attention to the simple wisdom of that modern proverb, "When all else fails, follow directions.[144]

One of Rabbi Ben Jochai's pupils once asked him, "Why did not the Lord furnish enough manna to Israel for a year, all at one time?"

The teacher said, "I will answer you with a parable. Once there was a king who had a son to whom he gave a yearly allowance, paying him the entire sum on the fixed date. It soon happened that the day on which the allowance was due was the only day of the year when the father ever saw his son. So the king changed his plan and gave his son day by day that which was sufficient for the day; and then the son visited his father every morning. How he needed his father's unbroken love, companionship, wisdom, and giving!"

Thus God dealt with Israel and deals with us in our daily walk.[145]

Imagine a field covered with freshly fallen snow. Off to the one side you notice two figures entering the field. The first is larger than the second—perhaps they are a father and his son. As they walk across the field, you notice that the father pays no particular attention to where he is going, but his son, on the other hand, follows directly behind, making a special effort to step in his father's footprints. After the two figures pass off the scene, you notice that there is only one set of tracks visible in the field, although two people had walked across it. The Christian life is that way. In our daily walk we ought to be following Christ's example, particularly in times when we are suffering. If someone were to observe the snow-covered fields of your life, would there be one set of tracks, those of Christ? Or would he see two sets, one belonging to Christ and the other distinctly yours?[146]

Christian Life, Failure in

Christian failure is seldom a blowout; it is usually a slow leak.[147]

Christian Life, Faith in

Telephone-pole climbing is an art. In order to climb, one must have a belt that goes around the pole and wear spiked shoes. The secret is to lean back and depend on the belt so the spikes can dig into the pole. Depending on the belt is hard to learn; often a beginner slides down the splintery pole because he won't depend on his equipment. It only takes a few such experiences to convince the beginner that it is better to depend on the belt.

In the Christian life, God wants us to climb by depending on him. When we are hurt by splinters, we should recognize that they are reminders that we need to depend on his strength and loving protection.[148]

Christian Life, Laziness in

When you become a sports spectator rather than a participant, the wrong things happen to your body. Your weight, blood pressure, resting heart rate, cholesterol, and triglycerides go up. Vital capacity, oxygen consumption, flexibility, stamina, and strength go down. Conclusion? Only the strongest can survive as spectators![149]

Christian Life, Motivation and

There is a story quoted in baseball circles about Earl Weaver (when he was manager of the Baltimore Orioles) and his experience with a born-again outfielder named Pat Kelly. As the story goes, Kelly is said to have told Weaver he had learned to walk with God, to which Weaver is reported to have glibly replied, "I'd rather have you walk with the bases loaded."

The Christian walk is incomprehensible to those who are not motivated by Christ.[150]

On March 11, 1830, a little English girl was doing her lessons with her tutor, and the lesson that day had to do with the royal family. As she studied the genealogical chart in the book, she became aware of the astounding fact that she was next in line for the throne! At first she wept, and then she looked at her tutor and said, "I will be good!" The fact that little Victoria would one day be queen motivated her to live on a higher level.[151]

Christian Life, Service in

A recently married man loved his young bride intensely. He wanted to provide her with the best home, nicest clothes, and everything else she might want. Though he had to hold down two jobs to do so, he did not mind, because they enabled him to provide for her many good things. Time together was hard to schedule, but he figured that later on, once they were set financially, there would be plenty. Yet, as so often happens, within a few years his wife left him, not for more money or material things, but for a man who would spend time with her.

We often serve God and obey him, expending much time and energy in doing things that we believe will please him. But this is not enough. God wants us to know him intimately, to develop a relationship through the time we spend with him.[152]

Christian Life, Source of

The moon shines in the night sky because of reflected light from the sun. Without that reflected light, the moon would become lost in the darkness of space.

The believer in Christ shines only because of the reflection of Christ's light. Without that reflected light, the believer becomes lost in the darkness of the world and sin.[153]

A young boy was doing his best to lift a rock that was too large for someone his size. He grunted and puffed as he tried various methods for lifting the rock. But, in spite of all his efforts, the rock wouldn't budge. His father walked by and, after watching his son's struggle, asked if he was having trouble. The boy answered, "Yes, I've tried everything, and it won't move." The father replied, "Are you sure you have tried every possibility, that you have used every resource at your disposal?" The boy looked up with frustration and exhaustion filling his face and grunted out a "Yes!" With kindness, the father bent over and softly said, "No, my son, you haven't. You haven't asked for my help."

How often are we like the little boy, struggling with our problems but unable to solve them—because we have not asked for our Father's help.[154]

Christian Life, Spirit's Role in

There are three ways in which a skier can get to the top of the ski slope. He can try to walk up on his own, or be pulled up as he holds on to a strap, or he can ride up in the chair lift. This illustration vividly depicts the various ways Christians try to live the victorious Christian life. Some try completely in their own strength; others try to combine their own effort with some degree of dependence on God. But the only way to know true victory in every situation is total dependence on the Holy Spirit.[155]

A piano sends forth beautiful melodies when played by a concert pianist. But when a piano is banged on by a child, it can send forth horrible sounds. A Christian is somewhat like a piano. They can have beautifully harmonious lives when controlled by the Master. On the other hand, that life can be one of discord when undisciplined and controlled only by self.[156]

On June 12, 1979, a young man made aviation history when he flew a pedal-powered plane across the English Channel. Taking off from England, he flew for three hours, rarely more than fifteen feet above the water. Finally, after covering twenty-two miles, he landed exhausted on the coast of France. As dramatic as this was, man-powered flight will never be practical. A man simply cannot maintain the necessary energy output for extended flights.

In the same way, no one can live the Christian life pedaling on his or her own power. It is only through the enabling power of the Holy Spirit that we can consistently live the Christian life.[157]

Christianity, Misconception about

A small boy sat in church with his mother and listened to a sermon entitled "What is a Christian?" Every time the minister asked the question, he banged his fist on the pulpit for emphasis.

The tension produced by the sermon built up in the boy and he finally whispered to his mother, "Mama, do you know? Do *you* know what a Christian is?"

"Yes, dear," she replied. "Now sit still and be quiet."

Finally, as the minister was winding up the sermon, he again thundered, "What is a Christian?" and banged especially hard on the pulpit. This time it was too much for the little boy, so he jumped up and cried out, "Tell him, Mama, tell him!"[158]

Christianity, Triumph of

One of the most famous books of all time is Edward Gibbon's *Decline and Fall of the Roman Empire,* in which this eighteenth-century historian traces what happened to that mighty empire and how it disintegrated from within. In that book is a passage that Winston Churchill memorized because he felt it so descriptive. Gibbon says this concerning the church within the empire:

"While that great body [Roman Empire] was invaded by open violence or undermined by slow decay, a pure and humble religion gently insinuated itself into the minds of men, grew up in silence and obscurity, derived new vigor from opposition, and finally erected the triumphant banner of the cross on the ruins of the Capitol."[159]

Christianity, Uniqueness of

A Chinese Confucian scholar, converted to Christ, told this story: "A man fell into a dark, dirty, slimy pit, and he tried to climb out of the pit and he couldn't. Confucius came along. He saw the man in the pit and said, 'Poor fellow, if he'd listened to me, he never would have got there,' and he went on.

"Buddha came along. He saw the man in the pit and said, 'Poor fellow, if he'll come up here, I'll help him.' And he too went on.

"Then Jesus Christ came. He saw the man and said, 'Poor fellow!' and jumped into the pit and lifted him out." (Cited by John Pollock, *A Foreign Devil in China*, p. 54.)[160]

Christmas

Christmas is a depressing time for most people. An article written by a director of the California Department of Mental Hygiene warns: "The Christmas season is marked by greater emotional stress and more acts of violence than any other time of the year."

Christmas is an excuse to get drunk, have a party, get something, give a little, leave work, get out of school, spend money, overeat, and all kinds of other excesses. But, for the church, Christmas is an excuse for us to exalt Jesus Christ in the face of a world that is at least tuned in to his name.[161]

A little boy and girl were singing their favorite Christmas carol in church the Sunday before Christmas. The boy concluded "Silent Night" with the words, "Sleep in heavenly beans."

"No," his sister corrected, "not beans, *peas.*"[162]

Sherwood Wirt captured the mood of that first Christmas in this description, which he wrote in a Christmas card:

> The people of that time were being heavily taxed, and faced every prospect of a sharp increase to cover expanding military expenses. The threat of world domination by a cruel, ungodly, power-intoxicated band of men was ever just below the threshold of consciousness. Moral deterioration had corrupted the upper levels of society and was moving rapidly into the broad base of the populace. Intense nationalistic feeling was clashing openly with new and sinister forms of imperialism. Conformity was the spirit of the age. Government handouts were being used with

increasing lavishness to keep the population from rising up and throwing out the leaders. Interest rates were spiraling upward in the midst of an inflated economy. External religious observances were considered a political asset, and abnormal emphasis was being placed upon sports and athletic competition. Racial tensions were at the breaking point. In such a time, and amid such a people, a child was born to a migrant couple who had just signed up for a fresh round of taxation, and who were soon to become political exiles. And the child who was born was called, among other things, Immanuel, God with us.[163]

Bishop Robinson says this about the Christmas story:

Suppose the whole notion of a God who visits the earth in the person of His Son is as mythical as the prince in the fairy story. Suppose there is no realm "out there" from which the man from heaven arrives. Suppose the Christmas myth (the invasion of this side by the other side), as opposed to the Christmas history (the birth of the man, Jesus of Nazareth), has to go. Are we prepared for that? Or are we to cling here to this last vestige of the mythological or metaphysical world view as the only garb in which to clothe the story with power to touch the imagination? Cannot perhaps the supernaturalist scheme survive at least as part of the "magic" of Christmas?—Robinson, John A., *Honest to God* (Philadelphia: Westminster, 1963).[164]

What a sad commentary on what the birth of our Lord has come to mean is this all-too-true parody of the wonderful words of Luke's Christmas narrative.

"And there were in the same country children keeping watch over their stockings by the fireplace. And, Lo! Santa Claus came upon them; and they were sore afraid. And Santa said unto them: "Fear not, for behold, I bring you good tidings of great joy which be to all people who can afford them. For unto you will be given great feasts of turkey, dressing and cake; and many presents; and this shall be a sign unto you, ye shall find the presents, wrapped in bright paper, lying beneath a tree adorned with tinsel, colored balls and lights. And suddenly, there will be with you a multitude of relatives and friends, praising you and saying, 'Thank you so much, it was just what I wanted.' And it shall come to pass as the friends and relatives have gone away into their own homes, the parents shall say to one another, 'Darn it! What a mess to clean up! I'm tired, let's go to bed and pick it up tomorrow. Thank goodness, Christmas only comes once a year!' And they go with haste to their cold bed and find their desired rest."[165]

The Lord Jesus Christ whom we exalt at Christmas is not just a baby in a manger. He is not a character in a children's story. He is far more.

The first time he came, he came veiled in the form of a child. The next time he comes, and we believe it will be soon, he will come unveiled, and it will be abundantly and immediately clear to all the world just who he really is.

The first time he came, a star marked his arrival. The next time he comes, the whole heavens will roll up like a scroll, and all the stars will fall out of the sky, and he himself will light it.

The first time he came, wise men and shepherds brought him gifts. The next time he comes, he will bring gifts, rewards for his own.

The first time he came, there was no room for him. The next time he comes, the whole world will not be able to contain His glory.

The first time he came, only a few attended his arrival—some shepherds and some wise men. The next time he comes, every eye shall see him.

The first time he came as a baby. Soon he will come as Sovereign King and Lord.[166]

Church, Attending

A Christian who says he worships God every Sunday morning on the golf course is really worshiping golf on God's course.[167]

An old farmer attending a Sunday-school conference commented: "I find it amusing, all those papers and discussion on how to get people to come to the meetings. I have never heard a single address at a farmer's convention on how to get the cattle to come to the rack. It's simple—we just use the best kind of feed."[168]

Many believers don't see the importance of regular church attendance. Members of Northend Prince of Peace Lutheran Church in Seattle received a special announcement in the mail, listing the many things that would be done for them at church on the following "no-excuse-to-stay-home Sunday."

According to the pastor, cots would be available for those who say Sunday is their only day to sleep. Eye drops would be supplied for those who have red eyes from watching late Saturday-night TV shows. There would be steel helmets for those who say the roof would cave in if they ever went to church, blankets for persons who think the church is too cold, fans for those who say it is too hot, scorecards for those wishing to list all the hypocrites present, TV dinners for those who can't go to church and also cook dinner. Finally, the sanctuary would be decorated with Christmas poinsettias and Easter lilies for those who have never seen the church without them.[169]

A certain parishioner who had previously been attending services regularly, suddenly stopped coming to church. After some weeks, the minister decided to visit the absent member. It was a chilly evening, and the minister found the man at home alone, sitting before a blazing fire. Guessing the reason for his pastor's visit, the man welcomed him, led him to a big chair by the fireplace, and waited.

The minister made himself comfortable and said nothing. In grave silence, he contemplated the play of the flames around the burning logs. After some minutes, he took the fire tongs, carefully picked up a brightly burning ember and placed it to one side of the hearth. Then he sat back in his chair, still silent. The host watched all this in quiet fascination. As the lone ember's flame diminished, there was a momentary glow, but then its fire was no more and it was cold and dead. Not a word had been spoken since the initial greetings. But as the minister rose to leave, the host said, "Thank you so much for your visit—and especially for your fiery sermon. I shall be at church next Sunday."[170]

Dear Sir:

You manufacture aspirin tablets that relieve sufferings, colds, and fevers. The mixture used in your tablets makes it possible for people to get out of bed and fight off headaches, bad nerves, and muscle spasms. I have noticed that these tablets work wonders on Monday, Tuesday, Wednesday, Thursday, Friday, and especially well on Saturday. But people who take them on Sunday seem to get no relief. They claim they cannot get rid of their aches and pains and are thus not able to attend Sunday school and church. Is it possible to put in an ingredient that will work on Sunday? Hopefully, *A Concerned Pastor*[171]

Church (Bride of Christ)

It was all that a young woman could do to maintain a conversation with a fellow Christian while waiting for her fiancé's jet to bring him home to her after a three-week separation. Once the plane was at the gate, conversation was impossible as the engaged woman stood watching, eagerly waiting for the moment when she could throw her arms around her loved one at last. As she peered down the passage, the friend with whom she had been talking earlier was heard to say, "What a beautiful picture of the church watching for the return of her bridegroom."[172]

Church, Discipline in

If someone has cancer, an operation is usually performed to cut out the malignancy. The reason is simple: if left alone, it will metastasize; that is, it will spread. No one wants a cancer to spread, so it is cut out or otherwise removed from the body so that the patient can be healthy again. And, of course, when the doctors tell the patient, "We got it all," everyone is encouraged and rejoices.

The same thing should be true in the church. The reason to excommunicate the one refusing to be disciplined is to protect the rest of the body from being infected with that disease. Sin, like cancer, needs to be cut out so it will not spread.[173]

Discipline in the church is kind of like a vaccination. You get a little dose of the disease and then you fight against it. And that builds immunity, whether it be against germs or sinning.[174]

If our physical bodies were like the body of Christ—the church—we would be in intensive care twenty-four hours a day.[175]

Church, Involvement in

An athlete who desires to be effective on game day must first be properly trained. He must spend many hours keeping himself in shape and developing his skills to a high degree. If he does not, he will not be able to accomplish all that he wishes when it is time to play the game.

Any Christian who desires to be effective in the work of ministry must also realize that the public moment of any effective ministry is always preceded by many hours of careful preparation. Effective ministry will never be done by a weak and unhealthy church whose members neglect regular participation and sacrificial service.[176]

Many churches have a *Beau Geste* view of spiritual gifts. In that movie, the Arabs were attacking a Legionnaire fort where only four Legionnaires were left alive. The Arabs were not aware of this, but if they were to realize it, the fort would fall for sure. Therefore, the Legionnaires devised a plan to disguise their weak condition. They set up the bodies of their dead comrades along the wall of the fort and ran back and forth, firing off the guns of their dead friends. From the outside, it all looked very convincing—but on the inside, there were only four men.

Likewise, in many of our churches, we have two or three or four "professionals" who run around and shoot off the guns of the spiritually inactive congregation. Outwardly the church looks like it is alive and well—but inwardly there are only a very few people doing the work of the whole body.[177]

The frenzied activities of Christians have become a joke. Someone has revised the old nursery rhyme to read:

> Mary had a little lamb,
> 'Twas given her to keep;
> But then it joined the Baptist Church,
> And died for lack of sleep![178]

Proverb: He who is faithful in a little shall be swamped with much![179]

Your local church is like a bank: the more you put into it, the greater the interest.[180]

The story is told of Oliver Cromwell who, when faced with a shortage of precious metal for coins, sent his troops out to find some. They reported that the only precious metal to be found was in the statues of saints standing in the corners of churches. Cromwell said, "Well, melt down the saints and put them in circulation."[181]

Bud Wilkinson, a famous football coach, was once asked, "What contribution does professional sport make to the physical fitness of Americans?" To no one's surprise, he answered, "Very little. A professional football game," he said, "is a happening where fifty thousand spectators, desperately needing exercise, sit in the stands watching twenty-two men on the field, desperately needing rest." That's also a description of the typical mid-twentieth-century church organization.[182]

Church, Love in *Church Conf. report 11/98*

There is a story about a man who was walking down the street. He passed a used-book store, and in the window he saw a book with the title *How to Hug*. He was taken by the title and, being of a somewhat romantic nature, went in to buy the book. To his chagrin, he discovered that it was the seventh volume of an encyclopedia and covered the subjects "How" to "Hug."

Everyone knows that the church is a place where love ought to be manifested, and many people have come to church hoping to find a demonstration of love—only to discover an encyclopedia on theology.[183]

Church, Membership in

There once was a mule who found himself between two haystacks, completely unable to decide which one to eat first. Because of his indecision, he didn't eat either one; he just stood there until he starved.

Many people are like the mule when deciding which church to attend. They wander back and forth, never committing themselves, and meanwhile going hungry.[184]

Someone asked Sir Winston Churchill, "Are you a pillar of the church?" He quipped, "I am more of a flying buttress: I support it from the outside."[185]

Church, Mission of

Frederick the Great, King of Prussia, won a strategic battle with comparative ease and little loss of men. When asked for the explanation of his victory over the enemy, he said, "The enemy had seven cooks and one spy, but I had seven spies and one cook."

Perhaps the church lacks power because it majors on the minors and minors on the majors.[186]

A generation ago, Dr. F. B. Meyer said this about the local church: "It is urgently needful that the Christian people of our charge should come to understand that they are not a company of invalids, to be wheeled about, or fed by hand, cosseted, nursed, and comforted, the minister being the Head Physician and Nurse; but a garrison in an enemy's country, every soldier of which should have some post or duty, at which he should be prepared to make any sacrifice rather than quitting."[187]

The hero of Mark Twain's *Connecticut Yankee in King Arthur's Court* was wise enough to install dynamite under the foundation of all the munitions plants and factories he had built. He realized that should there be an uprising against his "new" nineteenth-century ideas, these factories (once so helpful) might be taken over and used against him.

There is wisdom to this approach for the church. Every new building, and every new program ought to have ample dynamite poured into its foundation so that if in the future these things become obstacles to the mission of the church, they can be removed to clear the ground for greater works.[188]

Church, Separation in

The story has been told of a small church affiliated with an exclusive "splinter" denomination. The members had cut out some gold letters and fastened them on the wall in front of the church. The letters said: "JESUS ONLY."

One day a gust of wind blew away the first three letters. The sign then read, more accurately: "US ONLY."[189]

Church, Service to

This is a story about four people in the church whose names were Everybody, Somebody, Anybody, and Nobody.

The church had financial responsibilities and Everybody was asked to help. Everybody was sure that Somebody would do it. Anybody could have done it. But you know who did it? Nobody. It ended up that

Everybody blamed Somebody when Nobody did what Anybody could have done.

Then the church grounds needed some work, and Somebody was asked to help. But Somebody got angry about that, because Anybody could have done it just as well and, after all, it was really Everybody's job. In the end the work was given to Nobody, and Nobody did a fine job.

On and on this went. Whenever work was to be done, Nobody could always be counted on. Nobody visited the sick. Nobody gave liberally. Nobody shared his faith. In short, Nobody was a very faithful member.

Finally the day came when Somebody left the church and took Anybody and Everybody with him. Guess who was left. Nobody![190]

Church Strife

In Paul's Letter to the Philippians, there are named two ladies who could not get along with each other, Euodia and Syntyche (or, as it has been rendered, Odious and Soontouchy). They obviously had trouble working together. Then and now, the church is too often described in this little jingle:

> To dwell above with saints we love,
> O that will sure be glory.
> But to dwell below with saints we know,
> Well, that's another story![191]

9|18|94

The church filled with strife may do well to be reminded of Lord Nelson at Trafalgar who, coming on deck and finding two British officers quarreling, whirled them about and—pointing to the ships of their adversary—exclaimed, "Gentlemen, *there* are your enemies!"[192]

Church Unity

A visitor to a mental hospital was astonished to note that there were only three guards watching over a hundred dangerous inmates. He asked his guide, "Don't you fear that these people will overpower the guards and escape?"

"No," was the reply. "Lunatics never unite."[193]

For safety reasons, mountain climbers rope themselves together when climbing a mountain. That way, if one climber should slip and fall, he would not fall to his death. He would be held by the others until he could regain his footing.

The church ought to be like that. When one member slips and falls, the others should hold him up until he regains his footing. We are all roped together by the Holy Spirit.[194]

A man asked his young son to break a bundle of sticks. He returned a little later to find the lad frustrated in the task. He had raised the bundle high and smashed it on his knee, but he only bruised his knee. He had set the bundle against a wall and stomped hard with his foot, but the bundle barely bent.

The father took the bundle from the child and untied it. Then he began to break the sticks easily—one at a time.

So it is with the church: united we are strong, divided we can fail or be broken.[195]

Many years ago, two students graduated from the Chicago-Kent College of Law. The highest ranking student in the class was a blind man named Overton, and when he received his honor, he insisted that half the credit should go to his friend, Kaspryzak. They had first met one another in school when the armless Kaspryzak had guided the blind Overton down a flight of stairs. This acquaintance ripened into friendship and a beautiful example of interdependence. The blind man carried the books that the armless man read aloud in their common study, and thus the deficiency of each individual was compensated for by the other's ability.[196]

If you fell and severely injured your wrist, it would swell up and become very painful. The rest of your body might feel so bad about it that it would sit up all night to keep it company!

That is what the body of Christ should do when one member is hurt. When one hurts, all hurt—and all should respond.[197]

Two porcupines found themselves in a blizzard and tried to huddle together to keep warm. But because they were pricked by each other's quills, they moved apart. Soon they were shivering again and had to lie side by side once more for their own survival. They needed each other, even though they needled each other!

There are many "porcupine" Christians running around. They have their good points, but you can't get near them because the bad points prick too hard.[198]

Have you ever wondered what makes the difference between a spotlight and a laser beam? How can a medium-power laser burn through steel in a matter of seconds, while the most powerful spotlight can only make it warm? Both may have the same electrical power requirements. The difference is unity.

A laser can be simply described as a medium of excited molecules with mirrors at each end. Some of the excited molecules naturally decay into a less excited state. In the decay process they release a photon, a particle of light. It is here that the unique process of the laser begins. The photon moves along and "tickles" another molecule, inviting another photon to join him on his journey. Then these two photons "tickle" two more molecules and invite two more photons to join the parade. Soon there is a huge army of photons marching in step with each other. It is this unity that gives the laser its power. A spotlight may have just as many photons, but each is going its own independent way, occasionally interfering with other photons. As a result, much of its power is wasted and cannot be focused to do any useful work. However, the laser, because of its unity, is like an army marching in tight formation and is able to focus all its power on its objective.[199]

In any flesh-and-bones body, there are a variety of cells. There are nerve cells, blood cells, muscle cells, and many others, each having a distinct function. The body operates smoothly, not because the cells get together and vote on what to do, but because each one does what it was designed to do. It is the function of the head to bring all these different functions together, so that the body operates effectively as each cell gives itself to the task of functioning according to its design.

Certainly the body would not operate properly if its cells chose to go their own way. Do you know what we call a rebellion of the cells of your stomach? We call it indigestion! A revolt of your brain cells is called insanity. Any time the cells in our body don't operate properly, it means that the body is sick, that something is wrong with it.

Many of the problems in the church today are a result of our forgetting that the church is a *body* with a head, Jesus Christ. Instead we sometimes try to operate the church as an *organization.* As a result, the church has no more power than any other human organization at work in the world.[200]

The story is told of a time when a little child in an African tribe wandered off into the tall jungle grass and could not be found, although the tribe searched all day. The next day the tribal members all held hands and walked through the grass together. This enabled them to find the child, but due to the cold night he had not survived. In her anguish and through tears, the mother cried, "If only we would have held hands sooner."

It is not enough that we all share a common goal. We must all work together to accomplish it without hesitation.[201]

As members of the body of Christ, we can be compared to pieces in a jigsaw puzzle. Each piece has protrusions and indentations. The protrusions represent our strengths (gifts, talents, abilities), and the indentations represent our weaknesses (faults, limitations, shortcomings, undeveloped areas). The beautiful thing is that the pieces complement one another and produce a beautiful whole.

Just as each piece of a puzzle is important, so each member of the body of Christ is important and can minister to the other members of the body.

Just as, when one piece is missing from the puzzle, its absence is very obvious and damages the picture, so also is the whole weakened when we are absent from the body of Christ.

Just as, when each piece of a puzzle is in place, any one piece is not conspicuous but blends in to form the whole picture, so it should be in the body of Christ.[202]

The story is told that during the American Civil War, when the rival armies were encamped on the opposite banks of the Potomac River, the Union's band played one of its patriotic tunes, and the Confederate musicians quickly struck up a melody dear to any Southerner's heart. Then one of the bands started to play "Home, Sweet Home." The musical competition ceased, and the musicians from the other army joined in. Soon voices from both sides of the river could be heard singing, "There is no place like home."

In a similar way, the church, in spite of its many divisions, is bound together by that one strong link—we are all going home, and to the same home. We have a common destiny.[203]

Born in 1765 in France, James Smithson was the illegitimate son of a prominent English duke and a direct lineal descendant of King Henry VII through his mother. Branded as a bastard, James was refused British citizenship and denied a rich inheritance through his true father. Due to this rejection the young Smithson felt constrained to succeed at whatever he did, and he became one of England's leading scientists and a member of the Royal Society (the chief association of leading scientists) at the age of twenty-two.

In 1829 Smithson, who never married, died and left his considerable fortune to a nephew. Rumor had it that the terms of Smithson's will stipulated that his entire estate was to go to one recipient upon the nephew's death. The English scientific community hoped that he had made sizable grants to their favorite institutions. But when the terms of the will were made public they were shocked!

Smithson had written: "Just as England has rejected me, so have I rejected England." During Smithson's lifetime, England had fought two bitter wars with her rebellious colonies in America. So, to show his utter contempt for those who had mistreated him, he gave everything to the United States Government for the establishment of a scientific institution in the young nation's capital. To this day the Smithsonian Institution is recognized as one of the most prominent institutions of its kind in the world. England made the tremendous mistake of thinking that she had no need of this man, from whom she might have benefited greatly.

Let us be careful of saying to some member of the body of Christ, "I have no need of you," only to find that the same member could have met some of our greatest spiritual needs.[204]

Comfort

Merrill Womach, a brilliant Christian singer, was in a plane that struck a tree after takeoff in the winter of 1961. The plane caught fire and Womach tumbled out of the plane engulfed in flames. Some people found him and drove him to a hospital. On the way, to their amazement—from a body squealing with pain—came these words:

> I've found the dear Savior and I'm made whole,
> I'm pardoned and have my release.
> His spirit abiding and blessing my soul,
> Praise God in my heart there is peace.
> Wonderful peace, wonderful peace.
> When I think how he brought me from darkness to light,
> There's a wonderful, wonderful peace.[205]

A little girl lost a playmate in death and one day reported to her family that she had gone to comfort the sorrowing mother. "What did you say?" asked her parents. "Nothing," she replied. "I just climbed up on her lap and cried with her."[206]

The Joe Bayly family, in the course of several years, lost three of their children. In his book *View from A Hearse*, (Elgin, Ill.: Cook, 1973) Joe Bayly shared his honest feelings when one of his children died:

"I was sitting there torn by grief. Someone came and talked of God's dealings, of why it happened, of hope beyond the grave. He talked constantly. He said things I knew were true. I was unmoved, except to wish he'd go away. He finally did.

"Another came and sat beside me. He didn't talk. He didn't ask me leading questions. He just sat beside me for an hour and more, listened when I said something, answered briefly, prayed simply, and left. I was moved. I was comforted. I hated to see him go."[207]

Commitment

A certain dog had always boasted of his ability as a runner. Then one day a rabbit that he was chasing got away. This brought a lot of ridicule from the other dogs because of his previous boasting. His explanation: "You must remember that the rabbit was running for his life, while I was only running for my dinner."[208]

On August 11, 1978, *Double Eagle II*, a large helium balloon, and her crew of three eased into an almost windless sky above the potato fields of Maine. Their destination was Paris, France. The aerodynamics of ballooning are somewhat complex, but one thing is certain. In order for the balloon to stay aloft as the journey progressed, ballast (that which is used to add weight) had to be expelled. As they approached continental Europe six days later, one of the crew wrote, "We have been expending ballast wisely, but as we neared land, not cheaply . . . over went such gear as tape recorders, radios, film magazines, sleeping bag, lawn chairs, most of our water, food, and the cooler it was in."

Following Christ is the wisest choice a man can make, but it does not come cheap. Just as for these balloonists many important things had to be abandoned because they weighed them down, so for the believer.

P.S. The balloonists' mission was accomplished.[209]

For many days an old farmer had been plowing with an ox and a mule together and working them pretty hard. The ox said to the mule, "Let's play sick today and rest a little while." But the old mule said, "No, we need to get the work done, for the season is short."

But the ox played sick, and the farmer brought him fresh hay and corn and made him comfortable. When the mule came in from plowing, the ox asked how he made out. "We didn't get as much done, but we made it all right," answered the mule. Then the ox asked, "What did the old man say about me?" "Nothing," said the mule.

The next day the ox, thinking he had a good thing going, played sick again. When the mule came in again very tired, the ox asked, "How did it go?" The mule said, "All right, I guess, but we didn't get much done." Then the ox also asked, "What did the old man say about me?" "Nothing to me," was the reply, "but he did stop and have a long talk with the butcher."[210]

John Audubon, the well-known naturalist and artist, practiced great self-mastery in order to learn more about birds. Counting his physical comforts as nothing, he would rise at midnight night after night and go into the swamps to study certain nighthawks. He would crouch motionless in the dark and fog, hoping to discover just one more additional fact about a single species.

During one summer, Audubon repeatedly visited the bayous near New Orleans to observe a shy water bird. He would stand almost to his neck in the stagnant waters, scarcely breathing, while poisonous water-moccasin snakes swam past his face. It was not comfortable or pleasant, but he beamed with enthusiasm and is reported to have said, "But what of that? I have the picture of the birds." He endured all these things just for a picture of a bird!

If a man could be so disciplined for a temporal and physical reward, how much more committed should the child of God be for the imperishable prize before him?[211]

Many men of the world have understood the necessity for commitment if they are to accomplish great things. For example, when Spanish explorer Cortez landed at Vera Cruz in 1519 to begin his conquest of Mexico with a small force of seven hundred men, legend has it that he purposely set fire to his fleet of eleven ships. Presumably, his men on the shore watched their only means of retreat sink to the bottom of the Gulf of Mexico. There was now only one direction to move—forward into the Mexican interior to meet whatever might come their way.

As part of our commitment as Christ's disciples, we must purposefully destroy all avenues of retreat. We must resolve that whatever price is required for being his follower, we will pay it.[212]

In the 1976 Summer Olympics, Shun Fujimoto competed in the team gymnastics competition for Japan. In a quest for the gold medal, Fujimoto suffered a broken right knee in the floor exercise. But his injury did not stop him, for during the next week he competed in his strongest event, the rings. His routine was excellent, but he astounded everyone by squarely dismounting with a triple somersault twist on a broken right knee. When asked concerning his feat, he said, "Yes, the pain shot through me like a knife. It brought tears to my eyes. But now I have a gold medal and the pain is gone."[213]

Henry Thoreau, that rugged New England individualist of the nineteenth century, once went to jail rather than pay his poll tax to a state that supported slavery. Thoreau's good friend Ralph Waldo Emerson hurried to visit him in jail and, peering through the bars, exclaimed: "Why, Henry, what are you doing in there?"

The uncowed Thoreau replied, "Nay, Ralph, the question is, what are you doing out there?"[214]

The story is told that when James Calvert went out as a missionary to the cannibals of the Fiji Islands, the captain of the ship that had carried him there sought to turn him back by saying, "You will lose your life and the lives of those with you if you go among such savages." Calvert's reply well demonstrates the cost of commitment: "We died before we came here."[215]

A mission society is reported to have written to David Livingstone: "Have you found a good road to where you are? If so, we want to send other men to join you." Livingstone replied: "If you have men who will come only if they know there is a good road, I don't want them. I want men who will come if there is no road at all."[216]

Robert Chapman of Barnstaple, a great friend of the late George Muller of Bristol, was once asked, "Would you not advise young Christians to do something for the Lord?" "No," was the reply, "I should advise them to do everything for the Lord."[217]

Commitment, Communist

"If you ask me what is the distinguishing mark of the Communist, what is it that Communists most outstandingly have in common, I would not say, as some might expect, their ability to hate . . . , I would say beyond any shadow of doubt it is their idealism, their zeal, dedication, devotion to their cause and willingness to sacrifice" (Douglas Hyde, former head of the Communist Party of Great Britain, before his conversion to Catholicism).[218]

Commitment, Cost of

A hen and a pig approached a church and read the advertised sermon topic: "What can we do to help the poor?" Immediately the hen suggested they feed them bacon and eggs. The pig thought for a moment and said, "There is only one thing wrong with feeding bacon and eggs to the poor. For you it requires only a contribution, but for me it requires total commitment!"[219]

An elderly Christian man in Communist-controlled Budapest remarked when asked about the effects of persecution and discrimination on the lives of Christians: "It is like the deep, fast-flowing Danube River. The banks of the river were artificially narrowed throughout the city of Budapest. As a result the river's fast waters dug deeper and deeper into the river bottom."

Believers under restrictions and persecution have limited freedom and few political options, but their narrowed lives have found great depth by going deeper in Christ.[220]

Committees

A secretary burst into the office of a Detroit executive on May 21, 1927, and cried, "Mr. Murphy, a man has just flown from New York to Paris all by himself." When her employer continued to work calmly, she cried out, "Don't you understand? A man has just flown the Atlantic all by himself!"

Then Murphy looked up. "All by himself, a man can do anything," he said quietly. "When a committee flies the Atlantic, let me know."[221]

Communication

In 1963, Adlai E. Stevenson spoke to the students at Princeton University. "I understand I am here to speak and you are here to listen," he said. "Let's hope we both finish at the same time."[222]

There is a story about a man who wanted to train his mule. The first thing he did was to pick up a big stick and hit the mule a resounding wallop between the ears. As the mule staggered about, someone said to the owner, "What is the matter? Why did you do that?" And the man said, "In order to teach a mule, you must first get his attention."

That may not be true of mules, but there is a good deal of truth in it when dealing with humans. For any communication to be effective, interest must first be awakened.[223]

Communication, Clarity in

If Jesus came to certain theological schools today and asked the professors, "And you, who do you think I am?" what do you think they might reply?

Some might answer, "You are the eschatological manifestation of the kerygma in which we recognize the ultimate significance of our interpersonal relations."

And Jesus would probably say, "What?!"[224]

"The difference between the right word and the almost-right word is the difference between lightning and the lightning bug" (Mark Twain).[225]

A stranger was walking down a residential street and noticed a man struggling with a washing machine at the doorway of his house. When the newcomer volunteered to help, the homeowner was overjoyed, and the two men together began to work and struggle with the bulky appliance. After several minutes of fruitless effort the two stopped and just stared at each other in frustration. They looked as if they were on the verge of total exhaustion.

Finally, when they had caught their breath, the first man said to the homeowner: "We'll never get this washing machine in there!" To which the homeowner replied: "In? I'm trying to move it out of here!"[226]

Communication, Lack of

The story is told of two businessmen, an American and a Frenchman, who met on a transatlantic voyage. As the American was seated for lunch with the Frenchman, the latter raised his wine glass and said, "Bon appetit." To which the smiling American replied, "Johnson." Since neither spoke the other's language, no other words were exchanged during the meal. After the same thing happened at dinner, an observant waiter later explained to the American that the Frenchman was saying, "Hope you enjoy your meal."

The next day the American sought out the Frenchman to correct his error. After finding him at lunch, at the first opportunity the American raised his glass and said, "Bon Appetit"—to which the Frenchman replied, "Johnson."[227]

A department-store clerk was demonstrating the efficiency of a window-cleaning device by smearing margarine on glass and cleaning it off again. Quite impressed, one potential customer asked, "How much margarine do I have to use?"[228]

Communion

This story has been told of the famous Scottish theologian John Duncan, of New College in Edinburgh. At communion one Sunday, when the elements came to a sixteen-year-old girl, she suddenly turned her head aside. She motioned for the elder to take the cup away, that she couldn't drink it. John Duncan reached his long arm over, touched her shoulder, and said tenderly, "Take it, lassie, it's for sinners!"[229]

Complaining

The next time you feel like complaining, remember that your garbage disposal probably eats better than 30 percent of the world's population does.[230]

The story is told of a Christian who was reduced to such poverty that he had only one pair of shoes, with the soles worn through and his toes sticking out. Depressed and discouraged, he walked down the street mumbling to himself: "I might as well be barefooted as to wear these miserable, uncomfortable shoes." As he felt himself becoming more and more bitter, he came upon a man sitting on the sidewalk and begging. The poor fellow had no legs. After a moment, the discouraged Christian realized that there was something worse than having old shoes—having no feet upon which to wear the shoes.

Are you complaining? Think how much worse things could be.[231]

Compromise

The following is a Russian parable. A hunter raised his rifle and took careful aim at a large bear. When about to pull the trigger, the bear spoke in a soft, soothing voice, "Isn't it better to talk than to shoot? What do you want? Let us negotiate the matter."

Lowering his rifle, the hunter replied, "I want a fur coat." "Good," said the bear, "that is a negotiable question. I only want a full stomach, so let us negotiate a compromise."

They sat down to negotiate, and after a time the bear walked away alone. The negotiations had been successful. The bear had a full stomach, and the hunter had his fur coat.

Compromises rarely satisfy both sides in equal measure.[232]

Conclusions

Drawing unwarranted conclusions is like looking through a keyhole. The trouble is, you don't always see enough to warrant a conclusion, but once you've seen a little, it's difficult to resist trying.[233]

Conferences

John R. Mott was for many years head of the Student Volunteer Movement when it was a vital force for Christ and for worldwide evangelism. When asked to evaluate his life, Mott commented, "If I had my life to live over, I would give much more emphasis to student conferences and retreats, because the benefits are far out of proportion to the investment of time and money."[234]

Conformity

Merchandisers have found that customers find safety in numbers. One man in Utah bought several used cars and lined them up in front of his store. His business increased significantly. Because we are conditioned to conform, we tend to find the presence of others to be an assurance that what is available is good and right.[235]

On a bright sunny day, when you first walk into a dark movie theater, you usually remark about how dark it is. If there was no usher to show you to a seat, you probably had to stand in the back for a few minutes until the darkness seemed to clear and you began to see again. Before long, you could see without difficulty. Indeed, you seemed to be able to see normally. "Normally," that is, until you walked out into the sunlight again and the bright glare forced you to cover your eyes.

We Christians are often in the same predicament. We live in a dimly lighted world, where sin is the rule and not the exception. And yet we are really children of the light. We must always be on our guard that we do not become so accustomed to the darkness of our world that we think it is normal and conform to its dubious guidelines. It is *not* normal. The dim moral and spiritual insight of the world is not the standard that the Christian is to walk by.[236]

More than a hundred years ago, Soren Kierkegaard warned that the age of the crowd was upon us. In such an age, said Kierkegaard, people would not think of deciding for themselves. They would follow the advice given to children going off to a party: "Look and see what the others are doing and then behave like them." (Cited by Kenneth Hamilton, "The Irrelevance of Relevance," *Christianity Today*, March 1972.)[237]

A flock of wild geese was flying south for the winter, when one of the geese looked down and noticed a group of domestic geese by a pond on a farm. He saw that they had plenty of grain to eat, so he went down to join them. The food was so good, he decided to stay with the domestic geese until spring, when his own flock would fly north again. When spring came, he heard his old flock going by and flew up to join them. The goose had grown fat, however, and flying was difficult, so he decided to spend one more season on the farm and join the wild geese on their next winter migration. The following fall, when his former flock flew southward, the goose flapped his wings a little, but kept eating his grain. By the next time they passed overhead, the now-domesticated goose didn't even notice them.[238]

The major reason for teenage suicide, drug addiction, and alcoholism is that most young people are conformists. They, like their parents, do what "everybody else" does, feeling instinctively that if most people are doing it, then "it" must be good to do. In effect, we act like sheep.

A television documentary showed a lot about the behavior of sheep. One scene was of a packing house where sheep were slaughtered. The sheep had to walk from their large pen up a narrow ramp and then turn right. In order to get the sheep to move up the ramp, a "Judas goat" was trained to lead the sheep up the ramp to their death. The goat was placed among the sheep and then walked confidently to the ramp as the nervous sheep watched. After the goat got about five feet up the ramp, he stopped and confidently looked around at the nervous sheep, who then began to follow. Near the top of the ramp the goat turned left, as a gate was opened only for him and then closed. The sheep, however, continued up the ramp and turned right, to their death.[239]

Conscience

A mother was helping her son with his spelling assignment and came to the words *conscious* and *conscience*. When she asked him if he knew the difference between the two, he responded, "Sure, Mom, 'conscious' is when you are aware of something and 'conscience' is when you wish you weren't."[240]

The conscience is like a sharp square peg in our hearts. If we are confronted by a questionable situation, that square begins to turn, and its corners cut into our hearts, warning us with an inward sensation against doing whatever confronts us. If the conscience is ignored time after time, the corners of the square are gradually worn down, and it virtually becomes a circle. When that circle turns within our hearts, there is no inner sensation of warning, and we are left without a conscience.[241]

Have you recently flown on an airplane? Do you recall the ritual of walking through the electronic device to detect concealed weapons? "A marvel of modern technology," you might think.

Interestingly enough, centuries ago, one of the palaces of Chang-an, the ancient capital of what is now known as Thailand, had a similar device. Its gates were made of lodestone—a natural magnet. If a would-be assassin came in through the gate with a concealed dagger, the lodestone would pull at the hidden weapon like an invisible hand. Startled, the individual would involuntarily reach for the weapon. Trained guards, watching every movement, would then grab him.

A healthy conscience acts in much the same way: it tugs at the concealed sins in our lives as though it were God's hidden hand.[242]

The Internal Revenue Service received the following letter from a conscience-stricken taxpayer:

"Dear Sir: My conscience bothered me. Here is $175.00, which I owe in back taxes."

There was a P.S. at the bottom that read: "If my conscience still bothers me, I'll send in the rest."

This taxpayer's response to a red warning light is not only humorous but also illustrates an important truth: one's conscience can become insensitive.[243]

When Clare Boothe Luce, then seventy-five, was asked, "Do you have any regrets?" she answered: "Yes, I should have been a better person. Kinder. More tolerant. Sometimes I wake up in the middle of the night, and I remember a girlhood friend of mine who had a brain tumor and called me three times to come and see her. I was always too busy, and when she died, I was profoundly ashamed. I still remember that after fifty-six years."[244]

Contentment

Two little teardrops were floating down the river of life. One teardrop asked the other, "Who are you?"

"I am a teardrop from a girl who loved a man and lost him. But who are *you?*"

The first teardrop replied, "I am a teardrop from the girl who got him."

Life is like that. We cry over the things we can't have, but we might cry twice as hard if we had received them. Paul had the right idea when he said, ". . . . I have learned the secret of being content in any and every situation . . ." (Phil. 4:12, NIV).[245]

79

A little Swiss watch had been made with the smallest of parts and great skill. Yet it was dissatisfied with its restricted sphere of influence on a lady's wrist. It envied the position of the great tower clock on the city hall. One day as it passed with its owner by the city hall, the tiny watch exclaimed, "I wish I could go way up there! I could then serve many instead of just one." Now it so happened that its owner was in a position with the city that gave her access to the tower clock, so she said, "You shall have your opportunity, little watch."

The next day, a slender thread was let down from the tower and the little watch was tied to it. Slowly and carefully, the watch was pulled up the side of the tower, rising higher and higher each moment. Of course, when it reached the top, it was completely lost to view. In this dramatic way, the watch learned that its elevation had effected its annihilation!

Pray that you too may not lose the small influence you now have for Christ by coveting something larger for which you are not equipped, and which God constantly refuses you in his love. Learn to be content.[246]

A story is told of a king who was suffering from a mysterious malady and was advised by his astrologer that he would be cured if the shirt of a contented man was brought for him to wear. People went out to all parts of the kingdom looking for such a person, and after a long search they found a man who was really happy. But he did not even possess a shirt.[247]

A Puritan sat down to his meal and found that he had only a little bread and some water. His response was to exclaim, "What? All this and Jesus Christ, too!"

Contentment is found when we have a correct perspective on life.[248]

Conversion

How painful *almost* to get a situation, but to miss it.

How vexing *almost* to catch a plane, but to be left at the terminal.

How sad *almost* to escape drowning, but to be engulfed in the water.

But, oh, how above-all-things terrible to be *almost* a Christian and yet in the lake of fire for eternity!

It has been said that the road to hell is paved with good intentions.

May it not be said also that it will be trodden by millions of almost-Christians!

Oh, be warned, then, against being an almost-er, for to be *almost* saved is to be certainly lost![249]

Conversion, Consequences of

When many people are converted they make the mistake of thinking that the battle was already theirs, that the victory is now won. But, after serving Christ for a few months, we realize that conversion is like enlisting in the army: there is a battle at hand and many more in the future.[250]

In England there is a paper factory that makes the finest stationery in the world. One day a man touring the factory asked what it was made from. He was shown a huge pile of old rags and told that the rag content was what determined the quality of the paper. The visitor wouldn't believe it. In weeks he received from the company a package of paper with his initials embossed on it. On the top piece were written the words "Dirty rags transformed."

The same is true of the Christian life. It is a process of transformation from what we were into something new and wonderful.[251]

Conversion, Example of

Luis Palau tells of a woman in Peru whose life was radically transformed by the power of Christ. Rosario was her name. She was a terrorist, a brute of a woman who was an expert in several martial arts. In her terrorist activities she had killed twelve policemen. When Luis conducted a crusade in Lima, she learned of it and, being incensed at the message of the gospel, made her way to the stadium to kill Luis. Inside the stadium, as she contemplated how to get to him, she began to listen to the message he preached on hell. She fell under conviction for her sins and embraced Christ as her Savior. Ten years later, Luis met this convert for the first time. She had by then assisted in the planting of five churches; was a vibrant, active witness and worker in the church; and had founded an orphanage that houses over one thousand children.[252]

The discovery of Christ and the company of Christ is the key to happiness. There was a Japanese criminal called Tockichi Ishii. He was utterly and bestially pitiless. He had brutally and callously murdered men, women, and children in his career of crime. He was captured and imprisoned. Two Canadian ladies visited the prison. He could not be induced even to speak; he only glowered at them with the face of a wild beast. When they left, they left with him a copy of the Bible in the faint hope that he might read it. He read it, and the story of the crucifixion made him a changed man. Later, when the jailer came to lead the doomed man to the scaffold, he found not the surly, hardened brute he expected, but a smiling, radiant man, for Ishii, the murderer, had been born again. The mark of his rebirth was a smiling radiance. The life that is lived in Christ cannot be lived other than in joy. (From William Barclay, *The Gospel of Mark*, [Philadelphia: Westminster, 1975].)[253]

Augustine was in Milan when God touched his heart and changed his life. He then left his former life of license (he even had an illegitimate son). When he returned home, his former girl friend called to him: "Augustine, Augustine, it is I." He turned and said: "Yes, but it is not I."[254]

Convictions

At the outbreak of the Civil War, a Tennessee cotton-planter could not decide which cause to support, the North or the South. He had friends on both sides, so he decided to be absolutely neutral. He wore a gray jacket and blue trousers, thereby dressing for both the Confederacy and the Union.

One day this man was caught in the middle of a skirmish between the two armies. He stood up and shouted that he was neutral in this fight and expected to be allowed to leave the field before the battle closed in on him. But Union sharpshooters, seeing the gray jacket, riddled it with bullets. And Confederate marksmen, seeing the blue pants, filled them with lead.

The point is, you cannot serve two masters (Matt. 6:24).[255]

"In religion, the things about which men agree are apt to be the things that are least worth holding; the really important things are the things about which men will fight." (J. G. Machen, *Christianity and Liberalism* [Grand Rapids: Wm. Eerdmans, 1923], p. 2).[256]

George Norris, a Senator from Nebraska, after making a very unpopular decision in the view of his constituents, stated: "I would rather lie in the silent grave, remembered by both friends and enemies as one who remained true to his faith and who never faltered in what he believed to be his duty, than to still live, old and aged, lacking the confidence of both factions." (Cited in John F. Kennedy, *Profiles in Courage* [New York: Harper & Row, 1983, Commemorative], pp. 161–2.)[257]

82

Cooperation

During a hike in the woods a troop of Boy Scouts came across an abandoned section of railroad track. Each boy in turn tried walking the rails but eventually lost his balance and tumbled off. Two boys, after considerable whispering, suddenly offered to bet that they could both walk the entire length of the track without falling off. Challenged to make good their boast, the two boys jumped up on opposite rails, extended a hand to balance each other, and walked the entire section of track with no difficulty whatever. That in a nutshell is the principle of Christian living.[258]

Country

Carl Schurz, a nineteenth-century political reformer, put the statement "My country, right or wrong" into proper perspective: "Our country, right or wrong. When right, to be kept right; when wrong, to be put right."[259]

Covetousness

A father was walking down the street with his two small sons, both of whom were crying loudly. A neighbor passing by inquired, "What's the matter? Why all the fuss?" The father responded, "The trouble with these lads is what's wrong with the world. One has a piece of candy and the other wants it!"[260]

The trouble with this world is that too many people try to go through life with a catcher's mitt on both hands.[261]

The story is told of an elderly Quaker who, to teach his neighbors a lesson, put up a sign on a vacant piece of property he owned that read, "I will give this lot to anyone who is really satisfied."

A wealthy farmer read it as he rode by and said to himself, "Since my Quaker friend is going to give this piece of land away, I might as well have it as anyone else. I am rich and have all I need, so I am well able to qualify." He went up to the Quaker's door and, when the aged man appeared, the farmer explained why he had come.

"And art thou really satisfied?" asked the owner of the lot.

"I surely am," was the farmer's reply. "I have all I need, and I am well satisfied."

"Friend," said the other, "if thou art satisfied, then what dost thou want with my lot?" The question revealed the covetousness that was hidden in the man's heart.[262]

Creation, Complexity of

Dr. Carl Sagan, a famous astronomer and author who professes to have no belief in God or the Bible, has nevertheless recognized the complexity of the design of creation. In his book *The Dragons of Eden* (New York: Ballantine, 1978) he describes the complexity of a chromosome:

> A single human chromosome contains twenty billion bits of information. How much information is twenty billion bits? What would be its equivalent, if it were written down in an ordinary printed book in modern human language? Twenty billion bits are the equivalent of about three billion letters. If there are approximately six letters in an average word, the information content of a human chromosome corresponds to about five hundred million words. If there are about three hundred words on an ordinary page of printed type, this corresponds to about two million pages. If a typical book contains five hundred such pages, the information content of a single human chromosome corresponds to some four thousand volumes. It is clear, then, that the chromosome contains an enormous library of information. It is equally clear that so rich a library is required to specify as exquisitely constructed and intricately functioning an object as a human being.[263]

Creation/Creator

John Haldone, a scientist, once suggested to Monsignor Knox that in a universe containing millions of planets it was inevitable that life would appear by chance on one of them. "Sir," said Knox, "if Scotland Yard found a body in your Saratoga trunk, would you tell them, 'There are millions of trunks in the world—surely one of them must contain a body'? I think they still would want to know who put it there."[264]

Robert Jastrow, a scientist who calls himself "agnostic" in religious matters, has written in *God and the Astronomers* (New York: Norton, 1978) the following:

A sound explanation may exist for the explosive birth of our Universe, but if it does, science cannot find out what that explanation is. The scientist's pursuit of the past ends in the moment of creation. This is an exceedingly strange development, unexpected by all but the theologians. They have always accepted the word of the Bible, "In the beginning, God created the heaven and earth." To which St. Augustine added, "Who can understand this mystery or explain it to others?" The development is unexpected because science has had such extraordinary success in tracing the chain of cause and effect backward in time. . . . Now we would like to pursue that inquiry farther back in time, but the barrier to further progress seems insurmountable. It is not a matter of another year, another decade of work, another measurement, or another theory; at this moment it seems as though science will never be able to raise the curtain on the mystery of creation. For the scientist who has lived by his faith in the power of reason, the story ends like a bad dream. He has scaled the mountains of ignorance; he is about to conquer the highest peak; as he pulls himself over the final rock, he is greeted by a band of theologians who have been sitting there for centuries.[265]

The story is told of a science professor who constructed a planetarium, a precisely scaled model of the universe. A student came into his office and asked him who made it. The professor said, "No one."

The student laughed and asked again, "Come on, who made this fantastic piece of precise work?" The professor replied, "No one. It just happened."

The student became confused and angry, and the professor said, "Well, if you can go out of this class and look at nature around you and believe it just happened, you can also believe *this* precise piece of work just happened without a creator."[266]

"Is it hard to paint a picture?" a woman asked Salvador Dali.

"No," replied the artist. "It's either easy or impossible."

The same answer holds for the creation of the universe. For God, it was "easy." For any other person, it is "impossible!"[267]

Crisis

The Chinese word for "crisis" is a combination of the symbols for "danger" plus "opportunity."[268]

Criticism

Horse Sense
A horse can't pull while kicking,
This fact we merely mention,
And he can't kick while pulling,
Which is our chief contention.

Let us imitate the good horse,
And lead a life that's fitting;
Just pull an honest load, and then
There will be no time for kicking.[269]

Adventuresome and courageous pioneers have often faced the critical laughter of jealous observers.

The first American steamboat took thirty-two hours to go from New York to Albany. People laughed.

The horse and buggy passed the early motor car as if it were standing still (it usually was). People laughed.

The first electric light bulb was so dim that people had to use a gas lamp to see it. They laughed.

The first airplane came down fifty-nine seconds after it left the ground. People laughed.

If you try to tackle a big job, or if you have new ideas, expect criticism![270]

The story is told of an old man whose grandson rode a donkey while they were traveling from one city to another. The man heard some people say, "Would you look at that old man suffering on his feet while that strong young boy is totally capable of walking."

So then the old man rode the donkey while the boy walked. And he heard some people say, "Would you look at that, a healthy man making the poor young boy suffer. Can you believe it?"

So the man and the boy both rode the donkey, and they heard some people say, "Would you look at those heavy brutes making that poor donkey suffer." So they both got off and walked, until they heard some people say, "Would you look at the waste—a perfectly good donkey not being used."

Finally, the scene shifts and we see the boy walking and the old man carrying the donkey. No matter what you do, someone will always criticize it.[271]

The Critic
A little seed lay on the ground,
And soon began to sprout.
"Now, which of all the flowers around,"
It mused, "shall I come out?
The lily's face is fair and proud,
But just a trifle cold;
The rose, I think, is rather loud,
And then, its fashion's old.
The violet is all very well,
But not a flower I'd choose;
Nor yet the Canterbury bell—
I never cared for blues,"
And so it criticized each flower,
This supercilious seed,
Until it woke one summer morn,
And found itself—a weed.[272]

The following is attributed to Theodore Roosevelt:

"It's not the critic who counts, not the one who points out how the strong man stumbles or how the doer of deeds might have done better. The credit belongs to the man who is actually in the arena; whose face is marred with sweat and dust and blood; who strives valiantly, who errs and comes short again and again; who knows the great enthusiasms, the great devotions, and spends himself in a worthy cause; who, if he fails, at least fails while daring greatly, that his place shall never be with those cold and timid souls who know neither victory nor defeat."[273]

A man was applying for the job of private secretary to Winston Churchill. Before introducing him, an aunt of Churchill's told the man, "Remember, you will see all of Winston's faults in the first five hours. It will take you a lifetime to discover his virtues."[274]

Criticism, Ignoring

Sailors in the northern oceans have frequently observed icebergs traveling in one direction in spite of strong winds blowing in the opposite direction. The icebergs were moving against the winds, but how? The explanation is that the icebergs, with eight-ninths of their bulk under the water surface, were caught in the grip of strong currents that moved them in a certain direction, no matter which way the winds raged.

In the Christian life, no matter how strongly the winds of passing opinion blow in opposition, the believer who has a depth of living in the currents of God's grace should move toward righteousness.[275]

Crucifixion

The unnatural position used in crucifixion made every movement painful; the lacerated veins and crushed tendons throbbed with incessant anguish; the wounds, inflamed by exposure, gradually gangrened; the arteries—especially at the head and stomach—became swollen and oppressed with surcharged blood; and while each variety of misery went on gradually increasing, there was added to them the intolerable pang of a burning and raging thirst; and all these physical complications caused an internal excitement and anxiety, which made the prospect of death itself—of death, the unknown enemy, at whose approach man usually shudders most—bear the aspect of a delicious and exquisite release.[276]

Cults, Recruits of

Dr. Margaret Thaler Singer, a psychologist at the University of California at Berkeley, said of people the cults seek to recruit: "About one-third are very psychologically distressed people. The other two-thirds are relatively average people, but in a period of depression, gloom, being at loose ends, such people are vulnerable to well-planned recruitment techniques" (*Time,* September 4, 1978).[277]

Cults, Response to

When the FBI trains staff members to identify counterfeit bills, they are not required to study fake money. Instead they undergo a thorough study of genuine currency as the best preparation to identify counterfeit money. Believers should approach cults in the same way. If they do, they will experience similar results.[278]

Death

The story is told of a certain man who was walking in his neighborhood when he came face to face with Death. He noticed an expression of surprise on the creature's horrid countenance, but they passed one another without speaking. The fellow was frightened and went to a wise man to ask what should be done. The wise man told him that Death had probably come to take him away the next morning. The poor fellow was terrified at this and asked how ever he could escape.

The only solution the two could think of was that the victim should drive all night to a distant city and so elude Death. So the man drove to the other city—it was a terrible journey that had never been done in one night before—and when he arrived he congratulated himself on having eluded death.

Just then, Death came up to him and tapped him on the shoulder. "Excuse me," he said, "but I have come for you."

"Why," exclaimed the terrified man, "I thought I saw you yesterday near my home!"

"Exactly," said Death. "That was why I looked surprised—for I had been told to meet you today in this city."[279]

An Indiana cemetery has a tombstone over a hundred years old that bears this epitaph:

> Pause, Stranger, when you pass me by,
> As you are now, so once was I.
> As I am now, so you will be,
> So prepare for death and follow me.

An unknown passerby had read those words and scratched this reply below them:

> To follow you I'm not content,
> Until I know which way you went.

The passerby was right, the important thing about death is what follows. Where are *you* going?[280]

It has become fashionable in our culture to hold the view that death is a perfectly natural occurrence. The Bible teaches that it is not, and even those who deny the afterlife witness that God "has set eternity in the hearts of men." The following extract from Charlotte and Howard Clinebell's *The Intimate Marriage* (N.Y.: Harper & Row, 1970), p. 188, serves as a good illustration of this truth:

One of the roots of the need for spiritual relatedness is the experience of man as the animal who knows he will die. How can one cope constructively with the dizzy flight of the years, with the knowledge that every tick of the clock brings death closer? How can one confront the brevity of one's membership in the human family? How can one deal constructively with the ultimate threat of non-existence? The fact that a man knows he will die colors all of his life. . . . behind the will to relate is man's existential loneliness and anxiety—the normal, nonpathological anxiety which is a part of what Paul Tillich once called man's "heritage of finitude." Erikson calls this form of anxiety the "ego chill." It slips up on a self-aware human being whenever he becomes conscious of his fragile position in the face of sickness, nature, fate, and, ultimately, death.

There are echoes of such anxiety in any depth study of life or time. Consider this line from R. M. MacIver's *The Challenge of the Passing Years, My Encounter with Time:* "The deeds of men sink into the melting pot of time, with countless ripples that quickly disappear."[281]

The story is told of a time when the famed philosopher Diogenes looked intently at a large collection of human bones piled one on another. Alexander the Great stood nearby and became curious about what Diogenes was doing. When he asked the old man, the reply was, "I am searching for the bones of your father, but I cannot seem to distinguish them from those of the slaves." Alexander got the point: all are equal in death.[282]

Tom Howard, professor of Theology and Missions at Gordon College, captured something of the way humanity feels in the presence of death in these eloquent words:

> Like a hen before a cobra, we find ourselves incapable of doing anything at all in the presence of the very thing that seems to call for the most drastic and decisive action. The disquieting thought, that stares at us like a fact with a freezing grin, is that there is, in fact, nothing we can do. Say what we will, dance how we will, we will soon enough be a heap of ruined feathers and bones, indistinguishable from the rest of the ruins that lie about. It will not appear to matter in the slightest whether we met the enemy with equanimity, shrieks, or a trumped-up gaiety, there we will be.[283]

Death, Believer's Response to

The inevitable tomb is not a period at the end of the sentence of life, but a conjunction connecting us with the life to come.[284]

A father gave this counsel to his married daughter on the first anniversary of her mother's death:

"I had forty wonderful years with your Mom," he said, "the best years of my life. But that part of my life is over. Finished!"

"But Dad . . ." "No buts, listen to me." His clear blue eyes stared intensely into mine. I couldn't turn away from him as much as I wanted to. "They were the best years of my life," he repeated. "Your mother is no longer with me; this truth has to be faced. But I am alive and must live the time allotted me until she and I are together again." His voice trembled, but it was not uncertain. "She is gone, but no one can take away the wonderful memories. They are part of me, the happy memories and the sad ones. But only a part. I can't let them possess me or I couldn't get through my days. Every day is a gift from God. It must be lived with joy. It is just a taste of the joy to come when we will all be together again." I kissed him then, not realizing that our conversation would one day be one of my fondest memories. Recalling that day has always been a great strength to me, particularly today—the first anniversary of my dear father's death. [Cited in *Home Living*, May 1980.][285]

Dr. Donald Grey Barnhouse told of the occasion when his first wife had died. He, with his children, had been to the funeral service for her. As he was driving his motherless children home, they were naturally overcome with grief at the parting. Dr. Barnhouse said that he was trying to think of some word of comfort that he could give them. Just then, a huge moving van passed them. As it passed, the shadow of the truck swept over the car. And as the truck pulled on in front of them, an inspiration came to Dr. Barnhouse. He said, "Children, would you rather be run over by a truck or by its shadow?" The children said, "Well, of course, Dad, we'd much rather be run over by the shadow! That can't hurt us at all." Dr. Barnhouse said, "Did you know that two thousand years ago the truck of death ran over the Lord Jesus . . . in order that only its shadow might run over us?"[286]

I am standing on a seashore. A ship at my side spreads her white sails to the morning breeze and starts for the ocean blue. She is an object of beauty and strength, and I stand and watch her until at length she hangs like a speck of white cloud just where the sea and sky come down to meet each other. Then someone at my side says, "There, she is gone." Gone where? Gone from my sight, that is all. She is just as large in mast and hull and spar as she was when she left my side, and just as able to bear her load of living weights to its place of destination. Her diminished size is in me, not in her, and just at the moment when someone says, "There she is gone," on that distant shore there are other eyes watching for her coming and other voices ready to take up the glad shout, "Here she comes," and such is dying (From Loraine Boettner, *Immortality* [Phillipsburg, N.J.: Pres. & Reformed, 1956], pp. 29–30.)[287]

A little girl whose father had just died asked her mother where her father had gone. "To be with Jesus," replied the mother.

A few days later, talking to a friend, the mother said, "I am so grieved to have lost my husband."

The little girl heard her and, remembering what she had told her, asked, "Mother, is a thing lost when you know where it is?"

"No, of course not," said her mom.

"Well, then, how can Daddy be lost when he has gone to be with Jesus?"[288]

Years ago, Dr. Arthur John Gossip preached a sermon titled "When Life Tumbles In, What Then?" on the day after his beloved wife had died suddenly. He closed with these words:

"I don't think you need to be afraid of life. Our hearts are very frail, and there are places where the road is very steep and very lonely, but we have a wonderful God. And as Paul puts it, 'What can separate us from His love? Not death,' he writes immediately. No, not death, for standing in the roaring of the Jordan, cold with its dreadful chill and very conscious of its terror, of its rushing, I, too, like Hopeful in *Pilgrim's Progress*, can call back to you who one day in your turn will have to cross it, 'Be of good cheer, my brother, for I feel the bottom and it is sound.' "[289]

As the great Baptist missionary Adoniram Judson lay sick and about to die, he said, "I am not tired of my work, neither am I tired of the world; yet when Christ calls me home, I shall go with the gladness of a boy bounding away from his school. Perhaps I feel something like the young bride when she contemplates resigning the pleasant association of her childhood for a yet dearer home—though only a little like her, for there is no doubt resting on my future." (Cited in Edward Judson, *The Life of Adoniram Judson*, 1883, p. 540.)[290]

When Martin Luther's daughter, Magdelena, was fourteen years old, she was taken sick and lay dying. Luther prayed, "O God, I love her so, but nevertheless, Thy will be done."

Then he turned to his daughter and said, "Magdelena, would you rather be with me, or would you rather go and be with your Father in heaven?" And the girl said, "Father, as God wills." Luther held her in his arms as she passed away, and as they laid her to rest, he said, "Oh my dear Magdelenachen, you will rise and shine like the stars in the sun. How strange to be so sorrowful and yet to know that all is at peace, that all is well."

It is this hope in the hour of death that the resurrection gives to us.[291]

There are many instances of those whose faith has triumphed in the hour of death. D. L. Moody, the great evangelist of the past century, said on his deathbed, "Earth is receding; heaven is approaching. This is my crowning day!"[292]

This incident illustrates how the child of God can face the last enemy with confidence and courage:

Many years ago, the ship known as the *Empress of Ireland* went down with 130 Salvation Army officers on board, along with many other passengers. Only 21 of those Christian workers' lives were spared—an unusually small number. Of the 109 workers who drowned, not one body had on a life preserver! Many of the survivors told how those brave people, seeing that there were not enough lifebelts, took off their own and strapped them onto others, saying, "I know Jesus, so I can die better than you can." Their supreme sacrifice and faithful words set a beautiful example, which for many years has inspired the Salvation Army to carry on courageously for God. Millions have come to recognize that born-again individuals can face death fearlessly.

Death for someone who has not come to know God is a frightening prospect. And indeed it should be, for when one passes from this life, there is no longer the possibility of coming right with God. In contrast, the dark door of death for a Christian is only the other side of the shining gate of life.[293]

The dedicated missionary Jim Elliot once said: "I must not think it strange if God takes in youth those whom I would have kept on earth until they were older. God is peopling eternity, and I must not restrict Him to old men and women."[294]

Samuel Rutherford, a seventeenth-century Scottish pastor and theologian, wrote the following to a woman when her young daughter died:

"Remember what age your daughter was, and that just so long was your lease of her . . . your lease [has] run out, and you can no more justly quarrel against your great Superior for taking His own, at His just term-day, than a poor farmer can complain that his master taketh a portion of his own land to himself when his lease is expired." (From *Letters of Samuel Rutherford*, London: Banner of Truth, 1973, p. 13.)[295]

Death, Enoch's Translation to Heaven

Enoch lived to be 365 years old. The Bible says that he walked with God and God took him away. A little girl described this experience to her mother. "Mamma," she said, "one day Enoch and God took a walk together. They walked and they talked, and they talked and they walked, until Enoch finally said, 'Oh, my, dear Lord, it's getting late. I'd better go home.' And the Lord said, 'Why, Enoch, we've been walking so long together, I believe we're closer to my home than yours. Why don't you come home with me tonight?' " So Enoch went home with God.[296]

Death, Fear of

A dying man was fearful, even though he was a born-again Christian. He expressed his feelings to his Christian doctor. The physician was silent, not knowing what to say. Just then a whining and scratching was heard at the door. When the doctor opened it, in bounded his big beautiful dog, who often went with him as he made house calls. The dog was glad to see his master. Sensing an opportunity to comfort his troubled patient, the doctor said, "My dog has never been in your room before, so he didn't know what it was like in here. But he knew I was in here, and that was enough. In the same way, I'm looking forward to heaven. I don't know much about it, but I know my Savior is there. And that's all I need to know!"[297]

John Wayne, at age 71, explained that he sometimes had difficult moments watching his old movies: "It's kind of irritating to see I was a good-looking 40-year-old and suddenly I can look over and see this 71-year-old. . . . I'm not squawking . . . I just want to be around for a long time." (From interview with Barbara Walters, *ABC Special Report*, January 1979.)[298]

Death, Last Words

In Shakespeare's *Richard II*, the dying Duke of Lancaster tells the Duke of York: "O, but they say the tongues of dying men enforce attention like deep harmony: Where words are scarce they are seldom spent in vain, for they breathe their words in pain."[299]

Death, Ministry to Terminally Ill

David Banner—the main character in the T.V. series "The Incredible Hulk"—in talking to a terminal cancer victim, told this story: "A man being chased by a tiger came to a cliff. In desperation he jumped and grabbed a solitary limb. Below him, a second tiger roared, waiting for his fall. Above him, the first tiger lashed out, barely missing its prey. As the branch suddenly began to pull away from the cliff, the helpless man noticed on the cliff in a patch of soil a single bright red strawberry on a lonely plant. Hanging there, he reached out, grabbed the fruit, and ate it. And, oh, it tasted so good!"

Reach out for the strawberries.[300]

Death, Preparation for

Many people sleep under an electric blanket during winter. The only problem with this wonderful invention is that it is too good at what it does. That is, an electric blanket makes a bed so warm and comfortable that on cold mornings it is very hard to get up. Some people have found that the only thing that works for them is to turn off their electric blanket so that the bed becomes much less comfortable and thus it is easier to leave their cozy spot. Perhaps God lets us deteriorate physically in our late years so that we will be more willing to leave our ailing bodies for the unexplored future that he sets before us.[301]

When Corrie ten Boom was a girl, her first realization of death came after a visit to the home of a neighbor who had died. It impressed her that someday her parents would die. Corrie's father comforted her. "Corrie, when you and I go to Amsterdam, when do I give you your ticket?" he asked.

Corrie answered, "Why, just before we get on the train."

"Exactly," responded her father, "and our wise Father in heaven knows exactly when we're going to need things too. Don't run out ahead of him, Corrie. When the time comes that some of us will have to die, you will look into your heart and find the strength you need— just in time."[302]

Death, Sting Removed from

A boy and his father were traveling in a car when a bee flew through the open window. The boy was so highly allergic to bee stings that both he and his father knew that his life was in danger. As the boy frantically jumped around and tried to avoid the agitated bee, the father calmly reached out and grabbed the bee. When he opened his hand, the bee began to fly again, terrorizing the boy once more. The father then said, "Look, son," holding up a hand with an implanted stinger, "his stinger is gone; he can't hurt you any longer."

As a bee loses its stinger when it stings, so death lost its sting when it stung Jesus.[303]

Death, Unbeliever's Response to

Three "pop" postcards illustrate three aspects of the world's perspective on death:

Fear: A man is pictured standing directly beneath an enormous, needle-sharp dagger that is suspended from above by a very thin thread. The caption: "It's very inconvenient to be mortal—you never know when everything may suddenly stop happening."

False hope: A person is lying in bed. The caption: "Tell the scientist to hurry—I don't want to die before they discover how to save me."

Uncertainty: A health enthusiast is pictured jogging. The caption: "I'm doing what I can to prolong my life, hoping that someday I'll learn what it's for."[304]

For Roger

My sister is crying,
Why can't I?
I guess it hasn't hit me that my brother has died;
I feel nothing inside
My brother has died
It may hit me years from now
But when I found out
That he was gone I felt nothing
So I wrote down
This song.

Nothing I can do will bring him back
Why is it that I have no feeling—
It's no act I'm not hurt and I'm not down

I'm just sitting here writing this song
It's not sure it's not fact
But I still want my brother back.

Life ends tomorrow
Not for me
Just for my brother
Not for me
His life is over
Not for me.[305]

These are the words of a distraught father telling us of his reaction to the death of his son. He says:

The rays of a late morning South Carolina sun struck me full on the face as I stepped through the door of the hospital. The squint of my eyes, however, was not occasioned by the rays of the sun; it was the visible display of the anguish and despair that wracked my very life. I had spent several hours with my sobbing wife. Now I was about to keep the appointment that would prove to be the emotional climax of the day my world collapsed. On my way to the appointment, I stopped at a diner to have a cup of coffee and to bolster my courage. I was oblivious to everything except the appointment that awaited me. Leaving the diner, I made my way to a large white house, located on a corner in Columbia, South Carolina. I followed the owner into a large room, where he soon left me alone. I slowly made my way across a thick rug on the floor to a table on the far side of the room. Upon the table was a white box. I stood before that white box for endless eternities before I finally summoned enough courage to look over the top and down into the white box, at the lifeless body of my son. At that sight my world collapsed. I would have given up all of my academic and athletic awards. I would have given up the prestigious executive training program that I was engaged in with one of the largest international oil companies. I would have given anything. For the first time in my life, I had come to a hurdle I could not clear. My world collapsed.

This is the sting of death that the non-Christian is confronted with—and to which he has no answer.[306]

"It's not that I'm afraid to die. I just don't want to be there when it happens" (Woody Allen).[307]

97

Today, some people's fear of death is so strong and their confidence in technology so great that they are spending tens of thousands of dollars to have their bodies frozen at the time of death. Their hope is that they might be revived to live again when a cure is found for whatever caused their death.[308]

The story is told of an author, William Saroyan, who had achieved great success in his field. His works had been acclaimed in the literary world, his name was a familiar entry on best-seller lists, and he had even been awarded a Pulitzer Prize. But now he lay dying in New York City of cancer, which had spread to several of his vital organs.

One evening, as Saroyan reflected on his condition and what the future held for him, he placed a phone call to Associated Press. After identifying himself to the reporter who answered his call, he posed a question that revealed the honest, searching sensitivity that had characterized his career. It was a final statement to be used after his death (which occurred later in May of 1981).

He said, "Everybody has got to die. But I have always believed an exception would be made in my case. Now what?" And then he hung up the phone. (Cited in *Reader's Digest,* Dec. 1981, p. 136.)[309]

Literature is filled with the expressions of fear about death that grip the hearts of unbelievers. Socrates said, "No one knows whether death . . . may not be the greatest of all good," but men "in their fear apprehend it to be the greatest evil."

Francis Bacon wrote, "Men fear death as children fear to go in the dark. . . ."

Samuel Johnson told of his horror at the death of a friend: "At the sight of this last conflict, I felt a sensation never known to me before: a confusion of passions, an awful stillness of sorrow, a gloomy terror without a name."[310]

A missionary told an old Indian chief about Jesus Christ, describing him as God's only way to heaven. "The Jesus road is a good road," the aged chief agreed. "But I have followed the Indian road all my life, and I cannot change now." A year later, he lay in his hut, deathly sick. The missionary hurried to his side and once more told him of Christ. "Can I turn to Jesus now?" the dying chief asked. "My own road stops here. It has no way through the valley!"

Every road that a man walks in life ends at the grave. The roads of religion, fame, wealth, and success can never take you through the valley of the shadow of death. Only Christ can do that! And he will if you will but trust him.[311]

Deceit

A humorist told the story of a driver who put a note under the windshield wiper of a parked car. It read: "I have just smashed into your car. The people who saw the accident are watching me. They think I'm writing down my name and address. I'm not. Good luck."[312]

A little boy was lost during the Christmas shopping rush. He was standing in an aisle of the busy department store crying, "I want my mommy." People passing by kept giving the unhappy youngster nickels and dimes to cheer him up.

Finally a floorwalker came over to him and said, "I know where your mommy is, son."

The little boy looked up with his tear-drenched eyes and said, "So do I . . . just keep quiet!"[313]

In some resort towns in Arizona, it is the practice of various hotels or motels to spray-paint the grass green in the winter to lure tourists to what looks like a lush vacation spot. The problem is that the first spring rains wash the paint into the gutters, revealing how false was the image of the picture-perfect lawns.

That's the essence of hypocrisy—pretending to be what we are not.[314]

Deception

A deception is often something that looks good on the outside and makes great promises, but on the inside you find it is empty—and there is really not much to it.

Most of us at some time or other have bought into an empty deception. We put our money into a machine and pushed a button for a bag of potato chips that, judging from the appearance of the package, looked as if it were full of chips. When the bag comes out and we open it, it turns out to be mainly full of air and contains only a few chips. If we had examined the bag closely before making the purchase, we would have seen it as an empty deception.

The Colossians are an example of believers who were in danger of buying into an empty deception. The apostle Paul warned that they were being presented with religious philosophies and humanly imposed ideas that looked good on the surface. But, when examined on the inside, they were found to be hollow and empty of truth (Col. 2:8, 23).[315]

The story has been told of a woman who had acquired wealth and social prominence and decided to have a book written about her genealogy. The well-known author she engaged for the assignment discovered that one of her grandfathers was a murderer who had been electrocuted in Sing Sing. When he said this would have to be included in the book, the woman pleaded that he find a way of saying it that would hide the truth.

When the book appeared, the incident read as follows: "One of her grandfathers occupied the chair of applied electricity in one of America's best-known institutions. He was very much attached to his position and literally died in the harness."[316]

Several years ago on the *Saturday Evening Post* cover was a painting by Norman Rockwell that showed a woman buying a Thanksgiving turkey. The turkey was on the scales and the butcher was standing behind the counter. The customer, a lady of about sixty, stood watching the weigh-in. Each had a pleased look, but a quick glance at the painting shows nothing unusual going on.

Then we look closely at the entire cover. Rockwell has shown us their hands. The butcher is pressing down on the scales with a thumb while the woman is pushing up with a finger. Both would resent being called thieves, but neither saw anything wrong with a little deception.[317]

Decisions

It may be true that there are two sides to every question, but it is also true that there are two sides to a sheet of flypaper. And it makes a big difference to the fly which side he chooses![318]

Jim Elliot, a dedicated missionary in Ecuador who was killed by the Auca Indians in 1956, said it well: "Father, make of me a crisis man. Bring those I contact to decision. Let me not be a milepost on a single road; make me a fork, that men must turn one way or another on facing

Christ in me." (Cited by Elisabeth Elliot, *The Shadow of the Almighty* [New York: Harper & Row, 1979], p. 59.)[319]

Dedication

Suppose you gave a notebook to a friend and then later find a page that belongs in that notebook. You don't need to agonize over what to do with that page because that was decided when you gave the notebook away. The giving of the page is a reaffirmation of the first giving of the notebook.

So, too, is our dedication to the Lord a continuous act—an ongoing surrender to his power and love.[320]

The only problem with "living sacrifices" is that they keep crawling off the altar.[321]

Someone is reported to have asked a concert violinist in New York's Carnegie Hall how she became so skilled. She said that it was by "planned neglect." She planned to neglect everything that was not related to her goal.[322]

Dedication, Incomplete

Suppose you had a thousand-acre ranch and someone offered to buy it. You agree to sell the land except for one acre right in the center that you want to keep for yourself. In most parts of the country, the law would allow you to have access to that one lone spot by building a road across the surrounding property.

So it is with us as Christians if we make less than a full surrender to God. We can be sure that the devil will build roads to reach any uncommitted area of our life. When this happens, our testimony will be marred and our service will become ineffective.[323]

Defiance Toward God

Invictus
Out of the night that covers me,
Black as the Pit from pole to pole,
I thank whatever gods may be
For my unconquerable soul.

In the fell clutch of circumstance
I have not winced nor cried aloud.
Under the bludgeonings of chance
My head is bloody, but unbowed.

Beyond this place of wrath and tears
Looms but the Horror of the shade,
And yet the menace of the years
Finds, and shall find me, unafraid.

It matters not how strait the gate,
How charged with punishment the scroll,
I am the master of my fate:
I am the captain of my soul.

William E. Henley[324]

Depravity

"Total depravity" is a doctrine rarely preached anymore. Why don't we feel as wicked as the doctrine says we are? For the same reason that a fish doesn't feel wet—because it is immersed.[325]

The Bible says that man was created a little lower than the angels. One thing is clear today—he's been getting a little lower ever since.[326]

Nothing comes out of man's physical body that is either pleasing to look at or pleasing to smell. Likewise there is nothing that comes out of man's heart that is pleasing to God (for salvation).[327]

Suppose we pour a measure of salt into a container of pure water. The salt affects every drop of the water to the extent that all the formerly pure water becomes salty. From that time on, every bit of water drawn from that container is salty and no pure water can be drawn. This is similar to the depraved condition of man. The first sin was an act, one act that brought sin into the human race. Since that one act the very bloodstream of the human race has been polluted.[328]

Dr. Albert Einstein, in a lecture given in 1948, spoke of the nature of man in relation to the world: "The true problem lies in the hearts and thoughts of men. It is not a physical but an ethical one . . . . What terrifies us is not the explosive force of the atomic bomb, but the power of the wickedness of the human heart."[329]

"No clever arrangement of bad eggs will make a good omelet" (C. S. Lewis).[330]

"If only there were evil people somewhere insidiously committing evil deeds, and it were necessary only to separate them from the rest of us and destroy them. But the line dividing good and evil cuts through the heart of every human being. And who is willing to destroy a piece of his own heart?" (Aleksandr Solzenitsyn, *The Gulag Archipelago* [New York: Harper & Row, 1975]).[331]

Depression

A depressive is driving down a country road and has a flat tire. He looks in his trunk for a jack. Not finding one, he spots a farmhouse about a quarter-mile away with a truck in the front yard and says to himself, "I'll go borrow the farmer's jack." As the stranded motorist approaches the house, he is feeling bad—one, for failing to have a jack; two, for having to depend on someone else for help. As he gets nearer the farmhouse, he begins to expect rejection and to get angry over that expectation. As he becomes more and more angry at his unmet dependency needs in the past, he projects to the farmer the anger he feels toward himself for needing the jack and toward others for disappointing him. By the time he knocks on the door and the farmer opens it, the depressive yells, "Keep your jack!" This will most likely guarantee that he doesn't get the jack, so the motorist walks back, reconvinced that you can't depend on people.

Very often our outlook and expectations determine the results.[332]

A man and his wife who were on a long trip stopped at a full-service gas station. After the station attendant had washed their car's windshield, the man in the car said to the station attendant, "It's still dirty. Wash it again."

So the station attendant complied. After washing it again, the man in the car angrily said, "It's still dirty. Don't you know how to wash a windshield?"

Just then the man's wife reached over, removed her husband's glasses from his face, and cleaned them with a tissue. Then he put them back on and behold—the windshield was clean!

Our mental attitude has a great deal to do with how we look at things. The whole world can appear pretty bleak if we have a depressed mental attitude. Yet how bright the world can appear if we have a joyful attitude of hope.[333]

Karl Menninger, a famous psychiatrist, once gave a lecture on mental health and was answering questions from the audience. "What would you advise a person to do," asked one, "if that person felt a nervous breakdown coming on?"

Most people expected Menninger to reply: "Consult a psychiatrist." To their astonishment, he replied, "Lock up your house, go across the railway tracks, find someone in need, and then do something to help that person."[334]

Despair

Sometimes it gets extremely dark in the tunnel. All of a sudden, just when we think we see a light at the end, instead it turns out to be a train coming right at us! Such is the hopeless, fatalistic view of a desperate person.[335]

It is no accident that we describe lives without Jesus Christ as "empty," because that is exactly what they are. The world today is suffering from what Dr. Carl Jung calls "a neurosis of emptiness." He says, "When goal goes, meaning goes; when meaning goes, purpose goes; when purpose goes, life goes dead on our hands."[336]

A skeptic wrote in his autobiography: "What else is there to make life tolerable? We stand on the shore of an ocean, crying to the night, and in the emptiness sometimes a voice answers out of the darkness. But it is the voice of one drowning, and in a moment the silence returns and the world seems to be quite dreadful. The unhappiness of many people is very great, and I often wonder how they endure it."[337]

Devil

A materialist is one who does not believe in demons and has no interest in what they do. A magician is one who believes too much in demons and has an unhealthy interest in them. As for the demons, they care not which you are, for both are equally in error and thus leave you open to their efforts.[338]

Devil's Effect on Christians

While on a trip to the zoo one day, a boy and his father saw a huge lion. The lion was prowling around his enclosure and letting out chilling roars. The boy became very frightened and screamed in terror, but his father remained calm and unafraid. Why? The boy was frightened because he saw only the lion, while the father was unafraid because he saw the cage enclosing the lion.

The Christian's view of Satan should be like that of the father rather than that of the boy, for our fierce enemy is like a *caged* lion.[339]

In some ways the devil is like the villain in the old melodramas. Remember how the plot always develops? The heroine seems to be doomed, and the villain always appears to have the upper hand as he twirls his mustache and rubs his hands together. But at the critical moment the rescuing hero arrives and the plot line changes. The villain is beaten, his scheme fails, and he slinks off the stage muttering, "Curses! Foiled again!"

Of course that is exactly what happens to the devil when a Christian is willing to stand firm, fully outfitted in the armor God has provided (Eph. 6:10–17).[340]

An artist carved a woodcut titled "The Knight, the Devil, and Death." The woodcut pictures a gallant knight riding his stallion down a path in the middle of the night. Alongside the path are many creatures and monsters that seem to want to devour the knight. But they can gain no advantage over him because his eyes are on his home; he cannot be bothered.

Likewise, as long as we keep our eyes on Christ, we will not be devoured by Satan, though he is eagerly awaiting a moment when he might distract us and cause us to sin.[341]

Devil's Fall

In his classic work *Paradise Lost,* John Milton describes the fall of Satan from heaven with his host of rebel angels. He depicts this as a great war lasting three days. The first two days of the cataclysm are waged solely between Satan and his demons and the unfallen angels under the Archangel Michael. On the third day, the Father sends the Son in glorious power to do singlehanded combat with all the demonic host. The following is a brief excerpt from the scene:

> "Stand still in bright array, ye Saints; here stand,
> Ye angels armed; this day from battle rest. . . .
> Therefore to me their doom he hath assigned,
> That they may have their wish, to try with me
> In battle which the stronger proves. . . ."
> So spake the Son, and into terror changed
> His countenance, too severe to be beheld,
> And full of wrath bent on his enemies. . . .
> They, astonished, all resistance lost,
> All courage; down their idle weapons dropt. . . .
> And of the wonted vigour left them drained,
> Exhausted, spiritless, afflicted, fallen.
> Yet half his strength he put not forth. . . .[342]

Discipleship

"The demand for absolute liberty brings men to the depths of slavery." (Dietrich Bonhoeffer, *Cost of Discipleship* [Magnolia, Mass.: Peter Smith, 1983]).[343]

Discipleship, Need for

One weekend, three young fellows decided to take a bicycle trip into the countryside. Although inexperienced, they covered forty miles in three and a half hours and congratulated themselves on their good time. The next morning, as they prepared to head back to their starting point, they were met by a good friend, who had just cycled the forty-mile trip that morning and was ready to head back. He was an excellent cyclist, and with him pacing the young cyclists back to town, they made the return trip in just two and a half hours.

In the same way, young Christians need the "pacing" of older believers as they take their first "rides" in Christ if they are to progress as far in the Christian life as they should and as quickly as they can.[344]

Discipleship, Vision for

William Kelly was an outstanding student of the Bible whose scholarship and spirituality made him a real power for God in Great Britain at the close of the last century. Kelly had once helped a young relative prepare for Trinity College in Dublin and in this way came to the attention of the professors there. They urged him to take up work at the college and thus distinguish himself. When Kelly showed a compete lack of enthusiasm for their suggestion, they were nonplussed. One of them asked in exasperation, "But Mr. Kelly, aren't you interested in making a name for yourself in the world?"

To which Kelly adroitly replied, "Which world, gentlemen?"[345]

Discipline

A man came up to two boys fighting in the park. He took one aside and began to spank him for his inappropriate behavior. An observing bystander came up to the man and asked indignantly why he didn't do anything to the other boy. The man responded that this one was his own son and the other was not.[346]

Discipline, Purpose of

A young child accidentally took sleeping pills from the family's medicine cabinet. The doctor instructed the parents to keep the child awake by any means necessary for the next four hours—including the pain of slapping if necessary. That pain was necessary for the child's survival. So, too, in the Christian's journey: "No discipline seems pleasant at the time, but painful. Later on, however, it produces a harvest of righteousness and peace for those who have been trained by it" (Heb. 12:11, NIV).[347]

A boy's toy boat went out of reach on a pond one day and started floating away. A man on the side started throwing rocks at the boat and the boy became horrified at what might happen. But then he realized that the rocks were going over the boat and making ripples that finally pushed the boat back to shore and into the boy's hands.

Many times, when we stray away from God, it appears that he is throwing rocks at us. But he is really using the ripples to bring us back home.[348]

A woman visiting in Switzerland came to a sheepfold on one of her daily walks. Venturing in, she saw the shepherd seated on the ground with his flock around him. Nearby, on a pile of straw lay a single sheep, which seemed to be suffering. Looking closely, the woman saw that its leg was broken.

Her sympathy went out to the suffering sheep, and she looked up inquiringly to the shepherd as she asked how it happened. "I broke it myself," said the shepherd sadly and then explained. "Of all the sheep in my flock, this was the most wayward. It would not obey my voice and would not follow when I was leading the flock. On more than one occasion, it wandered to the edge of a perilous cliff. And not only was it disobedient itself, but it was leading other sheep astray.

"Based on my experience with this kind of sheep, I knew I had no choice, so I broke its leg. The next day I took food and it tried to bite me. After letting it lie alone for a couple of days, I went back and it not only eagerly took the food, but licked my hand and showed every sign of submission and affection.

"And now, let me say this. When this sheep is well, it will be the model sheep of my entire flock. No sheep will hear my voice so quickly nor follow so closely. Instead of leading the others away, it will be an example of devotion and obedience. In short, a complete change will come into the life of this wayward sheep. It will have learned obedience through its sufferings."

Many times it is the same in human experience. Through our suffering, God may be seeking to teach us obedience and reliance on his care.[349]

The two-year-old, normally a quite obedient little boy, was having an attack of stubbornness—a disease endemic to the species. Still, it was surprising to see such a severe case in one of such tender years. His mother had asked the lad to do something, but he was much too absorbed in his own activities to take time out for that. The father watched as the mother went over to impress on the little boy the importance of minding his parents promptly—to which he responded with a right hook to the jaw of his surprised mother! The father, realizing that his son's behavior was completely unacceptable and would become dangerous not only to the mother but to the child as well if it were allowed to continue, intervened at this point by giving the would-be boxer the worst spanking of his young life, after which he was sent to his room.

Ten minutes later, the child was back, tears still streaming down his cherub face, and crawled sobbing into the father's lap as he put his chubby little arms around his neck. What followed is one of the warmest and tenderest memories in this father's heart. What the child said was not "I'm sorry, Dad," or "I won't do it again," but—with a wisdom and perception far beyond his years—"I love you, Dad!"[350]

Discipline is not God's way of saying, "I'm through with you," or a mark of abandonment by him. Rather, it is the loving act of God to bring you back. C. S. Lewis said, "God whispers to us in our pleasures; he speaks to us in our work; he shouts at us in our pain."

Every one of us knows that there have been times when we would not listen to God or pay any attention to what his Word was saying, until finally he used a severe discipline to get our attention so that we *would* listen.[351]

Loose wires give out no musical notes, but when their ends are fastened, the piano, the harp, or the violin is born. Free steam drives no machine, but harnessed and confined with piston and turbine, it makes possible the great world of machinery. An unhampered river drives no dynamos, but dam it up and you can generate sufficient power to light a great city. So our lives must be disciplined if we are to be of any real service in the world.[352]

Discipline, Self-

Lord Joseph Duveen, American head of the art firm that bore his name, planned in 1915 to send one of his experts to England to examine some ancient pottery. He booked passage on the *Lusitania*. Then the German Embassy issued a warning that the liner might be torpedoed.

Duveen wanted to call off the trip. "I can't take the risk of your being killed," he said to his young employee.

"Don't worry," said the man, "I'm a strong swimmer, and when I read what was happening in the Atlantic, I began hardening myself by spending time every day in a tub of ice water. At first I could sit only a few minutes, but this morning, I stayed in that tub nearly two hours."

Naturally, Duveen laughed. It sounded preposterous. But his expert sailed, and the *Lusitania* was torpedoed. The young man was rescued after nearly five hours in the chilly ocean, still in excellent condition.

Just as this young man did, so Christians should condition themselves by practicing devotional discipline, behavioral discipline, and discipline in doing good. (Cited in *Christianity Today*, February 1979, p. 25.)[353]

Self-discipline is when your conscience tells you something and you don't talk back.[354]

Discipline, Success and

> "Why are men so great?" some ask. Well . . .
> The heights by great men reached and kept
> Were not attained by sudden flight;
> But they, while their companions slept,
> Were toiling upward in the night.[355]

Discouragement

The devil decided to have a garage sale. On the day of sale, his tools were placed for public inspection, each being marked with its sale price. There were a treacherous lot of implements: hatred, envy, jealousy, deceit, lust, lying, pride, and so on.

Set apart from the rest was a harmless-looking tool. It was quite worn and yet priced very high.

"What is the name of this tool?" asked one of the customers, pointing to it.

"That is discouragement," Satan replied.

"Why have you priced it so high?"

"Because it is more useful to me than the others. I can pry open and get inside a man's heart with that, even when I cannot get near him with the other tools. It is badly worn because I use it on almost everyone, since so few people know it belongs to me."

The devil's price for discouragement was high because it is still his favorite tool, and he is still using it on God's people.[356]

Divorce

Dissolving a marriage is not like dissolving a business partnership, or even like deserting from the army. Indeed, many psychologists have stated that it is second in emotional impact only to the death of a spouse.[357]

On a television show, "Divorce Wars," a thriving divorce lawyer found himself on the brink of divorce, even though he strongly believed in family life. As he began to ponder why his marriage was falling apart, he asked a friend the following question: "Max, how did you stay married for thirty-five years?"

Max, being older, had a rather illuminating answer: "I guess in our generation we didn't expect as much from each other—and we ended up getting more."[358]

"I will never marry again"—said by Barbara Hutton (who was at the time heiress to the forty-five-million-dollar Woolworth fortune), after divorcing her second husband, Count Kurt Heinrich Haughwitz-Hardenberg-Reventlow, in 1941.

"I will never marry again. You can't go on being a fool forever"—said by Barbara Hutton, after divorcing her third husband, Cary Grant, in 1945.

"This is positively my final marriage"—said by Barbara Hutton, after marrying her sixth husband, Baron Gottfried von Kramm, in 1955.

"He's a composite of all my previous husbands' best qualities without any of the bad qualities. . . . I have never been so happy in my life"—said by Barbara Hutton, after marrying her seventh husband, Prince Doan Vinh de Champacak of Vietnam, in 1964.

In November, 1966 Barbara Hutton and Prince Doan Vinh de Champacak of Vietnam filed for divorce.(Cited by Christopher Cerf and Victor Navasky, *The Experts Speak* [New York: Pantheon, 1984], p. 22.)[359]

Sylvester Stallone, filmdom's "Rocky," was quoted by *Sports Illustrated* (10/5/79) as saying, "Boxing is a great exercise—as long as you can yell 'cut' whenever you want to."

Many people go into marriage the same way. They figure it's great mental, emotional, or even physical exercise as long as you can cut out whenever you want to![360]

111

Divorce, Effect of

The results of a 1978 survey reveal that the main causes of loneliness usually have their origins in childhood. Children who were less than six years of age when parents were divorced were by far the loneliest as adults. (Cited in *Human Nature*, February 1979.)[361]

The conclusion of a five-year study by Mavis Hetherington of the University of Virginia on who is most hurt in a divorce is that "small boys are the worst victims of divorce and their painful attempts to adjust often lead them into a mutually destructive conflict with their mothers." (Cited in *Dads Only*, Vol. 2, No. 9, September 1979.)[362]

Divorce, Responsibility for

"As a pastor in three different churches, encompassing twenty-eight years, I'm beginning to wonder if there is such a thing as an innocent party" (Dr. Stephen Olford).[363]

Doctrine, False

I once saw a card that said: "Old fishermen never die—they only smell that way."

That surely describes false Christianity. It never dies—it only smells that way.[364]

Fire ants have virtually taken over the southern United States since they were accidentally transported here a few decades ago. They are amazingly adaptable, fiercely aggressive, and multiply seemingly overnight. Worst of all, insecticide sprays generally can't destroy the mound's inhabitants. Like a mighty army they have marched in, impervious to brute force.

Scientists have now found a rather crafty way to wipe out whole colonies. Pellets of the ants' favorite food are tainted with a special tasteless, odorless poison and sprinkled around the mound. The worker ants immediately begin gathering up the tainted treasure and take it down into the heart of the colony. Then they unwittingly feed the poisoned pellets to their queen, slowly killing her! When the queen dies, no more workers are produced, and so in a couple of weeks the entire colony starves to death. How ironic! Food that looked so good caused their starvation.

That is how it is with false doctrine. Those who lack discernment import it into the heart of the church, thinking it is harmless and in fact quite good. If any wise "ant" smells the poison and protests, he is ridiculed! And in the end the next generation starves to death spiritually.[365]

In an examination at a Christian school, the teacher asked the following question: "What is false doctrine?"

Up went a little boy's hand, and there came this answer: "It's when the doctor gives the wrong stuff to people who are sick."

Although the little boy had obviously confused *doctrine* with *doctorin'*, he arrived at the correct definition.[366]

The seriousness of errant doctrine can be compared to a missile aimed a mere one degree off target. The difference seems slight and negligible at first, yet the results of the error increase dramatically throughout the flight of the missile, until it totally misses its intended target.

So it is with false doctrine. At first it may seem to be a tolerable mistake, a little error—but not that serious. But, as with all errors, the effects compound over time until they become so serious that they may not be correctable.[367]

Doctrine, Sound

A *Peanuts* cartoon pictured Lucy and Linus looking out the window at a steady downpour of rain. "Boy," said Lucy, "look at it rain. What if it floods the whole world?"

"It will never do that," Linus replied confidently. "In the ninth chapter of Genesis, God promised Noah that would never happen again, and the sign of the promise is the rainbow."

"You've taken a great load off my mind," said Lucy with a relieved smile.

"Sound theology," pontificated Linus, "has a way of doing that!"[368]

Doubt

"To believe is to be 'in one mind' about accepting something as true; to disbelieve is to be 'in one mind' about rejecting it. To doubt is to waver between the two, to believe and disbelieve at once and so be 'in two minds' " (Os Guinness, *In Two Minds* [Downers Grove, Ill: Inter-Varsity, 1976], pp. 24–25).[369]

Drugs

> King Heroin is my shepherd,
> I shall always want,
> He maketh me to lie down in the gutters
> He leadeth me beside the troubled waters
> He destroyeth my soul.

This is an anonymous poem, quoted by Francis Schaeffer (*The God Who Is There* [Downers Grove, Ill: Inter-Varsity, 1968], p. 29).[370]

Edification

The church is not a gallery where we exhibit the finest of Christians. No, it is a school where we educate and encourage imperfect Christians.[371]

When geese migrate they can be seen flying in a V-shaped formation. While to us on the ground it is a thing of beauty, to the geese it is an essential for survival. If you watch them, you will observe that at certain intervals, relative to the strength of the headwind, the lead bird—who was doing the most work by breaking the force of wind—will drop off and fly at the end of the formation.

The reason for this is that the V-formation is much more efficient than flying close; up to 60 percent less work is required! It has been discovered that the flapping wings create an uplift of air, an effect that is greater at the rear of the formation. So the geese take turns "uplifting" one another. By cooperating—working together—the geese can achieve long migrations that would otherwise be exceedingly difficult for the strongest and deadly for the others.

In a similar manner, when believers in Christ actively uplift one another through prayer, sharing material means, and heart-to-heart friendship and caring, they can go further into godliness than if they attempt their pilgrimage alone.[372]

Education

"Soap and education are not as sudden as a massacre, but they are more deadly in the long run" (Mark Twain).[373]

Elect, Identity of

When C. H. Spurgeon preached on "election" somebody said to him, "Why don't you just preach to the called, to the elect?" He replied, "Well, if you'll run around and pull up everybody's shirttails so I can see if they have an 'E' stamped on their back, I will."

Only God knows who is elect and who is not.[374]

Election

There was a boy who did not have much athletic ability. Every time he and his friends would play some game he was always the last to be chosen. One day two new fellows came to play with them and were allowed to be team captains because they were older. The first team captain chose the boy who had always been chosen last before. Why? Because they were brothers, and he loved his brother.

So it is with God. He chose us not because of our abilities, but because he loves us.[375]

The mere preaching of the gospel does not save an individual. The gospel message must be activated by the election and calling of God for an individual to be drawn to him. It would be as if one had thrown a rope to a drowning man. The throwing of that rope could not save the man unless someone were at the other end drawing him into shore.

This is what God has done. By his election, God draws to himself the one who has heard the message. The man may have the rope, but he still needs the efficient force of God drawing him in. Who, therefore, deserves the praise for salvation, the man who grabbed the rope? No—the God who draws him in![376]

The resolution of election and free will has troubled theologians for centuries. One found an explanation in a picture of the door to heaven. On the side of the door facing the one who was about to enter heaven were written the words "Every one who calls upon the name of the Lord will be saved" (Rom. 10:13). On the side of the door facing those who were already in heaven were written the words "called through his grace" (Gal. 1:15).[377]

"The general call of the gospel is like the sheet lightning we sometimes see on a summer evening—beautiful, grand—but who ever heard of anything being struck by it? But the special call is the forked flash from heaven; it strikes somewhere" (C. H. Spurgeon, *Autobiography* [Carlisle, Penna.: Banner of Truth, 1975] p. 72).[378]

Many a young man thought that he had chosen the young lady who became his wife—only to find out after the wedding that she had first chosen him.[379]

"It is a good thing that God chose me before I was born, because he surely would not have afterwards!" (Attributed to C. H. Spurgeon).[380]

Election, Definition of

C. H. Spurgeon told of a time when he was preaching to a group of Methodist brethren. In his own words he gave us an account of what transpired:

> Preaching a few months ago in the midst of a large congregation of Methodists, the brethren were all alive, giving all kinds of answers to my sermon, nodding their heads and crying, "Amen! Hallelujah! Glory be to God!" My spirit was stirred, and I preached away with an unusual force and vigor, and the more I preached, the more they cried, "Amen, Hallelujah! Glory be to God!" At last a part of text led me to what is styled high doctrine. So I said, this brings me to the doctrine of Election. There was a deep drawing of breath, Now, my friends, you believe it. They seemed to say, "No, we don't!" But you do, and I will make you sing "Hallelujah" over it. I will so preach it to you that you will acknowledge it and believe it. So I put it thus: Is there no difference between you and other men? "Yes, yes, glory be to God!" There is a difference between what you were and what you are now? "Oh yes, yes!" There is sitting by your side a man who has been to the same chapel as you have, heard the same gospel; he

is unconverted, and you are converted. Who has made the difference, yourself or God? "The Lord!" said they. "The Lord! Glory! Hallelujah!" Yes, cried I, and that is the doctrine of Election; that is all I contend for, that if there be a difference, the Lord made the difference [C. H. Spurgeon, "Election and Holiness," March 11, 1860].[381]

Election, Predestination and

Election is God's deciding who gets on the plane bound for heaven.

Predestination is his charting the route the plane will take, the schedule, the accommodations both during and after the flight, and each passenger's safety. With God as the pilot of the plane and the plane itself, all who board the plane make it to heaven. Predestination means God himself makes sure the elect actually board the plane. Their response of faith in Christ is like checking in at the gate with a boarding pass.

The gospel call, in contrast, is like advertising for the trip. The church is commissioned to get the word to the whole world. Unfortunately most people treat God's free offer as "junk mail" and throw it in the trash. However, those whom God has elected to salvation he also moves to accept his free offer. Many are called, but few are chosen. Yet all who are chosen are predestined to end up in heaven.[382]

Election of Judas

A man once asked a theologian, "Why did Jesus choose Judas Iscariot to be his disciple?" The reply was insightful, "I do not know, but I have an even harder question: Why did Jesus choose me?"[383]

Emotions

The human personality is said to consist of roughly four-fifths emotions and one-fifth intellect. This means that our decisions are arrived at on the basis of 80 percent emotion and only 20 percent intellect. To engage in a confrontation, or even a discussion, without taking emotions into account is to be only 20 percent effective in your dealings with people.[384]

Encouragement

> I saw them tearing a building down,
> A gang of men in a dusty town.

117

> With a "yo heave ho" and a lusty yell,
> They swung a beam and the side wall fell.
>
> I asked the foreman if these men were as skilled
> As the men he'd hire, if he were to build.
> He laughed and said, "Oh, no indeed.
> Common labor is all I need."
>
> For those men can wreck in a day or two,
> What builders had taken years to do.
> I asked myself as I went my way,
> Which kind of role am I to play?
>
> Am I the builder who builds with care,
> Measuring life by the rule and square?
> Or am I the wrecker who walks the town,
> Content with the role of tearing down?[385]

Encouragement is like a peanut butter sandwich—the more you spread it around, the better things stick together.[386]

Said Bear Bryant, one of the greatest college football coaches ever, when he was pushed to explain his philosophy of coaching: "There's just three things I ever say [to my players]: 'If anything goes bad, then *I* did it. If anything goes semi-good, then *we* did it. If anything goes real good, then *you* did it.' That's all it takes to get people to win football games for you. I can do that better than anybody."[387]

In a 1978 interview, Lou Holtz, at the time the head coach of the then number-one rated Arkansas Razorbacks, modeled and stated his philosophy of coaching. At practice, Holtz grabs his players by their face masks and shakes them; he flails at them with his hat; he throws his hat in disgust; he smacks players on the rear with his omnipresent manila folder. "Once you get things going, then you begin to build confidence," he says. "You praise loudly and criticize softly."[388]

Dr. Paul Tournier received the supreme compliment of life one day when an acquaintance came to visit him in his home. The acquaintance relayed a message from a third party, who had never met Dr. Tournier but had been helped through many of his writings. The message was: "You're going to see Paul Tournier in Switzerland. No doubt

I shall never see him in this world, but tell him from me that he will be one of the first people I shall look out for in heaven."[389]

Encouragement, Parental

Evangelist Bill Glass asked a group of a thousand prison inmates, "How many of you had parents who told you that you would end up in prison one day?" Almost every one of the inmates raised his hand.[390]

When he was a young boy the great painter Benjamin West decided to paint a picture of his sister while his mother was not at home. He got out the bottles of ink and started, but soon had an awful mess. His mother eventually returned and of course saw the mess. Instead of scolding him, she picked up the portrait and declared, "What a beautiful picture of your sister!" Then she kissed him. Later in life he said, "With that kiss I became a painter."[391]

Encouragement, Spousal

In 1849, when Nathaniel Hawthorne was dismissed from his government job in the customs house, he went home in despair. His wife listened to his tale of woe, set pen and ink on the table, lit the fire, put her arms around his shoulders and said, "Now you will be able to write your novel." Hawthorne did—and literature was enriched with *The Scarlet Letter*.[392]

Katherine, the wife of Martin Luther, dramatically revived the depressed Reformer's confidence in God's providence. This has been versified by F. W. Herzberger:

> One day when skies loomed the blackest,
> This greatest and bravest of men
> Lost heart and in an oversad spirit
> Refused to take courage again,
>
> Neither eating or drinking nor speaking
> To anxious wife, children or friends,
> Till Katherine dons widow garments
> And deepest of mourning pretends.

> Surprised, Luther asked why she sorrowed.
>   "Dear Doctor," his Katie replied,
> "I have cause for the saddest of weeping,
>   For God in His heaven has died!"
>
> Her gentle rebuke did not fail him,
>   He laughingly kissed his wise spouse,
> Took courage, and banished his sorrow,
>   And joy again reigned in the house.[393]

Endurance

Several years ago a man reported his observations of the effects of a hurricane on a southeastern Gulf Coast town. As he walked up and down the ravaged streets, he observed that the palm trees had been uprooted and flung about. Once tall and majestic, their root systems were too shallow to withstand the hurricane force winds. But as he proceeded, he came upon a lone oak tree. The leaves had been blown away and some of the smaller branches ripped off, but the roots had gone deep, and the tree held its position. And in due season it would again produce leaves.

So it is with us. If we are to endure in times of great stress and difficulty, we must beforehand have put down a depth of character that will sustain the blows of the trial.[394]

"Our men were not braver than the enemy. They were brave five minutes longer" (attributed to Lord Wellington after the great victory won over Napoleon at Waterloo).[395]

Enemies

"If we could read the secret history of our enemies, we should find in each man's life sorrow and suffering enough to disarm all hostility" (Henry W. Longfellow, "Driftwood").[396]

Enemies, Love for

In the Shapra Indian tribe of Peru, an interesting event occurred. In this South American tribe, who once were headhunters, Christ has made a difference in those who became believers. One man used to kill his enemies when he captured them. After his conversion, he would hold them captive and teach them Scripture for three weeks! (Cited by Herbert Fuqua, missionary to Peru.)[397]

Envy

There is a fable that Satan's agents were failing in their various attempts to draw into sin a holy man who lived as a hermit in the desert of northern Africa. Every attempt had met with failure; so Satan, angered with the incompetence of his subordinates, became personally involved in the case. He said, "The reason you have failed is that your methods are too crude for one such as this. Watch this."

He then approached the holy man with great care and whispered softly in his ear, "Your brother has just been made Bishop of Alexandria." Instantly the holy man's face showed that Satan had been successful: a great scowl formed over his mouth and his eyes tightened up.

"Envy," said Satan, "is often our best weapon against those who seek holiness."[398]

Eternal Life

A child does not *begin* to exist when he (or she) is born. The child has already existed for nine months prior to this in the mother's womb. At the point of birth, only the conditions in which the child exists change. Before, he lived internally; now, he lives externally. Before, he was fed internally; now, he feeds externally. He does not begin to live at birth: he has lived all the time since conception, but conditions change at birth.

So also can the believer view death. At the point of death, the conditions of our eternal life change—but not the fact that we do indeed have eternal life.[399]

When the great Christian scientist Sir Michael Faraday was dying, some journalists questioned him about his speculations for a life after death. He purportedly replied: "Speculations! I know nothing about speculations. I'm resting on certainties. I know that my Redeemer liveth, and because He lives, I shall live also" (Job 19:25)[400]

B. J. Honeycutt, a character on the T.V. series "M.A.S.H.," gave this reason for why he didn't give in to temptation in the midst of the Korean

War: "I live in an insane world where nothing makes sense. Everyone around me lives for the now, because there may not be a tomorrow. But I have to live for tomorrow, because for me there is no now."

For B. J., his hope for the future was seeing his family again. That hope was sufficient to define how he would behave in an extremely difficult situation. How much more so should our future hope of the kingdom of God shape how we live?[401]

Eternal Security

It is said that D. L. Moody was once accosted on a Chicago street by a drunk who exclaimed, "Aren't you Mr. Moody? Why, I'm one of your converts!" Said Moody in reply, "That must be true, for you surely aren't one of the Lord's."

The gospel promises not only forgiveness of sins but also new life. When a person receives this new life, his or her life should begin to show some changes.[402]

Those who don't believe in eternal security say that the doctrine leads to license and sin. This is as absurd as saying that because we have Blue Cross/Blue Shield insurance, we will chew on razor blades or guzzle hydrochloric acid.[403]

Euthanasia

The following is from a story on "60 Minutes" (10/12/80) about the growing interest in euthanasia and its actual practice, including cases where it went unprosecuted:

> Dame Cicily, a woman given the equivalent of knighthood by Queen Elizabeth II for her years of work with the dying, and the founder of the Hospice Movement in England and the U.S., gave the estimation that the problem with granting or encouraging use of the "right" to die is that it will soon become the duty to die. Knowing the depravity of man, she said, it is unthinkable that once old people enlist the help of friends or family, they will soon be expected to enlist such help to "end it all." People will say to the ones dying and in pain, "You know, you don't have to go on like this. You could end it all painlessly and quickly, and stop your own pain and the hardship on your family."[404]

Evangelism

Evangelism has been described as one beggar telling another beggar where to find food.[405]

Holy boldness honors the gospel. In the olden times, when Oriental despots had things pretty much their own way, they expected all ambassadors from the West to lay their mouths in the dust if permitted to appear before his Celestial Brightness, the Brother of the Sun and Cousin of the Moon. Certain money-loving traders agreed to all this, and ate dust as readily as reptiles. But when England sent her ambassadors abroad, the daring islanders stood bolt-upright. They were told that they could not be indulged with a vision of the Brother of the Sun and Cousin of the Moon without going to their hands and knees. "Very well," said the Englishmen, "we will dispense with the luxury, but tell his Celestial Splendor that it is very likely that his Serenity will hear our cannon at his palace gates before long, and that their booming is not quite so harmless as the cooing of his Sublimity's doves." When it was seen that ambassadors of the English Crown were no cringing petitioners, the British Empire rose in respect of Oriental nations.

It must be just so with the cross of Christ. Our cowardice has subjected the gospel to contempt. To preach the gospel boldly is to deliver it as such a message ought to be delivered [C. H. Spurgeon, *Feathers for Arrows*, p. 23].[406]

The church ought to be a maternity ward where the cries of newborn babes in Christ are constantly heard.[407]

Evangelism, Clarity in

As the following dialogue illustrates, many times well-meaning Christians, including evangelists, fail to communicate the Good News to non-believers because they use terms that the non-believer doesn't use, or uses in a different way.

Evangelist: Are you a member of the Christian family?

Store clerk: No, they live two miles down the road, the white house on the left.

Evangelist: Let me try again. Are you lost?

Store clerk: No, I've lived in this town for over thirty years now. I know right where I am.

Evangelist: Let me put it this way—are you ready for the Judgment Day?

Store clerk: When will it be?

Evangelist: Could be today, could be tomorrow!

Store clerk: Well, when you know exactly, be sure to let me know. My wife will probably want to go on both days.[408]

Evangelism, Commitment to

Coca-Cola has fulfilled their own version of the Great Commission many times over. They have virtually put a bottle of Coke in everyone's hand. If they can do it with a soft drink, we can certainly do it with the gospel.[409]

Many Christians are like the Arctic River—frozen over at the mouth! In evangelism, the hardest thing seems to be to open your mouth to get the first word out.[410]

Each human soul is like a cavern full of gems. The casual observer glances into it through some cranny, and all looks dark and sullen and useless. But let light enter into it and lo! It will flash with crystals and amethysts and quiver under the touch of brightness. If souls do not shine before you it is because you bring them no light to make them shine. Throw away your miserable, smouldering, fuming torch of conceit and hatred, lift up to them the light of love, and lo! They will arise and shine; yea, flame and burn with an undreamt of glory" (Canon Farrar).[411]

When Henry Ford purchased a large insurance policy, the Detroit newspapers blazoned the fact, since the amount was so large and he was so prominent. The story was read by one of Ford's old friends, who happened to be in the insurance business. The old friend went to confront Ford to see if the story was true. When Ford assured him that it was, the friend asked him why the policy was not purchased from him, since he was a personal friend and had been in insurance for many years. Ford's reply was, "You never asked me."

How many of our friends can say to us, "You never asked me," as to our sharing Christ with them?[412]

Jehovah's Witnesses spend at least ten hours a month pounding the pavement in their hometown, looking for new members. "Our religion is not just a formality," said Jared K. Hardie, a public-relations officer for the Dallas Watchtower Convention. "Our whole lifestyle revolves around our obligation to follow the command of Jesus. We have five hours of meetings each week in addition to our personal study. And our door-to-door work is not an effort to pester or harass people. I think most people know that we do it because they know we are sincere." (Cited in *Dallas Times Herald*, 7/1/79, p. B-2.)[413]

Once, when walking down a certain street in Chicago, D. L. Moody stepped up to a man, a perfect stranger to him, and said, "Sir, are you a Christian?"

"You mind your own business!" was the reply.

Moody replied, "This *is* my business."[414]

Evangelism, Love and

This story is told of Harry Winston, who was one of the world's greatest jewel merchants. One day he watched one of his salesmen show a beautiful diamond to a rich Dutch merchant. The customer listened thoughtfully to the expert description, but he eventually turned away, saying, "It's a wonderful stone, but not exactly what I want."

Winston stopped the customer on his way out and asked, "Do you mind if I show you that diamond once more?" The merchant agreed. Winston took the stone in his hand. He did not repeat anything the salesman had said. He simply talked about the gem as an object of deep beauty. Abruptly the customer changed his mind and bought the diamond. While he was waiting for it to be brought to him, he turned to Winston and said, "Why did I buy it willingly from you, though I had no difficulty saying no to your salesman?"

Winston answered, "That salesman is one of the best men in the business. He knows diamonds—but I love them."[415]

Evangelism, Methods of

In an apparent effort to promote the spread of the gospel message, someone in a major city decided to take a can of spray paint and spray-paint the message "Trust Jesus" on sidewalks, overpasses, and even mailboxes in the downtown area.

This was not "evangelism," but rather, "evandalism." The right message does not justify the use of wrong means.[416]

Too many Christians are no longer fishers of men but keepers of the aquarium.[417]

Evangelism must be done where lost people are.

An old farmer fishing in a tub of water in his back yard was chided by his neighbor: "Man, there ain't no fish in that tub. Why are you wastin' your time like that?"

"Yeah," came the reply. "I know there ain't no fish in here, but it's just so powerful convenient."

Many churches are engaged in "convenience evangelism," which is really very little evangelism at all.[418]

A little girl asked her father why firemen stayed in the firehouse all day and polished their engines and other equipment. He explained that they did this to pass the time while waiting for fire calls.

Many Christians likewise stay close to the familiar surroundings of the church community, applying another coat of worship or getting a theological tune-up, while all the time waiting for some sinner to request a gospel presentation. The problem with this approach to evangelism is that the world is already ablaze, and the call went out two thousand years ago! A person in the midst of a fire doesn't need a beautiful, well-tuned, and shiny fire engine to be rescued.[419]

"It is better for most of us to fish with the rod than with the net. To angle for single souls rather than to try and enclose a multitude at once. Preaching to a congregation has its own place and value; but private and personal talk honestly and wisely done will effect more than the most eloquent preaching" (attributed to Alexander Maclaren, a widely known preacher).[420]

Many believers who would share Christ have more zeal than knowledge and offend more often than they communicate. You may have heard of the barber who was newly saved and was eager to witness to his experience with Jesus Christ. As he met his first customer the next day, he was sharpening his straight razor on the leather strap. His initial approach to his customer was, "Are you ready to die?" One can imagine what went through the customer's mind as he viewed the finely honed razor. As the cliché goes, "If we don't use tact, we may lose contact."[421]

Evangelism, Muslims and

A Christian man was looking for an opportunity to witness to a devout Muslim whom he knew. One day the chance came when the Muslim was preparing for prayer by carefully washing his arms and face and other parts of his body. When he was through, his Christian friend told him that he had forgotten one thing, washing his heart. The Muslim replied, "Don't be silly. I can't wash my heart!" The friend agreed, "That's right, that's why you need Christ."[422]

Evangelism, Motives for

Imagine that I have ten bags of money here, each containing a thousand dollars, and that I offer one of these bags to each of the first ten people who, by this time tomorrow, will share the gospel with a nonbeliever and invite him to receive Jesus Christ as Savior. The response of the non-believer would have no bearing on whether one gets the money.

What do you think would happen? We all know that there would be a mad rush to get out of here and be one of the first ten to tell somebody about Jesus. Are we more willing to witness out of impure motives than out of love for and obedience to the Lord?[423]

The story is told of the captain of a Mississippi riverboat who, as his ship passed another vessel, grabbed the first passenger he saw and said, "Look, look, over there on the other boat. Look at its captain." The man was somewhat bewildered and asked, "Why do you want me to look at that captain? What makes him so special?"

Then the captain told him the story of how he had collided one night with another boat. His own vessel was foundering and in the process he was thrown overboard. The captain of the other vessel saw his desperate plight and maneuvered close enough that he was able to dive into the water and save his life.

After telling the story, the once-saved captain then turned to the bystander and said, "Ever since that day, I want to point out my rescuer to others." Likewise, as those who have been saved, secured, and loved by Jesus, we should want to tell others of him.[424]

Evangelism, Necessity for

A young boy about seven years old went to Disneyland with his family, but in the excitement of going on all the rides, he was separated from them. He was having such a wonderful time that it was quite a while before he realized that he was lost. When he discovered the predicament he was in, he at first figured that he could find his way back to his family. But, after a time, it finally hit him that he didn't know where he was going or how to get there. He was lost, *really lost!*

The same is true for unbelievers. They may not know it yet, because they may still be having a wonderful time, but they are lost all the same. Sooner or later it's going to hit them that they don't know where they are going or how to get there.

Two things were necessary for the boy to be reunited with his family. First, he had to recognize his condition. Second, someone had to show him where he could find his family. So, too, in evangelism— the Holy Spirit will first convict individuals of their lostness (John 16:8–10), but we Christians are commissioned to show them the way of salvation.[425]

Evangelist Vance Havner, preaching at the Moody Bible Institute's Founder's Week in 1974, stated: "Evangelism is to Christianity what veins are to our bodies. You can cut Christianity anywhere and it'll bleed evangelism. Evangelism is vascular, it's our business. Talk about majoring on evangelism, you might as well talk about a doctor majoring on healing. That's our business."[426]

The following excerpt is from *A Quiet Revolution*, (Waco, Texas: Word, 1977) by John Perkins, a black evangelist and social worker in Jackson, Mississippi.

Many years ago, before the term "civil rights" was a household phrase, one Southern state was reforming its penal system. The latest refinement was the installation of the state's first gas chamber. The day had come for the chamber to be used for the first time. The victim, a black man, was brought into the chamber and strapped into the chair. He became hysterical and began to scream, "Save me, Joe Louis! Save me, Joe Louis!"

He had been found guilty by the courts. He paid the price. I don't find any meaning in that. But his words, his last words, could be the words of a whole generation of black people, few of whom have heard the real truth about salvation through Jesus Christ. They represent the majority of black people looking for something to save them, to make them whole, to give them meaning and peace and happiness, but who are without access to the central truths of the gospel.[427]

Hudson Taylor told of a Chinese pastor who always instructed new converts to witness as soon as possible. Once, upon meeting a young convert, the pastor inquired, "Brother, how long have you been saved?" The man answered that he had been saved for about three months.

"And how many have you won to the Savior?"

"Oh, I'm only a learner," the convert responded.

Shaking his head in disapproval, the pastor said, "Young man, the Lord doesn't expect you to be a full-fledged preacher, but he does expect you to be a faithful witness. Tell me, when does a candle begin to shine—when it's already half burned up?"

"No, as soon as it's lit," came the reply.

"That's right, so let your light shine right away."[428]

Evil, Problem of

Whatever the answer to why there is evil and suffering in the world, this much is true: God took his own medicine.[429]

Evil, Purpose of

A composer of a musical score sometimes includes some discords to create an overall pleasing effect. In a similar manner, God's ultimate purpose for the world was best served by a plan that allowed for the presence and activity of evil.[430]

Evil, Response to

A certain man purchased a paper at a newspaper stand. He greeted the newsman very courteously, but in return received gruff and discourteous service. Accepting the newspaper, which was rudely shoved in his face, the customer politely smiled and wished the newsman a nice weekend. A friend observed all of this and asked, "Does he always treat you so rudely?"

"Yes, unfortunately he does."

"And are you always so polite and friendly to him?"

"Yes, I am."

"Why are you so nice to him when he is so rude to you?"

"Because I don't want *him* to decide how *I* am going to act."[431]

Evolutionism, Impact of

In commenting on the medical challenges faced during the rapid urbanization of U.S. cities in the late 1800s, Columbia University historian John Garraty said the following about the negative influence of Darwinism upon medical science: "Efforts to do something about high infant mortality rates in poor districts ran into resistance from Darwinian evolutionists who argued that any attempt to reduce infant mortality might lead to the survival of too many 'weaklings' and thus to racial degeneration" (John Garraty, *The New Commonwealth* [New York: Harper & Row, 1968], p. 213).[432]

Example, Teaching by

The story is told of a T.V. repairman who didn't like to think about his job when he came home. As a result, he never bothered to properly install the T.V. antenna on the top of his house or fix it when one arm broke in a windstorm. One day a new family moved in next door, and the owner went up on his roof to install an antenna. Knowing that his neighbor was a T.V. repairman, he put his up exactly the same way and turned his antenna to face in the same direction as his neighbor's. Then, after studying his neighbor's antenna for a while, he reached up and broke one arm off his new antenna!

As disciples, we teach by example, whether we intend to or not![433]

As a boy, Dr. John Mitchell was familiar with the mountains and mine pits around his house. One night his Boy Scout troop was on a midnight hike. Since Mitchell knew the mountains and where the dangerous pits were, he took several private jaunts away from the troop. The scoutmaster admonished him, saying: "Although *you* know where the mine pits are and how to avoid them, when you go to them you make a path that others may follow to their death."[434]

Excellence

A true musician always does his best before every audience, be it of knowledgeable music lovers or unschooled listeners. A committee once asked Enrico Caruso, the great tenor, to sing at a concert that would benefit a charity. The chairman said, "Of course, Mr. Caruso, as this is a charity affair we would not expect much from you. Your name alone will draw a crowd and you can merely sing some song requiring little effort or skill." Caruso drew himself up and replied, "Gentlemen, Caruso never does less than his best."[435]

Excuses

An excuse has been defined as the skin of a reason stuffed with a lie.[436]

A farmer asked his neighbor if he might borrow a rope.
"Sorry," said the neighbor. "I'm using my rope to tie up my milk."
"Rope can't tie up milk."
"I know," replied the neighbor, "but when a man doesn't want to do something, one reason is as good as another."[437]

All of us are tempted to make rather ridiculous excuses to others, and sometimes even to God. If we would consciously examine our excuses, we would discover how ridiculous most of them sound. Someone has collected a few choice excuses that were offered to police officers in relation to automobile accidents:
"An invisible car came out of nowhere, struck my car and vanished."
"I had been driving my car for forty years when I fell asleep at the wheel and had the accident.
"I pulled away from the side of the road, glanced at my mother-in-law, and headed over the embankment."
"The pedestrian had no idea which direction to go, so I ran over him."
"The guy was all over the road; I had to swerve a number of times before I hit him."
"Suddenly a tree was there, where no tree had been before!"[438]

Experience

It has been said that there is not a man or woman alive who could not retire comfortably in their old age if they could sell their experience for what it cost them.[439]

Experience is a wonderful thing. It enables you to recognize a mistake when you make it again.[440]

A useful axe must be sharp, but to have a sharp axe you must be willing to allow it to suffer loss on the grindstone. In a similar way, if you want to live a life that is useful in service to God, you must be willing to allow him to put you on the grindstone of trials and testings so that you may be made sharp through loss.[441]

Facts

Facts are to be reckoned as true, even if we don't "feel" that they are. For example, you get up and look at the sun and say, "The sun rose this morning." But we know that the sun didn't rise; rather, the earth rotated into the plane of the sun's light. We have learned to accept this as a fact, even though our feelings indicate otherwise.[442]

Failure

John F. Kennedy said, "Success has many fathers, but failure is an orphan; no one wants to claim it."[443]

In 1879, a child was born to a poor Jewish merchant. In early life the lad suffered a haunting sense of inferiority because of the anti-Semitic feeling he encountered on every hand. Shy and introspective, the boy was so slow in learning that his parents had him examined by specialists to see if he was normal. In 1895, he failed his entrance examinations at the Polytechnicum in Zurich, Switzerland, though a year later he tried again and succeeded. Later he received a doctorate from the University of Zurich, yet obtained only an obscure job as a patent examiner in the Berne patent office at first.

Who was he? The man who formulated the theory of relativity,

Albert Einstein, one of the greatest geniuses who ever lived. He never let early failures defeat him![444]

Faith

Faith is the gift of God. So is the air, but you have to breathe it. So is bread, but you have to eat it. So is water, but you have to drink it.

So how do we accept this gift? Not by a feeling, for "faith comes by hearing, and hearing by the Word of God" (Rom. 10:17). It is not for me to sit down and wait for faith to come upon me with a strong feeling of some kind. Rather, faith comes when we take God at his word.[445]

Faith, Childlike

When a father picks up his little daughter and tosses her all around in the air, she laughs and enjoys it, for she trusts—has faith in—her father. Even though she finds herself in unusual situations, like being upside down four feet above the floor with nothing supporting her (normally an uncomfortable circumstance), she does not fear, for she trusts her father. That is the sort of faith we should have toward our heavenly Father, too.[446]

Faith is a little boy who ties a rope swing onto a tiny sapling's branch. Then, noticing that the seat of the swing rests on the ground, he goes to get the garden hose and begins to water the sapling.[447]

Five-year-old Jessica became a bit frightened as lightning flashed and thunder cracked just as she was stepping out of her evening bath. The lights began flickering as she was getting into her pajamas. She remembered the other times the electricity had gone out and they had lit candles. Now she asked if she could "please sleep in Mommy's room" because of the storm.

Before kissing her parents good-night, Jessica prayed: "Dear God, I hope it doesn't thunder and I hope the lights don't go out." After a brief pause she continued, "But I thought it over, and you can do what you want. In Jesus' name, Amen."

What better way to say, "Thy will be done"?[448]

133

Faith, Content of

It was the great Augustine who said, "If you believe what you like in the gospel and reject what you don't like; it is not the gospel you believe, but yourself."[449]

Many ethnic groups decorate eggs for special events, especially Easter. In some cases the decoration is so much work that to preserve it the egg is first emptied of its contents through small holes in both ends. When you see the eggshell it looks perfectly normal. But, although it is beautiful, it is not a real egg. For what would happen if you tried to make a cake, or cookies, or egg nog with one of those beautiful "eggs"? Of course, it wouldn't turn out right because the egg was empty of content. Like an egg, the real value of faith is its content.[450]

Faith, Definition of

Suppose there is a fire in the upper section of a house. As the people gather in the street below, a child is seen at the window of a room next to the fire. The fire trucks are at least five minutes away and so will be too late to help. How is the child to escape?

Now suppose that in the neighborhood lives a large man, well known for his strength and athletic ability. He arrives at the scene and shouts to the child, "Drop into my arms. Don't be afraid. I'll catch you."

It is one part of faith for the child to know that the man is there. It is another part of faith to believe that the man is strong and able to catch someone. But the essence of faith lies in his dropping down into the man's arms.[451]

Faith, Development of

The desert is seemingly void of all life, but given a little rainfall, life springs into existence and beauty. Life is there, but it is dormant. Unbelief is like that. It is the desert of one's being. But the potential for life is there and needs only to be watered by faith to spring into existence and beauty.[452]

George Muller, a great man of faith, once said, "God delights to increase the faith of His children. We ought, instead of wanting no trials before victory, no exercise for patience, to be willing to take them from God's hand as a means. I say—and say it deliberately—trials, obstacles, difficulties, and sometimes defeats, are the very food of faith."[453]

Faith, Example of

Faith is central to all of life. For example, you go to a doctor whose name you cannot pronounce and whose degrees you have never verified. He gives you a prescription you cannot read. You take it to a pharmacist you have never seen before. He gives you a chemical compound you do not understand. Then you go home and take the pill according to the instructions on the bottle. All in trusting, sincere faith![454]

At a burning building in New York City's Harlem, a blind girl was perched on the fourth-floor window. The firemen had become desperate. They couldn't fit the ladder truck between the buildings, and they couldn't get her to jump into a net, which she, of course, couldn't see.

Finally her father arrived and shouted through the bull horn that there was a net and that she was to jump on his command. The girl jumped and was so completely relaxed that she did not break a bone or even strain a muscle in the four-story fall. Because she trusted her father completely, when she heard her father's voice she did what he said was best.[455]

The story has been told of a man who was crossing a desert in the days of the pioneers. He ran into trouble and was dying of thirst when he spotted a pump near an abandoned shack. He had no water to prime the pump, but he noticed a jug of water near the pump with a note attached. It read: "There is just enough water in this jug to prime the pump, but not if you drink some first. This well has never gone dry, even in the worst of times. Pour the water in the top of the pump and pump the handle quickly. After you have had a drink, refill this jug for the next man who comes along."

What would the man dying of thirst do? To follow the instructions and prime the pump without first taking a drink would be an exercise of the kind of belief the Bible speaks of. Biblical belief requires that one stake his life on the truth of the promise. If the man follows the instructions, he takes the chance of pouring out all the water and getting none to drink if the pump fails. So he must trust that the message is right. He must act in belief, without first receiving, and must trust in the truth of the promise.[456]

Near the end of World War II, members of the Allied forces were often found searching farms and houses for snipers. At one abandoned house, which had been reduced to rubble, searchers found their way into the basement. There, on a crumbling wall, a victim of the Holocaust had scratched a Star of David. Beneath it was written the words, "I believe in the sun, even when it does not shine. I believe in love, even when it is not shown. I believe in God, even when He does not speak."[457]

Faith, Exercise of

Many years ago it was decided to put a suspension bridge across a wide gorge. How could they build a bridge across such a wide space? In fact, how could they even start? They shot an arrow from one side to the other. The arrow carried across the gulf a tiny thread, and thus the connection was established. By and by the thread was used to draw a piece of twine across; the twine carried after it a small rope; the rope soon carried a cable across—and in good time came the iron chains the bridge was to hang from.

Although often weak in its beginning stage, a seemingly small faith can draw us to a stronger and stronger faith that will accomplish greater and greater things.[458]

At a circus a huge elephant was tied to an eighteen-inch stake. Could he not easily have pulled it out of the ground and be free? Sure! But he had tried it when he was a baby and was unsuccessful. The elephant had concluded that he could never pull it out of the ground. So there he stood, a massive creature capable of lifting whole trees, yet held captive by a puny stake.

What small stake could faith release *you* from?[459]

A student once purchased a new mechanical pencil. After some time he found himself in the middle of an important test, and his pencil ran out of lead! There was a great deal of frustration and anguish as he wasted precious minutes going around to other students trying to borrow another pencil. Later the student found out that his new pencil was designed with a complete supply of extra lead inside that could be dispensed with a mere press of the button.

Christians are often like this student: although they have all of God's sufficiency available to them, because of lack of knowledge they do not draw on it in their time of need. Faith must be linked to knowledge to be exercised and to grow.[460]

The physics professor had just finished his lecture about the pendulum, wherein he had shown the mathematical proof that an untouched pendulum will always swing in ever-decreasing arcs.

He then asked for a volunteer to demonstrate this fact by standing against a wall with a pendulum bob against his chin, then releasing the bob and allowing the pendulum to swing naturally through its arc. The professor reminded the class that the bob would return almost to, *but not quite touching,* the chin. No one volunteered. Although the science students "believed" that this law of physics was true, they were unwilling to put it to the test.

How like many of us in our relationship with God! We know the facts, but are unwilling to risk a step of faith based on them.[461]

It was a bright, clear morning. A large crowd had gathered at Niagara Falls to see the famous Blondin walk over it on a tightrope. The sun glistened on the cascading torrent as it rushed over the precipice. From below came the ceaseless thunder of the plunging cataract.

The world's greatest tightrope walker briefly tested the taut strand that reached across to the opposite bank. Then he took his long pole and, balancing himself expertly, started across. The crowd followed every movement tensely. Step by step he moved forward. The people on the shore reacted nervously to every sharp motion of the balancing pole. But their fears and forebodings were unnecessary. The great Blondin not only went across safely, but returned as well—to the great relief and admiration of the spectators.

Turning to the audience, he then made a sensational offer. He would cross the falls again, this time with someone on his back. Who was willing to go? No one rushed forward to accept the offer. Picking out a man at random, Blondin asked, "Do you believe that I am able to carry you across?"

"Yes, sir," came the unhesitating reply.

"Well, then, let's go," Blondin urged.

"Not on your life!"—and the man withdrew into the crowd.

137

And so it went. One after another expressed great confidence in the tightrope walker, but no one would agree to let Blondin take him across. Finally, a young fellow moved toward the front of the crowd. Blondin repeated his question: "Do you believe I can carry you across safely?"

"Yes, I do."

"Are you willing to let me?"

"As a matter of fact, I am." The young man climbed onto the expert's back. Blondin stepped onto the rope, paused momentarily, then moved across the falls without difficulty.

There were many in that crowd who believed that Blondin could do it. But there was only one who was willing to trust him to do it.[462]

> Three men were walking on a wall,
> Feeling, Faith, and Fact.
> When Feeling got an awful fall,
> Then Faith was taken back.
> So close was Faith to Feeling,
> That he stumbled and fell too.
> But Fact remained and pulled Faith back,
> And Faith brought Feeling too.[463]

Faith, Lack of

A man was walking along a narrow path, not paying much attention to where he was going. Suddenly he slipped over the edge of a cliff. As he fell, he grabbed a branch growing from the side of the cliff. Realizing that he couldn't hang on for long, he called for help.

Man: Is anybody up there?

Voice: Yes, I'm here!

Man: Who's that?

Voice: The Lord.

Man: Lord, help me!

Voice: Do you trust me?

Man: I trust you completely, Lord.

Voice: Good. Let go of the branch.

Man: What???

Voice: I said, "Let go of the branch."

Man: [After a long pause] Is anybody else up there?[464]

Faith, Law and

Rabbi Shammai, in the third century of the present era, noted that Moses gave us 365 prohibitions and 248 positive commands in the law. David in Psalm 15 reduced them to eleven; Isaiah 33:14–15 made them six; Micah 6:8 binds them into three; and Habakkuk 2:4 reduces them all to one, namely, "The just shall live by faith."[465]

Faith, Object of

The degree of faith that one places in a given object is directly proportional to one's knowledge of the object. For example, consider a man terrified of flying. When he first arrives at an airport he buys insurance at those coin-operated insurance-policy machines. He has his seat belt buckled twenty minutes before take-off and is sure to listen carefully to the routine "emergency instructions." He has no faith in the ability of the plane to get him to his destination. But, as the journey progresses, this passenger begins to change. He first unbuckles his seat belt, then has some lunch, and pretty soon is talking to the person next to him and joking. Why the change? What happened? Is there more faith at 36,000 feet? Of course not. The more he learned about the object of faith, the plane, the more faith he exercised in that object.

So it is with believers. The more we learn of the Lord, the more faith we can place in him.[466]

During an earthquake some years ago, the inhabitants of a small village were generally very much alarmed, but they were at the same time surprised at the calmness and apparent joy of an old woman whom they all knew. At length one of them, addressing the old woman, said, "Mother, are you not afraid?"

"No," said the woman. "I rejoice to know that I have a God who can shake the world."[467]

Faith is only as good as its object. A small boy in England was asked by a scientific team to be lowered down the side of a cliff to recover some important specimens. Though the scientists offered to pay him greatly, the boy said no. They tried to persuade him further and he consented finally, but only on one condition—that his father would be the one to hold the ropes by which he would be lowered.[468]

The object of man's faith is more important than the amount of his faith. For example, you might have a tremendous volume of faith in the ability of a well-known general to fly you across the Atlantic Ocean, even though he has never flown before. Yet—even with all this faith— if you enter the plane and he does the flying, you will probably end up very wet, or even drowned. The problem with your faith was that the object was not reliable in that particular area. Conversely, you might have only the minutest faith in the ability of an unknown twenty-year vet with 29,000 hours of flying time, yet he would get you where you wanted to go, because now the object of your faith was reliable in the area of your concern.[469]

The power of faith rests in the reliability of its object. After the first cold week of a Northern winter, I might go down to the shores of the nearby lake and with the utmost confidence begin to stride across the newly formed layer of ice. Unfortunately, I would receive only a cold, wet shock for my trouble. As long as the ice was thin, my faith would be meaningless. But let the winter progress and the cold wind do its work, and eventually the ice will become several feet thick. Imagine that I return to the lake. Now, though I may be frightened because of my previous experience, even the smallest, most hesitating step will be rewarded by the solid feel of firmness underfoot. Faith can now accomplish its task, because its object is worthy.[470]

Faith is an essential element of life, but the faith must be in God. Sir Donald Malcolm Campbell, the British car- and boat-racer and holder of several world speed records, lost his life while racing a fast boat on one of the lakes of Scotland. The boat exploded and rapidly sank. The only thing that ever surfaced was a toy stuffed animal, Campbell's "good luck charm." It was powerless to help him in the final and fatal crisis of his life. Faith is only as good as its object is able.[471]

The comic Steve Martin once said, "It's so hard to believe in anything anymore. . . . I guess I wouldn't believe in anything if it weren't for my lucky Astrology Mood Watch."

No one believes in nothing. Everyone has faith. The only differences are in the object of our faith and its intensity.[472]

Faith, Works and

Faith and works are as inseparable as sun and sunlight. Faith is the sun; good works are its rays.[473]

I was hungry, and you formed a humanities club and discussed my hunger.

I was imprisoned, and you crept off quietly to your chapel in the cellar and prayed for my release.

I was naked, and in your mind you debated the morality of my appearance.

I was sick, and you knelt and thanked God for your health.

I was homeless, and you preached to me the spiritual shelter of the love of God.

I was lonely, and you left me alone to pray for me.

You seem so holy, so close to God, but I'm still very hungry, and lonely, and cold.[474]

A man who claims to have faith without works is like a man who puts all his effort into building the foundation of a house and never builds anything on it.

A man who displays great works but claims no faith is like a man who builds a house on sand without any foundation.[475]

As gloves are to a surgeon's hands, so are Christians in service for God. It is actually "God's hand" doing the work. We are but used by him and therefore have nothing to boast of.[476]

A minister was talking to a professing Christian and asked him if he was active in a local church. The man responded, "No, but the dying thief wasn't active in a church and yet he was still accepted." The minister then asked if he had been baptized. The man responded, "The dying thief was not baptized and he still made it to heaven." The minister then asked if he had partaken of the Lord's Table. The man responded, "No, but the dying thief didn't either, and Christ still received him."

The minister then commented: "The only difference between you and the dying thief is that he was dying in his belief and you are dead in yours."[477]

141

Doctrine and doing are like the two chemical ingredients of salt, which is composed of two poisons: sodium and chlorine. If we ingested either of the two poisons, we would die. But if we combine them properly, we have sodium chloride, which is the common table salt that gives flavor to our food and indeed life and health to our bodies. So, too, are faith and works inseparable.[478]

You've probably heard it said, "It doesn't matter what you believe; it's how you live that counts."

A. J. Gordon encountered this philosophy one time as he talked with a fellow passenger on a train. The man believed he could get to heaven by his good works. Pointing to the conductor who was making his way through the coach, Gordon asked his new friend, "Did you ever notice how carefully he always examines the ticket but takes no pains whatever to inspect the passenger?" The man immediately caught the significance of the question. He had just been saying that God was interested only in what we do and not in a "little bit of theological scrip called faith."

"You see," continued Gordon, "the passenger and the ticket are accepted together. If he doesn't have one, or has the wrong one, he will be asked to get off the train—no matter how honest he might appear to be. Just as the ticket stands for the man, faith stands for you."

Note that the "ticket" of faith was purchased at a great price, but not by you or me![479]

Martin Luther, who had made himself the apostle and champion of faith alone, wrote the following: "Faith is a living, busy, active, powerful thing; it is impossible for it not to do us good continually. It never asks whether good works are to be done, but has done them before there is time to ask the question, and it is always doing them."[480]

Faith, World's Definition of

In the classic movie *Miracle on 34th Street*, Santa Claus utters what much of the world thinks faith is: "Faith is believing in things when common sense tells you not to." In other words, faith is irrational, contrary to experience, logic, and knowledge, and is so even at the most common sense level.

Of course, the Bible knows of no "common sense" that is not sensible enough to recognize that God exists and can do anything.[481]

Faithfulness

When Pompeii was destroyed by the eruption of Mount Vesuvius, there were many people buried in the ruins. Some were found in cellars, as if they had gone there for security. Some were found in the upper rooms of buildings. But where was the Roman sentinel found? Standing at the city gate where he had been placed by the captain, with his hands still grasping his weapon. There, while the earth shook beneath him—there, while the floods of ashes and cinders covered him—he had stood at his post. And there, after a thousand years, was this faithful man still to be found.[482]

Faithful progress in the Christian life is a necessity. We should get "better" as time goes on. This is illustrated by what many consider to be the greatest horse race ever run. When Secretariat won the Kentucky Derby, each successive quarter-mile in the race was run faster than the one before. The longer the race went, the faster the horse ran.[483]

The story is told of an eleventh-century German king, King Henry III, who, having grown tired of court life and the pressures of being a monarch, applied to a monastery to be accepted for a life of contemplation. The religious superior of the monastery, Prior Richard, is reported to have said, "Your Majesty, do you understand that the pledge here is one of obedience? That will be hard because you have been a king."

Henry replied, "I understand. The rest of my life I will be obedient to you, as Christ leads you."

"Then I will tell you what to do," said Prior Richard. "Go back to your throne and serve faithfully in the place where God has placed you."

When King Henry III died, a statement was written: "The King learned to rule by being obedient."

Like King Henry, we too often tire of our role and responsibility. Like King Henry, we too need to be reminded that God has placed each of us in a particular place to be faithful there. Be it as a plumber, accountant, mother, father, or whatever, God expects us to be faithful where he has placed us.[484]

Do you apply the same standards of faithfulness to your Christian activities that you expect from other areas of your life?

If your car starts once every three tries, is it reliable?

If your paperboy skips delivery every Monday and Thursday, is he trustworthy?

If you don't go to work once or twice a month, are you a loyal employee?

If your refrigerator stops working for a day or two every now and then, do you say, "Oh, well, it works most of the time"?

If your water heater provides an icy-cold shower every now and then, is it dependable?

If you miss a couple of loan payments every year, does the bank say, "Ten out of twelve isn't bad"?

If you fail to worship God one or two Sundays a month, would you expect to be called a faithful Christian?

We expect faithfulness and reliability from things and other people. Does not God expect the same from us? The problem is that in our religious activities we see ourselves as volunteers rather than as duty bound (1 Cor. 9). For a volunteer, almost anything seems acceptable. For a bondservant who is duty bound, faithfulness is expected (Matt. 25:21).[485]

Faithfulness, Benefit of

A Persian legend tells us that a certain king needed a faithful servant and had to choose between two candidates for the office. He took both at fixed wages and told them to fill a basket with water from a nearby well, saying that he would come in the evening to inspect their work. After dumping one or two buckets of water into the basket, one of the men said, "What is the good of doing this useless work? As soon as we pour the water in, it runs out the sides."

The other answered, "But we have our wages, haven't we? The use is the master's business, not ours."

"I'm not going to do such fool's work," replied the complainer. Throwing down his bucket, he went away.

The other man continued until he had drained the well. Looking down into it, he saw something shining at the bottom that proved to be a diamond ring. "Now I see the use of pouring water into the basket!" he exclaimed. "If the bucket had brought up the ring before the well was dry, it would have been found in the basket. Our work was not useless."

When God's blessing does not fully coincide with your expectations, remember to wait until the well is dry. There may be something precious at the bottom.[486]

144

Fall of Man

At the base of the Tetons in Wyoming lies Jackson Lake. Sometimes, early in the morning when the lake is perfectly calm, the reflection of the Tetons is magnificently duplicated and mirrored on the lake's surface. The interesting thing is that if you were to take one little flat stone and skip it across the surface of the lake, the image of the Tetons would be distorted and marred. In the same way, when Adam committed one sin, God's image in man was distorted and marred.[487]

Fame

A brilliant but bitter agnostic writer toured Europe with his wife and small daughter. He received honors from schools, royalty, and friends. After the family returned home, his daughter, impressed with her father's fame, said: "Daddy, I guess pretty soon you will know everybody except God."[488]

A reporter once asked Walt Disney how it felt to be a celebrity. "It feels fine," he replied, "when being a celebrity helps me get a choice reservation for a football game. . . . As far as I can remember, being a celebrity has never helped me make a good picture, or a good shot in a polo game, or command the obedience of my daughter, or impress my wife. It doesn't even seem to help keep fleas off our dogs and, if being a celebrity won't give me an advantage over a couple of fleas, then I guess there can't be that much in being a celebrity after all."[489]

Family, Christian

A popular book of a few years ago, *Jonathan Livingston Seagull,* extolled the "virtues" of independence and individuality at any price. The seagull is a popular subject for photography, and many people who vacation at the shore end up with some kind of souvenir bearing the picture of a seagull. It is easy to see why people like this figure. A seagull exults in freedom. When flying alone, he thrusts his wings back with powerful strokes, climbs higher and higher, and then swoops down in majestic loops and circles.

In a flock, though, the seagull is a different bird. His majesty dissolves into in-fights and cruelty. Concepts of sharing and manners do not seem to exist among gulls. They are so fiercely competitive and jealous that if you tie a ribbon around the leg of a gull, making him stand out from the rest, you sentence him to death. The others in his flock will furiously attack him with claws and beaks, hammering through feathers and flesh to draw blood. They'll continue until he is a bloody heap.

If we must have a bird as a model for our society, there is certainly a better choice. Consider the wild goose. The V-formation they use in flying enables them to fly with more ease and speed. The point position is the most difficult because of wind resistance, so the geese rotate this position every few minutes. The easiest flight is experienced in the two rear sections of the formation, and the stronger geese permit the young, weak, and older birds to occupy these positions. It is also probable that the constant honking encourages the weaker geese.

The seagull teaches us to break loose and fly alone, but the wild goose teaches us to fly in a "family." We can fly further with our Christian family than we could ever fly alone—and, as we fly, our efforts constantly help others in our family.[490]

Family, Leadership in

American men received a stinging insult from British psychologist Dr. Joshua Bierer, who described them as a "bunch of weak-kneed, lily-livered sissies." In a previous survey made in 1964, he had judged women to be at fault and declared American women to be domineering. He explained his changed viewpoint:

> Before, I thought that the women wanted to rule the country. I changed that opinion. Women are compelled to take over, not fighting to take over. I thought the men who attended with their wives some seminars I spoke at would shoot me for my remarks—but instead they all agreed with me. It's still the fatherless society. The husbands are not husbands. All the women are crying out for a strong man and he's just not there. [Cited by Aubrey P. Andelin, *Man of Steel and Velvet* [Naperville, Ill: Caroline Hse., 1982], p. 12.][491]

Family, Spiritual Decline of

> To our forefathers, our faith was an experience.
> To our fathers, our faith was an inheritance.
> To us, our faith is a convenience.
> To our children, our faith is a nuisance.[492]

Fanatic

A fanatic is one who redoubles his efforts after he has lost sight of his goal.[493]

Father

used 6/19/94

A little boy, frightened by a thunderous lightning storm, called out one dark night, "Daddy, come. I'm scared."

"Son," the father said, "God loves you and he'll take care of you."

"I know God loves me," the boy replied. "But right now I want somebody who has skin on."

It is the role of the father to be and demonstrate God, with skin on.[494]

A little girl followed her father as he carefully stepped through a new garden. She stepped exactly where he stepped and said, "Daddy, if you don't get mud on *your* feet, I won't get any mud on me!"[495]

Father, Failure of

The story is told of a young man who stood before a judge to be sentenced for forgery. The judge had been a friend of the boy's father, who was famous for his books on the law of trusts. "Young man," said the judge sternly, "do you remember your father, that father whom you have disgraced?"

"I remember him perfectly," the young man answered quietly. "When I went to him for advice or companionship, he would say, 'Run away, boy, I'm busy.' Well, my father finished his book, and here I am."[496]

Family-life specialists Delmer W. Holbrook and his wife have been lecturing and conducting surveys across America. In a survey of hundreds of children, the Holbrooks came up with the three things fathers say most in responding to their kids.

"I'm too tired" took first place.

"We don't have enough money" was second.

"Keep quiet" was third. (Cited in *Christianity Today*, August 27, 1976.)[497]

Faults

Nothing is easier than faultfinding: no talent, no self-denial, no brains, and no character are required to set up in the grumbling business.[498]

Faults are like the headlights of a car: those of others seem more glaring than your own.[499]

Fear, Child's

A little boy had a part in the school play that read, "It is I; be not afraid." He came out on stage and said, "It's me and I'm scared."[500]

Fear, Student's

Scrawled in a nervous hand across a blackboard at Southern Methodist University during finals week was this message: "We have nothing to fear, but F itself."[501]

Fear, Thief's

A farmer looked out his window one day and saw several young fellows stealing watermelons from his field. He pulled out his gun and fired over their heads once or twice to scare the thieves off. Later, when the boys met, one said, "Did you hear those bullets?" Another replied, "I heard them twice, once when they passed me, and once when I passed them!"

The farmer accomplished his purpose, since fear kept the boys from further stealing. Fear is a powerful motive-directing behavior. Perhaps love is the most desirable motive, but fear will also do.[502]

Fear of Wasted Life

Ray Stedman told the story of a time when, after a Billy Graham crusade meeting, he slipped into a seat on a bus beside a young man who had gone forward in the meeting that night and given his heart to Christ. Pastor Stedman spoke to him of what his new life would mean, and mentioned that he could now be free from all fear of death. The young man turned and looked the older man in the eye and said, "I

148

have never been much afraid of death. But I'll tell you what I *am* afraid of—I'm afraid I'll waste my life."

Pastor Stedman then commented, "I believe that fear is deep within each of us. It has been put there by our Creator. No one wishes to waste his life." (Cited in Ray Stedman, *Authentic Christianity* [Portland, Or.: Multnomah Press, 1985], p. 152.)[503]

Fear of Witnessing

To overcome the fear we all experience when considering approaching someone with the gospel, we need to have a conviction that God has given us something to say that our audience needs desperately to hear. Such a conviction will free us from fear.

For example, consider a person walking down a street who notices a meeting of a large group of people inside a building. Then he sees a fire in the upper part of the building where the meeting is being held. He would immediately run in and tell the people to get out. And there would be no fearful thoughts and hesitation. Why? Because he knows that they needed to hear what he had to say. How convinced are we that people need to hear a word from God?[504]

Have you ever had to paint a second or third story of a house? You get about halfway up that double or triple extension ladder and it begins to bend and bounce with your every movement. Then you start wondering about the ladder and its footing and where you will end up when it crashes to the earth so far below you. So, in fear and terror, you stop where you are and cling to the ladder, looking neither up nor down.

Eventually you realize that you must paint the house and that you can't reach it from where you are. So, mustering up all your courage and recalling that you have never seen such a ladder fall over, you conquer the next rung and inch your way to the next, then the next. Finally you reach the top of the ladder and cling to it for your life. Now that you've arrived, you ask yourself how you can take one hand off the ladder to use the paintbrush and not plummet to the earth below. But you do. You begin. After a bit of scraping, the wood soaks up the paint. You whistle and admire the fine job you are doing. Soon the terror is forgotten.

You've learned an important lesson of life from this. No matter what high responsibility you take on, it's scary, very scary—until you start working.[505]

LeRoy Eims told of an event which he and his son, Randy, witnessed in Istanbul, Turkey. They were sitting in a restaurant and looked out the window in surprise and unbelief at a huge brown bear, muzzled and on a leash. When a crowd of people had gathered, the bear's owner shook a tambourine, and immediately the bear stood up on its hind legs and began to dance around. Then, on command, the bear lay on its back and rolled from side to side. As the crowd applauded in appreciation, the tambourine became a collection plate. Suddenly a small, mangy, mongrel dog came leaping out from behind the bushes and began barking at the bear. But the mighty bear, which should have been able to dispatch the dog with one swipe of its powerful paw, was both helpless and terrified and bounded around, trying to dart away to find a place to hide.

What was the problem? Why was this magnificent wild beast afraid of a scruffy little dog? There were two reasons—the bear was both muzzled and declawed. It was a pathetic sight, but what made it even more sad was that it was a picture of so many Christians: muzzled, for they feel unable to speak, and weaponless, for they are unable to use the Sword of the Spirit. As a result, we, like that bear, often find ourselves helpless and fearful as if under siege, whenever we attempt to share our faith.[506]

Fellowship

During World War II, the enemy conducted experiments to find the most effective type of punishment for eliciting information from prisoners. They found that solitary confinement was the most effective. After a few days of solitary confinement, most men would tell all.

That is why we need fellowship—without it we too become easy prey for temptation and abandonment of our values.[507]

After many months of waiting, a Russian girl finally obtained a visa to visit her relatives in Canada for three months. She arrived in Canada and was shown around the various attractions, amusements, and entertainments. The young Russian seemed immensely impressed by the amount of things that people were wrapped up with. As the three months drew to a close, everyone expected her to defect and seek political asylum in Canada. She surprised them all by expressing a desire to return to her family in Russia and the small group of believers to which they belonged. She explained that in North America everyone seems wrapped up in "things" and doesn't have time for people. In

Russia, they don't have as many material possessions and consequently they need each other. She wanted to return to a place where people relied on each other, where fellowship was important.[508]

Flattery

Flattery is like perfume: the idea is to smell it, not to swallow it.[509]

Following

Someday, watch a stream of ants stretching between their anthill and a food source. Some will be going to pick up their load; others will be returning to deposit their prize in the recesses of the anthill. The whole process will be very organized, very precise. Then ask yourself, "Why are these ants so organized in their task?" The reason is that ants are good followers, each dependent on the ant in front of him to lead him to the food supply. Because each ant follows the other, there is a straight line between the anthill and the food—no wasted energy, no unnecessary detours. There is a lesson in that for would-be disciples.[510]

Forgiveness

If the soap-opera ad writers were to compose a devotional, it might sound as sudsy as this:

"Are you soft soaping God about your TEXIZE problem? DUZ you DREFT along with the TIDE? VEL, you can CHEER up and have real JOY. The DOVE of peace is sending an S.O.S. to ALL. The TREND is to BREEZE to church regularly on Sunday morning. But, too many WOODBURY their heads in a pillow or work in the yard like HANDY ANDY, forgetting that the Lord's Day was made for LESTOIL.

"Don't trust your LUX or wait for us to DIAL you and remind you of those IVORY palaces up yonder. This is not just idle BAB-O. Worship will add to your LIFEBUOY, so WISK yourself out of bed Sunday morning, dress up SPIC 'N SPAN and DASH like a COMET to God's house. You will feel as FANTASTIK as IRISH SPRING and will have new ZEST and PRIDE of conscience if you make this PLEDGE. You, too, can be MR. CLEAN."

More than detergents are needed, however. The kind of filth that has soiled our souls demands some new miracle cleanser that Madison Avenue does not have. (John F. Anderson, Jr., *Dallas Morning News*, March 26, 1977).[511]

An unmarked tombstone outside of Sydney, New York, has but one word on it, three syllables: "Forgiven" (Cited by Dr. D. James Kennedy, founder of Evangelism Explosion).[512]

A father bequeathed a large inheritance to his son. Technically, it then belonged to the son, but the bequest was "in trust," which meant that the son was not immediately allowed to withdraw the entire amount from the bank. The father had included a stipulation temporarily limiting the withdrawal privilege to the interest that accrued, although the son would eventually be entitled to the principal.

So, also, when a person receives the grace of regeneration, this does not mean that all of that which Christ merited for him is immediately experienced by him. If it were, would it not overwhelm and crush his capacities? Rather, "He [God] giveth and giveth again."

In a similar manner, we need to daily ask for a portion of God's forgiving grace.[513]

Forgiveness, Basis of

Bondage to sin came by birth; deliverance from sin comes by death. But if we die, then what good is it to be delivered? There is another way to die and yet live. For example, consider a small piece of paper that is placed into a book. The paper has an identity all its own, separate from the book, but now it is in the book and shares something with the book. Let's say that the book is then mailed to another person. The paper was not mailed, but it had been put into the book. So where is the paper? Obviously, whatever the book goes through the paper will go through as well, for it is still there in the book. When Christ was crucified, we who are "in him," died and received all that he went through, including deliverance from the bondage of sin.[514]

Forgiveness, Difficulty of

Many reconciliations have broken down because both parties have come prepared to forgive and unprepared to be forgiven.[515]

A man named John Oglethorpe, in talking to John Wesley, once made the comment, "I never forgive." Mr. Wesley wisely replied, "Then, Sir, I hope that you never sin."[516]

Forgiveness, Forgetting and

A man who was telling his friend about an argument he'd had with his wife commented, "Oh, how I hate it, every time we have an argument; she gets historical."

The friend replied, "You mean hysterical."

"No," he insisted. "I mean historical. Every time we argue she drags up everything from the past and holds it against me!"[517]

A friend of Clara Barton, founder of the American Red Cross, once reminded her of an especially cruel thing that had been done to her years before. But Miss Barton seemed not to recall it. "Don't you remember it?" her friend asked.

"No," came the reply, "I distinctly remember forgetting it."

You can't be free and happy if you harbor grudges, so put them away. Get rid of them. Collect postage stamps, or collect coins, if you wish— but don't collect grudges.[518]

Prospero, when finally given a chance to punish those who had removed him of his rightful place as king, states, "Let us not burden our remembrance with a heaviness that's gone" (William Shakespeare, *The Tempest*).[519]

God is able to forget our past. Why can't we? God throws our sins into the depths of the sea and puts up a sign on the shore that reads, "No fishing."

In ancient times the depths of the sea were completely inaccessible to us. The limits were how far a man could dive with one lungful of air. In modern times we have submarines that can go anywhere on or below the sea's surface, so we do not fully appreciate this figure of speech. Perhaps the inaccessible aspect would be clearer if we changed the statement to "God has cast all of our sins into a nuclear waste dump." That's truly inaccessible! And that's forgiveness![520]

Forgiveness, Judgment and

Some people try to punish themselves for their sins, as opposed to standing on the promises of forgiveness.

The story is told of a time, many years ago, when a father and his daughter were walking through the grass on the Canadian prairie. In

153

the distance they saw a prairie fire, which would soon engulf them. The father knew there was only one way of escape: they must quickly build a fire right where they were and burn a large patch of grass. When the huge prairie fire drew near, they could stand on the section that had already burned. When the flames did approach them, the girl was terrified, but her father assured her, "The flames can't get to us. We are standing where the fire has already been."

So it is with the forgiven when they see the judgment of God approaching. They are where the flames have already been and therefore are safe.[521]

Forgiveness, Perfect

A wealthy English merchant who lived on the European continent was satisfied with nothing but the best. This attitude extended even as far as the cars he owned. His pride and joy was a Rolls-Royce coupe that he had owned for years and that had given great service all that time. One day, while driving down a bumpy road, his car hit a deep pothole, resulting in a broken rear axle.

The owner had the car shipped back to the Rolls plant in England and was surprised by the quick repair that was performed. He received no bill for the work and, knowing his warranty had run out, he had expected one. He waited for months and still no bill came. So he finally communicated with the company about the bill for his car repairs. Again the response from the factory was immediate. The reply said, "We have thoroughly searched our files and find no record of a Rolls-Royce axle ever breaking."

This is a case where the integrity and excellence of that company would not permit a flaw in workmanship or materials to be made known. The excellence of Christ does not permit our flaws to be made known to the Father. He accomplishes our forgiveness.[522]

Forgiveness, Results of

We all have seen and used those little electronic calculators. What happens if you get your information confused or make an error? You press the "clear" button and automatically all of the information is eliminated from the calculator. Then you begin again, without trying to sort out the previous mistake. In fact, there is no record of your mistake! It is lost forever!

That's what happens to our sins when God forgives us. The consequences may remain, but the guilt—the legal condemnation for the offense—is gone.[523]

Karl Menninger, the famous psychiatrist, says that if he could convince the patients in his psychiatric hospitals that their sins are forgiven, 75 percent of them could walk out the next day. So often we do not take God at his word![524]

Fornication

Fornication is like a cat's paw. When lightly stroked, it is quite soft and pleasurable, but increased pressure brings out the claws of sin that will shred your very life.[525]

> Vice is a monster of such terrible mien
> That to be hated needs but to be seen.
> Yet seen too often, familiar her face
> We first endure, then sanction, then embrace.[526]

Foundation, Importance of

If you have ever lived in or visited a large city, you probably have had the chance to watch a skyscraper under construction. For the first six months or so of the project, all the workmen do is make a great hole in the ground. To build a tall building by starting far below the surface level seems absurd, even crazy. But, as you would suspect, there is a good reason for the large hole. To build a mammoth building, it is first necessary to dig down until a strong foundation can be built, one that is capable of supporting the skyscraper.

A doghouse needs no foundation, and an ordinary house can be built on little more than a concrete slab. But a skyscraper, that's different. It requires a deep and solid foundation.

So it is in our Christian life. Our upward potential is totally dependent on the foundation underneath it.[527]

A very short man wanted to drive a nail in his wall to hang a picture. He stood on a chair, but it was not high enough. His wife placed a box on the chair, but he was still short of his goal. So a stool was piled on top of the box. Balancing himself precariously, the do-it-yourself picture hanger began to tap timidly with his hammer. "Why don't you hit it hard?" asked the wife. "You'll never drive the nail that way!"

Our hero looked down from his perch to reply, "How can a man hit anything hard on a shaky foundation like this?"[528]

Freedom, Consequences of

When a man decides to exercise his freedom to break God's laws, he is like a person who ascends to the top of a tall building and jumps off. For the first several stories he feels great. There are no restraints, no restrictions, no hang-ups. But suppose, ten stories from the ground, he realizes that a sudden stop awaits him and that he doesn't want to endure its consequences. Can he reverse the falling process? Can you or he stop the fall? Of course not. Thus, in the final ten stories, our tragic character will examine his definition of freedom and realize—too late—that it was wrong.[529]

Freedom, License and

Many people think that freedom is the license to do whatever a person wants, but true freedom is the ability to do what is right. It takes obedience in order to have true freedom. I can sit at a piano and be at liberty to play any keys that I want, but I don't have freedom, because I can't play anything but noise. I have no freedom to play Bach, or even "Chopsticks." Why? Because it takes years of practice and obedience to lesson plans to be truly free at the piano. Then, and only then, does one have the freedom to play *any* piece of music.

The same is true of freedom in living. To be truly free, we must have the power and ability to be obedient.[530]

Freedom, Morality and

"Men are qualified for civil liberties only to the extent that they are willing to put moral chains on their appetites" (attributed to Edmund Burke).[531]

Freedom, Security and

At the University of Oklahoma, for many years a project was underway to teach a fifteen-year-old female chimpanzee named Washoe to talk by combining sign language with simple recognition. Since 1966, this chimpanzee learned 140 signs.

Finally, the project directors decided that Washoe was prepared to "conceptualize." This meant that instead of merely imitating some human's words, the chimp would express thoughts of her own. Now, understand, Washoe was a pampered animal in the university's laboratory—well fed, physically comfortable, safe from harm. She had security. And yet, when she was able to put words together on her own into a phrase, these were the first three—and she has said them again, repeatedly—"Let me out."[52]

Friendliness to Enemies

The Civil War had just ended, and the opportunistic scalawags were busy lording it over their fellow Southerners. A hot-blooded contingency of die-hard former rebels gained an audience with President Lincoln. His gentle, friendly manner soon thawed the ice, and the Southerners left with a new respect for their old foe. A northern congressman approached the president and criticized him for "befriending the enemy," suggesting that instead of befriending them he should have had them shot for the traitors they were. Lincoln smiled and replied, "Am I not destroying my enemies by making them my friends?"[533]

While still a young boy, a certain Christian formed the habit of praying beside his bed before he went to sleep. Later, when he joined the army, he kept up this practice, though he became an object of mockery and ridicule in the barracks. One night, as he knelt to pray after a long, weary march, one of his tormentors took off his muddy boots and threw them at him one at a time, hitting him on each side of his head. The Christian said nothing, took the persecutor's boots, put them beside the bed, and continued to pray. The next morning, when the other soldier woke up, he found his polished and shined boots sitting beside his own bed. It so affected him that he asked for forgiveness and after a time became a Christian.[534]

Friends, Influence of

A farmer, troubled by a flock of crows in his corn field, loaded his shotgun and crawled unseen along the fence-row, determined to get a shot at the crows. Now the farmer had a very "sociable" parrot who made friends with everybody. Seeing the flock of crows, the parrot flew over and joined them (just being sociable, you know). The farmer saw the crows but didn't see the parrot. He took careful aim and BANG! The farmer crawled over the fence to pick up the fallen crows, and lo, there was his parrot—badly ruffled, with a broken wing, but still alive. Tenderly, the farmer carried the parrot home, where his children met him. Seeing that their pet was injured, they tearfully asked, "What happened, Papa?" Before he could answer, the parrot spoke up: "Bad company!"[535]

Friendship

A new homeowner's riding lawn mower had broken down, and he had been working fruitlessly for two hours trying to get it back together. Suddenly, one of his neighbors appeared with a handful of tools. "Can I give some help?" he asked. In twenty minutes he had the mower functioning beautifully.

"Thanks a million," the now-happy newcomer said. "And say, what do you make with such fine tools?"

"Mostly friends," the neighbor smiled. "I'm available any time."[536]

Friendship, False

It is easy to treat people as means to an end rather than as ends in themselves. As a gregarious man once boasted, "I have friends I haven't even used yet."[537]

A false friend is like your shadow. As long as there is sunshine, he sticks close by. But the minute you step into the shade, he disappears.[538]

Friendship, True

A friend has been defined as the first person who comes in when the whole world has gone out.[539]

Value a friend who, for you, finds time on his calendar—but cherish the friend who, for you, does not even consult his calendar.[540]

"Oh, the comfort, the inexpressible comfort, of feeling safe with a person, having neither to weigh thoughts nor measure words, but to pour them all out just as they are, chaff and grain together, knowing that a faithful hand will take and sift them, keep what is worth keeping, and then, with the breath of kindness blow the rest away" (George Eliot [Marian Evans Cross]).[541]

Gambling

With typical insight, C. S. Lewis summed up the problem some Christians have with gambling and offered a simple solution for those who are encouraged by friends, co-workers, and others to participate in an office pool or "friendly wager."

> Problem: "If it is a way in which large sums of money are transferred from person to person without doing any good (e.g., producing employment, goodwill, etc.), then it is a bad thing."
> Solution: "If anyone comes to me asking to play bridge for money, I Just say, 'How much do you hope to win? Take it and go away'" (C. S. Lewis, *God in the Dock* [Grand Rapids: Wm. B. Eerdmans Pub. Co., 170], pp. 59–60).[542]

Giving

A little girl was given two dollars by her father. He told her that she could do anything she wanted with one and that the other was to be given to God on Sunday at church. The girl nodded in agreement and asked if she could go to the candy store. With visions of all that she could buy with her dollar, she happily skipped toward the store, holding tightly to the two dollars in her hand. As she was skipping along, she tripped and fell and the wind blew one of the dollars into a storm drain at the curb. Picking herself up, the little girl looked at the dollar still in her hand and then at the storm drain and said, "Well, Lord, there goes your dollar."

Sadly, many of us Christians have the same attitude toward giving. First me, then God.[543]

Years ago, *The Sunday School Times* carried the account of a Christian school for the children of "untouchables" in India prior to World War II. Each year the children received Christmas presents from children in England. The girls got a doll, and the boys a toy. On one occasion the doctor from a nearby mission hospital was asked to distribute the gifts. In the course of his visit, he told the youngsters about a village where the boys and girls had never even heard of Jesus. He suggested that maybe they would like to give them some of their old toys as presents. They liked the idea and readily agreed. A week later, the doctor returned to collect the gifts. The sight was unforgettable. One by one the children filed by and handed the doctor a doll or toy. To his great surprise, they all gave the new presents they had just received several days earlier. When he asked why, a girl spoke up, "Think what God did by giving us his only Son. Could we give him less than our best?"[544]

Givers can be divided into three types: the flint, the sponge and the honeycomb. Some givers are like a piece of flint—to get anything out of it you must hammer it, and even then you only get chips and sparks. Others are like a sponge—to get anything out of a sponge you must squeeze it and squeeze it hard, because the more you squeeze a sponge, the more you get. But others are like a honeycomb—which just overflows with its own sweetness. That is how God gives to us, and it is how we should give in turn.[545]

Dwight L. Moody understood the place of money in the kingdom of God, and he wasn't timid about expressing it, either. He had gone to a certain Mr. Farwell time and time again and was finally back for another ten-thousand-dollar contribution.

Mr. Farwell said, "Mr. Moody, must you always be coming to me for money?" Moody replied, "Mr. Farwell, you grew up on a farm, just as I did. Did you ever take a pail to a dry cow?"[546]

Giving, Humorous

> Do your givin'
> While you're livin'
> Then you're knowin'
> Where it's goin'.[547]

A pastor was talking to his farmer friend, and he asked the farmer, "If you had one hundred horses, would you give me fifty?" The farmer said, "Certainly."

The pastor asked, "If you had one hundred cows, would you give me fifty?" The farmer said, "Yes."

Then the pastor asked, "If you had two pigs, would you give me one?" The farmer said, "Now cut that out, pastor; you know I have two pigs!"[548]

A family sat down at the dinner table following church one Sunday.

"The sermon was boring today," said the teenage son.

"Yeah, could you believe how the pastor stumbled over the reading of the Scripture?" his sister chimed in.

"I've got to admit it was an uninspiring day," said Mother. "The choir was terrible."

Finally, father, showing his leadership, said, "Hush, you guys. Quit complaining. What did you expect for a quarter?"[549]

A rich man once asked his friend, "Why am I criticized for being miserly? Everyone knows I will leave everything to charity when I die."

"Well," said the friend, "Let me tell you about the pig who was lamenting to the cow one day about how unpopular he was. 'People are always talking about your gentleness and your kind eyes,' said the pig. 'Sure, you give milk and cream, but I give more. I give bacon, ham, bristles. They even pickle my feet! Still, nobody likes me. Why is this?' The cow thought a minute and replied, 'Well, maybe it's because I give while I'm still living.'"[550]

For Cure of Cirrhosis of the Giver

The disease cirrhosis of the giver was discovered in A.D. 34 by the husband-wife team of Ananias and Sapphira (Acts 5:1–11). It is an acute condition that renders the patient's hands immobile when he is called on to move them in the direction of his wallet or her purse, and from thence to the offering plate. This strange malady is clinically unobservable in such surroundings as the golf club, supermarket, clothing store, or restaurant. Some try to use a fake remedy, pointing out to the patients that income tax deductions can be claimed for giving. The best therapy, and that which leads to a sure and lasting cure, is to get the individual's heart right with God. This affliction is actually a symptom of a more basic need of the soul.

Prescribed Medication: Frequent doses of Romans 12:1 and Luke 9:23, accompanied by a dash of 2 Corinthians 9:7. This dosage will become quite pleasant if swallowed with a heaping tablespoon of Philippians 4:19![551]

A wealthy Texan was in the habit of giving his dad unique gifts on Father's Day. One year it was lessons on hang-gliding. The year before that it was the entire record collection of Slim Whitman's hits. But this past year he felt he had outdone himself. He purchased a rare kind of talking bird that could speak five languages and sing "The Yellow Rose of Texas" while standing on one foot. The talented bird cost ten thousand dollars, but he felt it was worth every penny. This would be a Father's Day gift his dad would never forget.

A week after Father's Day he called his father. "Dad, how did you like the bird?" His father responded, "It was delicious!"[552]

Giving, Missions

Many years ago a certain woman was preparing a box to be sent to some missionaries in India. A child gave her a penny, which she used to purchase a tract for the box. Eventually this tract reached a Burmese chief and was used to lead him to a saving knowledge of Christ. The chief told the story of his conversion to his friends, many of whom believed. Eventually a church was established there and over 1,500 natives were converted to Christianity.

The lesson is plain: no gift for God is too small for him to use.[553]

Giving, Motivation for

A missionary returned to his home city, where he announced a collection for foreign missions. A good friend said to him, "Very well, Andrew, seeing it is you, I'll give five hundred dollars."

"No," said the missionary, "I cannot take the money since you give it, seeing it is me." His friend saw the point and said, "You are right, Andrew. Here is a thousand dollars, seeing it is for the Lord Jesus."[554]

A long time ago a very godly and generous businessman in London was asked for a donation for a charitable project. Very little was expected because the businessman had recently sustained a heavy loss from the wreck of some of his ships. To the amazement of the leaders of the charity, he gave about ten times as much as he was expected to give to the project.

When asked how he was able to give so much in light of his business difficulties the businessman replied, "It is quite true, I have sustained heavy loss by these vessels being wrecked, but that is the very reason why I give you so much; for I must make better use than ever of my stewardship lest it should be entirely taken from me." (Adapted from *George Muller of Bristol*.)[555]

John Bunyan, author of *The Pilgrim's Progress*, wrote, "A man there was, and they called him mad; the more he gave, the more he had."

Of course Bunyan was writing of the Christian. To the world, such a principle of giving is nonsense. Only to the Christian, who understands that true worth is also spiritual, does this make sense. Hence, in giving to God, the Christian looks for spiritual returns.[556]

"But our tokens of compliment and love are for the most part barbarous. Rings and other jewels are not gifts, but apologies for gifts. The only gift is a portion of thyself. Thou must bleed for me. Therefore the poet brings his poem; the shepherd his lamb; the farmer his corn; the miner a gem; the sailor, coral and shells; the painter his picture; the girl, a handkerchief of her own sewing" (Ralph Waldo Emerson, from his essay *Gifts*).[557]

Charles Spurgeon, the great English preacher, was once invited by a wealthy man to come to preach in a certain country church, to help the membership raise funds to pay off a debt. The man told Spurgeon he was free to use his country house, his town house, or his seaside home. Spurgeon wrote back and said, "Sell one of the places and pay the debt yourself."[558]

Giving, Proportional

Give according to your income, lest God make your income according to your giving.[559]

A well-known philanthropist was asked, "How is it that you give away so much, and yet have so much left?"

"I suppose it's like this," he replied. "I shovel out, and God shovels in, and he has a bigger shovel than I do!"[560]

A man came to his pastor for counseling. He felt convicted that he had not been faithful in giving God a portion of the generous thousand-dollar weekly salary he was making. The man explained, "I had no problem thanking God and giving him a liberal offering when I was making just two hundred and fifty dollars a week. Please pray for me."

The pastor then prayed, much to the man's dismay, "Father, please bring this man back to a two-hundred-and-fifty-dollar salary so that he can get back into your will."[561]

Giving, Regular

I have a regular time for washing my face, combing my hair, dressing, and brushing my teeth.

I do not have a regular time for washing my car. It shows.

Giving is like that. If it is not done regularly, it doesn't get done.[562]

Giving, Selfishness in

During a sermon, the country preacher said to his congregation, "Now let the church walk." Deacon Jones said, "Amen, let it walk."

"Let the church run," said the preacher. "Let it run," echoed Deacon Jones.

"Let it fly," said the preacher. "Amen, brother, let the church fly," said Deacon Jones.

"Now it's going to take money to let it fly, brother," said the preacher. "Let it walk," said Deacon Jones. "Let it walk."[563]

The pastor of a large and wealthy church in Texas broke out in laughter in the middle of singing a hymn during the Sunday-morning service. After the service was over, his wife asked what could have caused him to do such a thing. "Well," he said, "I couldn't help it. We were singing 'Take my life and let it be consecrated, Lord, to Thee,' and I noticed the words of the third verse: 'Take my silver and my gold, not a mite would I withhold.' It suddenly struck me, with all the millionaires sitting in the congregation, what if God would answer that prayer right then? Some of them would be very upset and angry with him. I've been encouraging them to give their silver and gold for a long time, but they've not been willing. But now they're singing, 'Take my silver and my gold, not a mite would I withhold.' "[564]

Martin Marty, in his *Context* newsletter, quoted Yale professor-preacher Halford Luccock: "You remember that among the Franks, whole armies were sometimes given baptism at one stroke, and many warriors went into the water with their right hands held high, so that they did not get wet. Then they could say, 'This hand has never been baptized,' and they could swing their battle axes just as freely as ever. The modern counterpart of that partial baptism is seen in many people who have been baptized, all except their pocketbooks. They held these high out of the water."[565]

Goals

The FBI went into one town to investigate the work of what appeared to be a sharpshooter. They were amazed to find many bull's-eyes drawn around town, with bullets that had penetrated the exact center of the targets. When they finally found the man who had been doing the shooting, they asked him about the technique he used to attain such accuracy. The answer was simple. He shot the bullet first, and drew the bull's-eye later.

That may be an easy way to have the appearance of hitting the mark, but it is at best a deception and at worst a lie. So it is with goals. We should use them to direct our work and determine if we have accomplished our purposes, not to defend what we happened to do.[566]

A novice duck hunter, tired of waiting in the blind, decided to forge out on his own and see if he could get better results. After several cold and tiring hours he returned to his friends with what *he* considered to be a display of his hunting skills, several prized mallards. His friends were not impressed, because all he had was a worthless bunch of "mudhens."

Because the young hunter did not have his goal clearly in mind, he wasted his time and efforts. Zeal, commitment, hard work—all are wasted if spent on accomplishing the "wrong" goal.[567]

The California coast was shrouded in fog the morning of July 4, 1952. Twenty-one miles to the west, on Catalina Island, a thirty-four-year-old woman waded into the water and began swimming toward California, determined to be the first woman to ever swim the twenty-one-mile strait. Her name was Florence Chadwick, and she had already been the first woman to swim the English Channel in both directions.

The water was numbing cold that morning, and the fog was so thick that Chadwick could hardly see the boats in her own party—there to scare away the sharks. As the hours ticked off, she swam on. Fatigue had never been a serious problem; it was only the bone-chilling cold of the water that was threatening. More than fifteen hours later, numbed with the cold, the swimmer asked to be taken out. She couldn't go on any longer. Her mother and her trainer, in a boat alongside her, urged Chadwick to go on, as they were getting close to shore. Yet all she could see was dense fog. A few minutes later, the swimmer was taken out of the water, and later, realizing that she had been within a half-mile of the shore, she blurted out, "I'm not excusing myself, but if I could have seen the shore, I might have made it."

Florence Chadwick had been licked, not by the cold or even by the fatigue, but by the fog! The fog had obscured her goal; it had blinded her reason and her eyes. As Christians, we must be careful not to allow ourselves to be blinded by other matters, so that we are prevented from reaching our goals.[568]

There's a well-worn story of a man who approached a laborer who was laying bricks and asked him, "What are you doing?" The laborer said, "Can't you see I'm laying bricks?"

The man then walked over to another bricklayer and asked, "What are you doing?" And the workman answered with pride, "I'm building a cathedral."

Both were physically doing the same thing. But the first laborer was occupied with the present task, and the other was concerned with the ultimate goal.[569]

God, Attributes of

One of the greatest books written on the nature of God was by Stephen Charnock. In it he observed that "the fountain of . . . evil practices [is] a denial or doubting of some of the rights of His nature." And ". . . when men deny the God of purity, they must needs be polluted in soul and body" (Stephen Charnock, *The Attributes of God*, I, p. 14).

It is for this reason that all believers ought to have a deep and thorough knowledge of God's attributes.[570]

God, Eternality of

Time is often represented by a straight line drawn on a page. We call this a time line. To get a grasp of what the eternality of God means, when you have drawn your time line you must picture God as the whole page on which the line is drawn.[571]

God, Evidence of

The argument for Creationism from design and order is clear in the following lines, written by Elizabeth Barrett Browning in *Aurora Leigh:*

> Earth's crammed with heaven,
> And every common bush afire with God;
> But only he who sees takes off his shoes;
> The rest sit round it and pluck blackberries.[572]

God's Glory

God's "glory" is how we describe the sum effect of all of his attributes. Grace, truth, goodness, mercy, justice, knowledge, power, eternality—all that he is. Therefore, the glory of God is intrinsic, that is, it is as essential to God as light is to the sun, as blue is to the sky, as wet is to water. You don't make the sun light; it is light. You don't make the sky blue; it is blue. You don't make water wet; it is wet. In all of these cases, the attribute is intrinsic to the object.

In contrast, man's glory is *granted* to him. If you take a king and take off all his robes and crowns and give him only a rag to wear and leave him on the streets for a few weeks, when put next to a beggar you'll never know which is which. Because there is no intrinsic glory. The only glory a king has is when you give him a crown and a robe and sit him on his throne. He has no intrinsic glory.

That's the point. The only glory that men have is granted to them. The glory that is God's is his in his essence. You can't de-glory God because glory is his nature. You can't touch his glory. It cannot be taken away. It cannot be added to. It's his being.[573]

"Almost everything said of God is unworthy, for the very reason that it is capable of being said" (Pope Gregory the Great, *Magna moralia*).[574]

In 1715, Louis XIV of France died. Louis, who called himself "the Great," was the monarch who made the infamous statement "I am the State!" His court was the most magnificent in Europe, and his funeral was spectacular. His body lay in a golden coffin. To dramatize the deceased king's greatness, orders had been given that the cathedral should be very dimly lighted, with only one special candle set above his coffin. Thousands waited in hushed silence. Then Bishop Massilon began to speak. Slowly reaching down, he snuffed out the candle, saying, "Only God is great!"[575]

God's Invisibility

Art Linkletter saw a small boy drawing a picture. He inquired, "What are you drawing?" The small boy replied, "A picture of God."

Linkletter told the lad that no one knows what God looks like, to which the boy confidently responded, "They will when I get through."[576]

God's Knowability

Trying to explain God is like trying to explain a kiss. You can check the dictionary definition: "A caress with the lips; a gentle touch or contact."

But does that really capture the essence of what a kiss is? Does that describe what a mother does when she tenderly places her lips on the forehead of her newborn child? Is that what the young lover does when he says good-night to his girl?

Just as words cannot completely capture all that is involved in what we know by experience and attempt to describe as a "kiss," we also cannot fully comprehend, explain, or define "God." We can, however, know him through experiencing his revelation of himself to us in his Word and in the person of Jesus Christ.[577]

A farmer repeatedly invited a friend into his apple orchard to taste the fruit and make some fresh cider. But, just as often, the friend said, "No, I would rather not."

Finally, the farmer said, "I guess you are prejudiced against my apples."

"Well, to tell the truth," his friend said, "I have tasted a few of them and they are very sour."

The farmer then asked which apples his friend had eaten. "Why, those apples which fell along the road over your fence," he replied.

"Ah, yes," said the farmer, "they are sour. I planted them to fool the boys who live around here. But, if you will come into the middle of my orchard, you will find a different taste."

On the edges of Christianity are some very sour apples—conviction, self-denial, and purity of life—which keep off hypocrites and mere professors. But in the middle of the orchard are delicious fruits, sweet and desirable. The nearer to God, the sweeter the joy.[578]

The pagan world was always haunted by the unknowability of God. At best, men could but grope after his mystery. "It is hard," said Plato, "to investigate and to find the framer and the father of the universe. And, if one did find him, it would be impossible to express him in terms which all could understand." Aristotle spoke of God as the supreme cause, by all men dreamed of and by no man known. The ancient world did not doubt that there was a God or gods, but it believed that such gods as there might be were quite unknowable and only occasionally interested in mankind. In a world without Christ, God was a mystery and power, desirable but never known.[579]

God's Love

One day a single friend asked a father of four, "Why do you love your kids?" The father thought for a minute, but the only answer he could come up with was "Because they're mine."

The children had no need to do anything to prove themselves to this father. He took them just as they were. So it is with God's love for us. He loves us as we are, and it is his love that motivates us to trust and obey him in return.[580]

The love of God is like the Amazon River flowing down to water one daisy.[581]

I asked Jesus how much he loved me. He stretched out his arms and said, "This much"—and died.[582]

A father was tucking in his six-year-old son for the night. The father asked him, "Son, when does Daddy love you the most? When you've been fighting with your sister and getting into a lot of trouble? Or when you've been real helpful to Mommy and real nice to everyone?"

The son thought for a moment and then said, "Both times!"

"Right," the father said, "and do you know why?"

"Cause I'm your special guy," replied the boy. For that was his daddy's pet name for him, "Daddy's Special Guy." The boy knew his father loved him, no matter what, because he was "Daddy's Special Guy."

God loves us the same way. He loves us unconditionally because we are his "special guys."[583]

On the whole, God's love for us is a much safer subject to think about than our love for him" (C. S. Lewis).[584]

God's Omnipotence

A young boy was waiting after church for his family. The pastor saw him standing around and struck up a conversation. Since the boy had just come from Sunday school, the pastor decided to ask him some questions to determine just how much the children were learning there. He said, "Young man, if you can tell me something that God can do, I'll give you a big shiny apple." Thoughtfully the boy replied, "Sir, if you can tell me something God can't do, I'll give you a whole box of apples."[585]

"The greatest single distinguishing feature of the omnipotence of God is that our imagination gets lost when thinking about it" (Pascal, *Pensees*, I, XV).[586]

On March 5, 1979, what was called "the most powerful burst of energy ever recorded" occurred. It was described as follows:

"The burst of gamma radiation picked up by the satellites lasted for only one tenth of a second. But in that brief instant it emitted as much energy as the sun does over a period of three thousand years. If the sun had belched out the same amount of energy, the earth would have vaporized instantly."

Reflecting on the event, astrophysicist Doyle Evans said, "Every time we think we understand the physical laws of the universe, nature seems bent on confounding us." Nature? Or God?[587]

God's Omniscience

The guillemot is a small arctic sea bird that lives on the rocky cliffs of northern coastal regions. These birds flock together by the thousands in comparatively small areas. Because of the crowded conditions, hundreds of females lay their pear-shaped eggs side by side on a narrow ledge, in a long row. Since the eggs all look alike, it is incredible that a mother bird can identify those that belong to her. Yet studies show that she knows her own eggs so well that when even one is moved, she finds it and returns it to its original location.

Scripture tells us that God is also intimately acquainted with each of his children. He knows our every thought and emotion, every decision we must make and problem we are going through. Therefore, an understanding of the full extent of God's omniscience should both evoke praise and bring comfort to believers.[588]

The story is told of an elderly grandfather who was very wealthy. Because he was going deaf, he decided to buy a hearing aid. Two weeks later he stopped at the store where he had bought it and told the manager he could now pick up conversation quite easily, even in the next room. "Your relatives must be happy to know that you can hear so much better," beamed the delighted proprietor.

"Oh, I haven't told them yet," the man chuckled. "I've just been sitting around listening—and you know what? I've changed my will twice!"

God is not like a dear old grandfather who hears only when we speak clearly and directly to him. He always hears us. And his attitude toward us is not changed by what he hears, because we stand before him by grace. But if God *were* like that grandfather—and if his attitude toward us were changeable—how would *your* conversations of the past week have affected his attitude toward you?[589]

Dr. James M. Gray, former president of the Moody Bible Institute, was convalescing from a severe illness. His physician, thinking that a change of scenery might bring the relaxation his patient needed, advised him to take an ocean voyage. But just when arrangements for the journey were completed, Dr. Gray experienced an unexpected physical setback. He was greatly disappointed and began to wonder why the heavenly Father had allowed this new affliction to come. About a week later, he picked up a newspaper that carried on the front page the tragic account of a steamer that had sunk after striking a reef in St. John's harbor. There were no survivors. When Gray read that this was the ship he would have taken, he realized how perfectly the Lord had directed his way. His temporary sickness had delivered him from certain death.[590]

God's Sovereignty

God rules in the affairs of men. Napoleon, at the height of his career, is reported to have given this cynical answer to someone who asked if God was on the side of France: "God is on the side that has the heaviest artillery."

Then came the Battle of Waterloo, where Napoleon lost both the battle and his empire. Years later, in exile on the island of St. Helena, chastened and humbled, Napoleon is reported to have quoted the words of Thomas à Kempis: "Man proposes; God disposes."

This is the lesson with which history confronts us all. God is able to work his sovereign will—despite man.[591]

C. S. Lewis in *God in the Dock* (Grand Rapids: Wm. B. Eerdmans, 1970) writes: "In 'Hamlet' a branch breaks and Ophelia is drowned. Did she die because the branch broke or because Shakespeare wanted her to die at that point in the play? Either—both—whichever you prefer. The alternative suggested by the question is not a real alternative at all—once you have grasped that Shakespeare is making the whole play."[592]

God's Trustworthiness

Two young girls were talking, and one said she had ten pennies. The other girl looked at her hand and only saw five. She said, "You only have five pennies." The first girl replied, "I have five and my father told me he would give me five more tonight. So I have ten."

She understood that her father's promise was as good as done.[593]

God's Work

The story has been told of a museum guide who would take his tour group to a darkened room, shine a light on a mass of string, color, and apparent chaos and ask the group, "What do you think this is?"

"I don't know," was the inevitable reply.

He would then say, "Stand over there and watch." As the group moved over to the other side of the room, he would turn on a spotlight. It was instantly apparent that the mass of jumbled colored string seen just a moment earlier was in fact an enormous tapestry—from the back side. The real work had to be seen from a different perspective to understand what the artist was creating.

So it is with God and his ways. We often look at them and ask questions such as "Why?" and "How?" not because there is no purpose in what God is doing, but because we are on the wrong side of eternity to be able to have the perspective that would enable us to see the order and pattern to God's work.[594]

God's Wrath

A little Scottish boy wouldn't eat his prunes, so his mother sent him off to bed saying, "God is angry at you."

Soon after the boy went to his room a violent storm broke out. Amidst flashes of lightning and peals of thunder, the mother looked into the boy's room, worried that he would be terrified. When she opened the door she found him looking out the window muttering, "My, such a fuss to make over a few prunes."[595]

Gospel, Content

"To preach a social gospel without the redemptive background of the individual salvation from sin of the individual sinner is like launching a glider instead of a high-powered plane. A glider may soar for awhile on the fickle currents of the wind, and climb high on some sudden up-draft, but it is the four whirl-wind motors that will carry a bomber to the stratosphere and jet-propulsion and rockets that will take a plane beyond the speed of sound" (Donald Grey Barnhouse, *Man's Ruin* [Grand Rapids: Wm. B. Eerdmans, 1952], pp. 161–162).[596]

God's work of salvation, according to a hard-line liberal, is summed up in the following quote:

"A God without wrath brought men without sin into a kingdom without judgment through the ministrations of a Christ without a Cross" (H. Richard Niebuhr, *The Kingdom of God in America* [New York: Harper & Row, 1959], p. 193).[597]

The minister of the gospel must not be afraid of conflict with the wisdom of the world. Gregory the Great said, "God first gathered the unlearned, afterwards philosophers, nor has He taught fishermen by orators, but has subdued orators by fishermen."[598]

Gossip

Christians don't gossip. They just share prayer requests![599]

The difference between news and gossip lies in whether you raise your voice or lower it.[600]

The difference between a gossip and a concerned friend is like the difference between a butcher and a surgeon. Both cut the meat, but for different reasons.[601]

The television program "60 Minutes" once reported on a widely circulated sensational weekly paper and interviewed people who were buying the paper at grocery-store checkout counters. "Do you believe what you read in this paper?" the reporter asked. "No," came the reply, "but we like to read it anyway."
Gossip holds a strange fascination for all of us.[602]

Some time ago, Dr. Albert H. Cantril, a professor at Princeton University, conducted a series of experiments to demonstrate how quickly rumors spread. He called six students to his office and in strict confidence informed them that the Duke and Duchess of Windsor were planning to attend a certain university dance. Within a week, this completely fictitious story had reached nearly every student on campus. Town officials phoned the university, demanding to know why they had not been informed. Press agencies were frantically telephoning for details. Dr. Cantril observed, "That was a *pleasant* rumor—a slanderous one travels even faster."[603]

John Dryden, a seventeenth-century British dramatist and poet, once commented on man's propensity to gossip:

There is a lust in man no charm can tame,
Of loudly publishing his neighbor's shame.
Hence, on eagles' wings immortal scandals fly,
While virtuous actions are but born and die.[604]

In *King Henry IV*, Shakespeare observed:

Rumor is a pipe
Blown by surmises, jealousies, conjectures,
And of so easy and so plain a stop
That the blunt monster with uncounted heads,
The still-discordant wavering multitude,
Can play upon it.

And how certain Christians can play that pipe![605]

The story is told of a young man during the Middle Ages who went to a monk, saying, "I've sinned by telling slanderous statements about someone. What should I do now?" The monk replied, "Put a feather on every doorstep in town." The young man did it. He then returned to the monk, wondering if there was anything else that he should do. The monk said, "Go back and pick up all the feathers." The young man replied, "That's impossible! By now the wind will have blown them all over town!" Said the monk, "So has your slanderous word become impossible to retrieve."[606]

Grace

The believer who seeks to live the Christian life through self-effort is like the man who, in attempting to sail across the Atlantic Ocean, found his boat becalmed for days. Finally, frustrated by his lack of progress, he tried to make his stalled boat move by pushing against the mast. Through strenuous efforts, he succeeded in making the boat rock and so created a few small waves on the otherwise smooth sea. Seeing the waves and feeling the rocking of the boat, he assumed that he was making progress and so continued his efforts. Of course, although he exerted himself a great deal, he actually got nowhere.

So it is in the Christian life. The source of the Christian's strength lies in God's grace, not in exertions of will-power, or in efforts of discipline, or any other self-effort.[607]

Grace, Common

"If you offered to give one dollar to a man whom you knew needed one hundred dollars and if he rejected your one dollar gift, you would doubtless consider his refusal sufficient grounds for declining to give him further assistance. If, on the other hand, the needy man accepted the one dollar gift gratefully, you might try to give him more. The dollar would be insufficient to meet his need, but if refused it would be sufficient to condemn him. That dollar is like common grace which is not able to save but which is able to condemn, if rejected" (Charles C. Ryrie, *Holy Spirit* [Chicago: Moody Press, 1965], p. 63).[608]

Grace, Example of

An old Indian, after living many years in sin, was led to Christ by a missionary. Friends asked him to explain the change in his life. Reaching down, he picked up a little worm and placed it on a pile of leaves. Then, touching a match to the leaves, he watched them smolder and burst into flames. As the flames worked their way up to the center where the worm lay, the old chief suddenly plunged his hand into the center of the burning pile and snatched out the worm. Holding the worm gently in his hand, he gave this testimony to the grace of God: "Me . . . that worm!"[609]

During the Spanish-American War, Theodore Roosevelt came to Clara Barton of the Red Cross to buy some supplies for his sick and wounded men. His request was refused. Roosevelt was troubled and asked, "How can I get these things? I must have proper food for my sick men."

"Just ask for them, Colonel," said Barton.

"Oh," said Roosevelt, "then I do ask for them." He got them at once through grace, not through purchase.[610]

Dr. H. A. Ironside in his book *In the Heavenlies* (Neptune, N.J.: Loizeau Bros., Inc.) tells the story of an attempted assassination of the first Queen Elizabeth of England. The woman who sought to do so dressed as a male page and secreted herself in the queen's boudoir, awaiting the convenient moment to stab the queen to death. She did not realize that the queen's attendants would be very careful to search the rooms before Her Majesty was permitted to retire. They found the woman hidden there among the gowns and brought her into the presence of the queen, after confiscating the poniard that she had hoped to plant into the heart of the sovereign.

The would-be assassin realized that her case, humanly speaking, was hopeless. She threw herself down on her knees and pleaded and begged the queen as a woman to have compassion on her, a woman, and to show her grace. Queen Elizabeth looked at her coldly and quietly said, "If I show you grace, what promise will you make for the future?" The woman looked up and said, "Grace that hath conditions, grace that is fettered by precautions, is not grace at all." Queen Elizabeth caught the idea in a moment and said, "You are right; I pardon you of my grace." And they led her away, a free woman.

History tells us that from that moment Queen Elizabeth had no more faithful, devoted servant than that woman who had intended to take her life. That is exactly the way the grace of God works in the life of an individual—he or she becomes a faithful servant of God.[611]

Two passages by C. S. Lewis illustrate the author's experience with God's grace:

You must picture me alone in that room in Magdalen, night after night, feeling, whenever my mind lifted even for a second from my work, the steady, unrelented approach of Him whom I so earnestly desired not to meet. That which I greatly feared had at last come upon me. In the Trinity Term of 1929, I gave in and admitted that God was God and knelt and prayed: perhaps that night, the most dejected and reluctant convert in all England. I did not then see what is now the most shining and obvious thing, the Divine humility which will accept a convert on even such terms. The prodigal son at least walked home on his own feet. But who can duly adore that Love which will open the high gates to a prodigal who is brought in kicking, struggling, resentful, and darting his eyes in every direction for a chance of escape? The words "compelle intrare," compel them to come in, have been so abused by wicked men that we shudder at them; but, properly understood, they plumb the depth of the Divine mercy. The hardness of God is kinder than the softness of men, and His compulsion is our liberation. [C. S. Lewis, *Surprised by Joy* (San Diego: Harcourt Brace, 1956), p. 228; Magdalen is one of the colleges of Cambridge University.]

I never had the experience of looking for God. It was the other way round: He was the hunter (or so it seemed to me) and I was the deer. He stalked me like a redskin, took unerring aim, and fired. And I am very thankful that this is how the first (conscious) meeting occurred. It forearms one against subsequent fears that the whole thing was only wish fulfillment. Something one didn't wish for can hardly be that. [C. S. Lewis, *Christian Reflections* (San Diego: Harcourt Brace, 1956), p. 169.][612]

Grace, False

An elderly woman was standing in the checkout line ready to pay for her merchandise: a quart of milk and a loaf of bread. She opened her purse. No money was there; neither was her checkbook. As she was about to ask the clerk to put her things back, suddenly a gentle voice said, "It looks like that is your lunch." A gentleman was standing right behind her, smiling. "Don't worry," he continued. "Today I want to treat you. Take your things with you." Then the man paid for her merchandise and his own. A week passed by, and the woman came back to the store. The checker knew about the incident and recognized her. She approached the woman and whispered, "Ma'am, maybe you'd be interested to know. That gentleman's check—it bounced!"[613]

Grace vs. Justice and Mercy

Grace is getting what we do not deserve.
Justice is getting what we do deserve.
Mercy is not getting what we do deserve.[614]

Great Commission

When Jesus ascended to heaven after his mission on earth, the angels asked him: "Did you accomplish your task?"

"Yes, all is finished," the Lord replied.

"We have a second question," said the angels. "Has the whole world heard of you?"

"No," said Jesus.

The angels next asked, "Then what is your plan?"

Jesus said, "I have left twelve men and some other followers to carry the message to the whole world."

The angels looked at him and asked: "What is your Plan B?"

Friends, there is no Plan B. Jesus desires to reach the world through men and women like you and me.[615]

Greatness

Rudyard Kipling wrote in *Recessional* about the British Empire:

> Far flung, our navies melt away,
> On dune and headland sinks the fire.
> Lo, all our pomp of yesterday
> Is one with Nineveh and Tyre!

So, too, will America's greatness fade, as will Russia's, and as will that of all the nations of this world.[616]

Two brothers were discussing their life goals after Sunday school. The first brother's goal was to be rich and famous. The second brother's goal was to follow Christ to the fullest. The second brother went on to reach his goal. His name was David Livingstone, the renowned medical missionary and explorer of Africa. The first went on to be rich, but his fame came from another. The epitaph on his tombstone reads: "Here lies the brother of David Livingstone."[617]

Greed

Many years ago a major American company had trouble keeping employees working in their assembly plant in Panama. The laborers lived in a generally agrarian, barter economy, but the company paid them in cash. Since the average employee had more cash after a week's work than he had ever seen, he would periodically quit working, satisfied with what he had made.

What was the solution? Company executives gave all their employees a Sears catalog. No one quit then, because they all wanted the previously undreamed-of things they saw in that book.[618]

An old method for catching raccoons is to place a piece of foil inside a small barred box that is staked to the ground. When a raccoon comes by, he reaches his paw into the box to get the foil. But, once he has grasped the foil, his paw changes shape and will not fit back through the bars on the box. Many times a raccoon would rather give up his freedom and perhaps his life—just for the sake of a shiny but useless piece of foil.[619]

The story is told of long ago when a great ship struck a reef and began to sink. It was obvious that the people on the ship had only a few minutes to escape, so all their belongings were abandoned as they fled to the lifeboats. However, one man on the ship ran and filled his pockets with gold from different staterooms and the ship's safe. This took just long enough that there were no lifeboats left. So the thief put on a life jacket and jumped overboard, happy with his new riches and his narrow escape. But, as his friends who had left quickly looked on, he hit the water and plummeted to the bottom like an anchor—the weight of the gold being too much to allow him to float.

Greed often fills us with that which becomes our own destruction.[620]

A reporter interviewed Lynette Fromme, the girl who took a shot at President Ford in Sacramento and who was also a member of the infamous Manson family. She said that the thing that attracted her to Charles Manson was his philosophy—"Get what you want whenever you want it. That is your God-inspired right."[621]

A little girl accompanied her mother to the country store where, after the mother had made a purchase, the clerk invited the child to help herself to a handful of candy. The youngster held back. "What's the matter? Don't you like candy?" asked the clerk. The child nodded, and the clerk smilingly put his hand into the jar and dropped a generous portion into the little girl's handbag.

Afterward the mother asked her daughter why she had not taken the candy when the clerk first offered some to her. "Because his hand was bigger than mine," replied the little girl.[622]

Greed can overpower nearly all elements of spiritual maturity. That is why giving is so important. Giving should not be like an overflow valve on our wealth, that is, giving what is excess. Rather, it should be like a loosened drain plug. You see, for wealthy people, tithing is actually an escape from real giving, since they can easily spare that 10 percent.[623]

Grudges

Madrid, Spain (AP) 7/23/81—King Juan Carlos and Queen Sofia decided to boycott the wedding of Prince Charles and Lady Diana to continue a protest dating to 1704. The Spanish government announced Tuesday that the king and queen declined the invitation to next week's wedding because the royal couple plan to go to Gibraltar to board the royal yacht *Britannia* for a honeymoon cruise. Gibraltar has been a British colony since 1704.

Two hundred and seventy-seven years seems like a long time to carry a grudge![624]

It is said that a rattlesnake, if cornered, will sometimes become so upset that it will bite itself. That is exactly what the harboring of hate and resentment against others is—a biting of oneself. We think that we are harming others in holding these grudges and hates, but the deeper harm is to ourselves.[625]

180

Guilt

"It seems that I know evil more intimately than I know goodness and that's not a good thing either. I want to get even, to be made even, whole, my debts paid (whatever it may take!), to have no blemish, no reason to feel guilt or fear. . . . I'd like to stand in the sight of God. To know that I'm just and right and clean. When you're this way, you know it. And when you're not, you know that, too. It's all inside of us, each of us." (From a letter by Gary Gilmore [executed by State of Utah] to his girlfriend.)[626]

The story is told of a time when Sir Arthur Conan Doyle decided to play a practical joke on twelve of his friends. He sent them each a telegram that read, "Flee at once. . . . all is discovered." Within twenty-four hours, all twelve had left the country.[627]

Bruce Narramore has described the two kinds of remorse:
"Two people are chatting over coffee. Reaching for the sugar, one of them accidentally knocks his cup in the other's lap. A typical guilt reaction would be, 'How stupid of me. I should have known better. Look at the mess I've made. I'm sorry.' The offender continues to berate himself and his misdeed. Constructive sorrow is very different. The offender might say, 'I'm so sorry. Here are some napkins. I'll get the table cleaned up.' And later he might offer to pay the cleaning bill."
Godly sorrow is constructive.[628]

Guilt, Universal

"It is indeed amazing that in as fundamentally an irreligious culture as ours, the sense of guilt should be so widespread and deep-rooted as it is." (Erich Fromm, *The Sane Society*, [New York: Fawcett, 1977], p. 181).[629]

Habits

Have you ever noticed a vine growing and spiraling around a chain-link fence? The fresh growth, the young green vine, is easy to remove with a simple twist of your wrist. But the old, brown, woody part of the vine is very difficult to remove. It takes a lot of time and effort to break it off, and sometimes it won't come off unless we are willing to also remove part of the fence itself.

Bad habits are like a vine on a chain-link fence. The sooner we get after them, the easier they are to remove. But the old ones, the ones we've let remain in our life for years, are hard to get rid of. And sometimes they can't be removed unless we also remove other parts of our life.[630]

Bad habits are like comfortable beds: easy to get into, but hard to get out of.[631]

Habits have a tendency to take our life in directions we would never have chosen. Good habits can guide us through treacherous times and situations where we aren't sure what to do and lack the foresight to realize the dangers ahead.

Bad habits are often seemingly fine at first, but they can lead us into treacherous waters. They are like a smooth river on which a young boy is floating—seemingly harmless—which then becomes swifter—very exciting—then becomes a rapids—somewhat scary—and finally goes crashing over a waterfall—devastating, possibly even fatal.[632]

Habits are like a cable. Each day we do something in a pattern we intertwine one thread with another. As the threads are woven together, a cable is formed. On any particular day, the thread we added was too small to be noticed. But, after many threads have been woven in, we find that together they have become a practically unbreakable cable.

So it is with habits. Daily practices over time become habits that are practically unbreakable—so be careful what you weave.[633]

Happiness

There is a tendency throughout life to search for the easy answer to every problem. We all search for Easy Street. Well, I am told that it actually exists. Just travel to Honolulu, Hawaii, and take the Pali Highway northbound. Travel about a third of the way to the Pali Pass and turn right on Park Street. Go one block and there it is: "Easy Street." The problem comes when you turn left and go one block more. There's another sign that says "Dead End."

Dead end—that's what happens in life, too, whenever we think we've found the easy way.[634]

If lasting happiness could be found in having material things and in being able to indulge ourselves in whatever we wanted, then most of us in America should be delirious with joy and happy beyond description. We should be producing books and poems that describe our state of unparalleled bliss. Our literature and art should rival that of the ancient Greeks and Romans and Renaissance craftsmen.

Instead we find those who have "things" trying to get more of them, for no apparent reason other than to have more. We find high rates of divorce, suicide, depression, child abuse, and other personal and social problems beyond description. We find housewives trading tranquilizer prescriptions. All this is surely proof that happiness is not found in the state of having all we want and being able to get more.[635]

Hatred

"Hate at its best will distort you; at its worst it will destroy you; but it will always immobilize you" (Alex Haley, author of *Roots*, speaking of hate in his own life).[636]

A pastor in Ireland told this story:
"I was telling a Protestant group of a boy in our city, Paul McGeown, age two, who on summer days loved to go with his mother to the park to watch the birds. 'Birdies! Birdies!' he would say with glee. On his way to the park one day, the blast of a terrorist bomb hurled Paul right across the road, inflicting severe head injuries. For sixteen days, he lay unconscious in the Belfast Children's Hospital. A brain surgeon operated, and when Paul regained consciousness, he could not see. Then a month later, a miracle happened. The nurse was holding Paul at the window. Suddenly he pointed. 'Birdies! Birdies!' Paul could see again.

"What was the reaction from the people to whom I was telling this story? Nearly all felt happiness for the child whose sight had been restored, I'm sure. But one woman angrily asked, 'But wasn't he a Roman Catholic?' "[637]

Heaven

A man who has a layover at an airport does not go into the bathroom, frown at its decor, and start redecorating! Why? Because he doesn't live there. He has a home in another place. While he is away he will get by with only what he absolutely needs, to have more money with which to furnish his permanent home.

183

Why do we Christians work hard at trying to make our life in this world more comfortable? This is just the airport and we are in transit. We should spend our energy on enhancing our eternal reward, and not worry so much about the bare walls in the airport restrooms.[638]

Dr. W. A. Criswell, the beloved pastor of First Baptist Church of Dallas, was once asked, "Will we know each other when we get to heaven?" His answer: "We won't really know each other *until* we get to heaven."[639]

William M. Dyke was a young man who became blind at the young age of ten. Despite this handicap, he grew to be a very intelligent, witty and handsome young man. While attending graduate school in England, William met the daughter of an English admiral. The two soon became engaged. Though never having seen her, William loved her very much. Shortly before the wedding, at the insistence of the admiral, William submitted to special treatment for his loss of sight. Hoping against hope, William wanted the gauze from his eyes removed during the ceremony. He wanted the first thing he saw to be his wife's face.

As the bride came down the aisle, William's father started unwinding the gauze from around his head and eyes—still not knowing if the operation would be a success. With the unwrapping of the last circumference, William looked into the face of his new bride for the first time. "You are more beautiful than I ever imagined," he said.

Like the young groom, though we have never seen Jesus, it will be worth the years of darkness to "see him as he is" (1 John 3:2).[640]

"There are a lot of questions the Bible doesn't answer about the Hereafter. But I think one reason is illustrated by the story of a boy sitting down to a bowl of spinach when there's a chocolate cake at the end of the table. He's going to have a rough time eating that spinach when his eyes are on the cake. And if the Lord had explained everything to us about what's ours to come, I think we'd have a rough time with our spinach down here" (Vance Havner).[641]

"When I get to heaven, I shall see three wonders there: The first wonder will be to see many there whom I did not expect to see; the second wonder will be to miss many people whom I did expect to see; the third and greatest of all will be to find myself there" (John Newton, author of hymn "Amazing Grace").[642]

Hell

Archimedes, one of the greatest of the ancient Greek mathematicians and scientists, was working on a math problem when his native city of Syracuse was conquered by the Roman general Marcellus in 212 B.C. The scientist ignored the final assault and continued working on his math while the enemy entered the gates of the city. As the Roman soldiers came down the street where Archimedes was, he continued to work the problem in the sand and offered no resistance, even as one of them ran him through with a sword and killed him.

Many unbelievers are somewhat like Archimedes, oblivious to what is really happening around them until it is too late to do anything about it.[643]

W. C. Fields, following the 1933 earthquake that struck Southern California, said: "We're crazy to live here, but there sure are a lot of us."

The same attitude is often displayed by non-Christians, who seem to think that hell will be more tolerable because there will be a crowd down there.[644]

"The watchman who keeps silent when he sees a fire is guilty of gross neglect. The doctor who tells us we are getting well when we are dying is a false friend, and the minister who keeps back hell from his people in his sermons is neither a faithful nor a charitable man" (J. C. Ryle).[645]

The Russian novelist Dostoevski once declared: "I ponder, 'What is hell?' I maintain it is the suffering of being unable to love."[646]

Margaret Evening (pseud.) relates the following in her book *Who Walk Alone* (p. 38):

Many years ago I had a dream. It was one of the few coherent dreams that I have ever had, but it was so vivid that even now I can remember the details of it clearly.

In the dream, I visited Hell, where the sub-Warden showed me round. To my surprise, I was led along a labyrinth of dark, dank passages from which there were numerous doors leading into cells. It was not like Hell as I had pictured it at all. In fact, it was all rather religious and "churchy"! Each cell was identical. The central piece of furniture was an altar, and

185

before each altar knelt (or, in some cases, were prostrated) greeny-grey spectral figures in attitudes of prayer and adoration. "But whom are they worshipping?" I asked my guide. "Themselves," came the reply immediately. "This is 'pure' self-worship. They are feeding on themselves and their own spiritual vitality in a kind of auto-spiritual-cannibalism. That is why they are so sickly looking and emaciated."

I was appalled and saddened by the row upon row of cells with their non-communicating inmates, spending eternity in solitary confinement, themselves the first, last and only object of worship.

The dream continued . . . but the point germane to our discussion here has been made. According to the teaching of the New Testament, *Heaven is community.* My dream reminded me that *Hell is isolation.*[647]

"Hell is truth seen too late" (Thomas Hobbes).[648]

An impressive modern statement of the principle of divine retribution is provided by C. S. Lewis in *The Problem of Pain* (New York: Macmillan, 1978): "The lost enjoy forever the horrible freedom they have demanded, and are therefore self-enslaved" (p. 115).

In *The Great Divorce* (New York: Macmillan, 1978) C. S. Lewis says hell is made up of people who live at an infinite distance from each other. Surely this is a graphic picture of the result of the loss of God in our life.[649]

Hell, Reality of

Walter Hooper, who was C. S. Lewis's personal secretary, laughed when he read the following grave inscription:

> Here lies an atheist,
> All dressed up with no place to go.

Lewis, however, did not completely share in his laughter. He responded soberly, "I'm sure he wishes now that were true." Hell is a sobering reality for those who don't believe.[650]

Hermeneutics

In all innocence, children have for centuries sung a nursery rhyme that is in truth anything but an innocent verse:

> Ring-a-ring o'roses,
> A pocket full of posies,
> A-tishoo! A-tishoo!
> We all fall down!

The rhyme arose about 1665 in the streets of London during a plague epidemic of the Black Death. Each phrase of the rhyme refers to an aspect of the plague.

"Ring o'roses" is a reference to the small, red rashlike areas that developed on people infected with the plague.

"Pocket full of posies" is a reference to the ancient belief that evil smells were the poisonous breath of demons who afflicted people with the disease. It was thought that sweet-smelling herbs and flowers would drive them off.

"A-tishoo! A-tishoo!" is a reference to the sneezing that was a symptom of the plague.

"We all fall down!" is a reference to death.

Thus, a common children's rhyme is in fact a sinister parody of one of the most dreaded plagues ever to strike—the Black Death.

The same loss of context and therefore of meaning can affect those who study the Scriptures. And that is why when we seek to interpret the word of God, we do so in part by studying its historical, grammatical context.[651]

In 1728, potatoes were outlawed in Scotland because they were not mentioned in the Bible.[652]

Holidays

During the holiday season, people become greatly concerned about what they are going to eat. Of course, there is nothing wrong with eating such favorite traditional foods as special cakes, cookies, meats, and so forth. But for some of us there is a tendency to let it get out of hand—and into the stomach! Perhaps we should institute a new award to be given out at each holiday: the No-belly Prize for abstinence.[653]

Holiness

Many trees appear to be healthy when we see them in summer. But, in the winter, after their leaves have all fallen off, we sometimes find that hidden underneath the lush green of the summer foliage was a

187

parasitic plant called mistletoe, which had been slowly sucking away some of the tree's vitality.

We as Christians sometimes have hidden sins, which—like the mistletoe—slowly suck away our spiritual vitality. Although not always evident in times of outward spiritual health and fruitfulness, we must always examine ourselves for those small, often unseen, parasites of sinful habits that will sap our vitality. And we must also remember that just because they are not apparent now does not mean that in another season of our life God will not reveal them for all to see.[654]

What do we mean when we say a thing is holy? Look at your Bible and it says, "Holy Bible." What makes it holy? The land of Israel is called "The Holy Land," and the city of Jerusalem is called "The Holy City." Why? There is a quality about all three that they share in common. They all belong to God. The Bible is God's book; Israel is God's land; Jerusalem is God's city. They are all God's property! That is why they are holy; they belong to God.[655]

The great missionary David Brainerd, who spent his brief life (he died before the age of thirty) ministering to American Indians, wrote in his journal these words: "I never got away from Jesus and him crucified. When my people were gripped by this great evangelical doctrine of Christ and him crucified, I had no need to give them instructions about morality. I found that one followed as the sure and inevitable fruit of the other."

He also said this in another place: "I find my Indians begin to put on the garments of holiness and their common life begins to be sanctified even in small matters when they are possessed by the doctrine of Christ and him crucified."

What Brainerd was saying was this: when a Christian realizes who Christ is and what Christ has done for him so graciously, as we have been seeing, it tends to have a dramatic effect on this life, not only in salvation but in holiness.[656]

"One day as I was reading the second chapter of I John, I realized that my personal life's objective regarding holiness was less than that of John's. He was saying, in effect, 'Make it your aim not to sin.' As I thought about this, I realized that deep within my heart my real aim was not to sin 'very much'—Can you imagine a soldier going into battle with the aim of 'not getting hit very much?' " (Jerry Bridges, *The Pursuit of Holiness* [Colorado Springs, Colo.: Nav Press, 1978], p. 96).[657]

Howard Hendricks wisely observed, "It is foolish to build a chicken coop on the foundation of a skyscraper." The Christian who fails to live a holy life is failing to utilize the foundation for his life that Christ has given him.[658]

C. S. Lewis once commented to an American friend, "How little people know who think that holiness is dull. When one meets the real thing, . . . it is irresistible. If even 10% of the world's population had it, would not the whole world be converted and happy before a year's end?" (C. S. Lewis, *Letters to an American Lady* [Grand Rapids: Wm. Eerdmans, 1967], p. 19).[659]

"A surgeon who selects a scalpel in the operating room rejects a scalpel with a minute spot of defilement on it as readily as one that was severely defiled, because even the smallest spot means the scalpel is defiled and cannot be used in surgery. The degree of defilement is inconsequential. The fact of defilement is what matters to the surgeon. A thing is sterile or defiled, clean or unclean. A person is holy or unholy. God is not concerned with degrees, only with the absolute" (J. D. Pentecost, *Design for Living* [Grand Rapids: Zondervan, 1977], p. 57).[660]

Holy Spirit

At the close of World War II, two pictures appeared in a magazine showing a soldier in conflict with a tank. The first showed a huge tank bearing down on a tiny soldier, about to crush him. The picture was proportioned to show the odds involved when a footsoldier with a rifle faced a tank. The next picture showed what happened to that soldier's odds with a bazooka, or rocket launcher, in his hands. This time the tank appeared to be shrunken in size and the soldier at least equal in size, if not a little larger.

Without the power of God released in our lives, when in conflict with sin we are like an infantry soldier in the presence of a tank. We cannot do a thing. But by trust in the power of the living God at work in us, we can say no and make it stick. We can turn and begin to live as God intended us to live.[661]

Holy Spirit, Filling of

> What God chooses, He cleanses.
> What God cleanses, He molds.
> What God molds, He fills.
> What God fills, He uses.
>
> *J. S. Baxter*[662]

A. J. Gordon, one of the founders of Gordon Conwell Divinity School, told of being out walking and looking across a field at a house. There beside the house was what looked like a man pumping furiously at one of those hand pumps. As Gordon watched, the man continued to pump at a tremendous rate; he seemed absolutely tireless, pumping on and on, up and down, without ever slowing in the slightest, much less stopping.

Truly it was a remarkable sight, so Gordon started to walk toward it. As he got closer, he could see it was not a man at the pump, but a wooden figure painted to look like a man. The arm that was pumping so rapidly was hinged at the elbow and the hand was wired to the pump handle. The water was pouring forth, but not because the figure was pumping it. You see, it was an artesian well, and the water was pumping the man!

When you see a man who is at work for God and producing results, recognize that it is the Holy Spirit working through him, not the man's efforts that are giving results. All he has to do—and all you have to do—is keep your hand on the handle.[663]

"To be filled with the Holy Spirit is to be filled with one who is already there, in our hearts. Take up a sponge and while it is in your hand squeeze it. In that condition, plunge it in water and submerge it, keeping it in there. It is now in the water and the water is in it. As you hold it in the water, you open your hand, and as you do so the water fills all the pores which you release in this way. It is now filled with the water. When we receive Christ we are born anew and put into that sphere where the Holy Spirit is operating and the Holy Spirit comes to reside in us!! (Romans 8:9)" (Roy Hession, *Be Filled Now* [Fort Washington, Penn.: Christian Lit., 1968], p. 12).[664]

Two Texans were traveling together on vacation. They decided to stop at one of the natural wonders of the world, Niagara Falls. As they took the beautiful drive from Lake Erie to the falls they were filled with

190

admiration and awe at the size and power of the Niagara River. They were particularly impressed with the rapids just above the falls and stopped there to look. From there they could see the massive mist cloud that always hangs over the precipice.

One of the men, having already been there, said, "Come and I'll show you the greatest unused power in the world." Taking him to the foot of Niagara Falls, he said, "There is the greatest unused power in the world."

"Ah, no, my friend, not so!" was the reply of the other. "The greatest unused power in the world is the Holy Spirit of the living God."[665]

Many people ask, "How do I know the Holy Spirit is living in me?" I know in the same way that I know there is music on a cassette tape, even though I don't see the music on the tape. I can know that in either of two ways. I can believe the label that says there is music, or I can play the tape and hear it. We can know the Holy Spirit indwells us by believing God, who tells us in his Word, or by seeing his results in our lives when we are obedient to him.[666]

Holy Spirit, Ministry of

On a particularly rough airplane flight, a lady became very airsick. Her shoulders drooped, and her head slumped forward—she was totally wiped out. The stewardess came by to help her. "Come, come now," she said, "buck up and get control of yourself. Sit up and take courage." She put her arm under the lady's arm and helped her sit upright in her seat, gave her gum to chew, and then went to get her some water. With the help of the stewardess, the lady finished the trip in far better condition than she began it in.

This is like the ministry of the Holy Spirit in our lives. He comes alongside to help us when we are in hopeless defeat. He admonishes us, encourages us, and restores hope and faith in our lives.[667]

Holy Spirit, Sealing of

The trucking industry has an interesting illustration of the sealing of the Spirit. For certain types of loads, when a truck is fully loaded and ready for its run, a plastic seal is put around the lock on the door. This seal cannot be broken before the truck reaches its destination without the penalty of loss of one's job.

This is similar to the sealing of the Spirit. The seal of the Spirit

191

cannot be broken before the Christian reaches his heavenly destination. It is our guarantee of reaching God's destination for us.[668]

Ranchers in West Texas make it their practice to round up all their year-old calves each spring for branding. The calf is held down, the branding iron is heated red hot, and the brand is placed on its flank. The brand is the rancher's mark of ownership. No one can dispute that the calf belongs to him.

In the same way God has placed his mark of ownership on us by sealing us with the Holy Spirit. The Holy Spirit is God's mark of ownership, authority, and security over us. No one can remove us from his ownership until the day of redemption.[669]

When a piece of registered mail is mailed from a post office, it is sealed until delivered. Actually, only two persons can open registered mail—the sender (if it is returned to him) and the designated recipient.

To draw a parallel for believers, God is the One who sends us on our way to heaven, and God in heaven is the recipient on our arrival. As with registered mail, only God can break the seal of our redemption. However, he has promised not to do so—and the guarantee of that promise is the presence of the Holy Spirit, who is the One in whom we have been sealed by God. (Adapted from Charles C. Ryrie, *The Holy Spirit* [Chicago: Moody Press, 1965] p. 82).[670]

Home Bible Studies

It is most significant that whenever spiritual awakenings have occurred throughout the Christian centuries, they have always been accompanied by a restoration of koinonia, of the confession of faults, and the bearing of one another's burdens. During the Wesleyan awakening in eighteenth-century England, the great evangelist George Whitefield wrote to his converts:

"My brethren, let us plainly and freely tell one another what God has done for our souls. To this end, you would do well, as others have done, to form yourselves into little companies of four or five each, and meet once a week to tell each other what is in your hearts; that you may then also pray for and comfort each other as need shall require. None but those who have experienced it can tell the unspeakable advantages of such a union and communion of souls. None, I think, that truly loves his own soul and his brethren as himself, will be shy of opening his heart, in order to have their advice, reproof, admonition and prayers, as occasions require. A sincere person will esteem it one of the greatest blessings."[671]

Honesty

On his way to school one day, a young man found two canvas sacks lying in the street. When he looked inside he was amazed to see that the sacks were full of money—$415,000, in fact! When he returned the money to the Princeton Armored Service, he received a reward of $1,000. The youth, however, was unhappy and said he had expected a larger reward. "I don't understand it," he complained. "If I had to do it over again, I'd probably keep the money." (Cited in *Dallas Times Herald*, March 11, 1979, p. A–2.)[672]

In 1924, *Liberty* magazine sent out a hundred letters to people selected at random throughout the U.S. Each letter contained a one-dollar bill and explained that it was an adjustment of an error that the addressees had complained of—which they had actually never done. Of the hundred recipients, only twenty-seven returned the dollar and said it was a mistake.

In 1971, *Liberty* conducted the same test. This time only thirteen returned the money.[673]

The story has been told of a bank employee who was due for a good promotion. One day at lunch the president of the bank, who happened to be standing behind the clerk in the cafeteria, saw him slip two pats of butter under his slice of bread so they wouldn't be seen by the cashier.

That little act of dishonesty cost him his promotion. Just a few pennies' worth of butter made the difference. The bank president reasoned that if an employee cannot be trusted in little things he cannot be trusted at all.[674]

Adam Clarke was an assistant in a dry-goods store, selling silks and satins to a cultured clientele. One day his employer suggested to him that he try stretching the silk as he measured it out; this would increase sales and profits and also increase Adam's value to the company. Young Clarke straightened up from his work, faced his boss courageously, and said, "Sir, your silk may stretch, but my conscience won't!"

193

God honored Adam Clarke for being an embodied conscience by taking him from the dry-goods store and fitting him to write a famous commentary on the books of the Bible.[675]

Dr. Madison Sarratt, who taught mathematics at Vanderbilt University for many years, before giving a test would admonish his class something like this: "Today I am giving two examinations; one in trigonometry and the other in honesty. I hope you will pass them both. If you must fail one, fail trigonometry. There are many good people in the world who can't pass trig, but there are no good people in the world who cannot pass the examination of honesty."[676]

Hope

All too often, hope is pessimistically defined as the little boy did when he said: "Hope is wishing for something you know ain't gonna happen."[677]

Some years ago a hydroelectric dam was to be built across a valley in New England. The people in a small town in the valley were to be relocated because the town itself would be submerged when the dam was finished. During the time between the decision to build the dam and its completion, the buildings in the town, which previously were kept up nicely, fell into disrepair. Instead of being a pretty little town, it became an eyesore.

Why did this happen? The answer is simple. As one resident said, "Where there is no faith in the future, there is no work in the present."[678]

In his book *Man's Search for Meaning*, Victor Frankl, successor of Sigmund Freud at Vienna, argued that the "loss of hope and courage can have a deadly effect on man." As a result of his experiences in a Nazi concentration camp, Frankl contended that when a man no longer possesses a motive for living, no future to look toward, he curls up in a corner and dies. "Any attempt to restore a man's inner strength in camp," he wrote, "had first to succeed in showing him some future goal."[679]

In 1965, naval aviator James B. Stockdale became one of the first American pilots to be shot down during the Vietnam War. As a prisoner of the Vietcong, he spent seven years as a P.O.W., during which he was frequently tortured in an attempt to break him and get him to denounce the U.S. involvement in the war. He was chained for days at a time with his hands above his head so that he could not even swat the mosquitoes. Today, he still cannot bend his left knee and walks with a severe limp from having his leg broken by his captors and never reset. One of the worst things done to him was that he was held in isolation away from the other American P.O.W.s and allowed to see only his guards and interrogators.

How could anyone survive seven years of such treatment? As he looks back on that time, Stockdale says that it was his hope that kept him alive. Hope of one day going home, that each day could be the day of his release. Without hope, he knew that he would die in hopelessness, as others had done.

Such is the power of hope that it can keep one alive when nothing else can.[680]

Hope, False

Probably nothing in the world arouses more false hope than the first four hours of a diet.[681]

Hospitality

To entertain some people, all you have to do is listen.[682]

A seminary student drove about thirty miles to church on Sunday mornings and he would frequently pick up hitchhikers. One day he picked up a young man who noticed that he was wearing a suit and asked if he could go to church with him. The student said, "Of course you can."

The stranger came to church and afterward was invited over to one of the members' home for lunch and fellowship. While there, he received a hot bath, some clean clothes, and a hot meal. In conversation with the youth, his hosts found that he was a Christian, but he had been out of fellowship with the Lord. His home was in another state and he was just passing through on his way back. Later in the evening, they bought him a bus ticket and sent him on his way.

A week later, the seminary student received a letter from the hitchhiker. Enclosed with the letter was a newspaper clipping with head-

195

lines reading, "Man turns himself in for murder." This young man had killed a teenage boy in an attempted robbery and had been running away from the law for some time. But the kindness and hospitality of Christians had convicted him. He wanted to be in fellowship with God, and he knew he needed to do the right thing about his crime.

Little did those Christians know that by their faithfulness to show hospitality they had influenced a man to do what was right in God's eyes and thereby help restore him to fellowship with his Lord.[683]

Hospitality and Churches

Singer John Charles Thomas, at age sixty-six wrote to syndicated columnist Abigail Van Buren:

"I am presently completing the second year of a three-year survey on the hospitality or lack of it in churches. To date, of the 195 churches I have visited, I was spoken to in only one by someone other than an official greeter—and that was to ask me to move my feet." (Cited by "Eutychus and His Kin," *Christianity Today*, June 3, 1977.)[684]

Hospitality and Entertaining

The following differentiation between "hospitality" and "entertaining" was made by Karen Mains in *Open Heart, Open Home* (Elgin, Ill.: Cook, 1976):

Entertaining says, "I want to impress you with my home, my clever decorating, my cooking." Hospitality, seeking to minister, says, "This home is a gift from my Master. I use it as He desires." Hospitality aims to serve.

Entertaining puts things before people. "As soon as I get the house finished, the living room decorated, my housecleaning done—then I will start inviting people. Hospitality puts people first. "No furniture—we'll eat on the floor!" "The decorating may never get done—you come anyway." "The house is a mess—but you are friends—come home with us."

Entertaining subtly declares, "This home is mine, an expression of my personality. Look, please, and admire." Hospitality whispers, "What is mine is yours."[685]

Hospitality and Missions

A Chicago businessman called his wife to get her okay for him to bring home a visiting foreigner as a guest for dinner that night. At the time, the wife had three children in school and one preschooler, so there were plenty of important things to do besides entertaining strangers. But she consented and the meal came off without a hitch. The foreigner, an important Spanish official, never forgot that meal.

Years later, some friends of that family went to Spain as missionaries. Their work was brought to a standstill, however, by government regulations. When the Spanish official got word that the missionaries were friends of that hospitable Chicago couple, he used his influence to clear away the restrictions. There is a church today in that province of Spain, due in part to that one meal![686]

Humanist Manifesto

"Humanism" is a term widely used within the church to describe the prevailing philosophy of today—the world's mold that Christians have to resist deliberately. But what, specifically, is "humanism"? Probably its clearest definition and most aggressive repudiation of Christianity appears in the *Humanist Manifesto II* (Sept. 2, 1973), which contains the following basic tenets:

We believe that traditional dogmatic or authoritarian religions that place revelation, God, ritual, or creed above human needs and experience do a disservice to the human species.

Promises of immortal salvation or fear of eternal damnation are both illusory and harmful. They distract humans from present concerns, from self-actualization, and from rectifying social injustices.

We affirm that moral values derive their source from human experience. Ethics is autonomous and situational, needing no theological or ideological sanction. Ethics stem from human need and interest. To deny this distorts the whole basis of life. Reason and intelligence are the most effective instruments that humankind possesses. There is no substitute; neither faith nor passion suffices in itself.

No deity will save us; we must save ourselves.[687]

Humility

The story is told of two brothers who grew up on a farm. One went away to college, earned a law degree, and became a partner in a prominent law firm in the state capital. The other brother stayed on the family farm. One day the lawyer came and visited his brother, the farmer. He asked, "Why don't you go out and make a name for yourself and hold your head up high in the world like me?" The brother pointed and said, "See that field of wheat over there? Look closely. Only the empty heads stand up. Those that are well filled always bow low."

Said differently, "The branch that bears the most fruit is bent the lowest to the ground."[688]

Humility is like a slippery watermelon seed. Once you get it under your finger and you think you have it, it slips away from your grasp.[689]

"When a certain rhetorician was asked what was the chief rule of eloquence he replied, 'Delivery.' What was the second rule, 'Delivery.' What was the third rule, 'Delivery.' So if you ask me concerning the precepts of the Christian religion, first, second, third, and always I would answer, 'Humility.' " (Augustine, quoted by John Calvin, *Institutes*, 2.2.11).[690]

An ardent music lover unexpectedly met the great Johannes Brahms. On recognizing the composer the man asked: "Master, would you please write here a small portion of a masterpiece and sign it so I can have a precious memory of this fortunate encounter?"

Brahms took the pencil and paper, scribbled the initial bars of *The Blue Danube* by Johann Strauss and signed: "Unfortunately not by me, Johannes Brahms."[691]

There is an old ditty that goes: "It needs more skill than I can tell / To play the second fiddle well."

In a similar vein, Leonard Bernstein was once asked which instrument was the most difficult to play. He thought for a moment and then replied, "The second fiddle. I can get plenty of first violinists, but to find someone who can play the second fiddle with enthusiasm—that's a problem. And if we have no second fiddle, we have no harmony."[692]

Dr. H. A. Ironside felt that he was not as humble as he thought he ought to be. Showing his concern, he asked an elder friend what he could do about it. His friend replied, "Make a sandwich board with the plan of salvation in Scripture on it and wear it, then walk through the business and shopping area of downtown Chicago for a whole day."

Ironside followed his friend's advice. Upon completion of this humiliating experience, he returned to his apartment. As he took off the sandwich board, he caught himself thinking, "There's not another person in Chicago that would be willing to do a thing like that."[693]

A well-known incident in the life of Robert E. Lee occurred while that southern gentleman was riding on a train to Richmond. The general was seated at the rear, and all the other places were filled with officers and soldiers. An elderly woman, poorly dressed, entered the coach at one of the stations. Having no seat offered to her, she trudged down the aisle to the back of the car. Immediately, Lee stood up and gave her his place. One man after another then arose to give the general his seat. "No, gentlemen," he said, "if there is none for this lady, there can be none for me!"

Being a Christian, General Lee knew that good manners and humility demand consideration for people in all walks of life, not merely for those of high social ranking like himself.[694]

We have plenty of people nowadays who could not kill a mouse without publishing it in the *Gospel Gazette*. Samson killed a lion and said nothing about it: the Holy Spirit finds modesty so rare that He takes care to record it. Say much of what the Lord has done for you, but say little of what you have done for the Lord. Do not utter a self-glorifying sentence! (C. H. Spurgeon, as quoted in *The Shadow of the Broad Brim* by Richard E. Day [Grand Rapids: Baker, 1976, repr.], p. 182).[695]

Corrie ten Boom was once asked if it was difficult for her to remain humble. Her reply was simple. "When Jesus rode into Jerusalem on Palm Sunday on the back of a donkey, and everyone was waving palm branches and throwing garments on the road, and singing praises, do you think that for one moment it ever entered the head of that donkey that any of that was for him?"

She continued, "If I can be the donkey on which Jesus Christ rides in His glory, I give him all the praise and all the honor."[696]

Humility, Definition of

Andrew Murray gave a near-perfect definition of humility:

Humility is perfect quietness of heart. It is to expect nothing, to wonder at nothing that is done to me, to feel nothing done against me. It is to be at rest when nobody praises me, and when I am blamed or despised. It is to have a blessed home in the Lord, where I can go in and shut the door, and kneel to my Father in secret, and am at peace as in a deep sea of calmness, when all around and above is trouble.

The humble person is not one who thinks meanly of himself, he simply does not think of himself at all.[697]

Humility, Knowledge and

"Never seem more learned than the people you are with. Wear your learning like a pocketwatch and keep it hidden. Do not pull it out to count the hours, but give the time when you are asked" (Lord Chesterfield, *Letters to His Son*).[698]

Humility, Test of

"The true way to be humble is not to stoop until you are smaller than yourself, but to stand at your real height against some higher nature that will show you what the real smallness of your greatness is" (Phillips Brooks).[699]

The Navigators are well known for their emphasis on having a servant attitude. A businessman once asked Lorne Sanny, president of the Navigators, how he could know when he had a servant attitude. The reply: "By how you act when you are treated like one."[700]

Hypocrisy

In any great forest you will find many huge trees. They tower above other trees and appear to be the very picture of strength and maturity. However, loggers will sometimes not even bother to cut down these huge trees. At first one wonders, "Why leave them? After all, a tree that big must contain twice or thrice the amount of lumber as a smaller tree."

The reason is simple. Huge trees are often rotten on the inside. They are the hollow trees that children's picture books show raccoons living in. And they are the trees that are often blown over in a strong windstorm because, while they appear to be the picture of strength, in fact their hollowness makes them weak.

This is the essence of hypocrisy—appearing strong on the outside but hollow and rotten on the inside.[701]

On the French Riviera, it is such an important status symbol to have a balcony on an apartment that it is quite common to see balconies painted on the walls of apartment houses. People even paint wet laundry hanging on a clothesline, just to give it a touch of reality.

Hypocrisy is a facade painted just to give it a touch of reality.[702]

Hypocrisy is like a pin. It is pointed in one direction, and yet is headed in another.[703]

When Howard Carter and his associates found the tomb of King Tutankhamen, they opened up his casket and found another within it. They opened up the second, which was covered with gold leaf, and found a third. Inside the third casket was a fourth made of pure gold. The pharaoh's body was in the fourth, wrapped in gold cloth with a gold face mask. But when the body was unwrapped, it was leathery and shriveled.

Whether we are trying to cloak a dead spiritual life, or something else, in caskets of gold to impress others, the beauty of the exterior does not change the absence of life on the interior.[704]

A father complained about the amount of time his family spent in front of the television. His children watched cartoons and neglected schoolwork. His wife preferred soap operas to housework. His solution? "As soon as the baseball season's over, I'm going to pull the plug."[705]

Identification with Christ

The story has been told of a girl who was the daughter of one of the royal families of Europe, but had a big, bulbous nose that in her eyes destroyed her beauty and resulted in her seeing herself as an ugly person. Finally her family hired a famous plastic surgeon to change the contour of the girl's nose. He did his work, and there came the moment when they took the bandages off and the girl could see the results. The doctor saw that the operation had been a total success. All the ugly contours were gone. Her nose was different. When the incisions healed and the redness disappeared, she would be a beautiful girl. He held up a mirror for the girl to see, but so deeply embedded was the girl's image of herself that when she saw herself in the mirror, she couldn't see any change. She broke into tears and cried out, "Oh, I knew it wouldn't work!"

It took six months before the girl would accept the fact that she was indeed an attractive person, and it wasn't until she had accepted this fact that her self-image and behavior began to change accordingly. So it is with those who are "in Christ." We must accept our new identity before we will change.[706]

When the final second had ticked away, and the thrilling football game had ended, an exhausted fan in the bleachers turned to his friend and exclaimed, "Boy, we really played well today!" The fact was that he hadn't played at all. He wasn't wearing the pads. He wasn't on the field. Yet he identified himself with the eleven men on the team.

So should it be for believers. Christ was the One who died on the cross, Christ was buried, and Christ rose again. Yet we are identified with him.[707]

Do you remember Clark Kent, that mild-mannered newspaper reporter, of whom no one ever expected anything out of the ordinary? But whenever there was a sudden demand for action far beyond the ability of mortal men, Clark stepped into a closet, stripped off his conservative business suit, and emerged complete with bulging muscles and spectacular costume as—Superman! Superman, the one who could do what otherwise could not be done.

That is exactly what the Word of God is teaching us, although perhaps you have not seen it in those terms before. As we who are believers step into our identity in Christ—who we are, to whom we belong, and who is within us—we will find love, motivation, and power available so that we are able to do what otherwise we could not do.[708]

Illumination

"The Bible without the Holy Spirit is a sun-dial by moonlight" (D. L. Moody).[709]

Immortality, Search for

The April 1985 issue of *Eternity* magazine contained the following news item. It is not known if these plans were or will be accomplished, but they do illustrate that men cannot bear the thought of being dead and forgotten:

202

The quest for pseudoimmortality took a giant leap forward with the announcement that you can send your remains "to the heavens" when you die. The Celestis Group of Melbourne, Florida, has received federal approval for a privately financed launch of a rocket in early 1987, with a nose cone containing the ashes of 10,330 paying customers. Each person's ashes will be chemically treated to fit inside a 2-by-⅝-inch titanium capsule. The nose cone will enter an orbit at about 1,900 miles up, and, thanks to a reflective surface, "it will be visible to earth-bound loved ones." The Celestis group isn't promising an eternal rest, though. The orbit may deteriorate in about 63 million years.[710]

Inadequacy, Feelings of

A sign found above an office desk read, "We, the unwilling, led by the unqualified, have been doing the unbelievable for so long with so little, that we now attempt the impossible with nothing."[711]

Indifference

Dante once said, "The hottest places in hell are reserved for those who remain neutral in a time of great moral crisis."[712]

"In Germany, they first came for the Communists, and I didn't speak up because I wasn't a Communist; then they came for the Jews, and I didn't speak up because I wasn't a Jew. Then they came for the Trade Unionists, and I didn't speak up because I wasn't a Trade Unionist. Then they came for the Catholics, and I didn't speak up because I was a Protestant. Then they came for me—and by that time no one was left to speak up" (Martin Niemöller, German pastor, victim of Nazi concentration camp).[713]

Ingratitude

Many years ago, a boat was wrecked in a storm on Lake Michigan at Evanston, Illinois. Students from Northwestern University formed themselves into rescue teams. One student, Edward Spencer, saved seventeen people from the sinking ship. When he was carried exhausted to his room, he asked, "Did I do my best? Do you think I did my best?"

Years later, R. A. Torrey was talking about this incident at a meeting in Los Angeles, and a man in the audience called out that Edward

Spencer was present. Dr. Torrey invited Spencer to the platform. An old man with white hair slowly climbed the steps as the applause rang. Dr. Torrey asked him if anything in particular stood out in his memory. "Only this, sir," he replied, "of the seventeen people I saved, not one of them thanked me."[714]

Insignificance, Feelings of

Sir Michael Costa was conducting a rehearsal in which the orchestra was joined by a great chorus. About halfway through the session, with trumpets blaring, drums rolling, and violins singing their rich melody, the piccolo player muttered to himself, "What good am I doing? I might as well not be playing. Nobody can hear me anyway." So he placed his instrument to his lips but made no sound. Within moments the conductor cried, "Stop! Stop! Where's the piccolo?"

Perhaps many people did not realize that the piccolo was missing, but the most important one did. So it is in the Christian life. God knows when we do not play the part assigned to us, even if others do not.[715]

Integrity

In ancient China, the people desired security from the barbaric hordes to the north. So they built the Great Wall of China. It was too high to climb over, too thick to break down, and too long to go around. Security achieved!

The only problem was that during the first hundred years of the wall's existence, China was invaded three times. Was the wall a failure? Not really—for not once did the barbaric hordes climb over the wall, break it down, or go around it.

How then did they get into China? The answer lies in human nature. They simply bribed a gatekeeper and then marched right in through a gate. The fatal flaw in the Chinese defense was placing too much reliance on a wall and not putting enough effort into building character into the gatekeeper.[716]

A pastor preached a sermon on honesty one Sunday. On Monday morning he took the bus to get to his office. He paid the fare, and the bus driver gave him back too much change. During the rest of the journey, the pastor was rationalizing how God had provided him with some extra money he needed for the week. But he just could not live with himself, and before he got off the bus he said to the driver, "You have made a mistake. You've given me too much change." And he proceeded to give him back the extra money. The driver smiled and said, "There was no mistake. I was at your church yesterday and heard you preach on honesty. So I decided to put you to a test this morning."[717]

"Sen. Sam Not Convinced" read the headline. Former Senator Sam Ervin, who had presided over the Senate Watergate Committee, took note of H. R. Haldeman's perjury conviction in commenting on the former White House aide's book *The Ends of Power:* "A man that would commit perjury under oath might possibly be tempted to commit it when he is not under oath. . . . I would say that before I would accept his book as credible, I would want it corroborated by all the apostles, except Judas" (*Dallas Times Herald*, February 17, 1978).[718]

In 1959, 40-year-old Ted Williams of the Boston Red Sox was suffering from a pinched nerve in his neck. "It was so bad that I could hardly turn my head to look at the pitcher," he said. For the first time in his remarkable career, he batted under .300, hitting just .254 and only ten home runs. Williams was the highest salaried player in sports that year, making $125,000. The next year, the Red Sox offered him the same contract. "I told them I wouldn't sign it until they gave me the full pay cut allowed, 28 percent. My feeling was that I was always treated fairly by the Red Sox. They were offering me a contract I didn't deserve." Williams cut his own salary by $35,000![719]

Jews, Conversion of

Some years ago, a clergyman of the Church of England attended an early-morning prayer meeting in behalf of Israel in an East London Jewish mission. Coming out on the street, he met another clergyman, who had attended a special service at St. Paul's Cathedral on the anniversary of the conversion of the apostle Paul. After greeting each other, the second minister asked the other where he had been. He told him he had attended a Jewish mission meeting, upon which the second minister showed some surprise that his friend should believe in the possibility of Jews coming to faith. The minister who had attended the mission service asked the other where he had been and was told that he had attended a special service in honor of St. Paul at the cathedral bearing his name.

The clergyman who had attended the Jewish service asked, "Who exactly was Paul?"

The hesitating reply was, "I suppose you would consider him a believing Jew."

"What music did they have at the service?"

"Why, Mendelssohn's *St. Paul*, of course."

"Who was Mendelssohn?"

"Why, a German."

"No, he was not, he was a believing Jew," was the reply.

The clergyman who did not seem to believe in the possibility of Jews coming to faith had been in a church dedicated to the memory of a Jewish believer, attending a service in honor of this Jew's acceptance of the Messiah, had been listening to music composed by a Jewish believer, and was talking to a fellow clergyman—who was the Rev. Aaron Bernstein, a believing Jew.[720]

At a meeting of the Hebrew Christian Alliance of America, over 90 percent attending said they were aroused to consider the claims of Christ because some Gentile Christian had showed them love.[721]

In discussing the conversion of Jews, C. S. Lewis once said, "In a sense, the converted Jew is the only normal human being in the world." He continued, "Everyone else is, from one point of view, a special case dealt with under emergency conditions."

That is a way of stating the truth about Gentile conversion. God opened a "back door" and let us in as emergency cases. There are a lot of us, but we remain "grafted-in branches."[722]

Judging   *of 1484*

Most of us are umpires at heart; we like to call balls and strikes on somebody else.[723]

> Judge not.
> The workings of the mind and heart
> Thou canst not see.
> What looks to thy dim eyes as stain
> In God's pure light may only be a scar,
> Bought from some well-won field
> Where thou wouldst only faint and yield.[724]

A lady in an airport bought a book to read and a package of cookies to eat while she waited for her plane. After she had taken her seat in the terminal and gotten engrossed in her book, she noticed that the man one seat away from her was fumbling to open the package of cookies on the seat between them. She was so shocked that a stranger would eat her cookies that she didn't really know what to do, so she just reached over and took one of the cookies and ate it. The man didn't say anything but soon reached over and took another. Well, the woman wasn't going to let him eat them all, so she took another, too. When they were down to one cookie, the man reached over, broke the cookie in half, and got up and left. The lady couldn't believe the man's nerve, but soon the announcement came to board the plane.

Once the woman was aboard, still angry at the man's audacity and puzzling over the incident, she reached into her purse for a tissue. It suddenly dawned on her that she really shouldn't judge people too harshly—for there in her purse lay her still-unopened package of cookies.[725]

Judgment, God's

In the choir of life, it's easy to fake the words—but someday each of us will have to sing solo before God.[726]

In the days of the pioneers, when men saw that a prairie fire was coming, what would they do? Since not even the fastest of horses could outrun it, the pioneers took a match and burned the grass in a designated area around them. Then they would take their stand in the burned area and be safe from the threatening prairie fire. As the roar of the flames approached, they would not be afraid. Even as the ocean of fire surged around them there was no fear, because fire had already passed over the place where they stood.

When the judgment of God comes to sweep men and women into hell for eternity, there is one spot that is safe. Nearly two thousand years ago the wrath of God was poured on Calvary. There the Son of God took the wrath that should have fallen on us. Now, if we take our stand by the cross, we are safe for time and eternity.[727]

Sometimes the cup of iniquity is full and the people are ripe for judgment. In such a case it may happen as it did in the flourishing and extraordinarily beautiful city of Messina, Italy. In the early morning of December 28, 1908, an earthquake struck, and 84,000 human beings

207

died. Only a few hours before that devastating earthquake, which laid Messina and the surrounding districts in ruins, the unspeakably wicked and irreligious condition of some of the inhabitants was expressed in a series of violent resolutions that were passed against all objections.

The journal *Il Telefono*, printed in Messina, actually published in its Christmas issue an abominable parody, daring the Almighty to make himself known by sending an earthquake! And in three days the earthquake came! (Cited by John Lawrence, *Down to Earth* [Wheaton, Ill.: Tyndale, 1983], p. 51.)[728]

Judgment, Leadership and

Two men once robbed a jewelry store. One was a lawyer and the other was a high-school dropout. After being arrested, convicted, and sentenced, the lawyer received a ten-year imprisonment. The dropout received three years. The counselors for the lawyer protested the harsh judgment but the judge insisted that the lawyer was under greater responsibility to be an example of the law.

In like manner are church leaders under a greater responsibility to be living examples of the Lord Jesus Christ.[729]

Justice

The story has been told of a man who was caught and taken to court because he had stolen a loaf of bread. When the judge investigated, he found out that the man had no job, and his family was hungry. He had tried unsuccessfully to get work and finally, to feed his family, he had stolen a loaf of bread. Although recognizing the extenuating circumstances, the judge said, "I'm sorry, but the law can make no exceptions. You stole, and therefore I have to punish you. I order you to pay a fine of ten dollars." He then continued, " But I want to pay the fine myself." He reached into his pocket, pulled out a ten-dollar bill, and handed it to the man.

As soon as the man took the money, the judge said, "Now I also want to remit the fine." That is, the man could keep the money. "Furthermore, I am going to instruct the bailiff to pass around a hat to everyone in this courtroom, and I am fining everyone in this courtroom fifty cents for living in a city where a man has to steal in order to have bread to eat." The money was collected and given to the defendant.

This is an excellent example of justice being meted out in full and paid in full—while mercy and grace were also enacted in full measure.[730]

Learning that her husband had betrayed her, Vera Czermak jumped out her third-story window in Prague. The newspaper *Vicerni Praha* reported that Mrs. Czermak was recovering in the hospital, after landing on her husband, who was killed.[731]

Justification

Merlin Carothers, author of the book *Prison to Praise*, had firsthand experience of what it is like to be declared righteous. During World War II, he joined the army. Anxious to get into some action, Carothers went AWOL but was caught and sentenced to five years in prison. Instead of sending him to prison, the judge told him he could serve his term by staying in the army for five years. The judge told him if he left the army before the five years ended, he would have to spend the rest of his term in prison. Carothers was released from the army before the five-year term had passed, so he returned to the prosecutor's office to find out where he would be spending the remainder of his sentence. To his surprise and delight, Carothers was told that he had received a full pardon from President Truman. The prosecutor explained: "That means your record is completely clear. Just as if you had never gotten involved with the law."[732]

Kindness

It takes a long time to fill a glass with drops of water. Even when the glass seems full, it can still take one, two, three, four, or five or more additional drops. But if you will keep at it, there is at last that *one* drop that makes the glass overflow.

The same applies to deeds of kindness. In a series of kindnesses there is at last one that makes the heart run over.[733]

One of the most difficult things to give away is kindness, for it is usually returned.[734]

"You can accomplish by kindness," wrote Publilius Syrus in the first century before the birth of Christ, "what you cannot by force."

William B. McKinley, President of the United States from 1897 to 1901, was a man who understood that principle. During one of his campaigns, a reporter from an opposition newspaper followed him constantly and just as persistently misrepresented McKinley's views. Eventually during this campaign, the weather became extremely cold, and even though the reporter didn't have sufficiently warm clothing, he still followed McKinley. One bitter evening, the president-to-be was riding in his closed carriage, and the young reporter sat shivering on the driver's seat outside. McKinley stopped the carriage and invited the reporter to put on his coat and ride with him inside the warm carriage. The young man, astonished, protested that McKinley knew that he was opposition and that he wasn't going to stop opposing McKinley during the campaign. McKinley knew that, but he wasn't out to seek revenge. In the remaining days of the campaign, the reporter continued to oppose McKinley, but never again did he write anything unfair or biased about the future president.[735]

Laughter

"It is really a natural trend to lapse into taking oneself gravely because it is the easiest thing to do . . . for solemnity flows out of men naturally, but laughter is a leap. It is easy to be heavy; hard to be light. Satan fell by force of gravity" (G. K. Chesterton).[736]

Law

A law is a set pattern of how things happen; it is a rule. The law of gravity deems that a heavy slab of concrete will remain where it is placed. Thus sidewalks stay in place. But we all have seen a sidewalk that is heaved up and twisted because once a small acorn fell between the slabs of the sidewalk and now has grown into a massive oak tree whose roots are powerful enough to move great weights.

That is what is meant by the triumph of one law over another—such as the law of life over the law of sin and death (Rom. 8:2).[737]

A man lived in another country whose laws were such that one could not walk on the sidewalks after 6:00 P.M. Eventually this man moved to the United States. After arriving here he decided to see the sights and so went for a long walk. Suddenly he realized it was getting close to 6:00 P.M. and he was far from where he was staying. In desperation, he stopped a stranger who was getting into an automobile and in halting English said, "Please, sir, help me! It is almost six and I am too far from my hotel to walk back before I will be arrested. Can you give me a ride?"

The stranger at first was confused but then realized that the man was new to the United States and so said to him, "Sir, let me assure you that in the United States we do not arrest people for being out after six."

This man knew he was in the United States, but he had not cast off his obedience to the laws of his old country and so was still being controlled by what no longer had any jurisdiction over him. He was a free man, needlessly bound to the rules and regulations of his former life.[738]

Law, Effect of

The Flagship Hotel in Houston, Texas, is built right next to the water. Large plate-glass windows adorn the dining room, which is on the lowest floor. However, the windows kept getting broken by guests fishing from the balconies above. Heavy sinkers had to be used to cast to the water, but the lines were often too short and so would crash against the windows below. Finally the management removed the "NO FISHING FROM BALCONY" signs from the rooms. The windows were safe at last.

The law always bears fruit in disobedience.[739]

Law, Function of

Many people are physiologically sensitive to chocolate. Certain of the larger benzene compounds present in chocolate are resisted by their bodies through an allergic reaction. Depending on the individual, this reaction may range from very mild, producing a minor skin rash, to very severe, producing medical shock and death. Chocolate is fatal for some persons not because chocolate is poisonous in and of itself but because of the biochemical makeup of their bodies.

In a similar way, the power of sin in man reacts to the law and brings death. As Paul says in Romans 7:7–12, this happens not because the law is evil but because of sin within us.[740]

Law, Grace and

An Indian pastor in Oklahoma was going to a pastors' conference. He went to the train station and caught a train to a mansion where the conference was being held. The theme of the conference was "Law and Grace." The Indian pastor listened intently to the lengthy theological discussions and arguments presented by each seminar leader. Finally, in a group-discussion period, he said, "It seems to me the train station we all came in at demonstrates law, and this house we are meeting in, grace. At the station was a sign 'Do not spit,' yet the men there did. Here there is no sign, yet no one spits."[741]

The law says, "Do this and live." It commands but gives us neither feet nor hands.

Grace bids us to fly and gives us wings.[742]

Law, Purpose of

A plumb line can only prove that a crooked wall is crooked. No matter how you use it, a plumb line can't make a crooked wall straight. The law was God's plumb line, designed to show all people that they are crooked, or sinful. It was never intended to *make* us straight or righteous—and, indeed, it never could.[743]

If you set aside a glass of water with dirt and garbage in it and left it undisturbed for a few days, the particles would settle to the bottom of the glass so that the water would begin to look drinkable. However, we all know that it would still be dangerous to drink, even though that wasn't readily evident. If you took a sterile spoon and stirred the water, it would become readily evident that the water was not clean.

The law is like the sterile spoon—though perfect in itself, it was intended to make evident to us the true nature that exists within us.[744]

One of the biggest flops the federal government has ever promoted was the Susan B. Anthony dollar. Literally millions of these coins are stored in the government's vaults, unused and unwanted. Even when they were first issued, no one wanted them, and they soon became the basis for seemingly endless jokes.

However, this rejection was not universal. A postal worker in one town put up a sign that said, "Susan B. Anthony dollars: limit of two per customer." He said he had been previously trading two or three per day, but when he put the sign up, he traded at least fifty daily.

That is exactly what the law does to us. It makes desirable what was undesirable before.[745]

Laziness

A farmer was sitting on the porch of his house when a stranger came by and asked, "How's things?"

"Tolerable," came the reply. He continued, "Two weeks ago a tornado came along and knocked down all the trees I would have had to chop down for this winter's firewood. Then last week lightning struck the brush I had planned to burn to clear the fields for planting."

The stranger responded, "That's remarkable, what are you doing now?"

The farmer answered, "Waiting for an earthquake to come along and shake the taters out of the ground."[746]

According to John Silling, a Purdue University entomologist, the ant is an exemplary worker. "Basically the ant's entire life, which can range up to seven years, is spent working," says Silling. "They gather food, bring it back to the nest, and use it for day-to-day meals as well as to store for the winter."

In addition, the amazing insects can be adept horticulturalists, states the professor. Some species "gather bits of grass or leaves and take them back to their nest. On this organic matter, which is used much like fertilizer, they place tiny mushroom spores and grow them for food." But ants as dairy-keepers? That's right. "Some ants get the majority of their food by 'milking' aphids or plant lice which are often known as 'ant cows,' says the scientist. "The ants sometimes herd the aphids down into the ant nests at night or when it starts to get cool; then when it gets warm again, they herd them back up to the plants."[747]

Humorist Ogden Nash captured the bitter truth about laziness:

> If you don't want to work
> You have to work
> To earn enough money
> So that you won't have to work.[748]

F.O. Walsh gave this basis for laziness:

> While other men paint,
> Or water or weed,
> I'm curled up in a chair,
> With a good book to read.
>
> While other men shop,
> Or shovel, or mow,
> I'm having a drink
> While watching some show.

213

> I offer to help,
> But my wife says, "Forget it,
> If you lend a hand,
> I know I'll regret it."
>
> And therein's my secret,
> I'm very adept
> At only one thing,
> And that's being inept.
>
> *F. O. Walsh*[749]

Leadership

An ancient Persian proverb offers the following excellent advice on developing leaders.

He who knows not, and knows not that he knows not is a fool—shun him.

He who knows not, and knows that he knows not is a child—teach him.

He who knows, and knows not that he knows is asleep—wake him.

He who knows, and knows that he knows is wise—follow him.[750]

The person who can't lead and won't follow makes a dandy road-block.[751]

An important rule of leadership "Don't allow the patient to prescribe the medicine."[752]

Stay one step ahead of your people and you are called a leader. Stay ten steps ahead of your people and you are called a martyr![753]

True leaders always rise to the top, especially in difficult times. They are like beans in a jar of peas. When you place peas and beans in a jar and shake them up vigorously, the peas always settle to the bottom while the beans always come to the top.

So it is with godly men. They can never be held down when shaken up. If they truly have leadership abilities and a love for God, they will always rise to the top.[754]

214

One day, Confucius was asked by one of his disciples about the ingredients of good government. His answer: "Sufficient food, sufficient weapons, and the confidence of the common people."

"But," asked the disciple, "suppose you had no choice but to dispense with one of those three, which would you forego?"

"Weapons," said Confucius.

His disciple persisted: "Suppose you were then forced to dispense with one of the two that are left, which would you forego?"

Replied Confucius, "Food. For from of old, hunger has been the lot of all men, but a people that no longer trusts its rulers is lost indeed" (Confucius, *The Analects*).[755]

Thomas Monaghan is founder, president, and chief executive officer of Domino's Pizza, Inc. From 1970 to 1985, Domino's grew from a small debt-ridden chain to the second largest pizza company in America, with sales of over one billion dollars in 1985.

When asked to account for the phenomenal growth of the company, Monaghan explained, "I programmed everything for growth." And how did he plan for growth? "Every day we develop people—the key to growth is developing people."

Not special cheese, not a tasty crust, not fast delivery schedules, but people! People are the key to all effective leadership.[756]

Harry Truman once commented on the importance of polls to leadership, with the following insight: "I wonder how far Moses would have gone if he'd taken a poll in Egypt? What would Jesus Christ have preached if he'd taken a poll in Israel? Where would the Reformation have gone if Martin Luther had taken a poll? It isn't the polls or public opinion of the moment that counts. It is right and wrong and leadership—men with fortitude, honesty, and a belief in the right— that makes epochs in the history of the world."[757]

A bumper sticker reads: "Don't follow me. I'm lost too." Motion does not always mean purpose. Be very careful if you follow the crowd, for they may not know where they are going.[758]

A leader is like a radio station's clock. That clock is actually much more important than our own watches because we set our watches by the radio station's clock. So, too, with the character of a leader—he sets the pace for our own standards of conduct.[759]

215

Over a century ago, a colleague submitted to Asahel Nettleton a list of qualifications to be possessed by those who should be encouraged to enter the ministry. It read thus: (1) Piety; (2) Talents; (3) Scholarship; (4) Discretion. "Change the order," said Nettleton, "put discretion next to piety."[760]

"One definition of leadership is the ability to recognize the special abilities and limitations of others, combined with the capacity to fit each one into the job where he will do his best" (J. Oswald Sanders, *Spiritual Leadership* [Chicago: Moody Press, 1974], p. 127).[761]

"I'd rather get ten men to do the job than to do the job of ten men" (D. L. Moody).[762]

Leadership by Example

Shepherds of God's flock are not to lord it over the flock, but to prove to be examples. They are to lead by their example. This is graphically illustrated in the U. S. Army. The symbol of the infantry (footsoldiers who do most of the front-line fighting) is a soldier with a rifle in one hand, helmet cocked, and head looking back behind him. The rifle is pointing forward, the other arm is giving a "Come on ahead" motion, and the leader is shouting back, "Follow me!" This symbol illustrates leadership-by-example, as this soldier calls his men to follow him into the heart of the battle.[763]

General Eisenhower would demonstrate the art of leadership with a simple piece of string. He'd put it on a table and say: "*Pull* it and it will follow wherever you wish. *Push* it and it will go nowhere at all. It's just that way when it comes to leading people. They need to follow a person who is leading by example."

At another time he said, "You do not lead by hitting people over the head—that's assault, not leadership."[764]

Legalism

Sometimes we tend to be amazed (and even snicker) at the minutia of Pharisaic legalism. We tend to forget, however, that sandwiched among our country's sound and workable statutes, there are hundreds of cockeyed ordinances that remain to clutter up our law books because the powers-that-be—from state legislators to town fathers—have not gotten around to repealing them. For instance, in Amarillo, Texas, it is against the law to take a bath on the main street during banking hours. In Portland, Oregon, it is illegal to wear roller skates in public restrooms. In Halethorpe, Maryland, a kiss lasting more than a second is an illegal act. The list goes on and on. Suffice it to say that down through history man has been inclined to live by and enforce the letter of the law rather than the spirit of the law.[765]

The sin of the Pharisees was paying attention to outward demonstrations of piety for appearance's sake rather than giving attention to inward obedience. This can be well illustrated by two eggs. One egg is a normal raw egg that, when placed under the palm of the hand and pressed evenly cannot be broken because of the structure of the egg itself. The second egg is exactly the same on the outside, but its insides have been removed. When it is placed under the same palm pressure, it breaks easily because it is internally weak. So, too, one who gives himself to the sin of the Pharisees is empty of substance and will eventually crack under pressure.[766]

The attitude one has toward doing what has to be done determines if the action is legalistic. An illustration makes this clear:
"A serious athlete has to keep training rules. Most athletes are glad to keep them, rigid as they may be, for the sheer love of the sport. A few athletes conform to make the team and glorify, show off, self. The former attitude is love, and the latter is legalism, but both attitudes are toward the same rigid code, and both result in conformity. Having to conform to a law is not of itself legalism" (Charles C. Ryrie, *The Grace of God* [Chicago: Moody Press, 1975], p. 7).[767]

Leprosy

William Barclay described what a leper looks like:
"The whole appearance of the face is changed, till the man loses his human appearance and looks, as the ancients said, 'like a lion or a satyr.' The nodules grow larger and larger. They ulcerate. From them there comes a foul discharge. The eyebrows fall out, the eyes become staring. The voice becomes hoarse and the victim wheezes because of the ulceration of the vocal chords. The hands and feet always ulcerate.

217

Slowly the sufferer becomes a mass of ulcerated growths. The average course of the disease is nine years, and it ends in mental decay, coma, and ultimately death. The sufferer becomes utterly repulsive—both to himself and to others."[768]

Liberty, Christian

Fire, depending on how it is used, can be either beneficial or destructive. When used correctly, it can warm a house, cook food, and create a romantic evening with your spouse. However, when fire is used incorrectly, it can lay waste to woodlands, destroy houses, or even devastate an entire city.

Christian liberty is the same. When used correctly, it can be extremely beneficial, but when used incorrectly, it has great potential for destruction.[769]

Sometimes, when you enter a main highway or come to an intersection, you will see a sign with the word "YIELD" in large letters. The sign means that the driver on one road is to yield the right to proceed to any driver on the other road. The latter driver does not own the right of way; rather, another driver yields it to him.

This is an excellent picture of what Christian liberty is all about. We are to yield our rights so that others may go on to greater maturity. No one can demand that another believer yield his rights; rather, as an act of maturity, he should see the need to give up his rights for the good of another. Perhaps we should make yield signs and put them up in our homes and churches—because it is a Christian philosophy to yield, to give way to other believers.[770]

If the law states that one may drive 55 m.p.h., one has the "liberty" to proceed at that speed. However, it is not always *wise* to drive at the lawful speed because of other factors, such as a severe snowstorm, or fog. In a similar manner, a Christian has liberty in many areas, but sometimes he wisely restrains his liberty.[771]

When a man is released from prison, he is not free to do anything he feels like doing, but he *is* free to obey the law. In the same way, when we are freed from sin by trusting in Christ, we are not given a license to sin, but rather are set free to obey him.[772]

218

One of the greatest times of turmoil in the history of the church was the Reformation. Men like Luther, Calvin, and Zwingli were strong personalities in difficult times. Not a few people in those days found themselves banished from their ancestral homeland or city because of their beliefs. In some cases, wars were fought over beliefs and seemingly (to us) minor doctrinal points.

In a day of fiery personality conflicts, major doctrinal deviation, and battles at every level, a lesser-known German theologian, Philipp Melanchthon, summed up Christian liberty in a superb fashion: "In essentials, unity; in non-essentials, liberty; in all things, charity."[773]

Lie

"A little lie is like a little pregnancy—it doesn't take long before everyone knows" (C. S. Lewis).[774]

"A lie can travel half way around the world while Truth is still lacing up her boots" (Attributed to Mark Twain).[775]

Life, Happiness in

Charlie Brown, pondering his plight in life, thought, "Yesterday, for one brief moment I was happy. But just when I thought I was winning in the game of life, there was a flag thrown on the play and life dealt me a blow."[776]

Life, Day-to-Day

Yard by yard, life is hard.
Inch by inch, it's a cinch.[777]

Life, Perspective of

In a "Peanuts" comic strip, there was a conversation between Lucy and Charlie Brown. Lucy said that life is like a deck chair. Some place it so they can see where they are going; some place it so they can see where they have been; and some place it so they can see where they are at present. Charlie Brown's reply: "I can't even get mine unfolded."[778]

Life's Purpose

Someone has aptly said, "Living without God's plan for our life is like sewing with a needle without thread, or writing one's biography with a pen empty of ink."[779]

Some time ago, psychologist William Moulton Marston asked three thousand persons, "What have you to live for?"

He was shocked to find that 94 percent were simply enduring the present while waiting for the future. They would describe this as waiting for "something" to happen—waiting for children to grow up and leave home, waiting for next year, waiting for another time to take a long-dreamed-about trip, waiting for tomorrow. They were all waiting without realizing that all anyone ever has is today because yesterday is gone and tomorrow never comes.[780]

> All have been given a bag of tools,
> A formless rock and a book of rules.
> And each must make ere life has flown,
> A stumbling block or a stepping stone.[781]

"He who has a *why* to live for can bear with almost any *how*" (Friedrich Nietzsche, a German nihilist).[782]

> Lord, make me an instrument of Thy peace;
> Where there is hatred, let me sow love;
> Where there is doubt, faith;
> Where there is despair, hope;
> Where there is darkness, light; and
> Where there is sadness, joy.
> O Divine Master, grant that I may not so much
> Seek to be consoled, as to console;
> To be understood as to understand;
> To be loved, as to love;
> For it is in giving that we receive;
> It is in pardoning that we are pardoned; and
> It is in dying that we are born to eternal life.

Attributed to Francis of Assisi[783]

Life's Purpose (for Unbeliever)

A father went into a toy store to buy his son a Christmas present. The salesman showed him a new educational toy. It came unassembled, but no matter how the child put the pieces together, they wouldn't fit. You see, the toy was designed to teach the child how to deal with life.

Such is the predicament of man without God. He is never able to put his life together. A life without Christ is a life of futility.[784]

"The universe is merely a fleeting idea in God's mind—a pretty uncomfortable thought, particularly if you've just made a down payment on a house" (Woody Allen).[785]

G. N. Clark is reported to have said in his inaugural address as president of Cambridge University, "There is no secret and no plan in history to be discovered. I do not believe that any future consummation could make any sense of all the irrationalities of preceding ages. If it could not explain them, still less could it justify them."[786]

In the introduction to his *A History of Europe*, H. A. L. Fisher writes:

> One intellectual excitement has been denied me. Men wiser and more learned than I have discovered in history a plot, a rhythm, a predetermined pattern. But these harmonies are concealed from me. I can see only one emergency following another, as wave follows upon wave, only one great fact with respect to which, since it is unique, there can be no generalization, only one safe rule for the historian—that he should recognize in the development of human destiny the play of the contingent and the unforeseen.[787]

"Only religion is able to answer the question of the purpose of life. One can hardly go wrong in concluding that the idea of a purpose in life stands and falls with the religious system" (Sigmund Freud, *Civilization and Its Discontents* [New York: Norton, 1963], p. 26).[788]

Andre Maurios said, "The universe is indifferent. Who created it? Why are we here upon this puny mud heap spinning in infinite space? I have not the slightest idea, and I am quite convinced that no one else has the least idea."[789]

221

Socialists usually offer an optimistic view of mankind, and so Orwell's *1984* ends surprisingly pessimistically—evil conquers.

Some have suggested this pessimism came because Orwell was dying as he wrote. Actually he was merely expressing a dilemma he had seen for some time. He knew that man's central problem was the death of Christian belief. In 1944 he wrote, "Since about 1930 the world has given no reason for optimism whatever. Nothing is in sight except a welter of lies, hatred, cruelty, and ignorance, and beyond our present troubles loom vaster ones which are only now entering into the European consciousness. It is quite possible that man's major problems will 'never' be solved. . . . The real problem is how to restore the religious attitude while accepting death as final. Men can be happy only when they do not assume that the object of life is happiness."

Before then, in 1940, he had written of Europe's rejection of God—which he approved—this way: "For two hundred years we had sawed and sawed and sawed at the branch we were sitting on. And in the end, much more suddenly than anyone had foreseen, our efforts were rewarded, and down we came. But unfortunately there had been a little mistake: The thing at the bottom was not a bed of roses after all, it was a cesspool full of barbed wire . . . It appears that amputation of the soul isn't just a simple surgical job, like having your appendix out. The wound has a tendency to go septic." (Cited in *Christianity Today*, January 13, 1984, pp. 25–26.)[790]

Do the events of history make any sense? Or is life, as Shakespeare had Macbeth describe it, "a tale told by an idiot, full of sound and fury, signifying nothing"? (*Macbeth*, Act V, v).[791]

A greatest possible impact a non-believer's life can have on eternity is on the order of a large ship's impact on the ocean. It leaves a wake, which may be very impressive for the moment, but which is gone without a trace within a few moments more.[792]

Life's Uncertainty

A young couple desiring to go into missionary work had invited a missionary couple to their home. The host couple kept mentioning that life was so "uncertain" for them because the husband had multiple sclerosis. He could either be eventually immobilized in a hospital bed, or live normally until death, or die unexpectedly.

After hearing the term *uncertain* so many times, the missionary turned to the couple and said, "All of our lives are uncertain. You just happen to know it, and most of us don't."[793]

Listening

The story has been told of a new commander who was sent to an army fort on the American frontier. He soon was involved in a conference with an important Indian chief. Working through a translator, he nervously asked the chief a number of questions and was surprised to get no reply. After the meeting, he asked the translator why he had gotten no response. The translator replied, "That's what we call Indian time. He has enough respect for your questions to go away and think about them before answering them."

Maybe we all need to practice more Indian time.[794]

> His thoughts were slow,
> His words were few and never formed to glisten.
> But he was a joy to all his friends,
> You should have heard him listen![795]

Listening is not just passive hearing. It is an active participating experience in which you pay genuine attention to what the other person is saying. Here are some principles that should help you become a better listener:

1. Don't grab the conversation: "Yes, now take me, for instance . . ."
2. Don't let your gaze wander from the other person's face except momentarily.
3. Validate the feelings of the other: "Yes, I see what you mean."
4. Don't interrupt.
5. Don't try to top the other person's story or joke.
6. Don't criticize.
7. Ask appropriate questions: "What happened then?" or "How did you feel?"
8. Don't argue.

These guidelines are cited by Cecil C. Osborne, in *The Art of Getting Along with People* (Grand Rapids: Wm. B. Eerdmans, 1982).[796]

223

Lord's Prayer

I cannot say "our" if I live only for myself.

I cannot say "Father" if I do not endeavor each day to act like his child.

I cannot say "who art in heaven" if I am laying up no treasure there.

I cannot say "hallowed be thy name" if I am not striving for holiness.

I cannot say "thy Kingdom come" if I am not doing all in my power to hasten that wonderful event.

I cannot say "thy will be done" if I am disobedient to his Word.

I cannot say "on earth as it is in heaven" if I'll not serve him here and now.

I cannot say "give us this day our daily bread" if I am dishonest or am seeking things by subterfuge.

I cannot say "forgive us our debts" if I harbor a grudge against anyone.

I cannot say "lead us not into temptation" if I deliberately place myself in its path.

I cannot say "deliver us from evil" if I do not put on the whole armor of God.

I cannot say "thine is the kingdom" if I do not give the King the loyalty due him from a faithful subject.

I cannot attribute to him "the power" if I fear what men may do.

I cannot ascribe to him "the glory" if I'm seeking honor only for myself, and I cannot say "forever" if the horizon of my life is bounded completely by time.

Author Unknown[797]

A minister parked his car in a no-parking zone in a large city because he was short of time and couldn't find a space with a meter. So he put a note under the windshield wiper that read: "I have circled the block ten times. If I don't park here, I'll miss my appointment. *Forgive us our trespasses.*"

When he returned, he found a citation from a police officer along with this note: "I've circled this block for ten years. If I don't give you a ticket, I'll lose my job. *Lead us not into temptation.*"[798]

Love

A four-year-old girl, hugging a doll in each of her pudgy little arms, looked wistfully up at her mother and said, "Mama, I love them and love them and love them, but they never love me back."

How true of some Christians who are loved and loved and loved by God, but never love him back.[799]

In a boiler room, it is impossible to look into the boiler to see how much water it contains. But running up beside it is a tiny glass tube, that serves as a gauge. As the water stands in the little tube, so it stands in the great boiler. When the tube is half full, the boiler is half full; if empty, so is the boiler. How do you know you love God? You believe you love him, but you want to know. Look at the gauge. Your love for your brother is the measure of your love for God.[800]

This was the reaction of the unbelieving Greek writer Lucian (A.D. 120–200) upon observing the warm fellowship of Christians:
"It is incredible to see the fervor with which the people of that religion help each other in their wants. They spare nothing. Their first legislator [Jesus] has put it into their heads that they are brethren."[801]

"It is our care for the helpless, our practice of lovingkindness, that brands us in the eyes of many of our opponents. 'Look!' they say. 'How they love one another! Look how they are prepared to die for one another' " (Tertullian).[802]

What is love?

It's *silence* when your words would hurt.
It's *patience* when your neighbor's curt.
It's *deafness* when the scandal flows.
It's *thoughtfulness* for another's woes.
It's *promptness* when stern duty calls.
It's *courage* when misfortune falls.[803]

Love, Example of

Once on a railway train an elderly man accidentally broke a minor regulation and was unmercifully bawled out by a young train employee. Later a fellow passenger nudged the old gentleman and suggested he give the employee a piece of his mind. But the old man just smiled. "Oh," he said, "if a man like that can stand himself for all of his life, I surely can stand him for five minutes."[804]

A thirty-six-year-old mother was discovered to be in the advanced stages of terminal cancer. One doctor advised her to spend her remaining days enjoying herself on a beach in Acapulco. A second physician offered her the hope of living two to four years with the grueling side effects of chemotherapy and radiation treatment. She penned these words to her three small children:

"I've chosen to try to survive for you. This has some horrible costs, including pain, loss of my good humor, and moods I won't be able to control. But I must try this, if only on the outside chance that I might live one minute longer. And that minute could be the one you might need me when no one else will do. For this I intend to struggle, tooth and nail, so help me God." (Cited in *Focus on The Family*, May 1985.)[805]

A young lady walked into a fabric shop, went to the counter, and asked the owner for some noisy, rustling, white material. The owner found two such bolts of fabric but was rather puzzled at the young lady's motives. Why would anyone want several yards of noisy material? Finally the owner's curiosity got the best of him and he asked the young lady why she particularly wanted noisy cloth.

She answered: "You see, I am making a wedding gown, and my fiancé is blind. When I walk down the aisle, I want him to know when I've arrived at the altar, so he won't be embarrassed."

Such love the young woman had for her man![806]

One night a two-month-old baby kept his mother and father awake with his fussing and crying. The father was at wit's end and had lost all patience. The mother, though, in her deep maternal love, picked up her son and, cuddling him, said, "That's all right. I'm sorry you don't feel better!" What an object lesson in self-giving love.[807]

After the U.S.S. *Pueblo* was captured by the North Koreans, the eighty-two surviving crew members were thrown into a brutal captivity. In one particular instance thirteen of the men were required to sit in a rigid manner around a table for hours. After several hours the door was violently flung open and a North Korean guard brutally beat the man in the first chair with the butt of his rifle. The next day, as each man sat at his assigned place, again the door was thrown open and the man in the first chair was brutally beaten. On the third day it happened again to the same man. Knowing the man could not survive, another young sailor

226

took his place. When the door was flung open the guard automatically beat the new victim senseless. For weeks, each day a new man stepped forward to sit in that horrible chair, knowing full well what would happen. At last the guards gave up in exasperation. They were unable to beat that kind of sacrificial love.[808]

During the season of Super Bowl I, the great quarterback Bart Starr had a little incentive scheme going with his oldest son. For every perfect paper Bart Junior brought home from school, Starr gave him ten cents. After a particularly rough game against St. Louis, in which Starr felt he had performed poorly, he returned home weary and battered, late at night after a long plane ride. But he couldn't help feeling better when he reached his bedroom. There attached to his pillow was a note: "Dear Dad, I thought you played a great game. Love, Bart." Taped to the note were *two* dimes.[809]

Love, Mature/Immature

Infantile love follows the principle:
"I love because I am loved."

Mature love follows the principle:
"I am loved because I love."

Immature love says:
"I love you because I need you."

Mature love says:
"I need you because I love you."
Erich Fromm[810]

Love, Power of

A man who had been the superintendent of a city rescue mission for forty years was asked why he had spent his life working with dirty, unkempt, profane, drunken derelicts. He said, "All I'm doing is giving back to others a little of the love God has shown to me."

As a young man, he himself had been a drunkard who went into a mission for a bowl of chili. There he heard the preacher say that Christ could save sinners, and he stumbled forward to accept the Lord Jesus as his Savior. Though his brain was addled by drink, he felt a weight lifted from his shoulders, and that day he became a changed person. A little later, seeking God's will for his life, he felt the Lord calling him to go back to the gutter and reach the people still wallowing there. The power of redeeming love enabled him to carry on his ministry for forty years.[811]

> He drew a circle that shut me out—
> Heretic, rebel, a thing to flout.
> But Love and I had the wit to win:
> We drew a circle that took him in.

> *Edwin Markham*[812]

Love, Romantic

Falling in love at first sight is rather like falling down a hole—sudden, intense—often with an unsatisfactory outcome.[813]

> I climbed up the door,
> and I shut the stairs.
> I said my shoes,
> and took off my prayers.
> I shut off my bed,
> and I climbed into the light,
> and all because he kissed me goodnight!

> *Faith A. Mills*[814]

Love, Unconditional

One Sunday a little boy looked up at his dad and asked, "Daddy, how does God love us?" His father answered, "Son, God loves us with an unconditional love."

The lad thought for a moment and then asked, "Daddy, what kind of love is unconditional love?" After a few minutes of silence his father answered, "Do you remember the two boys who used to live next door to us and the cute little puppy they got last Christmas?" "*Yes.*" "Do you remember how they used to tease it, throw sticks and even rocks at it?" "*Yes.*" "Do you also remember how the puppy would always greet them with a wagging tail and would try to lick their faces?" "*Yes.*" "Well, that puppy had an unconditional love for those two boys. They certainly didn't deserve his love for them because they were mean to him. But, he loved them anyway."

228

The father then made his point: "God's love for us is also unconditional. Men threw rocks at his Son, Jesus, and hit him with sticks. They even killed him. But, Jesus loved them anyway."[815]

Lust

Lust is the craving for salt of a man who is dying of thirst.[816]

Lying

A melon farmer's crop of melons was disappearing fast from his field. Thieves were continually stealing the melons under the cover of night's darkness. The farmer finally became desperate and in an attempt to save his crop from the vandals he decided to put up a sign.

The sign had on it a skull and crossbones, and it read:"ONE OF THESE MELONS IS POISONED"—only the farmer knew that it was not true.

Sure enough, for two nights not a melon was missing. But, after the third night, the farmer noticed that his sign had been altered. Someone had scratched out the word "ONE" and replaced it with another word so that the sign now read: "TWO OF THESE MELONS ARE POISONED."

Thinking to save his whole crop through deception, he lost it all, which just goes to illustrate Sir Walter Scott's observation:

> Oh, what a tangled web we weave,
> When first we practice to deceive![817]

> He said likewise
> That a lie which is half a truth is ever
>   the blackest of lies,
> That a lie which is all a lie may be met
>   and fought with outright,
> But a lie which is part a truth is a
>   harder matter to fight.
>
> *Alfred, Lord Tennyson*
>
> *"The Grandmother"*[818]

In Mark Twain's fascinating book about his travels in the West and Hawaii, *Roughing It,* there is an account of a man, a notorious liar, who was known in the community to be a spinner of tall tales. No one ever believed anything he said. One day they found him hanging dead, with a suicide note pinned on him, written in his own hand, and saying that he had taken his own life. But the coroner's jury pronounced it murder. They said that if the man himself said he had taken his own life, it was proof he hadn't![819]

Man, Nature of

We are all made of common clay and that is why we all have the same problems. As someone has well put it, "We're all made in the same mold—only some are moldier than others."[820]

Remember that man was made out of dust, and when dust gets stuck on itself it only turns into mud.[821]

As the old proverb puts it, you can bring a pig into the parlor, but that doesn't change the pig—though it certainly changes the parlor![822]

"Man's unhappiness, as I construe, comes of his greatness; it is because there is an infinite in him which with all his cunning he cannot quite bury under the finite" (Thomas Carlyle).[823]

G. K. Chesterton said, "Whatever else may be said of man, this one thing is clear: He is not what he is capable of being."[824]

After many years of studying human behavior at one of the finest universities in the world, Harvard psychiatrist Robert Coles remarked, "Nothing I have discovered about the makeup of human beings contradicts in any way what I have learned from the Hebrew prophets such as Isaiah, Jeremiah, and Amos, and from the Book of Ecclesiastes, and from Jesus and the lives of those he touched. Anything that I can say as a result of my research into human behavior is a mere footnote to those lives in the Old and New Testaments" (Robert Coles, *Christianity Today*, February 6, 1987, p. 20).[825]

"With the discovery of the atom, everything changed, except for man's thinking. Because of this, we drift toward unparalleled catastrophe" (Albert Einstein).[826]

I still struggle with the old Adam, and so do we all. Young Philipp Melanchthon, colleague of Martin Luther, once wrote to Luther and said, "Old Adam is too strong for young Philipp."[827]

Man, Value of

A man should carry two stones in his pocket. On one should be inscribed, "I am but dust and ashes." On the other, "For my sake was the world created." And he should refer to each stone as he needs it.[828]

Marriage

Marriage is like a violin; it doesn't work without the strings. And when the music stops, the strings are still attached.[829]

Even if marriages are made in heaven, humans have to be responsible for their maintenance.[830]

If a man has enough horse sense to treat his wife like a thoroughbred, she'll never turn into an old nag.[831]

Marriage is like flies on a screen door. Those on the outside want to get in, but some of those already inside want to get out.[832]

"Marriage is not finding the person with whom you can live, but finding that person with whom you cannot live without" (Howard Hendricks).[833]

Carl Sandburg's daughter Helga wrote of her parents: "There were never loud arguments back and forth in our house. My father raged and roared, and often. But it was one-way. Mother coaxed him out of it. Once when he was very old, I saw him pull at a door that was stuck. He rattled the handle and shouted. My mother, a small woman, looked up at him and patted his chest, 'What a fine strong voice!' she said. Disarmed, he stood there in love. It was a thread established early and woven through their life."[834]

A little girl had just heard the story *Snow White* for the first time. So full of enthusiasm that she could hardly contain herself, she retold the fairy tale to her mother. After telling about how Prince Charming had arrived on his beautiful white horse and kissed Snow White back to life, she asked her mother, "And do you know what happened then?"

"Yes," said her mom, "they lived happily ever after."

"No," responded Suzie, with a frown, "they got married."

With childlike innocence, the little girl had spoken a partial truth without realizing it. For you see, getting married and living happily ever after are not necessarily synonymous.[835]

Marriage, Adjustment to

A cynic once observed: "All marriages are happy. It's the living together afterward that causes all the trouble."[836]

Marriage has been described as the relationship of "two reasonable human beings who have agreed to abide by each other's intolerabilities."[837]

Marriage is like taking an airplane to Florida for a relaxing vacation in January, and when you get off the plane you find you're in the Swiss Alps. There's cold and snow instead of swimming and sunshine.

Well, after you buy winter clothes and learn how to ski, and learn how to talk in a new foreign language, I guess you can have just as good a vacation in the Swiss Alps as you can in Florida. But it is a surprise when you get off that honeymoon airplane and find that everything is far different from what you expected.[838]

Unhappy spouse to marriage counselor:

> When I got married
> I was looking for an ideal.
> Then it became an ordeal.
> Now I want a new deal.[839]

Someone has likened adjustment to marriage to two porcupines who lived in Alaska. When the deep and heavy snows came, they felt the cold and began to draw close together. However, when they drew close they began to stick one another with their quills. But when they drew apart they felt the cold once again. To keep warm they had to learn how to adjust to one another—very carefully.[840]

"For best results, follow instructions of maker." So advised a brochure accompanying a bottle of a common cold remedy. If such advice is good for the relief of a simple physical ailment, how much more it is needed for the relief of sick marriage relationships! God, the Author of marriage, has given us clear instructions in the Bible.[841]

All of us have seen two rivers flowing smoothly and quietly along until they meet and join to form one new river. When this happens they clash and hurl themselves at one another. However, as the newly formed river flows downstream, it gradually quiets down and flows smoothly again. And now it is broader and more majestic and has more power. So it is in a marriage: the forming of a new union may be tumultuous—but, when achieved, the result is far greater than either alone.[842]

Some time ago, the *Saturday Evening Post* ran a humorous article that traced the tendency for marriage partners to drift from a height of bliss into the humdrum of routine attitudes. Called "The Seven Ages of the Married Cold," the article likens the state of the marriage to the reaction of a husband to his wife's colds during seven years of marriage.

The first year: "Sugar dumpling, I'm worried about my baby girl. You've got a bad sniffle and there's no telling about these things with all this strep around. I'm putting you in the hospital this afternoon for a general checkup and a good rest. I know the food's lousy, but I'll bring your meals in from Rossini's. I've already got it arranged with the floor superintendent."

The second year: "Listen darling, I don't like the sound of that cough and I've called Doc Miller to rush over here. Now you go to bed like a good girl, please? Just for Papa."

The third year: "Maybe you'd better lie down, honey; nothing like a little rest when you feel punk. I'll bring you something to eat. Have we got any soup?"

The fourth year: "Look, dear, be sensible. After you feed the kids and get the dishes washed, you'd better hit the sack."

The fifth year: "Why don't you get yourself a couple of aspirin?"

The sixth year: "If you'd just gargle or something, instead of sitting around barking like a seal!"

The seventh year: "For Pete's sake, stop sneezing! Whatcha trying to do, gimme pneumonia?"[843]

People in our nation spend more time preparing to get their driver's license than they do preparing for marriage or parenting.[844]

Marriage, Commitment in

With the rising divorce rate and the trend toward total truthfulness these days, it is almost as though the marriage vows are being changed from "till death do us part" to "till something better comes along."[845]

The ties of a durable marriage are not like the pretty silken ribbons attached to wedding presents. Instead, they must be forged like steel in the heat of daily life and the pressures of crisis in order to form a union that cannot be severed.[846]

The comic strip said a lot about the world's view of marriage:

One character said, "You know, it's odd—but now that I'm actually engaged I'm starting to feel nervous about getting married!"

The other character replied, "I know what you're thinking. It's only natural to be nervous! Marriage is a big commitment. Seven or eight years can be a long time!"[847]

A good many years ago, I knew a workingman in the north of England whose wife, soon after her marriage, drifted in vicious ways, and went rapidly from bad to worse. He came home one Sunday evening to find, as he had found a dozen times before, that she had gone on a new debauch. He knew in what condition she would return after two or three days of a nameless life. He sat down in the cheerless house to look the truth in the face and to find what he must do. The worst had happened too often to leave him much hope for amendment, and he saw in part what might be in store for him. He made his choice to hold by his wife to the end and to keep a home for her who would not make one for him. Now that a new and terrible meaning had passed into the words "for better or for worse," he reaffirmed his marriage vow.

Later, when someone who knew them both intimately ventured to commiserate with him, he answered, "Not a word! She is my wife! I loved her when she was a girl in our village and I shall love her as long as there is breath in my body." She did not mend, and died in his house after some years in a shameful condition, with his hands spread over her in pity and prayer to the last.

W. R. Maltby, *Christ and His Cross*, (London: Epworth, 1938) pp. 54–55.[848]

There is a scientific law called the Second Law of Thermodynamics. This law states that any closed system left to itself tends toward greater randomness; that is, it breaks down. It takes an ordered input of energy to keep anything together.

This is readily seen with a house. Any homeowner knows that to maintain a house, one must daily, monthly, and yearly invest time and energy to keep the house enjoyable to live in. If no energy is expended on the house, it eventually comes to the point of needing a complete overhaul, or else it is knocked down.

Although it is a law designed to describe material systems, the Second Law of Thermodynamics seems to describe other systems also. For example, consider the marriage relationship. It must have a daily, monthly, and yearly investment of time and energy so that it is enjoyable to live in. If no energy is expended, eventually the relationship needs a complete overhaul, or else it is knocked down.

It is a wise couple who build into their marriage continually—rather than waiting passively for a complete overhaul in the counselor's office or a knockdown in the courtroom.[849]

Marriage, Communication in

Thomas Carlyle paid many pathetic postmortem tributes to his deceased wife, whom he sometimes neglected in life. In his diary there is what has been called the saddest sentence in English literature. Carlyle wrote: "Oh, that I had you yet for five minutes by my side that I might tell you all."[850]

Marriage, Cost of

It is often said that two can live as cheaply as one. That's true—as long as one doesn't eat and the other goes naked.[851]

Marriage, Role of Wife

Charles Swindoll tells of being married ten years before he became aware of the value of being grateful for the differences between his wife and himself. He was often irritated that she didn't view things exactly as he did. She wasn't argumentative, only expressive of her honest feelings. But he took this as a lack of submission and told her so. Time and time again they locked horns until finally God showed him from the Genesis 2:18–25 passage that his wife was different because God had made her different, and she was more valuable to him because of those differences. She was not designed to be his echo but to be his counterpart, a necessary and needed individual to help him become all God wanted him to be.[852]

Masturbation

"For me the real evil of masturbation would be that is takes an appetite which, in lawful use, leads an individual out of himself to complete (and correct) his own personality in that of another (and finally in children and even grandchildren) and turns it back; sends the man back into the prison of himself, there to keep a harem of imaginary brides. And his harem, once admitted, works against his ever getting out and really uniting with a real woman" (C. S. Lewis, unpublished letter, March 6, 1956).[853]

Materialism

If we lack basic nutrients in our diet we suffer malnutrition. The cure is simple: take vitamin tablets to insure you get the minimum level. Once the minimum is reached, however, additional tablets have little or no benefit. Unfortunately some people apply this logic: "If a little was good, a lot will be better." This simply is not true and in some cases is dangerous. On occasion people have even lost their lives from overdoses of vitamin A.

Sadly, this is often the case with earning money. If at one point we lacked money for basic necessities, then money—when it finally came—was a blessing. But many have applied the logic "If a little was good, a lot will be better." Many have lost their lives this way![854]

The story is told of a man who was given a tour of one of the most impressive homes in a particular city. The rooms seemed to go on without end, and each one was more wonderful than the one before it.

Marble, gold, and fine woods were everywhere. Finally the visitor was asked how he liked the house. He replied, "These are the things that make dying hard."

For those who have seen only the beauty of this world and who do not long for the beauty of that to come, dying is indeed hard.[855]

If you have something you can't live without, you don't own it; it owns you.[856]

Materialism has nothing to do with amount, it has everything to do with attitude.[857]

In this world there are only two tragedies. One is not getting what you want. The other is getting it.[858]

Someone has intuitively stated, "A bargain is something you cannot use, at a price you cannot resist!"[859]

The fly lands on the flypaper and says, "My flypaper," while the flypaper says, "My fly."[860]

An extremely rich real-estate tycoon in Dallas once said, "If you go into business with the idea of erecting an empire, all you do is make yourself a nicer cage. You're a prisoner of the monster you created. It's lonely."[861]

The story of a butterfly named *Maculinea arion* is most instructive. The creature lays its eggs on a plant, and after feeding on the plant for several weeks, the young caterpillar makes its way to the ground. In order to complete its development, it must meet a certain kind of ant. When such an ant meets the caterpillar, the ant strokes it with its antennae, and the caterpillar exudes a sweet fluid from a special gland on its tenth segment. Apparently the ant likes this substance, because it then carries the caterpillar home to its nest. There the ants drink the sweet fluid exuded by the caterpillar, and the caterpillar feasts on larval ants. The caterpillar spends the winter in a special cavity of the ant's

237

nest, and in the spring it continues eating young ants. Eventually it emerges as an adult butterfly and flies away to establish more of its kind. And the cycle starts all over again.

Some people are not much different from the ants. For you see, they cherish a luxury item to the injury of themselves.[862]

The preacher came over to visit unexpectedly. Wanting to make a good impression, the lady of the house instructed her little daughter, "Please run and get that good book we all love so much and bring it here."

The daughter tottered off and then returned in a minute with triumph on her face and the Sears catalogue in her hands![863]

An anonymous writer tells about an American tourist's visit to the nineteenth-century Polish rabbi Hofetz Chaim:

Astonished to see that the rabbi's home was only a simple room filled with books, plus a table and a bench, the tourist asked, "Rabbi, where is your furniture?"

"Where is yours?" replied the rabbi.

"Mine?" asked the puzzled American. "But I'm a visitor here. I'm only passing through."

"So am I," said Hofetz Chaim.[864]

John M. Keynes was the founder of the modern study of economics. He realized that worldly prosperity could come about only through a corruption of the moral laws. To bring this prosperity to full operation in the world Lord Keynes is credited with the following quote: "If we are to succeed, we must call good bad and bad good for a little while longer."[865]

When John D. Rockefeller died, one man was curious about how much he left behind. Determined to find out, he set up an appointment with one of Rockefeller's highest aides and asked, "How much did Rockefeller leave behind?"

The aide answered, "All of it."[866]

Maturity

As a Christian, you have everything you need to be what you ought to be. Spiritual maturity is not a process of gaining things that you did not have when you became a believer.

For example, consider a newborn baby. It isn't born without arms, and then gets them later. It's not a pollywog. It doesn't develop into a frog. When a baby is born, it has all the physical equipment it will ever have. In fact, the older we get, the more stuff we lose!

When you were born in Christ, you were made spiritually whole and have all you will ever need to become mature. It's only a matter of development until you function in a mature way. You have everything you need—there is no lack, you are complete in the Lord.

However, a Christian can arrest his development and even permanently damage himself by sinning. As damaging as sin is, we must acknowledge that we sin, not because we lack anything, but because we do not appropriate what we have. [867]

> Not, how did he die?
>   But, how did he live?
> Not, what did he gain?
>   But, what did he give?
> These are the merits
>   To measure the worth
> Of a man as a man,
>   Regardless of birth.
> Not, what was his station?
>   But, had he a heart?
> And how did he play
>   His God-given part? [868]

Many believers have difficulty in realizing and facing up to the fact that sometimes God uses time in his development of our Christian life. This truth is brought home by the following story.

One day in the House of Commons, British Prime Minister Disraeli made a brilliant speech on the spur of the moment. That night a friend said to him, "I must tell you how much I enjoyed your extemporaneous talk. It's been on my mind all day." "Madam," confessed Disraeli, "that extemporaneous talk has been on my mind for twenty years!" [869]

Kipling once offered the following tests for maturity. "If you can keep your head when all about you are losing theirs and blaming it on you, it you can trust yourself when all men doubt you, but make allowance for their doubting too, if you can wait and not be tired by waiting, or, being lied about, don't deal in lies, or, being hated, don't give way to hating. . . ." [870]

Mediocrity

"The highest order of mind is accused of folly, as well as the lowest. Nothing is thoroughly approved but mediocrity. The majority has established this, and it fixes its fangs on whatever gets beyond it either way" (Blaise Pascal).[871]

Mercy

Long ago, a poor woman from the slums of London was invited to go with a group of people for a holiday at the ocean. She had never seen the ocean before, and when she saw it, she burst into tears. Those around her thought it was strange that she should cry when such a lovely holiday had been given her. "Why in the world are you crying?" they asked. Pointing to the ocean she answered, "This is the only thing I have ever seen that there was enough of."

God has oceans of mercy. There is enough of it—and God delights to show his mercy and compassion (Micah 7:19).[872]

The story has been told of a mother who sought from Napoleon the pardon of her son. The emperor said it was the man's second offense, and justice demanded his death. "I don't ask for justice," said the mother. "I plead for mercy."

"But," said the emperor, "he does not deserve mercy."

"Sir," cried the mother, "it would not be mercy if he deserved it, and mercy is all I ask."

"Well, then," said the emperor, "I will show mercy." And her son was saved.[873]

The story is told of a politician who, after receiving the proofs of a portrait, was very angry with the photographer. He stormed back to the photographer and arrived with these angry words: "This picture does not do me justice!" The photographer replied, "Sir, with a face like yours, you don't need justice, you need mercy!"[874]

It is our misery that calls forth God's mercy.

A parent knows how this is. When a child is suffering from a severe cold with a sore throat, runny nose, severe congestion, and assorted aches and pains, and all he can do is throw his arms around your neck and cry—what does this evoke in you as a parent?

It awakens your pity, and you reach out and try to relieve the child's distress in any way you possibly can. Why? Because his misery has called forth your mercy.[875]

Messiah, Expectation of

Dr. Charles Fineberg, a noted Jewish-Christian scholar, says that in the course of Israel's history since the time of our Lord, sixty-four different individuals have appeared claiming to be the Messiah.[876]

Minister, Function of

Most of us have gone to a circus sideshow at some time or at least seen one on TV. One of the common feats of daring under the big top is performed by the man who attempts to get a large number of plates simultaneously spinning on the end of some sticks. Of course, the problem he faces is that just as he gets another plate spinning on its stick, one of the earlier ones begins to waver and appears ready to fall. So the performer has to rush to it and give it a booster spin to keep it going. Back and forth he rushes, trying to add plates and at the same time not let those already spinning fall.

This seems to be an apt illustration of many churches and the role of the pastor in them. Like our sideshow performer, the pastor has figured out the plates he wants to spin, and he looks through the congregation to find who could be the sticks. With great effort, he gets it all going and then discovers that the sticks don't keep the plates moving. So he has to run up and down from plate to plate, operating programs that the sticks are not motivated enough to keep going on their own.

A comedian once did the spinning plate trick, but with a different twist. He got his plates up and spinning, while his sidekick attempted to do the same. But then he watched his sidekick run around like crazy, trying to keep his plates spinning, while he himself did nothing. Finally the sidekick realized that something was not quite right, so he looked at the comedian's sticks. In fact he picked one up, and the plate kept spinning. He tipped it over, and the plate kept spinning. You see, the twist was that the comedian had figured out how to make the *stick* responsible for the plate's spinning.

How much better is it for the church and its leaders to concentrate on "perfecting the sticks." That way, as they grow, parishioners become motivated to get involved in certain ministries and take responsibility for services that are on their hearts and interest them.[877]

Spurgeon graphically illustrated the effect of Christian leaders upon a congregation:

". . . as a result of your own decline, everyone of your hearers will suffer more or less. It is with us and our hearers as it is with watches and the public clock; if our watch be wrong, very few will be misled by it, but ourselves; but if the Horse Guards or Greenwich Observatory should go amiss, half London would lose its reckoning. So it is with the minister; he is the parish clock. Many take their time from him, and if he be incorrect, then they all go wrongly, and he is in a great measure accountable for all the sin which he occasions" (C. H. Spurgeon, *Lectures to My Students,* [Grand Rapids: Zondervan, 1980], p. 1954).[878]

Minister, Qualities of

If you can't stand the smell of sheep, you shouldn't be a shepherd.[879]

A pastor-teacher who does not love people is like a shepherd who is allergic to sheep, or a woman who wants to have a family but can't stand children.[880]

A survey of many churches was taken by the American Association of Theological Schools. Each church sampled was to list the qualities desired in a minister they would consider employing. The results;

First: Humility

Second: Honesty

Third: Good example in daily living

Fourth: Excellence in ministerial skills (i.e., preaching, counseling, teaching, etc.)[881]

If you hired a gardener to take care of your lawn and then went past his house and saw that his own yard was sloppy and unkempt, would you trust him with the care of your lawn? Or, if you went to the dentist to get your teeth checked and sat down in the chair only to look up to see that the dentist had a mouthful of rotten teeth, would you trust him to work on your teeth?

How can a minister expect any positive response to his ministry if his life is not holy?[882]

"The preacher needs to be pastor, that he may preach to real men. The pastor must be preacher, that he may keep the dignity of his work alive. The preacher, who is not a pastor, grows remote. The pastor, who is not a preacher, grows petty" (Bishop Phillips Brooks, *Lectures on Preaching* [Grand Rapids: Baker, 1969], p. 77).[883]

"Power for service is second. Power for holiness and character is first. The first, second, and third requisite for our work is personal godliness. Without that, though I have the tongues of men and angels, I am harsh and discordant as sounding brass, monstrous and unmusical as a tinkling cymbal" (Alexander Maclaren).[884]

Spurgeon said that this prayer would be the very last one he would pray, if able: "Lord, send to thy Church men filled with the Holy Ghost and with fire. Give to any denomination such men and its progress must be mighty; keep back such men, send them college gentlemen, of great refinement and profound learning, but of little fire and grace, dumb dogs which cannot bark, and straightway that denomination must decline." (Cited by Iain Murray, *The Forgotten Spurgeon* [Carlisle, Penn.: Banner of Truth, 1978], p. 36.)[885]

After years of research, the profile of the "perfect pastor" has been developed. The perfect pastor preaches exactly fifteen minutes. He condemns sin, but never embarrasses anyone. He works from 8:00 A.M. until midnight and is also the church janitor. He makes $60 a week, wears good clothes, drives a new car, and gives $50 a week to the poor. He is twenty-eight years old and has been preaching for twenty-five years, is wonderfully gentle and handsome, loves to work with teenagers, and spends countless hours with senior citizens. He makes fifteen calls daily on parish families, shut-ins, and hospital patients, and he is always in his office when needed.

If your pastor does not measure up to this profile of the perfect pastor, simply send this description to six other churches that are tired of their pastor. Then bundle up your pastor and send him to the church at the top of the list. In one week you will receive 1,643 pastors. One of them should be perfect.[886]

Ministry, Preparation for

Shortly after a recent seminary graduate had assumed his first pastorate, he and his wife went to visit his family one Saturday. His mother sensed that her daughter-in-law was unhappy, but—not wishing to be meddlesome—pretended not to notice. As they departed, she heard her daughter-in-law say, "All right, we can go by the church and you can practice baptizing me just one more time. But remember this—when you have your first funeral, you are not going to practice burying me!"[887]

"If someone had told me I would be Pope one day, I would have studied harder" (Pope John Paul I, September 1978).[888]

Miracle

Kham Put, Thailand (EP). Khun Paot, a 19-year-old girl, escaped the Khmer Rouge rule in Cambodia after an arduous journey with 100 others through miles of jungle, canals, mountains, and rivers. Standing between them and freedom were Communist soldiers, the elements, and a stretch of jungle ground covered with thorns. Most of the escapees were barefoot or wore flimsy thongs.

A midnight-like darkness hampered the struggling group as it crossed a valley between two high mountain ranges. "We could see absolutely nothing," Paot later told a missionary, Maxine Stewart. "We didn't even know where to step." Suddenly hundreds of fireflies swarmed into view. Their glow made enough light for the people to see the path. The refugees reached the next mountain by "firefly light," said Mrs. Stewart in the April issue of the Commission Magazine.

After Paot was transferred to Kham Put refugee camp, she was invited to a Christian meeting. "I know that old man," she exclaimed at a picture on the wall of the chapel. "He is the one who led us and showed us the way to Thailand and freedom." She was pointing to a picture of Jesus.

The Recorder, September 1979, p. 25.[889]

Miracles of Jairus' Daughter

There was a time when the first-born daughter of that great English expositor of Scripture, Dr. G. Campbell Morgan, lay at the point of

244

death. Years later, speaking on the incident of the raising of Jairus' daughter, he said these words:

"I can hardly speak of this matter without becoming personal and reminiscent, remembering a time forty years ago when my own first lassie lay at the point of death, dying. I called for Him then, and He came, and surely said to our troubled hearts, "Fear not, believe only." He did not say, "She shall be made whole." She was not made whole on the earthly plane; she passed away into the life beyond. But He did say to her, 'Talitha cumi,' that He needed her, and He took her to be with Himself. She has been with Him for all these years, as we measure time here, and I have missed her every day. But His word, "Believe only," has been the strength of all the passing years."[890]

Ray Stedman has told the story of a time when he and his wife were driving through Oregon with his little daughter, Susan. She had developed a fever the night before, when they were staying in a motel, but it didn't seem serious. As they drove along, all of a sudden the little girl went into convulsions. Her eyes turned up, her body began to jerk, and she obviously was in great danger. Stedman's heart clutched. He stopped the car, grabbed Susan, and stumbled across the road to a farmhouse that happened to be visible nearby. It was about six in the morning, but the frantic father thundered on the door. When a woman appeared, he cried out, "My daughter is very sick—she's in convulsions. Do you have a bathtub where we can put her in warm water?"

The lady was so taken aback she hardly knew what to say. She motioned down the hall, and without waiting for any words, Stedman pushed the front door open, went down the hall, and started running water in the tub. Later he called a doctor and arranged to take his daughter to him for an examination.

It all turned out all right, but Stedman never forgot that moment when it looked as though his daughter was going to die. Later he found out this farm family had the only bathtub and the only phone for miles around!

This is the same emotion that drove Jairus, that agonized father, to Jesus—the fear that his little one, who had blessed their home and filled it with sunshine for twelve years, was to be taken from them.[891]

Missionaries

"It is a mistake to suppose that a dull and second-rate man is good enough for the heathen. The worst-off need the very best we have. God gave His best, even His only begotten Son, in order to redeem a lost

245

world. The most darkened and degraded souls need the best thinking."
(Adoniram Judson)[892]

Missions

Where do you like to fish best? Where thousands of people are stepping all over each other with oftentimes the same bait in a lake known to have been heavily fished day after day for decades? Where fish are gorged with bait, and most of them swim wearily or disdainfully away as bait aplenty splashes near them from hordes of fishermen jockeying desperately for position and stumbling all over one another?

Or would you prefer to fish where the terrain may be difficult, danger may lurk in the vicinity, the lake is attainable only after sacrifice and hardship, but, oh, the hungry fish!

Multitudes fight and starve for even one morsel of food, and many have never so much as seen one time the bait you have to offer. If you prefer the latter fishing scene, that is missions.

(The above excerpt by Floyd McElveen appeared in *I'd Love to Tell the World*, compiled by Harold J. Westing, Accent Books, 1977).[893]

A deacon was briefed beforehand on what his role would be at an upcoming missionary banquet and was told to be sensitive to the fact that there would be guests from foreign countries who were not accustomed to American culture.

During the banquet, the deacon found himself seated next to an African man who was hungrily devouring his portion of chicken. Trying to think of some way to communicate with the man, the deacon leaned over and said, "Chomp, chomp, good, huh?" The man, gazing back at the deacon, simply replied, "Mmmmm good!"

A few moments later, as the African man savored a delicious cup of coffee, the deacon leaned over and commented, "Glug, glug, good, huh?" The man, a little uncertain, replied, "Mmmmm good!"

To the deacon's dismay, when the speaker for the evening was announced, it happened to be the African gentleman next to him. The gentleman got up and delivered a flawless message in Oxford-accented English. Upon concluding, he headed toward the deacon, whose face was aglow with red. The speaker simply said, "Blab, blab, good, huh?"[894]

In the early days of Wycliffe Bible Translators in Mexico, Cameron Townsend, the founder, tried to get permission from the Mexican government to translate the Scriptures into the languages of the Indian tribes. But the government was adamantly opposed to it. The official to whom he had to appeal told him, "As long as I am in this office the Bible will never be translated into the Indian languages—it would only upset them." Townsend did everything he could think of, went to every official he could find, and had all his Christian friends praying that God would open this door. But it seemed to remain totally closed.

Finally, Townsend decided to give up pressing the issue. He and his wife went to live in a little, obscure Indian village, learned the language, ministered to the people as best they could, and waited for God to move. It was not very long before Townsend noticed that the fountain in the center of the village plaza produced beautiful, clear spring water, but that it ran off down the hill and was wasted. He suggested that the Indians plant crops in an area to which the water could easily be diverted and thus make use of it. Soon they were growing twice as much food as before, and their economy blossomed as a result. The Indians were grateful. Townsend wrote this up in a little article and sent it to a Mexican paper he thought might be interested.

Unknown to him, that article found its way into the hands of the President of Mexico, Lazaro Cardenas. The President was amazed that a *gringo* would come to live in and help a poor Indian village where he couldn't even get many of his own people to live. The President wanted to meet Townsend, so he, his limousine, and his attendants drove to that little Indian village and parked in the plaza.

Cameron Townsend is not one to miss an opportunity. He went up to the car and introduced himself and, to his amazement, heard the President say, "You're the man I've come here to see! Tell me more about your work." When he heard what it was, he said, "Of course you can translate the Scriptures into the Indian languages!" That began a friendship that continued throughout the lifetime of President Cardenas. His power and authority were used of God all those years to open doors to Wycliffe Translators throughout Mexico.[895]

Money

Money is an article that may be used as a universal provider of everything—except happiness![896]

A billboard advertisement for a savings-and-loan association in Dallas, Texas, read: "We Lend *Happiness* at Eighteen Locations."[897]

Money will buy a fine dog, but only love will make him wag his tail.[898]

There's a new golden rule in effect today: "He who has the gold, makes up the rules."[899]

Money, Debts and

Money is the number-one cause of domestic unhappiness. Many couples need to undergo plastic surgery. They need to have their credit cards cut off.[900]

Nowadays people can be divided into three classes:

> the Haves,
> the Have-Nots, and
> the Have-Not-Paid-for-What-They-Haves.[901]

"If the Word taught me anything, it taught me to have no connection with debt. I could not think that God was poor, that He was short on resources, or unwilling to supply any want of whatever work was really His. It seemed to me that if there were lack of funds to carry on work, then to that degree, in that special development, or at that time, it could not be the work of God" (*Hudson Taylor's Spiritual Secret*, p. 58).[902]

Money, Deceitfulness

One day a certain old, rich man of a miserable disposition visited a rabbi, who took the rich man by the hand and led him to a window. "Look out there," he said. The rich man looked into the street, "What do you see?" asked the rabbi.

"I see men, women, and children," answered the rich man.

Again the rabbi took him by the hand and this time led him to a mirror. "Now what do you see?"

"Now I see myself," the rich man replied.

Then the rabbi said, "Behold, in the window there is glass, and in the mirror there is glass. But the glass of the mirror is covered with a little silver, and no sooner is the silver added than you cease to see others, but you see only yourself."[903]

A businessman had an angel come to visit him who promised to grant him one request. The man requested a copy of the stock-market quotes for one year in the future. As he was studying the future prices on the American and New York stock exchanges, he boasted of his plans and the increased riches that would be his as a result of this "insider" look into the future.

He then glanced across the newspaper page, only to see his own picture in the obituary column. Obviously, in the light of his certain death, money was no longer important.[904]

Money will buy:

A bed, but not sleep.

Books, but not brains.

Food, but not appetite.

A house, but not a home.

Medicine, but not health.

Amusement, but not happiness.

Finery, but not beauty.

A crucifix, but not a Savior.[905]

In the June 14, 1968, issue of *Life* magazine appeared a picture of young David Kennedy sitting outside the White House. The picture had been taken several years before by his Aunt Jacqueline and was inscribed by his Uncle John with the words: "A future president inspects his property—John Kennedy."

Though he had name, status, wealth, and all that money could buy, in 1984 David Kennedy was found dead by his own hand at age twenty-eight. Money can buy the things of this world but cannot satisfy man's inner longing for peace.[906]

"I sit in my house in Buffalo and sometimes I get so lonely it's unbelievable. Life has been so good to me. I've got a great wife, good kids, money, my own health—and I'm lonely and bored. . . . I often wondered why so many rich people commit suicide. Money sure isn't a cure-all!" (O. J. Simpson, *People Magazine*, 1978).[907]

Money, Love of

An old Jack Benny skit illustrates how money can become more important to us than anything else. Jack was walking along, when suddenly an armed robber approached him and ordered, "Your money or your life!" There was a long pause, and Jack did nothing. The robber impatiently queried, "Well?" Jack replied, "Don't rush me, I'm thinking about it." (Incidentally, in real life, Jack Benny was known as a very generous man!)[908]

Morality

A few years ago, young women blushed if they were embarrassed. Today, they are embarrassed if they blush.[909]

In a schoolboy experiment, some young lads put a frog in a container of water and began to heat the water very slowly. The water finally reached the boiling point and yet the frog never even attempted to jump out. Why? Because the changes in the environment were so slight and slow to occur that the frog didn't notice them until it was too late.

As Christians, we can end up like the frog. There are changes in our moral environment that we don't even notice have occurred. We can be dying without even noticing it![910]

"But one has to have an ethical base for a society. Where the prime force is impulse, there is the death of ethics. America used to have ethical laws based in Jerusalem. Now they are based in Sodom and Gomorrah, and civilizations rooted in Sodom and Gomorrah are destined to collapse" (The Rev. Jesse Jackson, *Time*, Nov. 21, 1977).

So it is also with individual lives.[911]

Morality, Purpose of

"Morality seems to be concerned with three things. First, with fair play and harmony between individuals. Second, with what might be called tidying up or harmonizing the things inside each individual. Third, with the general purpose of human life as a whole; what man

250

was made for; what course the whole fleet ought to be on; what tune the conductor of the band wants it to play" (C. S. Lewis, *Christian Reflections* [Grand Rapids: Wm. B. Eerdmans, 1974], p. 18).[912]

Motherhood

A small boy invaded the lingerie section of a large department store and shyly presented his problem to a woman clerk in the lingerie department. "I want to buy a slip as a present for my mom," he said. "But, I don't know what size she wears."

"Is she tall or short, fat or skinny?" asked the clerk.

"She's just perfect," beamed the small boy. So the clerk wrapped up a size 34 for him.

Two days later, Mom came to the store by herself and changed the slip to a size 52.[913]

A London editor submitted to Winston Churchill for his approval a list of all those who had been Churchill's teachers. Churchill returned the list with this comment: "You have omitted to mention the greatest of my teachers—my mother."[914]

Motivation

The story has been told about a frog who fell in a large pothole and couldn't get out. Even his friends couldn't get him to muster enough strength to jump out of the deep pothole. They gave him up to his fate. But the next day they saw him bounding around just fine. Somehow he had made it out, and so they asked him how he did it, adding, "We thought you couldn't get out." The frog replied, "I couldn't, but a truck came along and I *had* to."[915]

In his book *Dedication and Leadership* (South Bend, Univ. of Notre Dame Press, 1966), on why Communism has more apparent success than Christianity in reaching out to new areas, Douglas Hyde said: "If, on the other hand, the majority of members, from the leaders down, are characterized by their single-minded devotion to the cause, if it is quite clear that the majority are giving until it hurts . . . then those who consider joining will assume that this is what will be expected of them. If they nonetheless make the decision to join they will come already conditioned to sacrifice till it hurts."[916]

Dr. Frederik Herzberg, writing in the *Harvard Business Review,* concluded from his research that six factors must be present to keep people highly motivated about sustained responsibility:

1. Achievement
2. Recognition
3. The task itself
4. Responsibility
5. Advancement
6. Opportunity for growth[917]

Motivation for Ministry

David Brainerd said this to Jonathan Edwards: "I do not go to heaven to be advanced but to give honor to God. It is no matter where I shall be stationed in heaven, whether I have a high or low seat there, but to live and please and glorify God. . . . My heaven is to please God and glorify Him, and give all to Him, and to be wholly devoted to His glory."[918]

Natural Man

"One might as well discuss nuclear physics with a wooden Indian in front of a cigar store as to discuss spiritual things with a natural man (Vance Havner)."[919]

Those who are old enough can remember the infamous "iron lung" machines that kept alive many children who were stricken with polio and other diseases that limited their ability to breathe. The iron lung was a huge, casket-like pumping contraption that aided the patients' respiration. It also made them totally dependent on others for everything. Persons in an iron lung had no freedom to come and go. Anything that they needed would have to be brought to them by others.

That's an apt illustration of the spiritual condition of the natural man. He is trapped in the iron lung of his own incapacity. Anything spiritual that comes to him will have to be brought to him from outside his realm of experience, since he isn't going anywhere on his own.

However, God did send his Son, and the Holy Spirit has come. They present spiritual truth to the man trapped in the iron lung of his own inability. And that truth can set him free![920]

Neighbor

A good neighbor is one who will watch your vacation slides all evening without telling you that he has been there too.[921]

Obedience

Selected obedience is not obedience at all; it it merely convenience.[922]

When God puts a period, do not change it to a question mark.[923]

A husband and wife were discussing the possibility of taking a trip to the Holy Land:
Husband: Wouldn't it be fantastic to go to the Holy Land and stand and shout the Ten Commandments from Mount Sinai?
Wife: It would be better if we stayed home and kept them.[924]

Nate Saint was one of five missionaries who were killed by the Auca Indians. He once said that his life did not change until he came to grips with the idea that "obedience is not a momentary option . . . it is a die-cast decision made beforehand."[925]

Obedience, Reasons for

There are many reasons why we may obey someone, including God. What are yours?
Fear! Obeying because you have to?
Reward! Obeying because you get something out of it?
Love! Obeying because you love Christ and your fellowman?[926]

Obedience, Results of

A little boy was riding his tricycle furiously around the block, over and over again. Finally a policeman stopped and asked him why he was going around and around. The boy said that he was running away from home. Then the policeman asked why he kept going around the block. The boy responded, "Because my mom said that I'm not allowed to cross the street."
The point is clear—obedience will keep you close to those you love.[927]

The doctors keep claiming that if I follow the regimen of regular exercise, I will achieve the desired results of weight loss and physical fitness. Well, I've tried it; and like so many of you, I had no immediate experience of these promised benefits. In fact, over the first few weeks I felt very weak and tired. The secret is perseverance. Over the long haul, exercise does produce better physical conditioning.

The same principle applies to obedience. It is not always comfortable, but over the long haul, it has good results.[928]

Objectives

In *Alice in Wonderland*, at one point Alice says to the Cheshire Cat, "Would you tell me, please, which way I ought to go from here?"
"That depends a good deal on where you want to get to," said the Cat.
"I don't much care where," said Alice.
"Then it doesn't matter which way you go," said the Cat.

As with Alice, so with us and the church. Without objectives, we will have nowhere to go, and we'll just keep wandering aimlessly.[929]

Opposition

The way is which we need to stand in the face of opposition is aptly described by a word the British use: "steady." To illustrate this word's meaning, picture a British commander in the nineteenth century as he and his regiment are being approached by a horde of Bedouins brandishing swords. As he awaits the battle, he reviews his past experiences in battle and his regiment's capabilities and—being confident of victory— also considers the future sense of accomplishment this experience will give him. And so he remains "steady."

As believers, we should learn to rely on the testimony of God's past accomplishments, his present work in our lives, and his promise of ultimate victory, and thus remain "steady" in the face of opposition.[930]

Optimism

The Marine officer, when he saw that he and his men were surrounded by the enemy, said, "Men, we are surrounded by the enemy; don't let a one of them get away."[931]

There are two rooms—one full of brand-new toys, the other full of hay and horse manure. Two children are taken into them, one a pessimist, the other an optimist.

254

The pessimist looked at the first room and cried because all those wonderful toys would soon be broken. The optimist was in the other room shoveling. "I know there's got to be a horse in here somewhere," he said.[932]

Somebody has well said that there are only two kinds of people in the world—there are those who wake up in the morning and say, "Good morning, Lord," and there are those who wake up in the morning and say, "Good Lord, it's morning."[933]

During the Battle of Britain, someone said to a man on the street in London, "Things look pretty dark, don't they?" The man replied, "But the King says there's 'ope, Sir!"[934]

It is written on a sundial on a pier at Brighton, England: "'Tis always morning somewhere in the world."[935]

A shoe salesman, upon finding out that in his new territory no one wore shoes, wrote his company and said, "Don't send any shoes, because no one here wears them."

Another salesman in the same territory wrote the company and said, "Send all the shoes you've got; nobody here has any."[936]

"I regard myself an an optimist. An optimist is a person who knows exactly how sad a place the world can be. A pessimist is one who is forever finding out" (Peter Ustinov).[937]

Pain, Purpose of

"There is an ancient Chinese philosophy which says: 'To be dry and thirsty in a hot and dusty land—and to feel great drops of rain on my bare skin—ah, is this not happiness? To have an itch in the private parts of my body—and finally to escape from my friends and to a hiding place where I can scratch—ah, is this not happiness?' Pain and pleasure are inextricably linked. The pleasure would not exist, or least be recognized, if it were not for pain" (Philip Yancey, *Where Is God When It Hurts* [Grand Rapids: Zondervan, 1978], p. 46).[938]

255

Pain can serve a definite purpose in our lives.

Dr. Paul Brand of Carville, Louisiana, one of the world's foremost experts on leprosy, describes how "leprosy patients lose their fingers and toes, not because the disease can cause decay, but precisely because they lack pain sensations. Nothing warns them when water is too hot or a hammer handle is splintered. Accidental self-abuse destroys their bodies." (Cited by Philip Yancey in "Pain: The Tool of the Wounded Surgeon," *Christianity Today*, March 24, 1978.)[939]

"Pain insists upon being attended to. God whispers to us in our pleasures, speaks in our conscience, and shouts in our pain. It is His megaphone to rouse a deaf world" (C. S. Lewis, *The Problem of Pain* [New York: Macmillan, 1978]).[940]

Parables

The story is told of an ancient Stoic philosopher, Epictetus (c. A.D. 50–120), who wanted to teach his students that truth understood is of no value; it is truth acted upon which changes things. This is, of course, a great truth. Sometimes we try putting it in a little saying like "Practice what you preach." The problem is that we tend to remember only the words in these little sayings and ignore the truth they are intended to communicate.

Epictetus once gathered his students around and said, "Have you ever noticed that a sheep does not vomit up the grass it ate at the feet of the shepherd in order to impress him? The sheep digests it to produce wool and milk." What a vivid illustration of the idea that it is *truth acted on* that changes things. Certainly it is a word picture that you are unlikely to forget!

This is exactly what a parable is. It is truth put into a form that is so succinct, compelling, and accurate that you will not forget it.[941]

Parents

Little Billy was allowed to sit in his father's place at the dinner table one evening when his father was absent. His slightly older sister, resenting the arrangement, sneered, "So, you're the father tonight. All right, how much is two times seven?"

Without a moment's hesitation, Billy replied nonchalantly, "I'm busy. Ask your mother!"[942]

Some children walk the high road
While others tread the low;
A parent's life determines
Which way a child will go.[943]

A young mother, feeling sorry for herself because of her many responsibilities as a parent, saw this sign on a local day-care center: "Attention all mothers—Let *me* love your children, while *you* work."

After seeing this, the mother went away grateful for the opportunity she had to love her children herself.[944]

Neglect is one of the most devastating ways a parent can abuse a child. O. Henry, in one of his short stories, tells of a little girl whose mother had died. When the father would come home from work, he would fix their meal, then he would sit down with his paper and pipe, put his feet up on the hassock, and read. The little girl would come in and say, "Father, would you play with me?" And he would say, "No, I'm too tired, I'm too busy. Go out in the street and play." This went on for so long that finally the little girl grew up on the streets and became what we would call a streetwalker, a prostitute. Eventually she died, and when, in the story, her soul appeared at the gates of heaven, St. Peter said to Jesus, "Here's this prostitute. Shall we send her to hell?" Jesus said, "No, no; let her in. But go find the man who refused to play with his little girl, and send *him* to hell."[945]

Tips to help teenagers understand parents:

1. Don't be afraid to speak their language. Try using strange sounding phrases like, "I'll help you with the dishes" and "Yes."

2. Try to understand their music. Play Glenn Miller's "Moonlight Serenade" on the stereo until you are accustomed to the sound.

3. Be patient with the underachiever. When you catch your dieting Mom sneaking salted peanuts, don't show your disapproval. Tell her you like fat Moms.

4. Encourage your parents to talk about their problems. Try to keep in mind that, to them, things like earning a living and paying off the mortgage seem important.

5. Be tolerant of their appearance. When Dad gets a haircut, don't feel personally humiliated. Remember, it's important to him to look like his peers.

6. Most important of all: If they do something you consider wrong, let them know it's their *behavior* you dislike, not *themselves*.[946]

Past, Living in

Our past, mistakes as well as worthwhile accomplishments, is like a car's rear-view mirror. While driving, we use the broad view through the windshield as we move ahead, but we also use the mirror for reference, making quick, periodic glances into it for information to aid in making driving decisions. Although we cannot effectively or safely move ahead by staring only into the mirror and ignoring the view from the windshield, "proper" use of the mirror does ensure a safer, smoother trip to our destination.

In the same way, we are not to dwell in our past, but live by using the lessons of the past as a reference to aid our journey into the future.[947]

Patience

Patience is letting your motor idle when you feel like stripping the gears.[948]

Patience on the part of young Clyde Tombaugh is what led him finally to discover the planet Pluto. Astronomers had already calculated a probable orbit for this "suspected" heavenly body, which they had never seen. Tombaugh took up the search in March 1929. He examined scores of telescopic photographs, each showing tens of thousands of star images in pairs under the blink comparator, or dual microscope. It often took three days to scan a single pair of photographs. It was exhausting, eye-cracking work, in Tombaugh's own words, "brutal, tediousness." The search went on for months. Star by star, Tombaugh examined twenty million images. Finally, on February 18, 1930, as he was blinking a pair of photographs in the constellation Gemini, "I suddenly came upon the image of Pluto!" It was the most dramatic astronomic discovery in nearly one hundred years and it was made possible by patience.[949]

No one treated Lincoln with more contempt than did Edwin Stanton, who denounced Lincoln's policies and called him a "low cunning clown." Stanton had nicknamed him "the original gorilla" and said that explorer Paul Du Chaillu was a fool to wander about in Africa trying to capture a gorilla, when he could have found one so easily in Springfield, Illinois. Lincoln said nothing in reply. In fact, he made Stanton his war minister because Stanton was the best man for the job. He treated him with every courtesy. The years wore on.

The night came when an assassin's bullet struck down Lincoln in a theatre. In a room off to the side where Lincoln's body was taken, stood Stanton that night. As he looked down on the silent, rugged face of the President, Stanton said through his tears, "There lies the greatest ruler of men the world has ever seen." The patience of love had conquered in the end.[950]

Hudson Taylor would tell those who wanted to be missionaries to China that there were three indispensable requirements for a missionary:

1. Patience
2. Patience
3. Patience[951]

A teacher had just finished putting the last pair of galoshes on her first-graders—thirty-two pairs in all. The last little girl said, "You know what, teacher? These aren't my galoshes."

The teacher removed them from the girl's feet. Then the little girl continued, "They are my sister's, and she let me wear them." The teacher quietly put them back on her pupil.

Now that's patience![952]

Chrysostom said that a patient man is one who, having the resources and opportunity to avenge himself, chooses to refrain from the exercise of these.[953]

Paul

Scarcely a greater contrast can be drawn than that between Paul and Nero. Nero was the Roman emperor, seated on a throne. His name was known throughout the empire. Paul was an obscure Jew, totally unimpressive in his physical appearance—he says so himself in his letters. In a distant corner of the Roman Empire, Paul was a leader in a small, heretical sect that was known only as a group of troublemakers. Virtually no one had heard of Paul, while everybody had heard of Nero.

The interesting thing is that now, two thousand years later, we name our sons Paul, and our dogs Nero.[954]

"On his numerous missionary journeys, the apostle Paul showed a greater accomplishment in distances traveled than any known general of the Roman army, official of the Roman Empire, or trader of his time" (*Encyclopedia Britannica Macropaedia*, 1974 edition, volume 4, p. 504).[955]

Peace

There is a painting titled "Peace." It depicts waves crashing against the jagged rocks. It portrays the violence of a crushing storm. It seems anything but peaceful. But down in a small corner of the painting, tucked away in the rocks, is a little bird sitting on her nest totally oblivious to the raging storm all about. That is peace.[956]

Picture a massive hurricane raging over the ocean. On the surface of the sea the violent winds whip the water into giant waves and create a scene of havoc and chaos. Yet, a mere twenty-five feet below the surface, the waters are clear and calm. The fish there go on living their lives totally unaware of the thunderous tumult just above them.

When there is "depth," there is peace. So it is in the Christian life.[957]

A hurricane is a storm with cyclonic winds that exceed 74 m.p.h. Rain, thunder, and lightning usually accompany the winds. Hurricanes can be very fierce storms with relentless pounding winds that continue hour after hour. But a very fascinating thing about a hurricane is its "eye"—a place of perfect calm in its center. Though the winds blow and rage all around it, there are none in the eye.

So with us in the storms of life. With the Lord as our center, there is calm and peace, even in the darkest of life's storms.[958]

Eric Barker was a missionary from Great Britain who had spent over fifty years in Portugal preaching the gospel, often under adverse conditions. During World War II, the situation became so critical that he took the advice to send his wife and eight children to England for safety. His sister and her three children were also evacuated on the same ship. Barker remained behind to conclude some mission matters. The Sunday after Barker's loved ones had left, he stood before the congregation and said, "I've just received word that all my family have arrived safely home." He then proceeded with the service as usual. Later, the full meaning of his words became known to his people. He had been handed a wire just before the meeting, informing him that a submarine had torpedoed the ship, and everyone on board had drowned. Barker knew that all on board were believers, and the knowledge that his family was enjoying the bliss of heaven enabled him to live above his circumstances in spite of his overwhelming grief.[959]

U Thant was once Secretary General of the United Nations. While speaking in 1965 before sixty-seven distinguished scholars and statesmen from nineteen countries of the world, who were convened to talk about the requirements for world peace, he asked these questions:

What element is lacking so that with all our skill and all our knowledge we still find ourselves in the dark valley of discord and enmity? What is it that inhibits us from going forward together to enjoy the fruits of human endeavor and to reap the harvest of human experience? Why is it that, for all our professed ideals, our hopes, and our skills, peace on earth is still a distant objective seen only dimly through the storms and turmoils of our present difficulties?"[960]

Perfection

The closest to perfection a person ever comes is when he fills out a job application form.[961]

Persecution

The way of this world is to praise dead saints and persecute living ones.[962]

On one occasion, following unspeakable sufferings in a filthy prison, missionary Adoniram Judson appeared before the king of Burma and asked permission to go to a certain city to preach.

"I am willing for a dozen preachers to go, but not you," was the king's answer. "Not with those hands! My people are not such fools as to take notice of your preaching, but they will take notice of those scarred hands."[963]

One of the most inspiring examples of courage in the history of the church was the martyrdom of Polycarp, who was burned at the stake for his faith. The aged Polycarp had been arrested by the Roman authorities and brought to the arena for execution in front of the cheering crowd. The proconsul pressed him hard and said, "Swear, and I will release you. Revile Christ." Polycarp replied, "Eighty and six years have I served him, and he never did me wrong; and how can I now blaspheme my King that has saved me?" (Cited in Eusebius, *Ecclesiastical History*, chapter 15.)[964]

During the Watergate scandal, some people regarded it as a compliment to be on Nixon's "enemies list." They took it as a credit to them that people in the administration opposed them.

In the same way, if you have enemies because of your righteousness, it will be a credit to you. You should be glad that you have that kind of enemies, and that they are persecuting you, because it means that you are not doing what *they* do and instead are doing what unrighteous men hate.[965]

Perseverance

> Two frogs fell into a can of cream,
> Or so I've heard it told.
> The sides of the can were shiny and steep,
> The cream was deep and cold.
> "Oh, what's the use?" croaked number one.
> "'Tis fate, no help's around.
> Good-bye, my friend!
> Good-bye, sad world!"
> And weeping still, he drowned.
>
> But number two, of sterner stuff,
> Dog-paddled in surprise.
> The while he wiped his creamy face,
> And dried his creamy eyes.
> "I'll swim awhile at least," he said,
> Or so I've heard he said;
> "It really wouldn't help the world,
> If one more frog were dead."
> An hour or two he kicked and swam,
> Not once he stopped to mutter,
> But kicked and kicked and swam and kicked,
> Then hopped out, via butter![966]

Sometime go out and watch a stonecutter hammering away at a rock. He might hit the rock a hundred times without so much as a crack showing in it. Then, suddenly, at the hundred and first blow the rock splits in two. Was it the one blow that split the rock? Only in an immediate sense, for that one blow would have accomplished nothing if it were not for all that had gone before.[967]

In the movie *Chariots of Fire*, young Harold Abrahams, a champion sprinter, had just suffered his first-ever defeat. After the race he sat alone, pouting in the bleachers. When his girlfriend tried to encourage him, he bellowed, "If I can't win, I won't run!" To which she wisely replied, "If you don't run, you can't win." Abrahams went on to win the 1924 Olympic Gold Medal in the hundred-meter run.[968]

By perseverance the snail reached the ark.[969] 3/9/95

"It is better to limp in the way, than to run with swiftness out of it" (John Calvin, *Institutes*, 6:3).[970]

William Carey, when asked about his great accomplishments in his work of translating the Bible into Indian languages and dialects, said: "I am not a genius, just a plodder." But what a plodder! In forty years of labor, he translated all or portions of the Bible into thirty-four of the languages and dialects of India.[971]

Many years ago in England there was a small boy who talked with a lisp. While growing up, he was never a scholar. When war came along, they rejected him because "we need *men.*" He once rose to address the House of Commons, and they all walked out. He often spoke to empty chairs and echoes.

One day he became prime minister of Great Britain and led his country to victory in a worldwide conflict. That man was Sir Winston Churchill, whose iron will to persevere rallied all of his countrymen to defend their land and eventually win the war.[972]

The following is attributed to "Gentleman Jim" Corbett, who held the heavyweight boxing title for five years at the end of the nineteenth century:

"Fight one more round. When your feet are so tired that you have to shuffle back to the center of the ring, fight one more round. When your arms are so tired that you can hardly lift your hands to come on guard, fight one more round. When your nose is bleeding and your eyes are black and you are so tired that you wish your opponent would crack you on the jaw and put you to sleep, fight one more round—remembering that the man who fights one more round is never whipped."[973]

Thomas Edison gave us some wise thoughts regarding failure. It is said that the famous inventor made thousands of trials before he got his celebrated electric light to operate.

One day, a workman to whom he had given a task said, "Mr. Edison, it cannot be done." Edison said, "How often have you tried?" The man replied, "About two thousand times." Edison responded, "Go back and try two thousand times more; you have only found that there are two thousand ways in which it cannot be done."

This is the same man who also said, "Genius is one percent inspiration and ninety-nine percent perspiration."[974]

At the close of the first day of the Battle of Shiloh, with serious Union reverses, General U. S. Grant was met by his greatly discouraged chief engineer, James McPherson, who said: "Things look bad, General. We've lost half our artillery and a third of the infantry. Our line is broken and we are pushed back nearly to the river." Grant made no reply, and McPherson impatiently asked what he intended to do. "Do? Why re-form the lines and attack at daybreak. Won't they be surprised!" Surprised they were. The Confederate troops were routed before nine o'clock that morning.

No one is defeated until he gives up.[975]

Here is the biography of a failure. . . .

A man who had less than three years of formal education failed in business in '31, was defeated for the legislature in '32, again failed in business in '33, was elected to the legislature in '34, defeated for speaker in '38, defeated for elector in '40, defeated for Congress in '43, elected to Congress in '46 and defeated in '48, defeated for Senate in '55, defeated for the Vice Presidential nomination in '56, defeated for the Senate in '58.

His name? Abraham Lincoln.[976]

Rocky, the motion picture that won three Academy Awards, tells the story of a small-time boxer given the opportunity of a lifetime—the chance to fight the undisputed world heavyweight boxing champ. After weeks of punishing, grueling training, on the evening of the fight Rocky finally admitted the futility of his effort. "Who am I trying to kid?" he pondered, "I'm not even in the same class with da guy. But I gotta go da distance. I gotta go da distance."

Rocky Balboa set as his goal to go all fifteen rounds. He wanted to hang in there when he knew every muscle in his body would scream to quit. He wanted to endure under pressure. As a fighter, he wanted to go the full distance. The fight began, but in round one Rocky was knocked down. The count commenced, but after wildly shaking his head back and forth, he struggled to his feet and lasted not just one or two more rounds, but all fifteen. He was able to go the distance because, during training, his body had been subjected to grueling preparation. Daily he had driven himself to the point of exhaustion. One-arm push-ups, back-bending sit-ups, sprinting, sparring—this had all been part of his schedule of training.

The design of a demanding training schedule enabled Rocky to endure. Perseverance in any great test comes as a result of disciplined preparation in the ordinary days.[977]

Babe Ruth struck out 1,330 times. So keep on swinging![978]

A teenager had decided to quit high school, saying he was just fed up with it all. His father was trying to convince him to stay with it. "Son," he said, "you just can't quit. All the people who are remembered in history didn't quit. Abe Lincoln, he didn't quit. Thomas Edison, he didn't quit. Douglas MacArthur, he didn't quit. Elmo McCringle. . . ."

"Who?" the son burst in. "Who's Elmo McCringle?"

"See," the father replied, "you don't remember him. He quit!"[979]

"I would rather fail in a cause that will someday triumph, than triumph in a cause that will someday fail" (Woodrow Wilson).[980]

Persistence

A common phenomenon in nature is "the path of least resistance." Electricity moving through a circuit will always travel where it has the "easiest" route. Cars are developed aerodynamically so there will be minimal wind resistance. Rivers always travel *around* a mountain because it is easier than going through one.

Frequently people are like that, too. It is easier to sit in front of the T.V. than to care for a neighbor's needs. It is easier to get angry at your mate and let that anger diminish (or smolder) over the course of time rather than sitting down and working the problem through. Thumbing through a *Reader's Digest* is much easier than a time of personal Bible study. And so we find that we humans are prone to take the "path of least resistance."

But there is one difference between ourselves and electricity or a river. They will never have to give an account of what they have done. We will. Thus, perhaps we should incline ourselves to take the path of greatest persistence.[981]

Perspective

A parent once described how her three children would respond to a spider web in the garden. The first child would examine the web and wonder how the spider wove it. The second would worry a great deal about where the spider was. And the third would exclaim, "Oh, look! A trampoline!"

There was only one spider web in the garden, only one reality. But how differently it can be perceived and understood.[982]

To the poet, a pearl is a teardrop of the sea or a drop of dew, solidified. To the ladies, it is a jewel they can wear on their finger, neck, or ear. To the chemist, it is a mixture of phosphate and carbonate of lime with a little gelatin. To the naturalist, it is simply a morbid secretion of the organ that among certain bivalves produces mother-of-pearl. To a believer, a pearl is a marvel in God's creation.[983]

The Texas *Driver's Handbook* has a drawing that helps illustrate the fact that the faster the pace of life, the less perspective one can achieve.

When not moving, a driver enjoys a field of vision of 180 degrees or more. At 20 m.p.h. the field of vision is reduced by approximately two-thirds. At 40 m.p.h. the field of vision is further reduced by two-fifths. And at 60 m.p.h. the field of vision is barely wider than the width of the beams of the headlights.[984]

When the soldiers of Israel saw Goliath, they thought to themselves, "He is so big that we can never kill him." When David saw Goliath, he thought to himself, "He is so big that I cannot miss him."[985]

The importance of choosing to think positively was captured by the owner of a doughnut shop when he put this roadside sign in front of his shop:

> When along life's journey you roll,
> Keep your eye on the doughnut and not on the hole.[986]

A canny Maine farmer was approached by a stranger one day and asked how much he thought his prize Jersey cow was worth. The farmer thought for a moment, looked the stranger over, then asked: "Are you the tax assessor or has she just been killed by your car?"[987]

Pessimism

An optimist said to a pessimist, "Isn't this a bright, sunny day?" The pessimist replied, "Yes, but if this heat spell doesn't stop soon, all the grass will burn up."

Two days later, the optimist said to the pessimist, "Isn't this rain wonderful?" The pessimist replied, "Well, if it doesn't stop soon, my garden will wash away."

The next day, the optimist invited the pessimist to go duck hunting. The optimist wanted to show off his new registered hunting dog that could do things no other dog could. The pessimist looked at the dog and said, "Looks like a mutt to me."

At that moment, a flock of ducks flew over. The optimist shot one of the ducks and it fell in the middle of the lake. He snapped his fingers and his new dog ran after the duck. The dog ran out on the water, picked up the duck, and ran back on the water. The optimist took the duck from the dog's mouth, turned to the pessimist, and said, "What do you think of my dog now?" The pessimist replied, "Dumb dog—can't even swim!"[988]

When someone is convinced that things can't be done, he will cling to that conviction in the face of the most obvious contradiction. The story is told of the time when Robert Fulton gave the first public demonstration of his steamboat. One of those "can't be done" fellows stood in the crowd along the shore repeating, "He can't start it."

Suddenly, there was a belch of steam and the boat began to move. Startled, the man stared for a moment and then began to chant, "He can't stop it."[989]

Philosophy

"Philosophers have only interpreted the world differently; the point is, however, to change it" (Karl Marx).[990]

"Philosophy has shown itself over and over again to be full of arguments but lacking in conclusions" (Hugh Silvester, *Arguing with God* [Minneapolis: Bethany House, 1972], p. 8).[991]

Philosophy, Existential

The current world philosophy is summarized by the following: A man sat waiting for the light to turn green when his car was unexpectedly rear-ended. The two drivers hopped out of their cars and a vicious argument ensued. The man at fault defended himself by saying, "I really felt like running into someone today to vent my frustrations, and your bumper sticker has given me license to crash into your car." The bumper sticker read: "If it feels good, do it."[992]

It is said that there is a tombstone from ancient Rome that has inscribed on it the following:

> I was not and I became;
> I was and am no more.
> This much is true;
> Whoever says other, lies;
> For I shall not be,
> And thou who livest, drink, play, come.

Although we are separated from the one buried under that inscription by many centuries, that is the philosophy of our generation. But the Christian message is that there is more than this life. Life does not end at death, and so it has a purpose greater than enjoyment and pleasure.[993]

Potential

Anyone can count the seeds in an apple, but only God can count the apples in a seed. All he needs is a seed yielded to him.

D. L. Moody, uneducated and untrained, yet yielded to God, led Mordecai Ham to the Lord. Mordecai Ham, though not a great evangelist, was faithful to his task and won William Graham to the Lord. And Billy Graham has won thousands.[994]

Poverty, Cycle of

John Perkins, black evangelist and social worker in Jackson, Mississippi, related a story concerning a black woman who was trapped in poverty. She had ten or twelve kids packed into a four-room house.

All her cupboard held was cornbread. When Perkins encouraged the small Oak Ridge Church outside of Mendenhall, Mississippi, to help this neighbor out, they began to send food. But it didn't produce much change. The church asked itself, "How could Christ's love deal with these needs?"

The answer began to surface when Perkins observed that in the summer, while it was hot and humid, the woman and her children tore wood off the outside of the house to use in their cooking fire. You could look right through the whole house. It seemed stupid to tear up the house when winter was just a few months away, so many of the people in the community quit trying to be charitable. They began to blame the woman for her own problems. To a certain extent, she was to blame, but Perkins recognized that she was trapped in the cycle of poverty.

The root problem was that for this woman and many folks like her, poverty had moved beyond her physical condition to claim her whole mind. To the poor, poverty leads to thinking just for the moment. It leads to an inability to think about the future because of the total demand to think about survival in the present. It is a culture, a whole way of life. Money can't help until there is reason to have hope for the future.[995]

Power

On May 18, 1980, Mount St. Helens in the Cascade Range of Washington exploded with what is probably the most visible indication of the power of nature that the modern world has ever seen. At 8:32 A.M. the explosion ripped 1,300 feet off the mountain, with a force of ten million tons of TNT, or roughly equal to five hundred Hiroshimas.

Sixty people were killed, most by a blast of 300-degree heat traveling at two hundred miles an hour. Some were killed as far as sixteen miles away.

The blast also leveled 150-foot Douglas firs, as far as seventeen miles away. A total of 3.2 billion board-feet of lumber were destroyed, enough to build 200,000 three-bedroom homes.[996]

Praise

The attention span of a typical human is ten praises, six promises, or one preachment.[997]

Praise is a natural and necessary response to fully enjoy the object that is praised. For example, when watching a football game on television, it is a natural response to praise a tremendous play. To shout WOW! after an acrobatic catch in the end zone is not only natural, but necessary to fully enjoy the spectacular play. If you do not believe that it is necessary, the next time you watch a football game try to *not* express yourself at all. You will quickly find that you do not enjoy the action nearly as much as you do when you have the freedom to express yourself in praise and excitement.[998]

"It is not out of compliment that lovers keep on telling one another how beautiful they are; the delight is incomplete till it is expressed. It is frustrating to have discovered a new author and not to be able to tell anyone how good he is; to come suddenly, at the turn of the road, upon some mountain valley of unexpected grandeur and then to have to keep silent because the people with you care for it no more than for a tin can in the ditch; to hear a good joke and find no one to share it with" (C. S. Lewis, *Reflections on the Psalms* [New York: Walker & Co., 1985], p. 95).[999]

One Sunday morning after the service a woman came up to the pastor and thanked him for the encouraging sermon he had preached. In response he said, "Why, don't thank me, thank the Lord."

She said, "Well, I thought of that, but it wasn't quite that good."[1000]

Prayer

A comparison of the following book titles on the subject of prayer points up some of the tensions of the subject:

Where Is the Lord of Elijah? (Cox) vs. *You Never Walk Alone* (Mesner)

How Can God Answer Prayer? (Biederwolf) vs. *Getting Things from God* (Blanchard)

Let's Pray Together (Fromer) vs. *The Hidden Life of Prayer* (McIntyre)

Saying Better Prayers (Karney) vs. *Prayer Without Pretending* (Townsend)

Teach Yourself to Pray (Winward) vs. *The Holy Spirit—Our Teacher in Prayer* (Walton)

Five Laws That Govern Prayer (Gordon) vs. *Beyond the Natural Order* (Best)

. . . and lastly, *Taking Hold of God* (Zwemer) vs. *Prayer: Conversing With God* (Rinker)[1001]

For the Christian, praying should be like breathing. Just as breathing is the response of physical life to the presence of air, so prayer should be the response of spiritual life to the presence of God.[1002]

The brother of a seminary student came to visit him one day. Unsure of directions, he turned to the first person who passed by and asked, "Is this Davidson Hall?" On hearing the man described later, the seminary student asked his brother if he had realized that he had been talking to a world-famous theologian. The brother couldn't believe it. He had the opportunity to ask *any* question—and he asked only where a building was.

Unfortunately that's how many of us pray. We talk to God and ask for inane little things that are really insignificant.[1003]

Prayer is much like a check to be countersigned by two parties. I sign the check and send it up to heaven. If Jesus Christ also signs it, it does not matter how large it is—it will be honored.[1004]

The elders of a certain church once came to a young man to criticize some of the theology and vocabulary he used in the prayers he prayed publicly in the church service. After they had laid their load on him, he turned to them and said, "Are you gentlemen finished? I have just one thing to say: I wasn't speaking to you."[1005]

271

Some people's prayers need to be cut short at both ends and set on fire in the middle.[1006]

Often we pray with our minds on hold and our mouths on automatic.[1007]

Eight-ninths of the bulk of an iceberg is below the waterline and out of sight. Only one-ninth is visible above the surface. Our prayer life should be like an iceberg, with about one-ninth showing in public group prayer and eight-ninths out of sight in our personal prayer time.[1008]

The story is told of a young girl who said, "Lord, I am not going to pray for myself today; I am going to pray for others." But at the end of her prayer she added, "And give my mother a handsome son-in-law!" We just can't seem to end a prayer without asking for something for ourselves![1009]

Thyra Bjorn told the story of accompanying her pastor father one evening to the shack of a poverty-stricken old man. He was crippled with age and pain, yet he offered them what hospitality he could, and when they prayed together, the old man's face came alive as the agony of his present life gave way to radiant joy. Rather than asking anything of God, the man thanked him in detail for his shack, his warm bed, his visitors, for everything that was a part of his seemingly cramped and limited existence. When he had finished, Bjorn wrote, "he looked as happy and contented as though he had no discomfort at all."

On the way home through the dark cold fall air, Thyra's father sighted the lamp being lit in their parsonage in the valley below and called his daughter's attention to it. Then the thought struck the young girl that this too was what the old man in the cabin had seen: "He had seen his Father's house and knew that he soon would be home. There would be no more sickness or pain or loneliness there, and no more sorrow. And the light of prayer would lead him home." (Cited in Thyra F. Bjorn, *Mama's Way* [New York: Bantam, 1976]).[1010]

"In prayer it is better to have a heart without words than words without a heart" (John Bunyan).[1011]

272

Martin Luther prayed: "Dear Lord, Although I am sure of my position, I am unable to sustain it without thee. Help thou me or I am lost" (Cited in Plass, Ewald, *This Is Luther* [St. Louis: Concordia, 1984], p. 479).[1012]

> Lord
> I crawled across the barrenness
>   to you with my empty cup
> Uncertain
>   in asking any small drop of refreshment.
> If only I had known you better
> I'd have come running with a bucket.

Nancy Spiegelberg [1013]

Chaplain Richard Halverson of the United States Senate told the story of a time when the subject of prayer in schools came up just before a Senator was to give a speech to several hundred men at a church's annual men's dinner. In response to the Senator's question about how many of the church men believed in prayer in the public schools, nearly every man present raised his hand in the affirmative.

Then the Senator asked, "How many of you pray daily with your own children in your home?" This time, only a few hands were raised.[1014]

"Prayer pulls the rope down below and the great bell rings above in the ears of God. Some scarcely stir the bell, for they pray so languidly; others give only an occasional jerk at the rope. But he who communicates with heaven is the man who grasps the rope boldly and pulls continuously with all his might" (C. H. Spurgeon).[1015]

Prayer, Answers to

Two Christian men lived near each other. The first was a farmer. Since there had not been any rain for several weeks, the farmer got up one morning and prayed for rain, but there was no rain that day.

His next-door neighbor was also up early, but he was praying that it would *not* rain, because he was taking an unsaved friend fishing that morning. There was no rain that day.

God hears both requests, but he can't answer both. He will do that which glorifies him the most.[1016]

I asked for strength that I might achieve;
He made me weak that I might obey.
I asked for health that I might do great things;
He gave me grace that I might do better things.
I asked for riches that I might be happy;
He gave me poverty that I might be wise.
I asked for power that I might have the praise of men;
He gave me weakness that I might feel a need of God.
I asked for all things that I might enjoy life;
He gave me life that I might enjoy all things.
I received nothing I had asked for;
He gave me all that I had hoped for.[1017]

Shortly after Dallas Seminary was founded in 1924, it came to the point of bankruptcy. All the creditors were going to foreclose at noon on a particular day. That morning, the founders of the school met in the president's office to pray that God would provide. In that prayer meeting was Harry Ironside. When it was his turn to pray, he prayed in his characteristically refreshing manner: "Lord, we know that the cattle on a thousand hills are thine. Please sell some of them and send us the money."

While they were praying, a tall Texan came into the business office and said, "I just sold two carloads of cattle in Fort Worth. I've been trying to make a business deal go through and it won't work, and I feel that God is compelling me to give this money to the Seminary. I don't know if you need it or not, but here's the check."

A secretary took the check and, knowing something of the financial seriousness of the hour, went to the door of the prayer meeting and timidly tapped. When she finally got a response, Dr. Lewis Chafer took the check out of her hand, and it was for the exact amount of the debt. When he looked at the signature, he recognized the name of the cattle rancher. Turning to Dr. Ironside, he said, "Harry, God sold the cattle!"[1018]

Prayer, Asking in Jesus' Name

A father took his children to the county fair one day. Since they were obviously not interested in the prize pig or calf, the father bought a whole roll of tickets for the various rides at the fair. As each of the children approached a ride, they would hold out a hand to get a ticket from their father. At one ride, after all his children had received tickets, a strange boy whom the father had never seen came up and held out his hand, obviously expecting a ticket.

274

The father drew back his roll of tickets. He wasn't about to give this boy a ticket. Upon seeing this, the man's son Stephen turned and said to his dad, "It's okay, Dad, this is my friend. I told him you would give him a ticket."

Do you know what the father did? He gave the boy a ticket in Stephen's name. That boy had no right to a ticket, but since his son had said he would do it, the father honored the name of his son by giving that strange boy a ticket.[1019]

Prayer, Belief and

A tavern was being built in a town that until recently had been dry. A group of Christians in a certain church opposed this and began an all-night prayer meeting, asking God to intervene.

Lightning struck the tavern building, and it burned to the ground. The owner brought a lawsuit against the church, claiming they were responsible. The Christians hired a lawyer, claiming they were not responsible. The judge said, "No matter how this case comes out, one thing is clear. The tavern owner believes in prayer and the Christians do not."[1020]

The story is told of a time when a great Scotch preacher prayed in the morning service for rain. As he went to church in the afternoon his daughter, said, "Here is the umbrella, Papa."

"What do we need it for?" he asked.

"You prayed for rain this morning. Don't you expect God to send it?" his daughter replied.

They carried the umbrella, and while they came home they were glad to take shelter under it from the drenching storm. Such should be our faith when we pray, just like that little child's—with no doubt, and expecting an answer.[1021]

Prayer, Confident Access in

In Saudi Arabia, according to Arab custom, reinforced by a 1952 decree of King Abdul Aziz, every subject has the right of access to his ruler—whether the ruler is a tribal sheik, a governor, or the monarch himself—to present petitions of complaint or pleas for help. Even the poorest Saudi can approach his sovereign to plead a cause. Crown Prince Fahd, speaking about this custom said, "Anyone, anyone can

275

come here. That gives them confidence in their government. . . . They know they may look to us for help."

Every Christian has the right to approach an even greater monarch, the King of kings.[1022]

Prayer, God's Will and

When children first start to color, they have two problems. First, they might choose colors that are inappropriate. Secondly, once the colors are chosen, they have a difficult time keeping the colors within the boundary lines. As they mature and keep on coloring, they learn to keep within the guidelines and to choose the appropriate colors, resulting in a satisfying picture.

As children of our Heavenly Father, our prayer life often resembles a child's coloring. At first, we don't know what to pray for nor do our prayers stay within the guidelines of His will. As we mature and continue praying, though, we pray for the right things and stay within His will, resulting in a satisfying prayer life.[1023]

Prayer, Guidance Through

An aircraft pilot was following a major highway and observing the traffic below. One particular car caught his attention. The driver was attempting to pass a large truck, but because of oncoming traffic and no-passing zones, he was not able to pass safely. Over and over again, just as he would pull out, an oncoming vehicle would force him to retreat. The pilot, being able to see several miles down the highway, thought to himself, "If I could only talk to the driver, I could tell when and where it is safe to pass."

God, of course, is the ultimate Pilot and his perfect knowledge is exactly what we need to guide our life. Prayer is how we talk to God, and as we learn to listen to his responses, we will find the guidance we seek.[1024]

A woman asked G. Campbell Morgan, "Do you think we ought to pray about even the little things in life?"

Dr. Morgan, in his typically understated British manner, replied, "Madam, can you think of anything in *your* life that is big to God?"[1025]

Prayer, Humorous

A little boy was saying his bedtime prayers with his mother: "Lord, *7/95* bless Mommy and Daddy, and God, GIVE ME A NEW BICYCLE!!!"

Mom: "God's not deaf, son.

Boy: "I know, Mom, but Grandma's in the next room, and she's hard of hearing!"[1026]

A boy, age six, was invited by a friend to have dinner. When his friend's family were all seated around the table, the food was served. The young guest was puzzled and—with the frankness children are so well known for—asked, "Don't you say any prayer before you eat?" The host was embarrassed by the question and mumbled, "No, we don't take time for that." The boy was silent for a moment and then said, "Oh, I see, you eat like my dog does. He just starts right in, too."[1027]

Prayer, Importance of

D. E. Host, the man who took over for Hudson Taylor, wrote a book titled *Behind the Ranges.* He was trying to analyze a problem he had seen while working in two different villages in China. The people with whom he lived and worked were not doing very well. But the people in the other village across the ranges were doing great! He visited them only now and then, but they were always doing fine, so he began to ask the Lord what was going on. How could those across the ranges be doing better than those with whom he lived and worked? The Lord showed Host the answer. Although he was spending much time counseling, preaching, and teaching with those with whom he lived, he spent much more time in prayer for those across the ranges. He concluded that there were four basic elements in making disciples: (1) prayer, (2) prayer, (3) prayer, (4) the Word—in that order and in about that proportion.[1028]

"I have so much to do that I must spend the first three hours of each day in prayer" (Martin Luther).[1029]

"The church has many organizers, but few agonizers; many who pay, but few who pray; many resters, but few wrestlers; many who are enterprising, but few who are interceding. People who are not praying and praying. The secret of praying is praying in secret. A worldly Christian will stop praying and a praying Christian will stop worldliness. Tithes may build a church, but tears will give it life. That is the difference between the modern church and the early church. In the matter of effective praying, never have so many left so much to so few. Brethren, let us pray" (Leonard Ravenhill).[1030]

Prayer, Length of

A man who prays much in private will make short prayers in public![1031]

Prayer, Need for

Many view God only as a kind of heavenly genie, ready when you rub the lamp of prayer to appear and say, "Yes, master; what do you want me to do?" But God is not like that. God is sovereign. God moves according to his own purposes, and he does not play games with us. He is not to be mollified and placated by a temporary return to him when we get into difficulty.[1032]

Do you ever play the game "how far"? Its rules are really simple—you fill up your gas tank and then drive to see how far you can go before you fill up again. You watch the gauge nervously as it falls closer and closer to the big E.

What about your spiritual gas tank—do you play "how far" with it, too, trying to see how far you can get on a single fill-up?[1033]

A four-year-old boy once saw a picture of Christ praying and asked what Jesus was doing in that picture. When he was told that Jesus was praying, the youngster responded by asking who Jesus was praying to. After being told that Jesus was praying to God, the young boy replied, "But Jesus IS God!"

This same thought was captured well by St. Cyprian who said, "If He prayed who was without sin, how much more it becomes a sinner to pray."[1034]

Prayer, Perseverance in

A woman left her diamond brooch in a hotel. When she got home she remembered her brooch and called the hotel. She told the manager what happened and he went to look for it. He found it, put it in the safe, and returned to the phone to tell her the good news, but she had hung up.

So many of us are like this. We aren't willing to wait on the Lord.[1035]

When Edmund Gravely died at the controls of his small plane while on the way to Statesboro, Georgia, from the Rocky Mount-Wilson Airport in North Carolina, his wife, Janice, kept the plane aloft for two hours. As the plane crossed the South Carolina/North Carolina border, she radioed for help: "Help, help, won't someone help me? My pilot is unconscious." Authorities who picked up her distress signal were not able to reach her by radio during the flight because she kept changing channels. Eventually Mrs. Gravely made a rough landing and had to crawl for forty-five minutes to a farmhouse for help.

How often God's people cry out to him for help but switch channels before his message comes through! They turn to other sources for help, looking for human guidance. When you cry out to God for his intervention, don't switch channels![1036]

A father related that during their family time each person was going to pray for one person. His son prayed to ask God to help his friend Eddie be better at school because he was so bad. When they got together the next week, the father asked his son if he was going to pray for Eddie again. "No," the son replied, "I prayed for Eddie last week and he is still bad."[1037]

A young man, who was obviously worried, stepped into an elevator to go to the second floor of a hospital where his father was in the intensive-care unit. Although the button labeled "2" was already lighted, he pushed it again and again. A doctor standing behind him said, "Pushing the button someone has already pushed is like reminding God you're still there when he hasn't answered your prayer immediately."

As the man thought of his father in intensive care, it was comforting to know that God does encourage believers to continue to pray the same prayers until he answers (Matt. 7:7–8).[1038]

In *Pilgrim's Progress* by John Bunyan, Christiana (the hero's wife), Mercy (a young pilgrim), and the children are graphically pictured knocking on the Wicker Gate. They knock and knock, but no one answers. Meanwhile, a ferocious dog comes and begins to bark—making the women and children very afraid. They simply do not know what to do. If they continue to knock, they must fear the dog. If they turn away, they fear the gatekeeper will be offended. They determine to knock again, ever so fervently. Finally they hear the voice of the gate-keeper asking, "Who is there?" And the dog ceases barking.

What dogs are barking in *your* life that the Lord can silence?[1039]

"For your desire is your prayer; and your desire is without ceasing; your prayer will also be without ceasing" (St. Augustine).[1040]

The story is told of a long-ago couple who said farewell to their home church as they were about to leave for an African mission field known as "The White Man's Grave." The husband said, "My wife and I have a strange dread in going. We feel much as if we were going down into a pit. We are willing to take the risk and go if you, our home church, will promise to hold the ropes." One and all promised to do so.

Less than two years had passed when the wife and the little one God had given the couple succumbed to the dreaded fever. Soon the husband realized his days were also numbered. Not waiting to send word of his coming, he started back home at once and arrived at the time of the Wednesday prayer meeting. He slipped in unnoticed, taking a back seat. At the close of the meeting, he went forward. An awe came over the people, for death was written on his face.

He said, "I am your missionary. My wife and child are buried in Africa and I have come home to die. This evening I listened anxiously as you prayed for some mention of your missionary to see if you were keeping your promise, but in vain! You prayed for everything connected with yourselves and your home circle, but you forgot your missionary. I see now why I am a failure as a missionary. It is because you have failed to hold the ropes."[1041]

Prayer, Power of

Prayer moves the hand that moves the world![1042]

Prayer is the only omnipotence God grants to us.[1043]

280

"Give me one hundred preachers who fear nothing but sin, and desire nothing but God, and I care not a straw whether they be clergymen or laymen; such alone will shake the gates of hell and set up the kingdom of heaven on earth. God does nothing but in answer to prayer" (John Wesley).[1044]

"Praying for particular things," said I, "always seems to me like advising God how to run the world. Wouldn't it be wiser to assume that He knows best?" "On the same principle," said he, "I suppose you never ask a man next to you to pass the salt, because God knows best whether you ought to have salt or not. And I suppose you never take an umbrella, because God knows best whether you ought to be wet or dry." "That's quite different," I protested. "I don't see why," said he. "The odd thing is that He should let us influence the course of events at all. But since He let us do it in one way, I don't see why He shouldn't let us do it in the other." [From C. S. Lewis, *God in the Dock* (Grand Rapids: Wm. B. Eerdmans, 1970), p. 217.][1045]

Prayer, Unanswered

A young boy saw a pack of cigarettes on the ground and decided to try them. He went to a field near his home and, after several fumbling attempts, got one to light up. It didn't taste good; indeed, it burned his throat and made him cough. But it made him feel very grown up.

Then he saw his father coming. Quickly he put the cigarette behind his back and tried to be casual. Desperate to divert his father's attention, the young boy pointed to a nearby billboard advertising the circus. "Can we go, Dad? Please, let's go when it comes to town."

The father quietly but firmly replied, "Son, never make a petition while at the same time trying to hide a smoldering disobedience."[1046]

Students at the university level are usually familiar with an experiment peformed with chickens. A chicken is placed in a cage. On one side of the cage are two buttons, one red and the other green. Every time the chicken pecks the green button, a small amount of chicken feed comes out of a slot below the buttons. However, when the chicken pecks the red button, nothing comes out. The chicken soon learns the game and will repeatedly peck the green button to receive grain.

The interesting thing is that if the experimenter reverses the effect of each button, the chicken eventually realizes that pecking the green button now does nothing, so it stops.

281

How like chickens we are when we pray! When we turn to God to ask him for something and are not granted our request immediately, we stop praying about it. Why? Because we think of prayer as a supernatural button to press to get what we want. We forget that unanswered prayer is still heard by God, and so his silence is for a purpose. Perhaps he wishes to do more than supply our requests. Perhaps he wishes to draw us closer to him, test the maturity of our faith, or force us to re-evaluate our request.[1047]

A newborn baby cries frequently when he or she has needs, and the mother comes immediately, day or night, to fill those needs. Thus, children learn to cry when they want Mother's presence. Later, Mother comes but does not pick up the child; she only softly says, "Hush, child, go back to sleep." Later she may not even come every time the baby cries. Of course, the baby does not like this one bit, but the feelings of "abandonment" lessen as he or she learns that Mother will always come in the morning. In the process, all babies learn that they cannot manipulate a mother, especially one who distinguishes between her baby's needs and wants.

So it is with prayer. When we are young believers, God often answers our prayers quickly. Later, as we mature, he uses unanswered prayer as a means of teaching us to rely on him—he who knows our real needs and who is always faithful.[1048]

Let us not be like the man who was lost in the deep woods. Later, in describing the experience, he told how frightened he was and how he had prayed. "Did God answer your prayer?" someone asked. "Oh, no!" was the reply. "Before God had a chance, a guide came along and showed me the path."

Was that prayer *really* unanswered?[1049]

Dr. Howard Hendricks tells of the time when he was a young man, before he was married. He was aware that certain mothers had set their caps for him on behalf of their daughters. One mother even said to him one day, "Howard, I just want you to know that I'm praying that you'll be my son-in-law."

Dr. Hendricks always stops at that point in the story and says, very solemnly, "Have you ever thanked God for unanswered prayer?"[1050]

282

George Muller wrote concerning his orphan ministry: "The funds are exhausted. We had been reduced so low as to be at the point of selling those things which could be spared. . . ." Then a woman arrived who had been traveling four days, bringing with her sufficient funds for the orphanage. Muller and his co-workers had prayed those four days for something God had already answered.

Under these circumstances, Muller made the following observation: "That the money had been so near the orphan house for several days without being given, is a plain proof that it was from the beginning in the heart of God to help us; but because he delights in the prayers of His children, He had allowed us to pray so long; also to try our faith, and to make the answer so much sweeter." (Cited in George Muller, *Autobiography* [Grand Rapids: Baker, 1981], p. 110.)[1051]

Prayer and Bible Study

"Little of the Word with little prayer is death to the spiritual life. Much of the Word with little prayer gives a sickly life. Much prayer with little of the Word gives emotional life. But a full measure of both the Word and prayer each day gives a healthy and powerful life" (Attributed to Andrew Murray).[1052]

Preachers

Someone has said that there are only two kinds of speakers: those who have something to say, and those who have to say something![1053]

A young preacher, looking up from his reading, asked his wife, "How many really great preachers do you think there are?" She replied, "Well, I don't know, but there is probably one less than you think."[1054]

"Some students never study but, like the spider, spin everything out from within, beautiful webs that never last. Some are like ants that steal whatever they find, store it away, and use it later. But the bee sets the example for us all. He takes from the many flowers, but he makes his own honey" (Francis Bacon).[1055]

"A good preacher should have these properties and virtues:

first, to teach systematically;

second, he should have a ready wit;

third, he should be eloquent;

fourth, he should have a good voice;

fifth, a good memory;

sixth, he should know when to make an end;

seventh, he should be sure of his doctrine;

eighth, he should venture and engage body and blood, wealth and honour, in the word;

ninth, he should suffer himself to be mocked and jeered by everyone" (Martin Luther, in *Table Talks* [Grand Rapids: Baker, 1979], p. 182).[1056]

A young minister who was asked to speak at his old seminary stood up and said, "What I have to say must be pretty good because my knees are already applauding."[1057]

Someone has said, "In periods of unsettled faith, skepticism, and mere curious speculation in matters of religion, teachers of all kinds swarm like the flies in Egypt. The demand creates the supply. The hearers invite and shape their own preachers. If the people desire a calf to worship, a ministerial calf-maker is readily found."

Paul says, "I proclaimed to you the testimony about God (1 Cor. 2:1, NIV). He did not tickle people's ears with giving them what they wanted to hear.[1058]

Preaching

Upon accepting his first church, a young pastor asked an elderly board member if he had any wise advice. The elderly man responded, "Son, a sermon is like a good meal; you should end it just before we have had enough."[1059]

Preaching has been described this way: "A mild-mannered man standing up before mild-mannered people and exhorting them to be more mild mannered."

The true function of preaching is to disturb the comfortable and to comfort the disturbed.[1060]

The story is told of a patient in a mental ward who attended chapel services with the other patients in the ward. The chaplain who spoke was so confusing that one of the patients going out was heard to say, "There, but for the grace of God, go I."[1061]

"I preached as never to preach again; as a dying man to dying men" (Robert Murray McCheyne).[1062]

Helena Modjeska (1844–1909) was one of the most popular actresses of her time because of her emotional style and superb ability. Once, to demonstrate the raw power of her ability, she gave a dramatic reading in her native tongue, Polish. No one at the sedate dinner party understood Polish, but all were in tears by the end of her performance. Such was the power of her presentation. Only later was it revealed that the piece that had moved the sophisticated audience to tears was the Polish alphabet.[1063]

Preaching, Content of

A preacher once confided to his head deacon that he was troubled by how few of the church members showed up for any given service. The deacon, a faithful farmhand who never missed a service, reflected on the years he had listened to his preacher's long-winded sermons and then replied: "Well, Preacher, if you pour only water into the feeding trough, the hogs don't come around to feed too often."[1064]

"If I profess with the loudest voice and clearest exposition every portion of the word of God except precisely that little point which the world and the Devil are at that point attacking, I am not confessing Christ, however boldly I may be professing Christ. Where the battle rages, there the loyalty of the soldier is tested. To be steady in all the battlefields besides is mere flight and disgrace, if the soldier flinches at that one point" (Martin Luther).[1065]

Preaching, Expository

Many people do not know what expository preaching is. Dr. Donald Campbell, president of Dallas Theological Seminary, recalled some early advice he received while a youth minister in a small Texas town. His pastor said to his young apprentice, "Son, there are two types of sermons: topical and suppository!"[1066]

Preaching Style

In a sermon, Greek and Hebrew are like underwear: they add a lot of support, but you don't want to let them show.[1067]

The story has been told of a young pastor who with great concern and sincerity ended his sermon like this: "And now, my friends, if you do not believe these truths, there may be for you grave eschatological consequences."

Afterward a layman went to him and asked, "Did you mean that they would be in danger of hell?"

"Why, yes," the preacher said.

"Then why in the world didn't you say so?" the layman asked.[1068]

Predestination

Dr. Harry Ironside told of a man who gave his testimony, telling how God had sought him and found him. How God had loved him, called him, saved him, delivered him, cleansed him, and healed him. It was a tremendous testimony to the glory of God.

After the meeting, one rather legalistic brother took him aside and said, "You know, I appreciate all that you said about what God did for you, but you didn't mention anything about your part in it. Salvation is really part us and part God, and you should have mentioned something about your part."

"Oh," the man said, "I apologize. I'm sorry. I really should have mentioned that. My part was running away, and God's part was running after me until he found me."[1069]

Prejudice

Mohandas K. Gandhi was the leader of the Indian nationalist movement against British rule and considered the father of his country. He is internationally esteemed for his doctrine of nonviolence to achieve political and social progress.

Gandhi says in his autobiography that in his student days he was truly interested in the Bible. Deeply touched by reading the Gospels, he seriously considered becoming a convert, since Christianity seemed to offer the real solution to the caste system that was dividing the people of India. One Sunday, he went to a nearby church to attend services. He decided to see the minister and ask for instruction in the way of salvation and enlightenment on other doctrines. But when he entered the sanctuary, the ushers refused to give him a seat and suggested that he go and worship with his own people. Gandhi left and never came back. "If Christians have caste differences also," he said to himself, "I might as well remain a Hindu."[1070]

Presuppositions

A certain mental patient was convinced that he was dead, so he was committed to the care of a psychiatrist. The psychiatrist had the man read an anatomy book and watch films to show him that dead men do not bleed. Then he took him into a room full of cadavers, where the man saw for himself that dead men do not bleed. "All right, I'm convinced, dead men don't bleed," he said.

Then the doctor took a pin and poked the man, and a tiny drop of blood appeared. "Well, what do you know," the man responded. "Dead men do bleed after all."[1071]

"Every period of intellectual history has some dogma which is regarded at the time not as dogma, but merely as what is evident" (James Cornman, *Philosophical Problems and Arguments: An Introduction* [New York: Macmillan, 1982]).[1072]

Pride

A life that is wrapped up in itself makes a very small package.[1073]

Pride is like a beard. It just keeps growing. The solution? Shave it every day.[1074]

A minister, a Boy Scout, and a computer expert were the only passengers on a small plane. The pilot came back to the cabin and said that the plane was going down but there were only three parachutes and four people. The pilot added, "*I* should have one of the parachutes because I have a wife and three small children." So he took one and jumped.

The computer whiz said, "*I* should have one of the parachutes because I am the smartest man in the world and everyone needs me." So he took one and jumped.

The minister turned to the Boy Scout and with a sad smile said, "You are young and I have lived a rich life, so you take the remaining parachute, and I'll go down with the plane."

The Boy Scout said, "Relax, Reverend, the smartest man in the world just picked up my knapsack and jumped out!"[1075]

Many Christians are like the woodpecker who was pecking on the trunk of a dead tree. Suddenly lightning struck the tree and splintered it. The woodpecker flew away unharmed. Looking back to where the dead tree had stood, the proud bird exclaimed, "Look what I did!"[1076]

Pride is the only disease known to man that makes everyone sick except the one who has it.[1077]

A conceited person is someone who does a crossword puzzle with a ballpoint pen.[1078]

An article titled "The Art of Being a Big Shot" was written by a very prominent Christian businessman named Howard Butt. Among many other insightful things he said were these words:

> It is my pride that makes me independent of God. It's appealing to me to feel that I am the master of my fate, that I run my own life, call my own shots, go it alone. But that feeling is my basic dishonesty. I can't go it alone. I have to get help from other people, and I can't ultimately rely on myself. I'm dependent on God for my next breath. It is dishonest of me to pretend that I'm anything but a man—small, weak, and limited. So, living independent of God is self-delusion. It is not just a matter of pride being an unfortunate little trait and humility being an attractive little virtue; it's my inner psychological integrity that's at stake. When I am conceited, I am lying to myself about what I am. I am pretending to be God, and not man. My pride is the idolatrous worship of myself. And that is the national religion of Hell! [from an undocumented source].[1079]

Albert Einstein once said, regarding pride of accomplishment: "The only way to escape the personal corruption of praise is to go on working. One is tempted to stop and listen to it. The only thing is to turn away and go on working. Work. There is nothing else."[1080]

A rich man once invited many honored guests for a feast. His own chair, richly decorated, was placed at one end of the long table. While he was away, each guest seated himself according to his own esteem of his position in sight of the master. When time came and all were seated, the master moved his chair to the *other* end of the table![1081]

Many Christians have wrongly concluded that sexual sins are the worst kind of sin. But that is not true. Sexual sins are not the worst kind of sins. C. S. Lewis has caught this fact very accurately. In a paragraph from his book *Mere Christianity* (New York: Macmillan, 1986), Lewis says:

> If anyone thinks that Christians regard unchastity as the supreme vice, he is quite wrong. The sins of the flesh are bad, but they are the least bad of all sins. All the worst pleasures are purely spiritual. The pleasure of putting other people in the wrong, of bossing and patronizing and spoiling sport, and backbiting; the pleasures of power, of hatred. For there are two things inside me competing with the human self which I must try to become; they are the animal self, and the diabolical self; and the diabolical self is the worst of the two. That is why a cold, self-righteous prig, who goes regularly to church may be far nearer to hell than a prostitute. But, of course, it's better to be neither.[1082]

According to *Life* magazine, Muhammed Ali spoke of himself before his 1971 fight with Joe Frazier thus:

> There seems to be some confusion. We're gonna clear this confusion up on March 8. We're gonna decide once and for all who is king! There's not a man alive who can whup me. (He jabs the air half a dozen blinding lefts.)
> I'm too smart. (He taps his head.)
> I'm too pretty. (He lifts his head high in profile, turning as a bust on a pedestal.)
> I AM the greatest. I AM the king! I should be a postage stamp—that's the only way I could get licked!

P.S. Ali lost to Frazier![1083]

When the nineteenth-century American evangelist Asahel Nettleton was asked what he considered the best safeguard against spiritual pride, he replied: "I know of nothing better than to keep my eye on my great sinfulness."[1084]

In Charles Colson's book *Born Again,* which details his experiences related to Watergate, Colson shares one of President Nixon's problems—he could never admit he was wrong in anything. In fact, Colson says, even when Nixon obviously had a cold—nose running, face red, sneezing, all the symptoms—he would never admit it.[1085]

When circus acrobat Philippe Petit was rehearsing in Bayfront Auditorium in St. Petersburg, Florida, he fell about thirty feet to a concrete floor. According to a witness, Petit rolled over on his stomach, began pounding the floor with his fists, and cried, "I can't believe it! I can't believe it! I don't ever fall!"[1086]

The story is told of a laborer who was a mature Christian and gave a solid testimony before all who knew him. His boss came to him one day and said, "You know, whatever you've got, I want. You have such peace and joy and contentment. How can I get this?"

The laborer said, "Go to your home, put on your best suit, come down here, and work in the mud with the rest of us—and you can have it."

"What are you talking about? I could never do that. I'm the boss, you're the worker. I can't do that. That's beneath my dignity." The boss came back a couple of months later and said, "I ask you again, what is it that you have and how can I get it?"

"I told you, go put on your best suit, come down and work in the mud with us, and you can have it." Again the boss became furious and walked off.

Finally, in desperation he came back to the laborer and said, "I don't care what it takes! I'll do anything." The laborer said, "Will you put on your best suit and come down and work in the mud?" The boss agreed that he would do even that. Then the laborer said, "You don't have to."

Do you see the point? The laborer knew what was standing between the boss and Christ—pride and self.[1087]

Principles vs. Rules

Some people confuse principles with rules. A principle is something that comes from inside a person. A rule is an outward restriction. To obey a principle you have to use your mental and moral powers. To obey a rule you have only to do what the rule says.

Dr. Frank Crane pointed out the difference neatly: "A rule supports us by the armpits over life's mountain passes. A principle makes us surefooted."[1088]

Priorities

Lewis Sperry Chafer, referring to a friend who was devoting most of his time and energy in pursuit of an insignificant matter, said, "He reminds me of a bulldog chasing a train: what's he going to do with it if he catches it?"[1089]

During the Byron Nelson Golf Tournament in Dallas in May 1981, a massive tree limb broke off and fell on a spectator, who was killed instantly.

It happened near the third hole where Charles Coody was playing at the time. Shortly after the accident, Coody was interviewed on the radio and, in talking to the reporter, he said, "After running over and seeing the accident, I tried to play golf, yet I had no desire to play after that. All of a sudden those three-foot putts didn't seem all that important."[1090]

During a flood in the hill country of Texas in 1978 there was a lady who needlessly lost her life. Her daughter told reporters, "My mother did not climb the tree with us. She lost her way before we got to the tree. See, she always kept every little bill and slip and stuff. She would not let go of her purse with those papers in it."

It was revealed that the family was trying to make a chain, holding hands to get through the water. But the mother had her insurance papers all gathered up in her hands and wouldn't drop those documents. So she just washed away.[1091]

At the Milan Cathedral there are three inscriptions over the respective doorways. Over the right-hand door there is this motto: "All that pleases is but for a moment." Over the left-hand door the words are: "All that troubles is but for a moment." But over the central door there is a simple sentence: "Nothing is important save that which is eternal."[1092]

If you give your child a quarter for the Sunday offering and later give him three dollars to go to the movies, you may be teaching him a set of values he will keep the rest of his life.[1093]

When asked why he had been so successful, Tom Landry responded to a crowd of more than two thousand students at Baylor University, "In 1958, I did something everyone who has been successful must do, I determined my priorities for my life—God, family, and then football." (Cited in *Dallas Morning News*, March 2, 1978).[1094]

Among the classified ads in the *Quay County Sun* was this ad: "Farmer with 160 irrigated acres wants marriage-minded woman with tractor. When replying, please show picture of tractor" (AP release, June 1978, Tucumcari, New Mexico).[1095]

Problems

The story has been told of a bricklayer who was hurt on the job and sent the following letter to his boss requesting sick leave:

> I arrived at the job after the storm, checked the building out and saw that the top needed repairs. I rigged a hoist and a boom, attached the rope to a barrel and pulled bricks to the top. When I pulled the barrel to the top, I secured the rope at the bottom. After repairing the building, I went back to fill the barrel with the leftover bricks. I went down and released the rope to lower the bricks, and the barrel was heavier than I and jerked me off the ground. I decided to hang on. Halfway up, I met the barrel coming down and received a blow to the shoulder. I hung on and went to the top, where I hit my head on the boom and caught my fingers in the pulley. In the meantime, the barrel hit the ground and burst open, throwing bricks all over. This made the barrel lighter than I, and I started down at high speed. Halfway down, I met the barrel coming up and received a blow to my shins. I continued down and fell on the bricks, receiving cuts and bruises. At this time I must have lost my presence of mind, because I let go of the rope and the barrel came down and hit me on the head. I respectfully request sick leave.[1096]

Procrastination

Procrastination is the assassination of motivation.[1097]

While cleaning out his desk, a man found a shoe-repair ticket that was ten years old. Figuring that he had nothing to lose, he went to the shop and gave the ticket to the repairman, who began to search the back room for the unclaimed shoes. After several minutes, he reappeared and gave the ticket back to the man.

"What's wrong?" asked the man. "Couldn't you find my shoes?"

"Oh, I found them," replied the repairman, "and they'll be ready next Friday."

Procrastination is not the result of lack of time to complete a task. It is an attitude and must be dealt with as such.[1098]

The story is told of an infidel who died after willing his farm to the devil. This gave the court cause for some head scratching, but after several months of deliberation it handed down the following decision: "It is decided that the best way to carry out the wish of the deceased is to allow the farm to grow weeds, the soil to erode, and the house and barn to rot. In our opinion, the best way to leave something to the devil is to do nothing."

Therein lies a truth. Few of us would ever admit to such infidelity, but many will procrastinate and postpone the great decisions of life and end up having willed our soul to the devil.[1099]

"Perhaps the most valuable result of all education is the ability to make yourself do the thing you have to do, when it ought to be done, whether you like it or not; it is the first lesson that ought to be learned; and however early a man's training begins, it is probably the last lesson that he learns thoroughly" (Thomas Huxley, *Technical Education*).[1100]

Prodigal Son

One of the most beautiful stories of the Scriptures is that of the prodigal son, the youth who left home, got into deep difficulty, wasted his life in riotous living, and ended up in the pigpen.

Dr. J. Vernon McGee once asked, "Do you know the difference between the son in that pigpen and the pig? The difference is that no pig has ever said to himself, 'I will arise and go to my father.' "

He is right; only sons say that. That is why there will be no condemnation, no rejection by God of his children. All believers, even prodigal sons, are his children, not his enemies.[1101]

Promises, God's

When Crowfoot, the great chief of the Blackfoot confederacy in southern Alberta, gave the Canadian Pacific Railroad permission to cross the Blackfoot land from Medicine Hat to Calgary, he was given in return a lifetime railroad pass. Crowfoot put it in a leather case and carried it around his neck for the rest of his life. There is no record, however, that he ever availed himself of the right to travel anywhere on the CPR trains.

The promises of God are often treated in this way by Christians. They hang them on their walls in beautiful plaques; they treasure them in little promise boxes that play invitingly, "Standing on the Promises of God." But they do not claim the promises for themselves in times of need. Of what use are they on plaques and in boxes if they are not in our hearts?[1102]

Prophecy

The Chinese say that it's very difficult to prophesy, especially about the future.[1103]

There is a sense in which prophecy does for us what traveling in space has done. Much has been learned about the earth from going out there and looking back—things about weather patterns, location of natural resources, and so forth, which we could never have known from earth, where we are too close to really see what is there.

In a similar fashion, prophecy takes us out of the limitations of seeing only what our immediate circumstances allow and helps us to see the big picture. The result should be that we become better stewards of our time and other resources now and that we live our life on eternal values.[1104]

Dr. Charles C. Ryrie has pointed out that, by the law of chance, it would require two hundred billion earths, populated with four billion people each, to come up with one person who could achieve one hundred accurate prophecies without any errors in sequence. But the Bible records not one hundred but over three hundred prophecies fulfilled in Christ's first coming.[1105]

Propitiation vs. Expiation

The difference between propitiation and expiation is not always easy to understand, even though we all experience it.

Consider the case of a certain factory worker who was seriously injured on the job. After the doctors had done all they could, he was

294

still left partially paralyzed. An investigation revealed that the company was at fault because it did not provide a safe work place nor the proper safety equipment for its employees. Thus, it was liable for the dangerous conditions that resulted in this man's injury and permanent paralysis.

As we all have seen in similar situations, the court will probably award the injured man a great sum of money for his pain, suffering, and permanent injury. Once the company pays the judgment against it, it has expiated its wrongdoings. The demands of justice have been satisfied. The company no longer has any responsibility toward the injured man. That is expiation.

But we have not dealt with how the injured man feels toward the company. He may be filled with resentment, bitterness, even hatred. He may spend the rest of his life abhorring the name of that company, even though it has been directed to give him all the money he could possibly use. The *debt* that the wrong incurred has been expiated or paid for, but the *wrath* that the wrong incurred has not been propitiated.

When Christ died, he not only paid the debt for our sins but reconciled us to God by satisfying the Father's wrath. He was both an expiation and a propitiation for our sins.[1106]

Prosperity

The danger of prosperity is simple: it binds us to the world. Prosperity leads us to think that we have found our place in the world. Of course, the reality is that the world has found its place in us.[1107]

Protection, Divine

The story has been told of a believer, Frederick Nolan, who was fleeing from his enemies during a time of persecution in North Africa. Pursued by them over hill and valley with no place to hide, he fell exhausted into a wayside cave, expecting his enemies to find him soon.

Awaiting his death, he saw a spider weaving a web. Within minutes, the little bug had woven a beautiful web across the mouth of the cave. The pursuers arrived and wondered if Nolan was hiding there, but on seeing the unbroken and unmangled piece of art, thought it impossible for him to have entered the cave without dismantling the web. And so they went on. Having escaped, Nolan burst out and exclaimed:

"Where God is, a spider's web is like a wall,
Where God is not, a wall is like a spider's web."[1108]

Quiet Time

Michael E. DeBakey, heart surgeon, once observed: "For me, the solitude of early morning is the most precious time of day. There is a quiet serenity that disappears a few hours later with the hustle and bustle of the multitude. Early morning hours symbolize for me a rebirth; the anxieties, frustrations, and woes of the preceding day seem to have been washed away during the night. God has granted another day of life, another chance to do something worthwhile for humanity."[1109]

Rapture

Martin Luther said he only had two days on his calendar—today and "that day."[1110]

The story is told of a generation ago when an old farmer brought his family to the big city for the very first time. They had never seen buildings so tall or sights so impressive. The farmer dropped his wife off at a department store and took his son with him to the bank—the tallest of all the buildings. As they walked into the lobby, they saw something else they had never seen before. Two steel doors opened. A rather large and elderly woman walked in, and the big doors closed behind her. The dial over the door swept to the right and then back to the left. The doors opened and a beautiful young lady came walking out. The farmer was amazed. He turned to his son and said, "You wait right here. I'm going to get your mother and run her through that thing."

At the Rapture, we will be taken up. But we will be transformed and come back with resurrection bodies.[1111]

Reason

"He that will not reason is a bigot; he that cannot reason is a fool; and he that dares not to reason is a slave" (Sir William Drummond [1585–1649]).[1112]

We must always recognize what Blaise Pascal put so beautifully when he said, "The ultimate purpose of reason is to bring us to the place where we see that there is a limit to reason."[1113]

Reconciliation

Elizabeth Barrett Browning's parents disapproved so strongly of her marriage to Robert that they disowned her. Almost weekly, Elizabeth wrote love letters to her mother and father, asking for a reconciliation. They never once replied. After ten years of letter writing, Elizabeth received a huge box in the mail. She opened it. To her dismay and heartbreak, the box contained all of her letters to her parents. Not one of them had ever been opened!

Today those love letters are among the most beautiful in classical English literature. Had her parents opened and read only a few of them, a reconciliation might have been effected.

The Bible is God's letter of reconciliation to us. We should open and read it thoroughly and often.[1114]

Reconciliation, Ministry of

The Ministry of Reconciliation . . .
Originates with God, not man
Is personally experienced
Is universally inclusive
Is without condemnation
Is delivered by men
Is owned and accredited by God
Is voluntarily accepted
Achieves what otherwise is impossible
Is experienced moment by moment.

Ray Stedman
Authentic Christianity (Portland, OR: Mutnomah, 1985)[1115]

Redemption

A pastor of a church in Boston met a young boy in front of the sanctuary carrying a rusty cage in which several birds fluttered nervously. The pastor inquired, "Son, where did you get those birds?"

"I trapped them out in the field," the boy replied.

"What are you going to do with them?"

"I'm going to play with them, and then I guess I'll just feed them to an old cat we have at home."

When the pastor offered to buy them, the lad exclaimed, "Mister, you don't want them, they're just little old wild birds and can't sing very well."

The pastor replied, "I'll give you two dollars for the cage and the birds."

"Okay, it's a deal, but you're making a bad bargain."

The exchange was made, and the boy went away whistling, happy with his shiny coins. The pastor walked around to the back of the church property, opened the door of the small wire cage, and let the struggling creatures soar into the blue.

The next Sunday he took the empty cage into the pulpit and used it to illustrate Christ's coming to seek and to save those who—like the birds—were destined for destruction. The difference was that Christ had to purchase our freedom with his own life.[1116]

The story has been told of an orphaned boy who was living with his grandmother when their house caught fire. The grandmother, trying to get upstairs to rescue the boy, died in the flames. The boy's cries for help were finally answered by a man who climbed an iron drain pipe and came down with the boy hanging tightly to his neck.

Several weeks later, a public hearing was held to determine who would receive custody of the child. A farmer, a teacher, and the town's wealthiest citizen all gave the reasons they felt they should be chosen to give the boy a home. As they talked, the lad's eyes remained focused on the floor.

Then a stranger walked to the front and slowly took his hands from his pockets, revealing scars on them. As the crowd gasped, the boy cried out in recognition. This was the man who had saved his life and whose hands had been burned when he climbed the hot pipe. With a leap the boy threw his arms around the man's neck and held on for dear life. The other men silently walked away, leaving the boy and his rescuer alone. Those marred hands had settled the issue.[1117]

There was a young boy who lived in a New England seaport and loved to watch the boats come in from their daily catch. One day he decided to build a little sailboat all of his own. He worked for weeks, making sure each detail was just right. Finally the big day arrived. He went down to the wharf and proudly put his boat into the water. As he triumphantly observed his new sailboat, he noticed that the wind had suddenly changed, and the tiny boat was being swept out of sight. The little boy was heartbroken. Every day for a month he went back to see if his boat had been washed up on shore.

Finally, one day in the market he saw his boat in a store window. He excitedly ran into the store and told the proprietress that it was his boat. The woman only responded by saying that the boat would cost him two dollars. After pleading with her to no avail, the boy finally pulled out the money and gave it to the storeowner. As the boy was leaving the store, he said, "Little boat, you are twice mine. You are mine because I made you, and now you are mine because I bought you."[1118]

One of the clearest contemporary examples of what redemption means is found in "green stamps." Certain stores give you so many trading stamps for each dollar you spend at their store. You save up the stamps, and when you have enough, you can go to a redemption center and trade in stamps for something you want.

This transaction has two parts: purchasing the right of redemption and then claiming your merchandise. You buy the right of redemption when you make your original purchase and the store gives you the stamps as a token. Later you take the stamps to the redemption center and use them to claim something you want. Those items you redeem are not free, because in reality you already paid the price for them when you made your original purchase.

In the same way, God—by Christ's blood—has already purchased us from the power of sin, and we are redeemed. Yet God does not come for his merchandise immediately. Instead, he has given us a token of our redemption, the Holy Spirit. So we have redemption: the forgiveness of sin.[1119]

Regeneration

Many unregenerate men consider themselves to be God's children, or "sons of God." But being a product of God's handiwork does not qualify one for a sonship relationship.

A cabinetmaker constructs a cabinet. But this does not make the cabinet a "child" of the cabinetmaker. A birth process would be necessary for this. The unregenerate man who claims sonship with God "because he made me" is basing his claim merely on the fact that he is a product of God's handiwork. Like the cabinet, he lacks the new birth necessary for a sonship relationship.[1120]

We may sweep the world clean of militarism, we may scrub the world white of autocracy, we may carpet it with democracy and drape it with the flag of republicanism. We may hang on the walls the thrilling pictures of freedom: here, the signing of America's Independence; there, the thrilling portrait of Joan of Arc; yonder, the Magna Carta; and on this side, the inspiring picture of Garibaldi. We may spend energy and effort to make the world a paradise itself where the lion of capitalism can lie down with the proletarian lamb. But if we turn into that splendid room mankind with the same old heart, deceitful and desperately wicked, we may expect to clean house again not many days hence. What we need is a peace conference with the Prince of Peace.

Arthur Brisbane [1121]

Rejection

G. Campbell Morgan was one of a hundred and fifty young men who sought entrance into the Wesleyan ministry in 1888. He had passed his written exam but faced the test of giving a trial sermon in front of a panel. When the results were released, Morgan's name was among the hundred and five who were rejected.

He wired his father with one word: "Rejected." Then he sat down and wrote in his diary: "Very dark. Everything seems still. He knoweth best." The reply to his wire was quick to arrive. It read, "Rejected on earth, accepted in heaven. Dad."

As G. Campbell Morgan went on to prove, rejection on earth is often of little consequence. As his father wisely recognized, rejection on earth is of no consequence in heaven.[1122]

Religion, False

Long ago, a pastor was visiting at a couple's new home out in the country. The pastor spent the night. He was awakened the next morning by the soft voice of a soprano singing, "Nearer, My God, to Thee." He was impressed by the piety of the young hostess, since she evidently began her day in such a religious manner. At breakfast he spoke to her about it and told her how pleased he was. "Oh," she replied, "that's the hymn I boil the eggs by; three verses for soft and five for hard."[1123]

Repentance

The difficulty some have in entering the doorway to the kingdom of God is like the experience of the boy who got his hand caught inside an expensive vase. His upset parents applied soap suds and cooking oil, without success. When they seemed ready to break the vase as the only way to release the hand, the frightened boy cried, "Would it help if I let loose of the penny I'm holding?"

So it is all too often with us. We cause others great anguish and risk the truly valuable because we will not let go of the insignificant things we possess today.[1124]

Noah's message from the steps going up to the Ark was not, "Something good is going to happen to you!"

Amos was not confronted by the high priest of Israel for proclaiming, "Confession is possession!"

Jeremiah was not put into the pit for preaching, "I'm O.K., you're O.K.!"

Daniel was not put into the lion's den for telling people, "Possibility thinking will move mountains!"

John the Baptist was not forced to preach in the wilderness and eventually beheaded because he preached, "Smile, God loves you!"

The two prophets of the tribulation will not be killed for preaching, "God is in his heaven and all is right with the world!"

Instead, what was the message of all these men of God? Simple, one word: "Repent!"[1125]

George Whitefield mentioned in his journal that during his first voyage to Georgia, the ship's cook had a bad drinking problem. When the cook was reproved for it and other sins, he boasted that he would be wicked until the last two years of his life, and then he would reform.

Whitefield added that within six hours of the time the cook made his boastful statement, he died of an illness related to his drinking.[1126]

Reputation

Rabbi Simon said, "There are three crowns: the crown of [the study of] the Law, the crown of priesthood, and the crown of royalty, but the crown of a good name surpasses them all" (*Mishnah Avoth* 4.13).[1127]

We may be known by the following, according to A. W. Tozer:

1. What we want most
2. What we think about most
3. How we use our money
4. What we do with our leisure time
5. The company we enjoy
6. Who and what we admire
7. What we laugh at[1128]

Resentment

Leonard Holt was a paragon of respectability. He was a middle-aged, hard-working lab technician who had worked at the same Pennsylvania paper mill for nineteen years. Having been a Boy Scout leader, an affectionate father, a member of the local fire brigade, and a regular church attender, he was admired as a model in his community. Until that image exploded in a well-planned hour of bloodshed one brisk October morning.

A proficient marksman, Leonard Holt stuffed two pistols in his coat pockets and drove to the mill. He stalked slowly into his shop and began shooting with calculated frenzy. He filled several co-workers with two or three bullets apiece, firing more than thirty shots, killing some men he had known for more than fifteen years. When the posse found him standing defiantly in his doorway, he snarled, "Come and get me, you _____. I'm not taking any more of your _____ !" Bewilderment swept the community.

Puzzled policemen and friends finally found a train of logic behind his brief reign of terror. Down deep within the heart of Leonard Holt rumbled the giant of resentment. His monk-like exterior concealed the seething hatred within. The investigation yielded the following facts. Several victims had been promoted over him while he remained in the same position. More than one in Holt's carpool had quit riding with him due to his reckless driving. The man was brimming with resentment—rage that could be held no longer. Beneath his picture in *Time*, the caption told the story: "Responsible, Respectable, and Resentful."[1129]

Responsibility

When a flock of crows invades a field of corn, the birds customarily station two sentries in a nearby tree to keep watch and warn the rest of any danger. In *Character Sketches*, Bill Gothard relates the story of two people who succeeded in sneaking up on the flock and scaring them before the sentries had given warning. The birds burst into flight, immediately attacked and killed the two sentries, and only then flew off.[1130]

Restitution

New York—A 31-year-old accountant repaid the $40 he stole 15 years ago from an amusement park—and added $286 interest to atone for his previous theft. Jeff Street was a 16-year-old parking lot attendant at the amusement park in 1969. Recently, he said, "I was praying at my desk and reading the Word, and it just came to me. It wasn't the Lord's voice, but it came from within me—I had to pay back the money," Street said. [Cited in *Dallas Morning News*, November 11, 1984.][1131]

Resurrection, Believers'

Chrysostom, early church father and orator, deplored the ostentatious public lamentations that were made at Christian funerals in his day: "When I behold the wailings in public places, the groanings over those who have departed this life, the howlings and all the other unseemly behavior, I am ashamed before the heathen and the Jews and heretics who see it, and indeed before all who for this reason laugh us to scorn."

He complained that such conduct had the effect of nullifying his teaching on the resurrection and encouraged the heathen to continue in unbelief. He asked what could be more unseemly than for a person who professes to be crucified to the world to tear his hair and shriek hysterically in the presence of death.

"Those who are really worthy of being lamented," Chrysostom admonished, "are the ones who are still in fear and trembling at the prospect of death and have no faith at all in the resurrection." Then he drove home his point with these arresting words: "May God grant that you all depart this life unwailed!"[1132]

John G. Paton, a nineteenth-century missionary to the South Seas, met opposition to leaving his home in Scotland and going to preach to the cannibalistic peoples of the New Hebrides Islands. A well-meaning church member moaned to him, "The cannibals, the cannibals! You will be eaten by the cannibals!"

Without hesitation, Paton replied, "I confess to you that if I can live and die serving my Lord Jesus Christ, it makes no difference to me whether I am eaten by cannibals or by worms; for in that Great Day of Resurrection, my body will rise as fair as yours in the likeness of our risen Redeemer!"[1133]

Resurrection, Christ's

Dateline Jerusalem—On the eve of the annual celebration of the resurrection of Jesus of Nazareth, the 1 million inhabitants of this city were shocked by the announcement that a body, identified as that of Jesus, was found in a long-neglected tomb just outside the boundary of the city.

Rumors had been circulating the last week that a very important discovery was about to be announced. The news, however, far outstrips all of our wildest guesses. The initial reaction of Christians here and around the world has been one of astonishment, bewilderment, and defensive disbelief. We will have to wait and see just what effect this discovery will have on the 2,000-year-old religion. To the mind of this unbelieving writer, it appears that Christianity will have to take its place on the same level with the other religions of the world. No longer can its followers claim that, unlike other religions, the tomb of its founder is empty. Evidently a 2,000-year-old lie has come to an end.

Paul states that IF the above were true, your faith in Christ is worthless and you are still under the curse of your sins. Has your mind and heart grasped the eternal significance of the resurrection of Jesus Christ?[1134]

John Singleton Copley, one of the great legal minds in British history and three times High Chancellor of England, wrote, "I know pretty well what evidence is, and I tell you, such evidence as that for the resurrection has never broken down yet."[1135]

General Wellington commanded the victorious forces at the great battle of Waterloo that effectively ended the Napoleonic Wars. The story has been told that when the battle was over, Wellington sent the great news of his victory to England. A series of stations, one within sight of the next, had been established to send code messages between England and the continent. The message to be sent was "Wellington defeated Napoleon at Waterloo." Meanwhile a fog set in and interrupted the message sending. As a result, people only saw news of "Wellington defeated—" Later, the fog cleared and the full message continued, which was quite different from the outcome that the people originally thought had happened!

The same is true today. When many look at what happened on Good Friday, the death of Christ, they see only "defeat." Yet, on Easter, at the Resurrection, God's message was completed. The resurrection spelled "victory."[1136]

Hugh Schonfield's *Passover Plot* is one of the literary attempts to explain away the events of the crucifixion and the resurrection. But it, like all the others, relies on that ancient lie circulated in the very first century by the soldiers who were paid to say that the friends of Jesus had come and stolen his body away. But no one has ever been able to explain how that could happen.[1137]

The originator of a new religion came to the great French diplomat-statesman Charles Maurice de Talleyrand-Périgord and complained that he could not make any converts. "What would you suggest I do?" he asked.

"I should recommend," said Talleyrand, "that you get yourself crucified, and then die, but be sure to rise again the third day."[1138]

Revelation, General

There is nothing like nature to unfold truth about God. Nature is constantly shouting to us about the wisdom and the power of God. It gives a sense of awe and mystery to life. Even atheists cannot fully escape this.

Robert Browning has written a verse about a certain young man who has determined that he is going to build his life without God. He has his philosophies all worked out, and none of them include God. But then he admits to an older friend:

> Just when we are safest, there's a sunset-touch,
> A fancy from a flower-bell, someone's death,
> A chorus-ending from Euripides.
> And that's enough for fifty hopes and fears;
> The Grand Perhaps.[1139]

God's revelation in nature may be likened to a concert performed by an orchestra. Some people who come to listen hear only the instruments as they express the melody and harmony of the music. But others who come are familiar with the composer and know the words that go with the music. These hear more than the music.

In much the same way, only those who have a personal relationship with the Creator through Jesus Christ can really see in all of creation the fullness of what God intended to communicate through it.[1140]

Revival

A man once came to Gipsy Smith, the celebrated English evangelist of an earlier time, and asked him how to have revival. Asked Gipsy, "Do you have a place where you can pray?"

"Yes," was the reply.

"Tell you what to do, you go to that place, and take a piece of chalk along. Kneel down there, and with the chalk draw a complete circle all around you—and pray for God to send revival on everything inside of the circle. Stay there until He answers—and you will have revival."[1141]

Reward, Eternal

Our eternal reward reflects the amount of God's glory that we have allowed to shine through us. It is like a chandelier that has many light bulbs, some 25 watt, some 50 watt, and some 100 watt. The light bulbs as a whole all give and contribute light to the room. That's the way it will be in heaven, but some of us will be contributing only 25 watts, others 50 and still others a full 100 watts. How much of God's light do you want to shine through you?[1142]

"We must not be troubled by unbelievers when they say that this promise of reward makes the Christian life a mercenary affair. There are different kinds of reward. There is the reward which has no natural connection with the things you do to earn it, and is quite foreign to the desires that ought to accompany those things. Money is not the natural reward of love; that is why we call a man a mercenary if he married a woman for the sake of her money. But marriage is the proper reward for a real lover, and he is not mercenary for desiring it. . . . The proper rewards are not simply tacked on to the activity for which they are given, but are the activity itself in consummation" (C. S. Lewis, *The Weight of Glory* [New York: Macmillan, 1980]).[1143]

Henry C. Morrison, after serving for forty years on the African mission field, headed home by boat. On that same boat also rode Theodore Roosevelt. Morrison was quite dejected when, on entering New York harbor, President Roosevelt received a great fanfare as he arrived home. Morrison thought he should get some recognition for forty years in the Lord's service.

Then a small voice came to Morrison and said, "Henry—you're not home yet."[1144]

Rewards, Loss of

In the 1980 Boston Marathon, a young unknown runner named Rosie Ruiz was initially declared the winner in the women's division of

306

the 26-mile race. An investigation followed and it was discovered that this was only the second marathon in which she had ever run, she had no coach, she trained on an exercise cycle (others did 120 miles of road work per week), and she had not been seen by any of the other women runners in the race. It was speculated that she probably rode a subway for 16 miles to get near the finish line. Rosie was disqualified and lost the reward—not just the prize for finishing first, but the more lasting satisfaction of attaining a difficult goal.[1145]

Righteousness, Believers'

If we look through a piece of red glass, everything is red. If we look through a piece of blue glass, everything is blue. If we look through a piece of yellow glass, everything is yellow, and so on.

When we believe in Jesus Christ as our Savior, God looks at us through the Lord Jesus Christ. He sees us in all the white holiness of his Son. Our sins are imputed to the account of Christ and his righteousness to our account.[1146]

The Chinese character for "righteousness" is most interesting. It is composed of two separate characters—one standing for a lamb, the other for me. When "lamb" is placed directly above "me," a new character—"righteousness" is formed.

This is a helpful picture of the grace of God. Between me, the sinner, and God, the Holy One, there is interposed by faith the Lamb of God. By virtue of his sacrifice, he has received me on the ground of faith, and I have become righteous in his sight.[1147]

Righteousness, National

The instructive motto of the State of Hawaii is a result of the influence of the Protestant missionaries who first came to Hawaii in 1820. It expresses a great truth in the Hawaiian language: *Ua mau ke ia o ka aina i ka pono*, which means, "The life of the land is preserved in righteousness."

Righteousness is what preserves a nation, not a Declaration of Independence or a Constitution, and not even Congress or its laws. What sustains and perpetuates a national identity is the righteousness of its people—the reflection of their recognizing their need for God, worked out in their relationships with one another.[1148]

Righteousness, Personal

Blackmailers once sent C. H. Spurgeon a letter to the effect that if he did not place a certain amount of money in a certain place at a certain time, they would publish some things in the newspapers that would defame him and ruin his public ministry. Spurgeon left at that station a letter in reply: "You and your like are requested to publish all you know about me across the heavens." He knew his life was blameless in the eyes of men and, therefore, they could not touch his character.[1149]

Righteousness, Quest for

"He who would gain righteousness by faith and works is as the dog who runs along a stream with a piece of meat in his mouth, and, deceived by the reflection of the meat in the water, opens his mouth to snap at it, and so loses both the meat and the reflection" (Martin Luther, *Treatise on Christian Liberty* [Philadelphia: Fortress, 1943]).[1150]

Rights

During a heated debate at a church's board meeting, one of the overheated deacons rose to his feet and with clenched fists declared, "I have my rights!"

Quickly and sensitively, one of the older men replied, "You don't mean that. If we had our rights we would all be in hell."[1151]

Rivalry

On the American frontier, denominational differences were taken seriously. The story is told of a young Methodist minister who was asked to conduct a funeral for a Baptist. Since ministers were in short supply and he was the only one for miles around, he was unsure what to do. He performed the funeral and wrote to his bishop, asking if he had made the right decision and requesting some general guidelines for the future. His bishop's reply was brief. "Bury all the Baptists you can."[1152]

Roles

A woman had just returned from a meeting of the National Organization for Women (NOW) when her five-year-old daughter greeted her with the news that she wanted to be a nurse when she grew up. "A nurse!" her mother exclaimed. "Listen, Lisa, just because you're female doesn't mean you have to settle for being a nurse. You can be a surgeon, a lawyer, a banker, President of the United States. You can be anything!"

The daughter looked a little dubious as she asked, "Anything? Anything at all?" As she thought about it, her face was filled with ambition and enthusiasm. "All right," she said. "I'll be a horse."[1153]

Rulers

Remember that the powers-that-be will someday be the powers-that-have-been.[1154]

Sacrifice

Back in the days of the Great Depression a Missouri man named John Griffith was the controller of a great railroad drawbridge across the Mississippi River. One day in the summer of 1937 he decided to take his eight-year-old son, Greg, with him to work. At noon, John Griffith put the bridge up to allow ships to pass and sat on the observation deck with his son to eat lunch. Time passed quickly. Suddenly he was startled by the shrieking of a train whistle in the distance. He quickly looked at his watch and noticed it was 1:07—the Memphis Express, with four hundred passengers on board, was roaring toward the raised bridge! He leaped from the observation deck and ran back to the control tower. Just before throwing the master lever he glanced down for any ships below. There a sight caught his eye that caused his heart to leap poundingly into his throat. Greg had slipped from the observation deck and had fallen into the massive gears that operate the bridge. His left leg was caught in the cogs of the two main gears! Desperately John's mind whirled to devise a rescue plan. But as soon as he thought of a possibility he knew there was no way it could be done.

Again, with alarming closeness, the train whistle shrieked in the air. He could hear the clicking of the locomotive wheels over the tracks. That was his son down there—yet there were four hundred passengers on the train. John knew what he had to do, so he buried his head in his left arm and pushed the master switch forward. That great massive bridge lowered into place just as the Memphis Express began to roar across the river. When John Griffith lifted his head with his face smeared with tears, he looked into the passing windows of the train. There were businessmen casually reading their afternoon papers, finely dressed ladies in the dining car sipping coffee, and children pushing long spoons into their dishes of ice cream. No one looked at the control house, and no one looked at the great gear box. With wrenching agony, John Griffith cried out at the steel train: "I sacrificed my son for you people! Don't you care?" The train rushed by, but nobody heard the father's words, which recalled Lamentations 1:12: "Is it nothing to you, all who pass by?"

(Condensed and adapted from "Is It Nothing to You?" by Dr. D. James Kennedy, March 19, 1978, Coral Ridge Presbyterian Church, Ft. Lauderdale, Florida.)[1155]

Sacrificial Lamb

When telling his young daughter the story of Abraham and Isaac, a father related how God had finally told Abraham not to kill Isaac and had provided a sacrificial lamb instead. The little girl looked up with a sad expression and said, "I don't like killing lambs." The father was speechless for a moment and then realized what traumatic and memorable events such sacrifices were. How serious the killing of a lamb for sacrifice and how destructive the reason for the sacrifice: sin. If the killing of a pure white lamb seems horrendous, how immeasurably more was the crucifixion of the Lamb of God![1156]

Saints

A little boy attended a church that had beautiful stained-glass windows. He was told that the windows contained pictures of Saint Matthew, Saint Mark, Saint Luke, Saint John, Saint Paul, and other saints. One day he was asked, "What is a saint?" He replied, "A saint is a person whom the light shines through."[1157]

The word *saint* has come far from its original New Testament meaning. When we think of a "saint," we think of some stylized human figure depicted in stained glass, or of a person long dead who has been officially declared as an ecclesiastical relic. However, one of the clearest definitions is "A saint is a dead sinner, revised and edited."[1158]

Salvation, Assurance of

Several years ago one of the astronauts who walked on the moon was interviewed and asked, "What do you think about as you stood on the moon and looked back at the earth?" The astronaut replied, "I remembered how the spacecraft was built by the lowest bidder."

We as Christians can rejoice that the work of salvation did not go to the "lowest bidder" but was performed by an infinite God. There will never be a deficiency in his work. Our salvation is as sure as the architect of that salvation, Almighty God.[1159]

Picture a small lake in the north when winter has just made itself at home. A wooden dock juts out into the thin shell of ice on the pond. Over the whole scene lies a cotton cushion of snow. A young lad walks out onto the dock, long familiar to him from lazy summer days of fishing. He daydreams at the end of the dock, but suddenly his sister's call from shore arouses him. As he turns around to see her, he loses his balance, one of his feet lands on the ice, and he crashes into the icy water.

You see, as long as both his feet were solidly planted on the wooden dock, the boy stood securely. But as soon as he shifted one foot to the ice, even though by mistake, he toppled into the water.

As long as we keep our trust totally on Christ's finished work on the cross, we stand assured of God's promise of eternal life. But as soon as we rest any weight on the thin ice of our own efforts, we will topple into the icy waters of insecurity.[1160]

There is a commonly known story that comes from the life of Martin Luther. It is said that the devil approached Luther one day and tried to use the fact that every person is fallible. He presented the Reformer with a long list of sins of which he was guilty. When he had finished reading, Luther said to Satan, "Think a little harder; you must have forgotten some." This the devil did and added other sins to the list. At the conclusion of this exchange, Martin Luther simply said, "That's fine. Now write across that list in red ink, 'The blood of Jesus Christ, His Son, cleanses us from all sin.' " There was nothing the devil could say to that.[1161]

There is a story about a boy flying a kite. The kite was so high that it had disappeared into the clouds. A man came by and asked, "Why are you holding on to that string?" The boy said, "I've got a kite up there." The man looked up and said, "I don't see it." The boy replied, "Well, I know it's there because I can feel the tug."

That's like the witness of the Holy Spirit within us. We may not

311

always see the evidence, but we feel a tug in our hearts constantly, letting us know that we are in touch with God.[1162]

C. H. Spurgeon is quoted as saying that he was so sure of his salvation that he could grab on to a cornstalk and swing out over the fires of hell, look into the face of the devil, and sing, "Blessed assurance, Jesus is mine!"

When the storms of life, the winds of trouble, and the sea of discomfort and emotional agony seem to overwhelm, we have to say with the songwriter, "Our hope is built on nothing less than Jesus' blood and righteousness. . . . We dare not trust the sweetest frame, but wholly lean on Jesus' name."[1163]

Salvation, Consequences of

The movie *The Hanging Tree* was set in a western gold-mining camp in the late 1800s. Gary Cooper played the role of doctor for the camp. One day, a young boy was seen robbing gold from the camp. He was shot from a distance but managed to hobble into hiding. All hands in the camp spread out to see who would be the first to kill him for this offense. The doctor found the hurt, frightened youth. He took him into his cabin, nursed him, and removed the bullet. After the boy regained consciousness, he inquired what the doctor would do with him now. The doctor held the slug in the boy's face and said, "You will be my servant for as long as I want you to be, maybe forever, because that is how long you would be dead if this slug had remained in you."

That is the length of condemnation for the slug of sin if it remains in us. The Great Physician has already performed the surgery to remove the slug. The painless operation of trust in him is the only requirement. It is our privilege to be servants of the One who healed us forever, for without his healing, we also would be dead forever.[1164]

Salvation, Day of

The story is told of a time when Satan held a strategy session for subverting those who were close to salvation. "What shall we do?" asked Satan. A daring demon stood and shouted, "I have it! I know what we can do! We can tell men that there is no life after death, that they die like animals." Satan's face fell as he answered, "It will never work. Man is not ignorant; even atheists admit of times when they sense a tomorrow after death."

Another demon spoke, "Here's the solution! Let's say there is no God or if there ever was, he is dead—because even if he started the universe, he has left it now." Satan replied in dismay, "That won't work either; most of them know there *is* a God, even though they don't seek him."

Other ideas were presented, but none brought hope to Satan and his underlings. Finally, as they were about to give up, one demon leaped in glee, "I have it! A sure solution!" The other demons crowded around to hear the plan. "Go tell them that God is real and the Bible is God's Word." A gasp came from the audience as the demon continued, "And tell them that Jesus is God's Son and frees men from sin." The other demons were horror-stricken, thinking that their associate had gone bananas, until, with a smile, he added, "*Then* tell them that this is not the best time to choose Christ. Help them make excuses for delaying their decision. Tell them there is no hurry!" The demons danced in delight, realizing a workable plan had been discovered.[1165]

Salvation, Desire for

The well-known scientist and author Carl Sagan, in a PBS documentary titled "Chariots of the Gods," commented on the new optimism that there is life elsewhere in the universe: "It's nice to think that there is someone out there that can help us."

Unfortunately, this remark implies that for Sagan there is no God, and so his hope of help from other beings is a blind hope, a hope that assumes that other beings exist and that their race will not be affected with the depravity that is so evident in all human endeavor. And that they would be interested in helping us.[1166]

Salvation, Gift of

A group of believers was meeting by a river when one of their group fell into the water. It was obvious that the poor fellow couldn't swim, as he thrashed about wildly. One of the believers was a strong swimmer and was called on to jump in and save the man before he drowned. But though able to save the drowning man, he just watched until the wild struggles subsided. Then he dove in and pulled the man to safety.

When the rescue was over, the rescuer explained his slowness to act. "If I had jumped in immediately, he would have been strong enough to drown us both. Only by waiting until he was too exhausted to try to save himself, could I save him."

It seems to be all too easy for us to be like that drowning man. Our self-efforts can actually prevent us from being saved! Unfortunately, some people must reach the point of being too exhausted to continue trying to save themselves (by dealing with their own sin) before they become willing to trust in the Savior and accept his gift of salvation.[1167]

Suppose your best friend came by one day with a special gift for you. How would you respond? Would you immediately pull out your purse or wallet for some money to help pay for the gift? Of course not. To do so would be a great insult!

A gift must be accepted for what it is—something freely given and unmerited. If you have to pay for a gift or do something to deserve or earn it, it is not a gift. True gifts are freely given and freely received. To attempt to give or receive a gift in any other manner makes it not a gift.

So it is with our salvation. God offers us salvation as a free gift. He does not attach strings to it, because to do so makes it something other than a gift. In addition, any attempt on our part, no matter how small, to pay for our salvation by doing something or giving up something is an insult to God. No one in heaven will ever be able to say, "Look at me! I made it! With a little help from God, I made it!" Salvation is all by God. Not even the smallest part of it is the result of what we do or do not do. As God says in his Word, "For it is by grace you have been saved through faith—and this not from yourselves, it is the gift of God—not by works, so that no one can boast" (Eph. 2:8–9, NIV).[1168]

The story has been told of a wealthy man who became a Christian. He tried to reach his friends for Christ and told them, with tremendous enthusiasm, what had happened to him, how the Lord had changed his whole life and even saved his marriage. But he found that his words seemed to fall on deaf ears. His friends were not interested.

Since this man had great wealth, he developed a plan that would use this wealth to reach his friends. First he wrote out a check for a million dollars, which everyone knew he would easily be good for. He then visited his friends in turn and said, "I have always highly regarded you as a friend and have wanted to do something for you. Would you receive this check as a gift from me?"

People would look at the check and, when they saw the amount of it, they would hand it back and say, "I can't take that from you." He tried to give the check to many of his friends, but no one would take it, although it was a valid and sincere offer. Finally the man realized that people are not willing to receive great gifts without having some part in it.

That may be why some people hesitate to accept God's offer of eternal life as a free gift.[1169]

The story has been told of a missionary who became a good friend of an Indian pearl diver. The two had spent many hours together discussing salvation, but the Indian could not understand anything so precious being free. Instead, in making preparation for the life to come, the diver was going to walk the nine hundred miles to Delhi on his knees. He thought this would buy entrance into heaven for him. The missionary struggled to communicate to his friend that it is impossible to buy entrance into heaven because the price would be too costly. Instead, he said, Jesus had died to buy it *for* us.

Before he left for his pilgrimage, the Indian gave the missionary the largest and most perfect pearl he had ever seen. The missionary offered to buy it, but the diver became upset and said that the pearl was beyond price, that his only son had lost his life in the attempt to get it. The pearl was worth the life blood of his son. As he said this, suddenly the diver understood that God was offering him salvation as a priceless gift. It is so precious that no man could buy it. It had cost God the life's blood of his Son. The veil was lifted; he understood at last.[1170]

Salvation, Need for

A little boy came running into the house after playing outside. His mother stopped him and asked what was on his right hand. He replied, "Oh, just a little mud." His mother then asked if he was planning on getting it off his hand. He thought for a moment and said, "Sure, Mom. I'll just wipe it off with my other hand." There was only one problem with the plan, one dirty hand plus one clean hand equals two dirty hands.

Many people are like that little boy, they see the evil and wrongs in their life and think they can make themselves clean by bringing the good in their life to bear on the problem. But it doesn't work that way. We all need a way to be made morally and spiritually clean, and we will never succeed in doing it ourselves. The only solution is to be found in the blood of Jesus Christ, which cleanses us from all of our sins.[1171]

> Humpty Dumpty sat on a wall,
> Humpty Dumpty had a great fall;
> All the king's horses
> And all the king's men
> Couldn't put Humpty together again.

315

It is claimed that "Humpty Dumpty" was a story about a certain political situation in England, but it is also a parable about man. Man has had a great fall. The evidence is the havoc in all our lives. And we all are helpless to put ourselves back together again. But there is someone who can: it is Jesus, the One who made everyone Humpty Dumpty to begin with. He is the One who can take the shattered, scattered fragments of your life and put them back together again. If you are not yet a Christian, it is Jesus who can forgive your sins and create you anew. If you are a Christian, but your life is in disarray, he will restore things to order.[1172]

Before going to a dentist we usually brush our teeth with extra care to ensure their spotlessness under examination. But later the dentist can swish a red liquid around our mouth, which reveals (to our horror) a tremendous amount of plaque and other undesirable material that we could not remove in spite of all our brushing. The dentist alone has the equipment to adequately remove it.

Likewise, we may try on our own to be clean before God and may even do a good job of convincing ourselves that we are in good shape. But God's Spirit has a way of exposing both our sinfulness and the need for a divine "dentist" to make us clean.[1173]

Salvation, Rejection of

Scene: Big Thompson Flood on July 31, 1976, in the 35-mile-long, mountain-rimmed canyon linking Estes Park and Loveland, Colorado. A 19-foot wall of water, resulting from a furious thunderstorm, roared through the canyon and killed 129 people. This account is given by the wife of one of the victims. The name of the husband has been altered to conceal identities:

> Gary was an engineer, and to his trained eye the narrowness of the canyon and the rapidly rising river spelled trouble. Anyhow, he came over to tell me that he was going to our friends' cabin to warn them and the people in cabins across the way to leave at once for higher ground.
>
> Although I asked to go with him, Gary insisted that I stay at the hotel. He said that he would be back for me, but if he didn't return in thirty minutes, I was to climb to the top of the mountain without him. He said he'd catch up with me there. He told the hotel owner and his wife (where we were staying) to be sure to get their two youngsters, an eleven-year-old boy and eight-year-old girl, out of bed and dressed right away. Then

Gary drove off in such a hurry that he forgot to kiss me good-bye. I have no last kiss to remember.

In exactly thirty minutes, I followed Gary's instructions and started to climb up the rough, rocky side of the mountain. . . . In the canyon down below, now filled with water, I saw the tops of cars bob by; even a Greyhound bus swept past. I saw the hotel where we were to meet our friends break apart and float away. I wondered if the hotel owner, his wife, and their children were safe. All four, I later learned, were killed.

The warning of disaster and death was clear, the offer of an available salvation understood, the rejection tragic. In retrospect, we can all see the foolishness of those who rejected Gary's warning. But can we see the foolishness of rejecting the Bible's warning about what will happen to those who do not accept God's offer of salvation?[1174]

A certain atheistic barber was conversing with a minister as they rode through the slums of a large city. Said the unbeliever, "If there is a loving God, how can he permit all this poverty, suffering, and violence among these people? Why doesn't he save them from all this?"

Just then a disheveled bum crossed the street. He was unshaven and filthy, with long scraggly hair hanging down his neck. The minister pointed to him and said, "You are a barber and claim to be a good one, so why do you allow that man to go unkempt and unshaven?"

"Why, why . . ." the barber stuttered, "he never gave me a chance to fix him up."

"Exactly," said the minister. "Men are what they are because they reject God's help."[1175]

In the year 1829, a Philadelphia man named George Wilson robbed the U. S. mails, killing someone in the process. Wilson was arrested, brought to trial, found guilty, and sentenced to be hanged. Some friends intervened in his behalf and were finally able to obtain a pardon for him from President Andrew Jackson. But, when he was informed of this, George Wilson refused to accept the pardon!

The sheriff was unwilling to enact the sentence—for how could he hang a pardoned man? An appeal was sent to President Jackson. The perplexed President turned to the United States Supreme Court to decide the case. Chief Justice Marshall ruled that a pardon is a piece of paper, the value of which depends on its acceptance by the person implicated. It is hardly to be supposed that a person under the sentence of death would refuse to accept a pardon, but if it *is* refused, it is then not a pardon. George Wilson must be hanged. So George Wilson was executed, although his pardon lay on the sheriff's desk.

So, too, do some of us reject the gift of salvation by refusing the pardon thereby offered.[1176]

Salvation, Understanding of

I don't understand electricity, but I'm no fool—I'm not going to sit around in the dark till I do. I don't understand the thermodynamics of internal combustion and the hydraulics of an automatic transmission either, but I'm no fool—I'm not going to stay in one place until I do. The truth is that I don't understand a great deal of the things that are part of my everyday life, but I make them a part of my life anyway.

The same is true of salvation. No one will fully understand how God could become man, how he could die, how his death could be the basis for our forgiveness, how he could give you and me a new life, and all of the other aspects of salvation. But only a fool would ignore such a great opportunity just because he didn't understand it.[1177]

Salvation, Works and

You would not scramble five good eggs and one rotten egg and serve the mixture to guests, expecting it to be acceptable. Even less can you serve up to God a life that has the good things in it tainted with deeds and thoughts that are rotten, and expect it to be acceptable to God.

If you wanted to get to heaven by your good works, then you would have to be perfect, which means complete obedience to God *at all times.* But all of us have fallen short of this![1178]

A leading manufacturing company developed a new cake mix that required only water to be added. Tests were run, surveys were made, and the cake mix was found to be of superior quality to the other mixes available. It tasted good, it was easy to use, and it made a moist, tender cake. The company spent large sums of money on an advertising campaign and then released the cake mix to the general market. But few people bought the new cake mix.

The company then spent more money on a survey to find out why the cake mix didn't sell. Based on the results of this survey, the company recalled the mix, reworked the formula, and released the revised cake mix. The new cake mix required that one add not only water, but also an egg. It sold like hot cakes and is now a leading product in the field. You see, the first cake mix was just too simple to be believable. People would not accept it. The same is true of salvation by grace.[1179]

An old parable says, "A silly servant who is told to open the door sets his shoulder to it and pushes with all his might; but the door stirs not, and he cannot enter, use what strength he may. Another comes with a key and easily unlocks the door and enters right readily."

Those who would be saved by works are pushing at heaven's gate without result; but faith is the key that opens the gate at once.[1180]

Do you recall the last time you went to a nice restaurant with a friend? Perhaps, after a great meal, the waiter brought the check, and before you knew it your friend had paid the tab.

Do you remember how you felt? That you wanted somehow to even the score? Perhaps you vowed to pick up the tab the next time you went out? These feelings are quite natural. We like to be independent, not obligated to anyone for anything. For the natural man, the same principle carries over into the way he views religion, for the natural man tries to earn his way into God's favor.[1181]

The last words of the Buddha, as he was dying, are given as, "And now, O priests, I take my leave of you; all the constituents of being are transitory; work out your salvation with diligence."

As John Noss, the noted religion scholar explains, "Like Mahavira (founder of Jainism), the Buddha showed each disciple how to rely for salvation upon himself, on his own powers, focused upon redemption by spiritual self-discipline. Here was the strictest sort of humanism in religion." (Cited in John Noss, *Man's Religions* [New York: Macmillan, 1984], pp. 127, 129.)[1182]

"I began to fast twice a week for thirty-six hours together, prayed many times a day and received the sacrament every Lord's Day. I fasted myself almost to death all the forty days of Lent, during which I made it a point of duty never to go less than three times a day to public worship, besides seven times a day to my private prayers. Yet I knew no

319

more that I was to be born a new creature in Christ Jesus than if I had never been born at all." (Cited in Arnold Dalimore, *George Whitefield* [Westchester, Ill.: Good News, 1980], Vol. 1, p. 60.)[1183]

Sanctification

The story has been told of a do-it-yourselfer who went into a hardware store early one morning and asked for a saw. The salesman took a chain saw from the shelf and commented that it was their "newest model, with the latest in technology, guaranteed to cut ten cords of firewood a day." The customer thought that sounded pretty good, so he bought it on the spot.

The next day the customer returned, looking somewhat exhausted. "Something must be wrong with this saw," he moaned. "I worked as hard as I could and only managed to cut three cords of wood. I used to do four with my old-fashioned saw." Looking confused, the salesman said, "Here, let me try it out back on some wood we keep there." They went to the woodpile, the salesman pulled the cord, and as the motor went *Vvvrooommm*, the customer leaped back and exclaimed, "What's that noise?"

The customer trying to saw wood without the power of the saw to help him is very much like the believer who attempts to live the Christian life without the daily empowerment of the Spirit.[1184]

Sanctification, Instant

Charlie Waters, former strong safety for the Dallas Cowboys football team, tells a story about Frank Howard, who had been Charlie's college coach. When Frank Howard was head coach at Clemson University, he went out to practice one Monday before a big game with his first- and third-string quarterbacks out with injuries. That left him with his second-, fourth-, and fifth-string QB's to play the coming Saturday. In the first five minutes of practice, his starting quarterback (previously second-stringer) hurt his knee. That elevated the fourth-stringer to first-string position and put the fifth-stringer on the second team. About ten minutes later, that replacement QB hurt his knee. Well, the fifth-stringer was now next in line for the first team.

Coach Howard blew the whistle and gathered all the players around him. He took the one remaining QB, put his arm around him, and said in his gruff voice, "Son, do you believe in magic?" The QB said in a halfhearted way, "Well, sort of." Coach Howard looked at him, pointed his five fingers at him like a magician, and said, "Poof! You are now a first-string quarterback."

Many people expect the Christian life to work in the same manner— "Poof! All your problems are now solved!"[1185]

Sanctification, Process of

God deals with some people like grapes. He seems to take them in one bite, to take hold of their whole life all at once. Others are dealt with more like onions. God seems to take them one layer at a time.[1186]

Construction activity is going on as God is building his church. You probably have seen the button given out at the Basic Youth Conflicts Seminars that has the letters "PBPGINTWMY" on it. It is designed, of course, to evoke the question, "What do all of those letters mean?" The answer is: "Please Be Patient, God Is Not Through With Me Yet." It is true that we are "under construction."[1187]

God's work of grace apparently moves downward through our physical body. The last part of us to experience full salvation seems to be our *right foot!* Actually, the way we act behind the wheel of a car is often more indicative of our walk with God than the way we act praying in a pew or smiling over a well-marked Bible. So, if we occasionally *must* speed, maybe it would help to sing loudly:

At 45 m.p.h.—"God Will Take Care of You"
At 55 m.p.h.—"Guide Me, O Thou Great Jehovah"
At 65 m.p.h.—"Nearer, My God, to Thee"
At 75 m.p.h.—"Nearer, Still Nearer!"
At 85 m.p.h.—"This World Is Not My Home"
At 95 m.p.h.—"Lord, I'm Coming Home"
Over 100 m.p.h.—"Precious Memories"[1188]

The process of sanctification is something like the springtime ritual of "scalping" a lawn. After months of inactivity and apparent deadness the thick and tangled thatch of dead and decaying grass must be violently removed to allow the fresh, new, green growth to appear.

So God uses the trials and problems of our Christian life to strip away the worthless and self-defeating habits of our old nature. This allows the glorious new nature, God's own loving, holy character, to appear and triumph through us.[1189]

The process of sanctification can be compared to an iceberg, which is almost 90 percent under water. As the sun shines on the iceberg, the exposed part melts, moving the lower part upward.

In the same way, we are usually aware of only a small part of our sinfulness and need, which is all we can deal with at any one time. However, as the light of God's work in our lives changes us in the areas we know about, we become aware of new areas needing the work of God.[1190]

A little boy had a toothache and knew that if he went to his mother, she would give him something to deaden the pain and let him get to sleep that night. But he did not go to his mother, at least not until the pain was very bad, because he knew she would also do something else—take him to the dentist the next morning. He could not get what he wanted, immediate relief from pain, without getting something more, having his tooth repaired. And, since he knew dentists, he knew that something else would probably happen to his mouth, because dentists tend to fiddle about with other teeth, those that have not yet begun to ache.

Our Lord is like a dentist. People go to him to be cured of some particular sin. Well, he will cure us of that sin, all right, but he will not stop there. That may be all you asked for, but if you call him in, he is likely to give you the full treatment.[1191]

Satan

Some people think that there is no Satan. Perhaps the following story will be instructive to them.

Once there was a boxer who was being badly beaten. Battered and bruised, he leaned over the ropes and said to his trainer, "Throw in the towel! This guy is killing me!"

The trainer said, "Oh, no, he's not. He's not even hitting you. He hasn't laid a glove on you!"

At that point the boxer wiped the blood away from his eye and said, "Well, then, I wish you'd watch that referee. *Somebody* is sure hitting me!"[1192]

Savior

Two construction workers once fell into a deep pit. One said to the other, "Save me from this wretched place. Please get me out of the dirt and mud." The other replied, "You idiot, how can I? I am in the same plight as you." Since they were both in the pit, neither one could help the other. Then they heard a voice from above calling to them to grasp a rope. A third worker had not fallen into the pit, so he was the only one who could save them. He brought help from above.

The very best man among the prophets could not save us from the pit of sin because he, too, was a sinner just as we are. He landed in the same pit we did. But Jesus was God and thus was not sinful. He came from above to save us from the horrible mess we are in. Like the two workmen, we cannot save ourselves. Only Jesus Christ can save us.[1193]

A man decided he would swim from Los Angeles to Hawaii. He hired the finest swim coach to train him and worked out with Olympic gold-medal winners. He left no detail of preparation undone. Finally the big day arrived. He plunged into the Pacific Ocean and began to swim. Five . . . ten . . . fifteen . . . twenty miles he went. Now the ocean seemed to be getting more intimidating. The waves were becoming rather high and the water cold.

He began to realize that he could never swim to Hawaii; it was just too far. In vain he searched his mind for an alternative, but there was none. Then, as he was gasping for air and about to go down for the third time, a motorboat pulled up alongside him. With his last ounce of energy he called out, "Save me! Please, save me!" The owner of the motorboat looked down at our drowning swimmer and said, "Friend, you're in trouble. What you need is the waterproof edition of my book on swimming to Hawaii. It will tell you everything you need to know. Here, catch it." And then, *vrooom, vrooom,* off he goes in his boat to Hawaii. Obviously, our swimmer needs more than a book.

Well, let's suppose that as our swimmer was gasping for his last breath and the motorboat pulled alongside him and he cried out, "Save me! Please, save me!" the owner said, "Friend, you're in trouble. What you need is someone to show you how to swim. Here, watch me." At that, the boater jumps in and says, "The secret is the Australian crawl. Watch my head. See, it's breathe—blow, breathe—blow, breathe—blow. Now, friend, it won't be easy, but if you'll just follow my example, you are sure to make it." And then he climbs back into his boat and, *vrooom, vrooom,* off he goes to Hawaii. Obviously, our swimmer needs more than an example, a model.

Well, let's try again. This time as our swimmer was gasping for his last breath and the motorboat pulled alongside him and he cried out, "Save me! Please, save me!" suppose that the owner leans over the rail and says, "Friend, you're in trouble! Even worse, you're drowning! Here, let me save you." Then the owner reaches over and grabs the drowning swimmer, pulls him into the boat, sets him down in a chair, and gives him some chocolate-chip cookies to eat and chocolate milk to drink. After some time, the owner reappears on deck and says to the well-rested swimmer, "You know, I saved you from certain death back there. I pulled you out of the water, set you in my chair, and fed you my chocolate-chip cookies and chocolate milk. Now we are only a few hundred miles from Hawaii, and I think it's time that you did something. So, you lazy fellow, get back in the water and swim!" Obviously, our swimmer friend is right back where he started, and he surely needs more than an occasional boost or help when things get rough.

Let's give it one more try. This time as our swimmer is gasping for his last breath and the motorboat pulls alongside him and he cries out, "Save me! Please, save me!" the owner leans over the rail and says, "Friend, you're in trouble! Even worse, you're drowning! Here, let me save you." And the owner reaches over and grabs the drowning swimmer and pulls him into the boat. Then he sets him down in a chair and gives him some chocolate-chip cookies and chocolate milk. Eventually Hawaii comes into view and the owner heads for the dock. He ties up his boat, picks up the swimmer, carries him across the dock, and puts him down on the golden sands of Hawaii.

Now, which of these was truly the savior of our drowning swimmer? Why, the last one, of course. He was the only one who rescued the swimmer from certain death and took him to a place where there was no threat of drowning again. In a similar manner, God did not write the Bible to give us an instruction book on "How to Get to Heaven." Nor did Christ come to show us how to live a life that would be acceptable to God. Nor did Christ come to help us out when we needed a little extra boost but who still expects us to do our part. No, Christ was like the owner who did it *all* for the drowning swimmer and so became his savior.[1194]

Science

"I grew up as a disciple of science. I know its fascination. I have felt the godlike powers man derives from his great machines. Now I have lived to experience the early results of scientific materialism. I have watched men turn into human cogs in the factories they believed would enrich their lives. I have watched pride in workmanship leave and human character decline as the efficiency of production lines increased . . ." (Charles Lindbergh, *Of Flight and Life*).[1195]

Self-control

Self-control is the capacity to break a chocolate bar into four pieces with your bare hands—and then eat just one of the pieces.[1196]

Self-examination

There is a proverb in the business world that the man who takes no inventories finally becomes bankrupt.[1197]

The druggist of the town drugstore overheard a young boy talking on a pay telephone. "Hello, sir, I was calling to see if you needed a lawn boy. Oh, you have one. Well, is he adequate? Oh, he is! Thank you, I was just checking," said the young boy.

The druggist then said to the boy, "Sorry you didn't get the job, son."

"Oh, no sir," said the boy. "I've *got* the job. I was just calling to check up on myself."[1198]

Self-image

Some people feel a need to cover up a lack of self-confidence by trying to make a big impression. A newly promoted Army colonel moved into his new and impressive office. As he sat behind his new big desk, a private knocked at his door. "Just a minute," the colonel said, "I'm on the phone." He picked up the phone and said loudly, "Yes, sir, General, I'll call the President this afternoon. No, sir, I won't forget." Then he hung up the phone and told the private to come in. "What can I help you with?" the colonel asked. "Well, sir," the private replied, "I've come to hook up your phone."[1199]

At twenty, we worry about what people think about us.

At forty, we don't care what people think about us.

At sixty, we find out that people haven't been thinking about us at all.[1200]

"I have often wondered how it is that every man sets less value on his own opinion of himself than on the opinion of others. So much more respect have we to what our neighbors think of us than to what we think of ourselves" (Marcus Aurelius).[1201]

The famous actor Peter Sellers, who played in the "Pink Panther" movies, once said he lacked a personality. "As far as I'm aware, I'm nothing," he once said. "I have no personality of my own whatsoever. I have no character to offer the public. I have nothing to project." In spite of his notable professional image on the screen, Sellers saw himself as a person without an identity of his own.[1202]

Self-pity

Self-pity weeps on the devil's shoulder, turning to Satan for comfort. His invitation is: "Come unto me all you that are grieved, peeved, misused, and disgruntled, and I will spread on the sympathy. You will find me a never-failing source of the meanest attitudes and the most selfish sort of misery. At my altar you may feel free to fail and fall, and there to sigh and fret. There I will feed your soul on fears, and indulge your ego with envy and jealousy, bitterness and spite. There I will excuse you from every cross, duty, and hardship, and permit you to yield unto temptation."[1203]

Self-reform

No matter how much a man tries to reform himself, he can never achieve the newness of life that God wants him to have in Christ. Although a man can make changes in his life, even positive changes, he still remains the same person and often goes from one kind of problem to another.

Sports broadcaster Harry Kalas once introduced a Philadelphia Phillies baseball player, Garry Maddox, with the following words: "He has turned his life around. He used to be depressed and miserable. Now he's miserable and depressed."[1204]

Self-reliance

Without thinking about it, often our reasoning is this: "I—by my stupidity—got into this mess; therefore I—by my stupidity—will get out of it."[1205]

The story is told of a carpenter who was nailing shingles on the roof of a house. He lost his footing and started to slide off. As he was sliding he began praying, "Lord, oh, Lord, help me!" Still he kept sliding. Again the man prayed, "Lord, oh, Lord, help me!" He kept sliding until he got to the edge and a nail sticking up caught hold of his pants. After he came to a stop he said, "Never mind, Lord. The nail's got hold of me now."[1206]

Self-righteousness

Self-righteousness is like a bottomless cup: though you pour and pour, you will never be able to fill it. Why? Because pouring yourself into yourself adds nothing to you. Nothing plus nothing always equals nothing.

Instead, accept God's righteousness rather than trying to accumulate your own. You will find that the righteousness he offers is real. And that is what fills the cup of sanctification.[1207]

Self-sacrifice

A little girl's first-grade class held its "track and field" day. She won quite a few ribbons, among them one blue ribbon for a first place. Later that day, when she came home, the blue ribbon was missing, and her mother asked what had happened to it. "Oh," she said, "Bruce was crying because he didn't win a first place ribbon, so I gave it to him." Her mother hugged her and told her she thought it was very generous to give Bruce the ribbon. "Why not?" she asked. "After all, I know that I won it."

If only all of us, adults included, had such a clear idea of what things are really important in life, and what things are just decorations![1208]

Self-worth

We all frequently compare ourselves favorably with someone else. We all think of someone we consider to be less mature, less competent, or less able than we are. That person is a great comfort to us because he or she enables us to keep our self-image intact by saying, "Well, at least I'm not like so-and-so." The only problem with determining our self-worth by comparing ourselves with others is that we are using the wrong measuring stick.

A little boy came up to his mother one day and said to her, "Mother, guess what! I'm eight feet, four inches tall!" His mother, greatly surprised, inquired into the matter and found he was using a six-inch ruler to measure a "foot." The boy was actually only a few inches over four feet.

This is exactly what we do, we measure ourselves by one another, an imperfect prototype, rather than by the standard of the Word of God.[1209]

In his autobiography, cellist Gregor Piatigorsky tells about a time he was soloist at a concert conducted by Arturo Toscanini: "The maestro paced the dressing room in which I practiced, repeating, 'You are no good; I am no good.' 'Please, Maestro,' I begged, 'I will be a complete wreck.' Then, as we walked on stage, he said, 'We are no good, but the others are worse. Come on, caro, let's go.' "

To Toscanini, it did not matter what he said about himself and the cellist. So long as he could compare himself and the soloist with "the others" and say that the others were less, he felt that they themselves could walk forward with great confidence, feeling full of self-worth. But there is great danger here. For what happens when one looks out and finds the others better? To use comparison with others as a measure for self-worth and confidence is to use a false standard. It puts us at the mercy of the external situation and the circumstances in which we find ourselves. Our sufficiency must be in Christ alone. And our relationship with him should be the sole determinant for our feelings of self-worth and confidence.[1210]

Self-worth, Evaluation of

Suppose that during the past week a young wife gave birth to her first baby. Now suppose that as she held her new baby in her arms and was enjoying the pleasure of motherhood, someone came up to her and said, "How much do you want for the child?" Of course she would show no interest in the offer and would be offended at even a suggestion that her precious babe was for sale. But the stranger is persistent and offers ten thousand dollars, then a hundred thousand dollars, and finally one million dollars. The offers are in vain because the mother will simply press the baby closer to her and reply, "My baby is worth more to me than all the world!"

Of course, if she didn't say that, we would question whether she had the proper attitude for motherhood. But *why* does she say it? Because she looks forward to thousands of dirty diapers, sleepless nights with a sick child, and the costs of raising that child? Because the child will bring her fame and fortune? Of course not. Rather, it is because she has chosen to value this tiny person, to deem the small one to be of worth, and to love that baby of hers. Such worth resides in the very identity of a person, not in their performance. And such worth, coming from the image of God in all of us, must be the basis for our concept of ourselves, too, if our self-portrait is to be durable and worthwhile.[1211]

Selfishness

Too many people conduct their lives cafeteria-style: self-service only.[1212]

One-half of our problems come from wanting our own way. The other half come from getting it![1213]

A little boy and his younger sister were riding a hobby horse together. The boy said, "If one of us would just get off this hobby horse, there would be more room for me."[1214]

Selfishness, Destructive

"The things that will destroy America are peace at any price, prosperity at any cost, safety first instead of duty first, the love of soft living, and the get-rich-quick theory of life" (Attributed to Theodore Roosevelt).[1215]

Sermons, Preparation of

Someone once asked Woodrow Wilson how long he took to prepare a ten-minute speech. "Two weeks," was the answer.
"How long for a one-hour speech?"
"One week," replied the President.
"A two-hour speech?"
"I am ready now!"[1216]

Servanthood

D. L. Moody once said, "The measure of a man is not how many servants he has, but how many men he serves."[1217]

The Navigators are well known for their emphasis on having an attitude of servanthood. A businessman once asked Lorne Sanny, then

329

president of the Navigators, how he could know when he had a servantlike attitude. The answer was, "By how you act when you are treated like one."[1218]

A sign read, "There is no limit to the good that a man can do, if he doesn't care who gets the credit."

If you really don't care who gets the credit, then you can just enjoy yourself and do all kinds of good deeds for others. Just be glad that it is done, and don't worry about who gets the credit on earth, because your heavenly Father knows.[1219]

A student at a Bible school in the Philippines became disturbed over the condition of the men's rest rooms, since they always seemed to be neglected in the cleaning routine. When nothing was done to eliminate the filth, he took matters into his own hands and complained to the principal of the school. A little while later, the student noticed that the problem was being corrected, but he saw with amazement that the man with the mop and pail in hand was the principal himself!

Later the student commented, "I thought that he would call a janitor, but he cleaned the toilets himself. It was a major lesson to me on being a servant and, of course, it raised a question in my own mind as to why *I* hadn't taken care of the problem!"[1220]

> You know Lord how I serve You,
>   with great emotional fervor,
>   in the limelight.
> You know how eagerly I speak for You,
>   at a women's club.
> You know how I effervesce when I promote
>   a fellowship group.
> You know my genuine enthusiasm
>   at a Bible study.
>
> But how would I react, I wonder,
>   if You pointed to a basin of water,
>   and asked me to wash the calloused feet
>   of a bent and wrinkled old woman,
>   day after day,
>   month after month,
>   in a room where nobody saw,
>   and nobody knew?
>
> *Ruth Harms Calkin*[1221]

A. E. Whitham has an imaginary preacher give the following report of a visit to the New Jerusalem:

"In my wandering, I came upon the museum in the city of our dreams. I went in, and an attendant conducted me round. There was some old armor there, much bruised with battle. Many things were conspicuous by their absence. I saw nothing of Alexander's or of Napoleon's. There was no pope's ring, nor even the ink bottle that Luther is said to have thrown at the devil. I saw a widow's mite and the feather of a little bird. I saw some swaddling clothes, a hammer and three nails and a few thorns. I saw a sponge that had once been dipped in vinegar and a small piece of silver. Whilst I was turning over a simple drinking cup which had a very honorable place, I whispered to the attendant: 'Have you got a towel and basin among your collection?' 'No,' he said, 'not here. You see, they are in constant use.' "[1222]

Service

There's a clever young guy named Somebody Else,
There's nothing this guy can't do.
He is busy from morning till way late at night,
Just substituting for you.

You're asked to do this or you're asked to do that
And what is your ready reply?
Get Somebody Else to do that job,
He'll do it much better than I.

So much to do in this weary old world—
So much and workers so few,
And Somebody Else, all weary and worn,
Is still substituting for you.

The next time you're asked to do something worthwhile,
Just give this ready reply:
If Somebody Else can give time and support,
My goodness, so can I![1223]

Service, Priority of

When Dr. W. A. Criswell, pastor of the largest Southern Baptist church in the world, was preaching in the North Shore Baptist Church in Chicago, he was entertained at the home of deacon James L. Kraft, who was superintendent of the Sunday school and founder of Kraft Foods. Kraft said that as a young man he had a desire to be the most famous manufacturer and salesman of cheese in the world. He planned on becoming rich and famous by making and selling cheese and began as a young fellow with a little buggy pulled by a pony named Paddy. After making his cheese, the youth he would load his wagon and he and Paddy would drive down the streets of Chicago to sell the cheese. As the months passed, the young Kraft began to despair because he was not making any money, in spite of his long hours and hard work.

One day he pulled his pony to a stop and began to talk to him. He said, "Paddy, there is something wrong. We are not doing it right. I am afraid we have things turned around and our priorities are not where they ought to be. Maybe we ought to serve God and place him first in our lives." Kraft then drove home and made a covenant that for the rest of his life he would first serve God and then would work as God directed.

Many years after this, Dr. Criswell heard James Kraft say, "I would rather be a layman in the North Shore Baptist Church than to head the greatest corporation in America. My first job is serving Jesus." (Adapted from W. A. Criswell, *Acts* [Grand Rapids: Zondervan, 1983], pp. 187–88.)[1224]

Service, Qualifications for

D. L. Moody aptly observed, "We may easily be too big for God to use, but never too small."[1225]

Service, Rewards of

Many years ago a humble pastor served a church in a little country town. His ministry was quiet, and few souls were brought to Christ there. Year in and year out, the work became more and more discouraging. It was only years later that the faithful minister found great joy in the knowledge that one of those he had won to Christ was Charles Haddon Spurgeon, a man who was later used by God to bring multitudes to his Son. Humble service is rewarded now and certainly will be rewarded even more when Christ comes.[1226]

Sex

Sexual intercourse outside of marriage is always wrong. Why? Because those who indulge in it are trying to isolate one aspect of union— the physical—from all the other aspects that were intended to make a *total* union of two people. There is nothing wrong with sexual pleasure, any more than there is with the pleasure of eating. However, just as attempting to enjoy the pleasures of eating and tasting without swallowing and digesting is abhorrent and wrong, so attempting to enjoy sex as an isolated physical sensation is wrong.[1227]

Sex is like fire. In a fireplace, it's warm and delightful. Outside the hearth, it's destructive and uncontrollable.[1228]

You can usually get a large audience together to watch a striptease. There is no question about it, a lot of people would come to watch a woman undress on the stage, thus indulging and misusing their sexual appetites.

Now suppose you visited a country where an auditorium is packed to the walls with people watching, not a girl undressing, but a guy walking out with a big tray covered with a veil. Then music begins to play, lights begin to flash, and all of a sudden, after some rather enticing maneuvers, the veil is lifted and there on the tray is an orange. Next, in a teasing way, the fellow begins to peel the orange while the crowd goes wild! Wouldn't you think that in this country something had gone wrong with the people's appetite for food?

The Bible clearly speaks regarding the proper use of the body. In 1 Corinthians 6:13, Paul says, "The body is not meant for sexual immorality, but for the Lord" (NIV). And yet, what happens in our society? The body is distorted to the place of perversion![1229]

A wealthy couple desired to employ a chauffeur. The lady of the house advertised, the applicants were screened, and four suitable candidates were brought before her for the final selection. She called the prospective chauffeurs to her balcony and pointed out a brick wall alongside the driveway. Then she asked the men, "How close do you think you could come to that wall without scratching my car?"

The first man felt that he could drive within a foot of the wall without damaging the car. The second felt sure that he could come within six inches. The third believed that he could get within three inches. The fourth candidate said, "I do not know how close I could come to the wall without damaging your car. Instead, I would try to stay as far away from that wall as I could." This candidate had a different focus. He understood that true skill in driving is not based so much on the ability to steer the car to a narrow miss as on the ability to keep a wide margin of safety.

333

Like the fourth candidate, there are many aspects of human nature, such as sexual temptation, that are best dealt with by keeping a wide margin of safety. When we decide what to do in a doubtful area, such as going to a particular movie, we should be as wise as that man.[1230]

Christians should view sex with reverence. Therefore, they should not joke about it. Just as all Christians view communion with reverence and thus never joke about it, in like manner is sex considered sacred—and to joke about it is a form of profanity.[1231]

Silence

One of the lessons of history is that nothing is often a good thing to do and always a clever thing to say.[1232]

Sin

Sin is like a woodpecker. Each particular attack makes noise but doesn't seem to do much damage. But, like a woodpecker, if you let it chip away at your life long enough, it will leave many an ugly hole that never fills in.[1233]

If you have to do wrong to stay on the team, you are on the wrong team.[1234]

> He that falls into sin is man.
> He that grieves at sin is a saint.
> He that boasts of sin is a devil.
> He that forgives our sin is God.[1235]

A flippant youth asked a preacher, "You say that unsaved people carry a weight of sin. I feel nothing. How heavy is sin? Is it ten pounds? Eighty pounds?"

The preacher replied by asking the youth, "If you laid a four-hundred-pound weight on a corpse, would it feel the load?"

The youth replied, "It would feel nothing, because it is dead."

The preacher concluded, "That spirit, too, is indeed dead which feels no load of sin or is indifferent to its burden and flippant about its presence."

The youth was silenced.[1236]

"There is something of a secret atheism in all, which is the fountain of evil practices in their lives, not an utter disowning of the being of God, but a denial or a doubting of some of the rights of His nature. . . . Evil works are a dust stirred up by an atheistical breath" (Stephen Charnock, *Attributes of God* [Grand Rapids: Baker, 1979]).[1237]

"Sin is believing the lie that you are self-created, self-dependent, and self-sustained" (Augustine).[1238]

A small boy drew a picture of a car with a man in the driver's seat and a man and a woman in the back. When asked who was in the car, the boy replied, "That is God driving Adam and Eve out of the Garden of Eden."[1239]

"The very animals whose smell is most offensive to us have no idea that they are offensive, and are not offensive to one another. And man, fallen man, has just no idea what a vile thing sin is in the sight of God" (J. C. Ryle, *Holiness*).[1240]

There is always an advertised price for sin. But that price is always lower than the actual price it carries.[1241]

Sin, Avoidance of

A wife came to the conclusion that carbonated drinks were having negative physical effects on her family and herself and so decided that they should give them up. But how would she convince her three-year-old daughter, who liked them so much, that it was necessary to stop drinking them?

As the wife was telling her husband of her decision, the little girl

335

piped up to ask, "Mommy, we don't like pop any more?" Mommy said "That's right!"—and that was all it took.

Oh, for such a readiness to give up something when we learn that God does not want us to do it.[1242]

Sin, Confession of

A college freshman went to the dorm laundry room with his dirty clothes bundled into an old sweatshirt. But he was so embarrassed by how dirty his clothes were that he never opened the bundle. He merely pushed it into a washing machine and when the machine stopped pushed the bundle into a dryer and finally took the still-unopened bundle back to his room. He discovered, of course, that the clothes had gotten wet and then dry, but not clean.

God says, "Don't keep your sins in a safe little bundle. I want to do a thorough cleansing in your life—all the dirty laundry of your life."[1243]

Sin, Definition of

The story is told of two men who were trying to escape from an erupting volcano. As the fiery molten rock gushed out of its gaping crater, they fled in the only direction open to them. All went well until they came to a stream of hot, smoking lava about thirty feet across. Sizing up their situation, they realized that their only hope was to get over that wide barrier. One of the men was old; the other was healthy and young. With a running start, they each tried to leap to safety. The first man went only a few feet through the air before falling into the bubbling mass. The younger, with his greater strength and skill, catapulted himself much farther. Though he almost made it, he still missed the mark. It did not matter that he out-distanced his companion, for he, too, perished in the burning lava.

Sin is falling short of a standard, the glory of God (Rom. 3:23). Though some may fall short of the standard by far more than others, all fall short nevertheless.[1244]

> Man calls it an accident;
>   God calls it an abomination.
> Man calls it a blunder;
>   God calls it blindness.
> Man calls it a defect;
>   God calls it a disease.

> Man calls it a chance;
> God calls it a choice.
> Man calls it an error;
> God calls it an enmity.
> Man calls it a fascination;
> God calls it a fatality.
> Man calls it an infirmity;
> God calls it an iniquity.
> Man calls it a luxury;
> God calls it leprosy.
> Man calls it a liberty;
> God calls it lawlessness.
> Man calls it a trifle;
> God calls it tragedy.
> Man calls it a mistake;
> God calls it madness.
> Man calls it a weakness;
> God calls it willfulness.[1245]

Sin, Effects of

A famous preacher of many years ago had a clock in his church that was well known for its inability to keep the time accurately. Sometimes too fast, sometimes too slow, it resisted all attempts to solve the problem. Finally, after its dubious fame became widespread, the preacher put a sign over the clock, reading, "Don't blame the hands—the trouble lies deeper."

The same is true of people: the real trouble lies deeper than what shows on the surface.[1246]

There is an old saying that goes like this: "It isn't the mountain ahead that wears you out, it's the grain of sand in your shoe." Many a man, worried for fear he would not be able to cross a mountain, has had to stop some miles before he crossed the foothills because he had not taken time to clean out his shoes.

That has been the source of failure in many Christian lives. Eager to avoid the big sins, your life may outwardly be one of extreme piety, but if there are hidden imperfections—little pebbles in your shoe—these will cause failure in your Christian life.[1247]

One tiny piece of dirt in the carburetor can keep the most powerful truck from climbing a mountain road. A rather small impurity—but all-important in making the ascent.[1248]

In St. Louis there is a railroad switchyard. One particular switch begins with just the thinnest piece of steel to direct a train away from one main track to another. If you were to follow those two tracks, however, you would find that one ends in San Francisco, the other in New York.

Sin is like that. Just a small deviation from God's standards can place us far afield from our intended destination.[1249]

The *St. Petersburg Times* once carried a news item about a hungry thief who grabbed some sausages in a meat market, only to find they were part of a string fifteen feet long. Tripping over them, he was hindered in his getaway and the police found him collapsed in a tangle of fresh sausages.

So it is with sin: we always come away with more of it than we expected, and it tends to entangle us until it brings us down.[1250]

A Jewish father took his little boy to the ritual bath for the first time. When they jumped into the pool the little boy began to shiver with cold and cried, "Oy, papa, oy!" His father led him out of the pool, rubbed him down with a towel and dressed him. "Ahh, papa, ahh!" purred the little fellow, tingling with pleasant warmth.

"Isaac," said the father thoughtfully, "Do you want to know the difference between a cold bath and a sin? When you jump into a cold pool you first yell 'oy!" and then you say 'ahh!' But when you commit a sin you first say 'ahh!' and then you yell 'oy!' "[1251]

Like a piece of wood in a pond, a Christian can "float" on the surface of sin and not get too wet. But, just as wood that is in the water for too long gets waterlogged and sinks to the bottom, so also does the Christian who spends too much time in sin.[1252]

A workman on a road construction crew told this story of a time when he was working on a project deep in the mountain area of Pennsylvania. Every morning as he drove to work in his pickup, he would see a young boy at a fishing hole near the road. He would wave and speak to the boy each day. One day, however, as he drove slowly past the fishing spot and asked how the boy was doing, he got a strange reply: "The fish aren't bitin' today, but the worms sure are."

When he pulled into the local gas station down the road a few minutes later, he jokingly related the boy's comment to the attendant. For a moment the man laughed, but then a look of horror crossed his face, and without another word he ran to his truck, jumped in, and drove hurriedly away.

Later that day, the man on the construction crew found out what had happened. The gas station attendant had arrived on the scene too late to save the boy, who had somehow mistaken a nest of baby rattle-snakes for earthworms and had been bitten to death.

Baby rattlesnakes, you see, are born with their full venom. And so it is with many of the sins that tempt us. They may appear harmless, even colorful, yet they contain the full venom of Satan's poison and will destroy us if we handle them.[1253]

Anyone who has witnessed the felling of a giant redwood tree is left with a feeling of sadness. As the saw moves through the heart of the giant, it begins to sag down on the side where the wound is gaping. Presently, it is apparent that the tree is beginning to lean away from the cutters. They continue their work a moment longer; then is heard the cracking of wood fibers in front of the saw's teeth. Another swish of the saw, and the noises increase. The sounds, getting even more rapid, presently become a continuous roar. Then, if you are standing nearby, and the tree is large, you will get the impression that everything above is coming to earth. The great mass starts slowly to topple, crackling and exploding even louder at the base, until it comes sprawling down with a fearful momentum.

Sometimes we see a man come down like that. He had stood out, apparently so strong and forceful before all the world, carrying his head high. Young men had envied him, but the sappers were at his heart. The deadly saw of appetite or lust or passion steadily cut away the supports under him until he came crashing down to earth.[1254]

Lord Byron, a brilliant poet, spent his life in a mad search for pleasure. Moderns would say, "He tried to live it up." Then in despair he wrote:

> The thorns I have reaped are of the tree I planted.
> They have torn me and I bleed.
> I should have known what fruit would spring
>   from such a tree.[1255]

One of the hardest things for the Christian of our day is to recognize the presence of sin in his own life and all around him. In fact, we often try to minimize the presence of sin and to make light of its effects on us.

Dr. J. Wilbur Chapman told of a distinguished Methodist minister in Australia who preached on sin. One of his church officers came afterward to talk with him in his study. He said to the pastor, "Dr. Howard, we don't want you to talk so plainly as you do about sin, because if our boys and girls hear you talking so much about sin, they will more easily become sinners. Call it a mistake if you will, but do not speak so plainly about sin."

The minister went to a utility closet and brought back a small bottle of strychnine that was clearly marked "Rat Poison." He said, "I see what you want me to do. You wanted me to change the label. Suppose I take off this label of 'Poison' and put on some milder label, such as 'Essence of Peppermint.' Don't you see what might happen? The milder you make the label; the more dangerous you make the poison."[1256]

The sins of our youth will catch up to us—usually in middle age! There is no escape. As Kipling once said, "The sins ye do by two and two, ye must pay for one by one."[1257]

When we are in a state of sin, it is like riding a bicycle into the wind—God appears to be against us. Yet, like the bicyclist who turns around and finds that the wind is helping him, if we repent and change the direction of our lives, we will find God working with us. God didn't change—*we* did.[1258]

In an upholstering shop, if a piece of material is cut too short, there is no way it can be stretched to fit the part for which it was intended. However, while the material is too small for its original purpose, it can probably be used elsewhere on the chair, so it needn't be discarded.

Some sins have consequences that disqualify us for certain forms of ministry, but Christ can still use you if you will serve where he puts you.[1259]

Sin, Evidence of

It is always a somewhat surprising characteristic for believers who have grown in holiness to increasingly feel themselves to be sinners. Why? Consider the air in a room. It looks fresh and clean, but when it is penetrated by the sunlight we see that in reality it is full of dust and other impurities. In a similar way, as we draw nearer to God and are penetrated by his light, we can more clearly see our own impurities and begin to feel something of the same hatred for sin that God feels.[1260]

An old Chinese proverb declares: "There are two good men—one is dead and the other is not yet born."[1261]

"Near our vineyard there was a pear tree, loaded with fruit, though the fruit was not particularly attractive either in color or in taste. I and some other wretched youth conceived the idea of shaking the pears off this tree and carrying them away.

"We set out late that night (having, as we usually did in our depraved way, gone on playing in the streets till that hour) and stole all the fruit that we could carry. And this was not to feed ourselves; we may have tasted a few. But then we threw the rest to the pigs. I had no wish to enjoy what I tried to get by theft; all my enjoyment was in the theft itself and in sin. Our real pleasure was in doing something that was not allowed." (Cited in *The Confessions of St. Augustine* [New York: NAL, n.d.], p. 45. Translated by Rex Warner.)[1262]

In addition to being one of the most successful baseball manager of his day, John J. McGraw may have been responsible for there being a third-base umpire. Long before he became a famous manager of the New York Giants, as a young third baseman with the old Baltimore Orioles the intensely competitive McGraw had a habit of hooking his finger in the belt of a base runner who was tagging up to score after a long fly ball. This trick usually slowed the runner enough so that he was thrown out at home plate.

Despite violent protests, McGraw got away with his ploy for some months—until one base runner secretly unbuckled his belt. When the runner dashed for home, he left his belt dangling from McGraw's finger. The need for a third-base umpire could hardly have been made clearer.[1263]

A correspondent of the *London Times* quite a while back, researching and reporting on many of the same problems we now have, ended every article with this statement: "What's wrong with the world?" G. K. Chesterton once wrote a famous reply:
Dear editor:
What's wrong with the world?

341

I am.

Faithfully yours,

  G. K. Chesterton.

At the base of most of the world's problems is the sinfulness of man.[1264]

One evening a couple was entertaining some company in their home. After their two young daughters had been put to bed, the older child returned and told her parents that her two-year-old sister was not in bed but was playing with her toys. The parents told the girl to return to her room and to send her sister out to the living room.

The two-year-old girl, knowing full well that she was supposed to be sleeping and that she had been acting contrary to her parents' wishes, began the slow walk, but with both eyes closed. As she approached some steps at the end of the hall, she raised one eyelid only long enough to see them and to step down. With both eyes quickly shut again, she proceeded a bit further.

At this point, the mother asked the little girl, "Betsy, what are you doing?" In accord with what she was *supposed* to be doing, the child replied, "I'm sleeping, Mommy."

Children do not need to be taught to sin; they have sin bound up in their hearts.[1265]

"Certain it is that, while men are gathering knowledge and power with ever-increasing speed, their virtues and their wisdom have not shown any notable improvement as the centuries have rolled. Under sufficient stress—starvation, terror, war-like passion, or even cold intellectual frenzy—the modern man we know so well will do the most terrible deeds, and his modern woman will back him up" (Attributed to Winston Churchill).[1266]

Several years ago, there was a massive volcanic explosion in the state of Washington when Mount St. Helens erupted. Sheriff Bill Closner said, "People were in the danger areas around the mountain because they refused to obey roadblocks. The bottom line is that nobody would listen." As a result, there were needless deaths and injuries.

Even though danger was physically imminent, people still refused to obey the regulations. Sin or disobedience always has consequences. If people refused to listen in the midst of dangerous circumstances like the Mount St. Helens eruption, we should not be so shocked at the depravity and stubbornness of men in spiritual matters.[1267]

Sin, Illustration of

If there are mice or rats in a cellar, you are most likely to see them if you go in very suddenly. The suddenness of your entry did not create the rodents, it only prevented them from hiding.

In the same way, the best evidence for what sort of person you (or anyone else) are lies in what you do when taken off your guard. For example, the suddenness of a provocation does not make you or me ill-tempered, it only shows what ill-tempered persons we are.[1268]

Some fraternity members put Limburger cheese very gently on a brother's moustache while he slept. He woke up about an hour later and said, "This room stinks!" He walked into the hall and said, "This hall stinks!" He walked into the living room and said, "This living room stinks!" Then, greatly perplexed as to where the smell was coming from, he walked outside and exclaimed, "This whole world stinks!" And the real problem was right under his own nose—just like the sin in our lives.[1269]

Every baby starts life like a little savage—completely egotistic and self-centered. Babies want what they want, when they want it, be it a bottle, mother's attention, or a dry diaper. Deny a baby these "wants" and he or she is seized with rage. Babies have no morals, no knowledge, no skills for survival. All children, not just certain children, are potential delinquents! If permitted to continue in the self-centered world of their infancy, where they gave free rein to every impulse and had every want instantly gratified, all children would grow up in that mold of depravity. That is the stuff out of which are made criminals, killers, and rapists.[1270]

To those individuals acquainted with the Holocaust of World War II, the name of Simon Wiesenthal is certainly a most familiar one. World-famous for his ceaseless pursuit of Nazi war criminals, he often speaks to college audiences about his activities.

"Could it happen again, even in the United States?" Wiesenthal is asked by American college audiences. His reply is, "Yes. All you need is a government program of hatred and a crisis. If it happened in a civilized nation like Germany, which was a cultural superpower, it can happen anywhere. When I was a young man in the 1920s, our answer to Hitler was to laugh and make jokes. How could a man with such

343

crazy ideas succeed?" (Simon Wiesenthal, *Dallas Times Herald*, April 22, 1979).[1271]

Sin, Imputation of

If one football player jumps offside, the whole team is penalized. So it is with sin. Because one man, Adam, sinned, the whole human race was penalized.[1272]

Sin, Original

A young boy and his father were walking in an apple orchard. The father pulled an apple from a tree and, cupping his hands around it, asked his son what he saw. The son replied, "A beautiful red apple. May I have it?" The father then handed the apple to his son for examination. The boy touched it and immediately dropped it. Why? Because the apple appeared to be perfect only when viewed from one side. You see, on the other side it had been attacked by an insect and was rotten throughout. Yet the skin on the first side still had wholeness.

All people are like that apple. They may appear to be beautiful, but, once we examine them thoroughly, we see that all of us are rotten and marred because of our sin nature.[1273]

Imagine that you have a lemon tree in your yard. All it can produce is sour lemons. If you wanted to grow oranges, you might decide to pull off all the lemons from your tree and then tie on some sweet, juicy oranges in their place. In a few minutes your tree could be covered with the sweetest oranges in town. Everyone would see your "orange tree"— but in reality all you have is a lemon tree with dead oranges on it. You have not changed the nature of the tree at all.

So it is that the reason we cannot perfectly keep God's commandments is that we do not have the nature to act according to his will. We have no inner ability to keep God's laws.[1274]

The Pelagians believed that sin spread from Adam to the whole human race, not by derivation, but by imitation. In other words, there was no original sin; man is good but chooses evil and thus becomes in need of salvation.

In contrast, Paul affirms that we are born with sin, just as serpents bring their venom from the womb, and thus we are in need of salvation.[1275]

Sin is like a man's beard. Although we daily destroy its manifestations, it constantly reappears.[1276]

Your "death warrant" is, as it were, written into your own "birth certificate."[1277]

Have you ever bitten into an apple and found a worm in it, and yet the outside of the apple showed no hole or entry point for the worm? How did the worm get inside the apple? Clearly he could not have burrowed in from the outside. No, scientists have discovered that the worm can come from inside. But how does he get in there? Simple! An insect lays an egg in the apple blossom. Some time later, the worm hatches in the heart of the apple, then eats his way out. Sin, like the worm, begins in the heart and works out through a person's thoughts, words, and actions.[1278]

"A beautiful geranium plant that adorned the window was killed by the frost. Leaves and flowers withered, leaving only a mass of mildew and decay. What was the cause? Merely the loss of the sun's light and heat. But that was enough, for those belong to the nature of the plant, and are essential to its life and beauty. Deprived of them, it remains not what it is, but its nature loses its soundness, and this causes decay, mildew, and poisonous gases, which soon destroy it.

"So of human nature: in Paradise, Adam was like the blooming plant, flourishing in the warmth and brightness of the Lord's presence. By sin, he fled from that presence. The result was not merely the loss of light and heat, but since these were essential to his nature, that nature languished, drooped and withered. The mildew of corruption formed upon it; and the positive process of dissolution was begun, to end only in eternal death" (Abraham Kuyper, *The Work of the Holy Spirit* [Grand Rapids: Wm. B. Eerdmans, 1956], p. 90).[1279]

Sin, Response to

Many of us who are trying to get rid of sin are like housewives who destroy the spiders' webs without destroying the spiders.[1280]

What would you think of a doctor who, on discovering you had a tumor buried deep in your body, responded, "Take two aspirin and you'll be just fine"?

How about a fireman who responded to a three-alarm fire by saying, "It'll probably burn itself out soon enough," or a policeman who, on arriving at the scene of a robbery, merely shook his head and said, "Boys will be boys"!

In each case the response is inappropriate to the situation. Is your response to sin also inappropriate?[1281]

French aristocrat Baron Richard d'Arcy kept a strange pet in his home: a two-year-old lion. One night in 1977, the baron tried to make his pet enter the bathroom, where it usually spent the night, but it refused to go and leaped on its master. In a matter of minutes, the lion had clawed the baron to death.

Christians should deal with sin definitely and drastically. We must not permit any "pet" sins, since that means we are playing with evil. Only by severe dealing with a sin can we be sure that we will not become the victim of it.[1282]

For a saint to desire sin is as ridiculous as a rodeo where cowboys ride calves to rope horses. Not only is the experience unnatural, it is also extremely unproductive.[1283]

One of every 400,000 babies is born each year with Severe Combined Immunodeficiency Disease, or SCID, a disease that leaves the child with no body-chemistry defenses to fight infection from the germs that constantly attack one's body. For such children, life is often short and always filled with danger.

In a similar manner, the Christian who is not protected by the armor of God is defenseless against the attacks of the flesh, the world, and Satan. Sin, like an infection, can eat its way into his life because he has no defense against it.[1284]

A certain man used to come home dead drunk each night. He was always so inebriated that he would fall into bed fully clothed, pass out, and then snore loudly all night long. His wife was losing so much sleep because of his snoring that she went to a doctor and said, "Doctor, I can't stand it any longer. If you will tell me how to keep him from snoring, I will pay you anything!" The doctor told her that whenever her husband passed out and started snoring, she was to take a ribbon and tie it around his nose, and his snoring would stop.

That night, her husband came in as usual, fell across the bed fully dressed, passed out, and started snoring. The wife got up, pulled a blue ribbon from her dresser, and tied it around his nose. Sure enough, the snoring stopped. The next morning, the wife woke up refreshed from a solid night's sleep. She asked her husband as he was awakening, "Where were you last night?" The husband, still fully clothed, looked in the mirror and seeing the blue ribbon around his nose, replied, "I don't know, but wherever I was, I won first prize!"

This was the attitude of the early church that Paul referred to in 1 Corinthians 5:1–2. Immorality was in their midst, yet they were puffed up with pride. They had become so arrogant, thinking themselves first in spirituality, that they had become oblivious to their condition.[1285]

Sin, Source of

We are all like the moon. On one side all looks well, but the other side is dark.[1286]

Satan once came dejected before God and wailed, "Almighty God, I want you to know that I am bored—bored to tears! I go around doing nothing all day long. There isn't a stitch of work for me to do!"

I don't understand you," replied God. "There's plenty of work to be done, only you've got to have more initiative. Why don't you try to lead people into sin? That's your job!"

"Lead people into sin! Why, Lord, even before I can get a chance to say a word to anyone, he has already gone and sinned!"[1287]

Sin, Struggle Against

Near Watsonville, California, there is a creek that has a strange name: Salsipuedes Creek. *Salsi puedes* is Spanish for "Get out of it, if you can." The creek is lined with quicksand, and the story is that many years ago, in the early days of California, a Mexican laborer fell into the quicksand. A Spaniard, riding by on a horse, saw him and yelled out to him, "*Salsi puedes!*" which was not very helpful. The creek has been so named ever since. That is what the flesh is like. We struggle to correct these tendencies—to get out of the effects of our sinful nature—but we cannot do it.[1288]

Sin, Toleration of

For two years the hydraulic earthquake stabilizers in the thirteen-story "Nuevo Leon" apartment building in Mexico City were left out of service. Then, unexpectedly, at 7:30 A.M. on September 19, 1985, a devastating earthquake shook Mexico City. The thirteen-story building began to sway. Without hydraulic stabilizers to cushion the shocks, the building continued to sway until finally a third of it broke loose at the foundation and fell over sideways. Another third came crumbling down, floor on floor, crushed like a tin can. Only one third was left standing. For fifteen days rescuers dug through the rubble to search for survivors. Unfortunately, for most, the results of neglecting the inner defects were tragic.

So it is with our inner spiritual life and sin. To neglect the one is to open ourselves to the tragic results of the other.[1289]

Slavery, Spiritual

Some years ago in Los Angeles a man was walking down the street with a sign on his shoulders. The front of it said, 'I'M A SLAVE FOR CHRIST." The back of it read, "WHOSE SLAVE ARE YOU?"

That is a good question, because all of us are slaves to one or the other of two masters—sin or righteousness. We have no other choices. By the very nature of our humanity, we are made to serve and to be controlled by forces beyond our power.[1290]

Social Action

Many non-evangelicals have criticized evangelical Christians for not "caring," that is, for what they perceive to be too-little social involvement. In 1979 the Gallup Poll organization surveyed a cross section of Americans. The facts speak for themselves.

The question was "Do you as an individual happen to be involved in any charity or social service activities, such as helping the poor, the sick, or the elderly?"

The affirmative response by religion was proportioned as follows:

Non-Church Members	19%	Protestants	27%
Church Members	30%	Non-Evangelicals	26%
Catholics	26%	Evangelicals	42%[1291]

William Booth could not sleep one evening, so he went for a walk in the night. He walked down to the poor side of London and there, in the cover of darkness, saw the impoverished and beaten half-lives that existed in that setting. The rain was beating down on some of London's derelicts who were sleeping near the curbsides. When Booth returned home, he told his wife, "I've been to hell." Out of that nightmarish experience came the dream of the Salvation Army.

Had Booth not left the security of his own home, he might never have become aware of the needs of the homeless masses.[1292]

The following parody was written by two Englishmen after converting to Christianity from Communism.

The Socialist's 23rd Psalm

The Government is my shepherd,
Therefore, I need not work.
It allows me to lie down on a good job;
It leads me beside still factories.
It destroys my initiative;
It leads me in the path of a parasite for politics' sake.
Yea, though I walk through the valley of laziness and deficit spending,
I fear no evil; for the Government is with me.
It preparest an economic utopia for me;
By appropriating the earnings of my own grandchildren.
It fills my head with false security;
My inefficiency runneth over.
Surely the Government should care for me all the days of my life;
And I shall live forever in a fool's paradise.[1293]

Sorrow

You may soon forget those with whom you have laughed, but you will never forget those with whom you have wept.[1294]

Dr. R. A. Torrey was one of the great Bible teachers of a past generation and founder of the Bible Institute of Los Angeles (BIOLA University). He and Mrs. Torrey went through a time of great heartache when their twelve-year-old daughter was accidentally killed. The funeral was held on a gloomy, miserable, rainy day. They stood around the grave and watched as the body of their little girl was put away. As they turned away, Mrs. Torrey said, "I'm so glad that Elisabeth is with the Lord, and not in that box."

349

But, even knowing this to be true, their hearts were broken. Dr. Torrey said that the next day, as he was walking down the street, the whole thing broke anew—the loneliness of the years ahead without her presence, the heartbreak of an empty house, and all the other implications of her death. He was so burdened by this that he looked to the Lord for help. He said, "And just then, this fountain, the Holy Spirit that I had in my heart, broke forth with such power as I think I had never experienced before, and it was the most joyful moment I had ever known in my life! Oh, how wonderful is the joy of the Holy Ghost! It is an unspeakable glorious thing to have your joy not in things about you, not even in your most dearly loved friends, but to have within you a fountain ever springing up, springing up, springing up, always springing up three hundred and sixty-five days in every year, springing up under all circumstances unto everlasting life!"[1295]

Sorrow, Lessons from

Until I learned to trust,
　I never learned to pray;
And I did not learn to fully trust
　Till sorrows came my way.

Until I felt my weakness,
　His strength I never knew
Nor dreamed 'til I was stricken
　That he could see me through.

Who deepest drinks of sorrow,
　Drinks deepest, too, of grace;
He sends the storm so he himself
　Can be our hiding place.

His heart, that seeks our highest—GOOD—
　Knows well when things annoy;
We would not long for heaven
　If earth held only joy.

William G. Coltman[1296]

Oh, you tears,
I'm thankful that you run.
Though you trickle in the darkness,
You shall glitter in the sun.
The rainbow could not shine if the rain refused to fall;
And the eyes that cannot weep are the saddest eyes of all.

Charles Mackay[1297]

I walked a mile with Pleasure;
She chatted all the way,
But left me none the wiser
For all she had to say.

I walked a mile with Sorrow
And ne'er a word said she;
But, oh, the things I learned from her
When Sorrow walked with me!

Robert Browning Hamilton[1298]

Speaking

"Blessed are they who have nothing to say and cannot be persuaded to say it" (James Russell Lowell).[1299]

The six most important words: "I admit I made a mistake."

The five most important words: "You did a good job."

The four most important words: "What is your opinion?"

The three most important words: "If you please."

The two most important words: "Thank you."

The most important word: "We"

The least important word: "I"[1300]

Spiritual Gifts

The Christian church is composed of many different kinds of people with different gifts and different ministries. The manner in which these are combined is not like a melting pot but like a salad bowl. Within the church, there is no loss of individual identity, but rather the complementing of distinct elements to create a new, special, and united body.[1301]

On Christmas morning, the children in a family do not usually all receive the same gifts. One gets a football, one a puzzle, another receives a dollhouse, and another a table game. Yet, although each child does not receive the same gifts as the others, the parents intend the gifts to be enjoyed by all the children as they use them together.

The same is true of the gifts God gives his children. We do not all

351

have the same gift, but we are all to use our gift for the good of all in God's family.[1302]

A modern army is fitted with a strategic mix of various weapons to maximize its effectiveness in fulfilling its purpose. Some soldiers receive a rifle and some are given pistols or ride in a tank armed with a cannon and machine guns. Others operate missiles, jet fighters, bombers, or ships. To win the war, it takes the unified effects of all these weapons, operated by the shared efforts of all the variously equipped soldiers.

God, as the wise Commander-in-Chief in our spiritual warfare, has likewise given to each of his children in the body of Christ spiritual gifts so that they can work together to be effective in fulfilling his will. And, as in a physical war, if Christian "soldiers" work together and use their gifts, the task of the church on earth will be accomplished.[1303]

A young schoolboy was trying out for a part in the school play. His mother knew that he had set his heart on it, though she was afraid he would not be chosen. On the day the parts were awarded, she drove to school to pick him up. The young lad rushed up to her, eyes shining with pride and excitement. Then he said some words to her that should remain a lesson to us all: "I have been chosen to clap and cheer!" In the same way, God has lovingly chosen each of us for different and special tasks.[1304]

When Niccolo Paganini willed his finely crafted and lovingly used violin to the city of Genoa, he demanded that it never be played again. It was a gift designated for preservation, but not destined for service.

On the other hand, when the resurrected Christ willed his spiritual gifts to the children of God, he commanded that they be used. They were gifts not designated for preservation, but destined for service.[1305]

Imagine how a parent would feel if on Christmas Day when the gifts for their children were handed out, the children just took them, said "Thank you," and laid them aside with no attempt to open the gifts, not even to find out what they were!

Imagine how the Lord must feel when he has given gifts to us that he intends for us to use, and yet we never take the trouble to find out what they are, never put them to work, and then excuse ourselves from serving the church by saying that we can't do anything![1306]

The mountain does not speak ill of the river just because it is high and mighty. Nor does the river scorn the mountain just because it moves swiftly and gracefully. They both are great in their own way.[1307]

When a speck of dust blows into an eye, instinctively the eye is rubbed with a finger. There is no debate with the finger about whether to help the eye. Later, after pulling down the lid, causing the eye to water, the speck is washed out. In a short time the eye is back to normal. But without the hand, including its specially functioning fingers, the irritant would have remained. Each member in the body of Christ is equally important. We all need each other.[1308]

Imagine the Master Carpenter's tools holding a conference:

Brother Hammer presides, but several suggest he leave the meeting because he is too noisy. Brother Hammer replies, "If I have to leave this shop, Brother Screw must go also. You have to turn him around again and again to get him to accomplish anything."

Brother Screw then speaks up. "If you wish, I'll leave. But Brother Plane must leave, too. All his work is on the surface. His efforts have no depth."

To this, Brother Plane responds, "Brother Rule will also have to withdraw, for he is always measuring folks as though he were the only one who is right."

Brother Rule then complains about Brother Sandpaper: "He ought to leave, too, because he's so rough and always rubbing people the wrong way." And so goes the discord.

In the midst of all this discussion, in walks the Carpenter of Nazareth. He has arrived to start his day's work. Putting on his apron, he goes to the bench to make a pulpit from which to proclaim the gospel. He uses Brothers Hammer, Screw, Plane, Rule, Sandpaper, and all the other tools. After the day's work, when the pulpit is finished, Brother Saw arises and remarks, "Brethren, I observe that all of us are workers together with the Lord."[1309]

A man broke his left arm. One night when he couldn't sleep, he imagined a dialogue between his right and left hands. Right Hand said, "Left Hand, you are not missed. Everybody's glad it was you that was broken and not me. You are not very important."

Left Hand asked, "How are you superior?"

353

Right Hand replied, "Why, my owner cannot write a letter without me."

Left Hand: "But who holds the paper on which he writes?"

Right Hand: "Who swings the hammer?"

Left Hand: "Who holds the nail?"

Right Hand: "Who guides the plane when the carpenter smooths a board?"

Left Hand: "Who steadies the board?"

Right Hand: "When our owner walks down the street and lifts his hat to greet someone, which of us does it?"

Left Hand: "Who holds the briefcase while he does it?" Then he continued, "Let me ask you a question. When our owner shaved yesterday, you held the razor, but his face is cut because I wasn't there to help. Also, our owner's watch has stopped. Why? You may do the winding, but if I'm not there to hold it, the watch won't get wound. You can't take money out of his wallet to pay for something because I'm not there to hold it. The master can do very few things without me."

So, too, does each of us have a place of service for the Lord. None is greater—just different.[1310]

One snowy morning at 5:00 A.M., a missionary candidate rang the bell at a missionary examiner's home. Ushered into the office, he sat three hours past his appointment time waiting for his interview. At 8:00 A.M. a retired missionary appeared and began his questioning. "Can you spell?"

Rather mystified, the candidate answered, "Yes, sir."

All right, spell 'baker.' "

"B-A-K-E-R."

"Fine. Now, do you know anything about numbers?" the examiner continued.

"Yes, sir, something."

"Please add two plus two."

"Four," replied the candidate.

"That's fine," said the examiner. "I believe you have passed. I'll tell the board tomorrow.

At the board meeting, the examiner reported on the interview. "He has all the qualifications for a fine missionary. First, I tested him on self-denial, making him arrive at my home at five in the morning. He left a warm bed on a snowy morning without any complaint. Second, I tested him on promptness. He arrived on time. Third, I examined him on patience. I made him wait three hours to see me. Fourth, I tested him on temper. He failed to show any anger or aggravation. Fifth, I tried his humility by asking him questions that a seven-year-old child could answer, and he showed no indignation. So you see, I believe the candidate meets the requirements. He will make the fine missionary we need."

Spirit-given abilities are needed, but Spirit-produced fruit is more significant.[1311]

Dr. H. A. Ironside often spoke of the pathetic situation of those who felt they had the gift of preaching but complained that no one had the gift of listening.[1312]

Spiritual Growth

One night, a mother fixed a special meal for her family: turkey with mashed potatoes and gravy, corn, green beans, cranberry sauce, and apple pie for dessert. It was everyone's favorite meal, especially when it came at a time other than Thanksgiving. The aroma filled the house, and as the children came in from playing they could hardly wait for dinner to begin. The last child appeared only a few minutes before dinner time and sat through the meal without eating, even though he especially loved those foods. Why? Because he had filled up on peanut butter at a friend's house. In settling for something good, he had lost his appetite for the best.

The same applies to our spiritual appetites. Some people don't have much of an appetite for spiritual truth because they have satisfied themselves with lesser things.[1313]

Spiritual Growth, Evidence of

We have all been driving down a highway and noticed bright orange signs that state, "BEGIN CONSTRUCTION" and "END CONSTRUCTION." One thing about these signs is that they tend to remain around long after the construction work is over.

If one of us were to announce that—for the time being—God's construction in our lives was going to be halted, would our friends say, "I didn't know any construction was going on"?[1314]

Spiritual Growth, Source of

Some years ago, a study was done by an agricultural school in Iowa. It reported that production of a hundred bushels of corn from one acre of land required 4,000,000 lbs. of water, 6,800 lbs. of oxygen, 5,200 lbs.

of carbon, 160 lbs. of nitrogen, 125 lbs. of potassium, 75 lbs. of yellow sulphur, and other elements too numerous to list. In addition to these ingredients are required rain and sunshine at the right times. Although many hours of the farmer's labor are also needed, it was estimated that only 5 percent of the produce of a farm can be attributed to the efforts of man.

So it is in spiritual realms: God causes the growth (1 Cor. 3:6–7).[1315]

When James Garfield, later to become President of the United States, was principal of Hiram College in Ohio, one father asked him if the course of his studies could not be shortened so that his son might be able to complete his studies in less time. "Certainly," Garfield replied. "But it all depends on what you want to make of your boy. When God wants to make an oak, he takes one hundred years. When he wants to make a squash, he requires only two months."[1316]

Spiritual Pride

There was a godly Christian woman who startled her friends by saying, "There isn't a sin of which I am not capable. I could be a prostitute; I could murder; I could embezzle."

Most of her friends were not impressed with her frankness. Instead they thought that she was displaying a false humility. Then she added, "You don't really believe what I just said. I mean it—because I realize that any particular sin that crops up in someone else's life expresses itself in me, but in different ways. Until I accept that, I am self-righteous, proud, and arrogant."[1317]

Spiritual Warfare

A letter from a missionary out in the jungles of New Guinea writing to his friends at home caught the nature of spiritual warfare:

"Man, it is great to be in the thick of the fight, to draw the old devil's heaviest guns, to have him at you with depression and discouragement, slander, disease. He doesn't waste time on a lukewarm bunch. He hits good and hard when a fellow is hitting him. You can always measure the weight of your blow by the one you get back. When you're on your back with fever and at your last ounce of strength, when some of your converts backslide, when you learn that your most promising inquirers are only fooling, when your mail gets held up, and some don't bother to answer your letters, is that the time to put on mourning? No, sir.

That's the time to pull out the stops and shout Hallelujah! The old fellow's getting it in the neck and hitting back. Heaven is leaning over the battlements and watching. 'Will he stick with it?' And as they see who is with us, as they see the unlimited reserves, the boundless resources, as they see the impossibility of failure, how disgusted and sad they must be when we run away. Glory to God! We're not going to run away. We're going to stand!"[1318]

Bobby Leach, an Englishman, startled the world some years ago by his daring feat of going over Niagara Falls in a barrel. He came through the experience miraculously unscratched. Some time later, Leach was walking down the street and slipped on a small orange peel. He was rushed to the hospital with a badly fractured leg.

Believers are more frequently brought down by a minor skirmish than by a major battle.[1319]

The story has been told of a mental hospital that many years ago devised an unusual test to determine when their patients were ready to go back into the world. They brought a candidate for release to a room where a water faucet was left on so that the sink overflowed and was pouring water all over the floor. Then they handed the patient a mop and told him to mop up the water. If the patient had enough sense to turn off the faucet before mopping up the water, he was ready to be released. But if, as in the case of many, the patient started mopping while the water was still flowing, they kept the patient for more treatment.

As Christians, all of us face the world in which we live and are confronted with the need to do battle with the evil that dominates it. But, like the patients in the mental hospital, until we realize where the source of that evil is, we will make no real contribution. To see less evil in the world means that we must conquer the evil that is pouring forth from our own heart. That is conversion. Then, to deal with the evil around us, we need a "mop and bucket," the spiritual armor that God has provided for us.[1320]

Stewardship

First Corinthians 4:1 tells us to be "stewards of the mysteries of God" (RSV). If you have ever been on a ship, you know what a ship's steward is. Or if you have ever been on an airplane, you know what a

357

steward or a stewardess is. That person does not own the airplane or anything on the plane. The company owns everything, but he or she is entrusted with its care. That steward has been given the responsibility of taking the goods that belong to a higher authority and dispensing it to the people for their benefit. That is a steward—on an airplane or ship—and in the spiritual realm as well.[1321]

Epictetus, a Stoic philosopher, is recorded as having said the following:

"Never say about anything, 'I have lost it,' but only 'I have given it back.' Is your child dead? It has been given back. Is your wife dead? She has been given back. 'I have had my farm taken away.' Very well, this too has been given back. Yet it was a rascal who took it away. But what concern is it of yours by whose instrumentality the Giver called for its return? So long as He gives it to you, take care of it as of a thing that is not your own, as travelers treat their inn" (*The Encheiridion*, 11).

If this non-Christian could see all of life as a stewardship, how much more should we believers?[1322]

In the movie *Papillon*, the main character was a criminal who was imprisoned for life for crimes against the French state. The movie portrayed the dreams he had while in prison. In one dream, he stood before a tribunal for a crime. He pleaded with the judge that he was not guilty of the crime for which he was being tried. The judge replied that he was not being tried for that crime, but for a crime that is the most heinous crime of the human race. Papillon asked what crime it was. He replied, "The crime of a wasted life." Papillon wept, "Guilty, guilty." The judge pronounced the sentence of death.[1323]

Stress

As everyday experience often shows, stress and trials can strengthen a person. A seed that falls into a mere handful of soil next to a boulder can sometimes grow into a large tree by sending its roots down to the earth, roots that firmly wedge it onto the rock. The sequoia, the greatest of trees, grows best when forest fires periodically threaten its existence. The fires may scar it deeply, but they assure the proper composition of the soil needed for the tree's survival.[1324]

The head of the Menninger Institute has stated that up to 70 percent of minor ailments such as colds and fatigue are psychosomatic reactions to day-to-day stress, and also that they can lead to more serious problems.[1325]

Substitution, Example of

A man was lost in the Alps. The owner of the lodge where he had been staying sent out his best rescue dog to look for him. The dog found the man half-conscious, grabbed him, and started to shake him in order to wake him up. On coming to his senses the man, seeing the dog and thinking it was a wolf, stabbed the animal. The dog let go and returned to the lodge, where it died shortly thereafter. The dog's owner followed the trail of blood, came to the lost man, and saved him. The dog had given his life so that another might live.[1326]

"One day a certain farmer saw that a fire had ignited in his wheat fields, and was being blown toward his barns by the wind. To save the stored grain there, he lit a backfire, in hopes that it would impede the progress of the other flames. After both fires had subsided—and the barns had been saved—the farmer walked out through the smoldering ashes of the nearby fields. There he discovered the dead body of one of his hens, which had been caught in the blaze. Sadly, he turned over her black, charred body with his foot—and out from underneath ran four baby chicks. Her sacrifice saved her young ones. Such is the work of Christ on the cross, a place where the love of God dealt with the justice of God, where God's mercy matched God's wrath. Our Lord's sacrifice has saved us" (Attributed to Donald Grey Barnhouse).[1327]

In the winter of 1975, the *Chicago Sun Times* pictured a couple at a table kissing. The caption read: "Roderick A. Hinson gets a snack and a smack from Jacqueline Y. Nash in East Cleveland, Ohio, after he served her three-day jail sentence for possession of an unregistered gun." Hinson said it was his fault that she had the gun and that "a jail is not a good place for a lady." The judge said the substitution was unusual, but legal.[1328]

In one of Billy Graham's evangelistic films, *Shiokari Pass*, a young Christian became a hero. He was working with a railroad company, far away from his fiancée. He worked hard every day and finally the time came to go back to his fiancée and marry her. On the way back home, just before the peak of a steep hill, the train suddenly shook hard and stopped. When the young man went to the front of the passenger car on which he was riding, he found that it was disconnected from the rest of the train. It then began to roll backward down the steep slope. Since he had worked on the railroad, he knew there was a sharp curve behind them that the passenger car could not handle. It would be thrown off the tracks, killing the passengers. He tried to stop the car with the hand brake, but he failed. Our hero then remembered his favorite verse in the Bible: "Greater love has no one than this, that one lay down his life for his friends." Although this man had everything to live for, he jumped on the train tracks and stopped the passenger car with his body. He literally laid down his life to save the lives of many.[1329]

During a war between Britain and France, men were conscripted into the French Army by a kind of lottery system. When someone's name was drawn, he had to go off to battle. On one occasion, the authorities came to a certain man and told him he was among those who had been chosen. He refused to go, saying, "I was shot and killed two years ago." At first the officials questioned his sanity, but he insisted that was indeed the case. He claimed that the military records would show that he had been killed in action. "How can that be?" they questioned. "You are alive now!" He explained that when his name first came up, a close friend said to him, "You have a large family, but I am not married and nobody is dependent upon me. I'll take your name and address and go in your place." And that is indeed what the record showed. This rather unusual case was referred to Napoleon Bonaparte, who decided that the country had no legal claim on that man. He was free. He had died in the person of another![1330]

A number of years ago, a news story told of a dramatic incident that occurred in a small midwestern town. The residents of this town were warned to take cover because a tornado had been sighted. Living in this town was a young couple with a small baby. Knowing the tornado was upon them and that they had no time to take cover, they laid the tiny infant on the floor of their living room and covered the baby with their own bodies. The tornado struck with devastating force and leveled a row of homes, including theirs. The next morning, as rescue workers were rummaging through the destroyed homes, they heard a muffled crying. They came upon the lifeless bodies of the young couple, with their baby still safe beneath their shattered bodies.

They gave their lives for their child. This is what Christ has done for us.[1331]

A wise and just ruler established a series of laws for his people to follow. One day his mother broke one of the laws and was brought to the ruler after being caught. The penalty was twenty lashes. How could the ruler remain just and still fulfill the demands of his love for his mother? He took the lashes on his own back. Justice was satisfied, while love was revealed in full measure.[1332]

During the Civil War, a company of irregulars known as "bush-whackers" was arrested by the Union soldiers. Because they were guerrilla fighters and not in uniform, they were sentenced to be shot.

A courageous young boy in the Union Army touched his commanding officer on the arm and pleaded, "Won't you allow me to take the place of one of the men you have just condemned? I know him well—he has a large family who needs him badly. My parents are dead and I have few friends. No one will miss me. Please let me take his punishment!" The officer hesitated, but finally gave his consent. Pulling the husband and father to one side, the young man filled his position in the death line. On the stone that marks his grave in a little southern town are these words: "Sacred to the memory of Willy Lear. He took my place."[1333]

In Dickens's novel *A Tale of Two Cities*, a young French aristocrat was condemned to die by the guillotine during the bloody French Revolution. His punishment was based solely on his forefathers' crimes against the peasantry. The hour before his execution he was visited by a young English friend who could have passed for his twin. After the guard had left, the friend overpowered the doomed man with an anesthetic and exchanged clothes with him. Then, pretending to be the one condemned to die, he called the jailor and asked that his unconscious "visitor," supposedly overcome with grief, be removed and returned to his home. The nobleman was thus saved from death.

On his way to the guillotine, the young Englishman spoke these final words: "It is a far, far better thing that I do, than I have ever done. . . ." And he comforted himself with these words: "I am the Resurrection and the Life, saith the Lord: he that believeth in me, though he were dead, yet shall he live" (John 11:25). [1334]

361

Auschwitz was the first German concentration camp to become an extermination camp. The gas chambers were in constant use. But because of the great influx of new prisoners daily, the Germans began to use firing squads as well.

One day, the commandant selected ten men from one barracks to be executed by the firing squad. One of those selected was the father of a large family. When he was pulled from his place in line, he fell to the ground, begging the commandant to spare his life. The commandant was unresponsive until the man standing next to the fallen one, a Catholic priest named Maximillian Kolbe, stepped forward to offer his life in exchange for the man on his knees. Surprisingly, the commandant agreed to such an arrangement. But, instead of being led away to the firing squad, Father Maximillian was thrown into a tiny damp cell where he suffered the agonizing death of starvation. Today, Maximillian Kolbe is honored by millions of people because he died in the place of one man.

Jesus Christ, through an agonizing death on the cross, died not for one man, or a few, or even several—but for *all* men.[1335]

One Thanksgiving afternoon, while waiting for the expected feast, two sisters went outside to play. Being a bit mischievous, they soon found something that looked like fun to do, which all too soon led them to something they had been told not to do. Their father came into the backyard and found the evidence of their disobedience and called them to him. He explained to the girls that they must go to their room and that neither would be allowed to eat Thanksgiving dinner until the one who had disobeyed him confessed. The girls went to their room.

A while later the girls heard their mother calling them for dinner. Not knowing what was going to happen, they went and took their usual places around the table. The girls noticed that their father was not seated at the table as usual and asked, "Where is Daddy?"

The mother replied, "Daddy said that you girls could not eat Thanksgiving dinner with us today until one of you came to him and confessed your disobedience. Since neither of you came, Daddy decided that he would take your punishment himself—and so he will not be eating Thanksgiving dinner with us today."[1336]

Success

The only place where success comes before work is in the dictionary.[1337]

In August 1978, the first successful transatlantic balloon flight became a reality when *Double Eagle II* touched ground in a barley field in the small village of Miserey, France. But success in this accomplishment did not come easy. During the years from 1873 through 1978, thirteen attempts had been made—all ending in failure. After an unsuccessful attempt in 1977, in which *Double Eagle* ended up in Iceland, *Double Eagle II* was successful in making that historic six-day trip from Presque Isle, Maine, to Miserey, France.

What made the difference between the unsuccessful trip and the successful one? One difference was the addition of another man. A second difference was experience. Maxie Anderson, one of the crew, put it this way, "I don't think that you can fly the Atlantic without experience, and that's one reason it hadn't been flown before. Success in any venture is just the intelligent application of failure." (Cited in *National Geographic*, December 1978, pp. 858–882.)[1338]

Success, Measure of

"A measure of a man's success is not what he achieves, but what he overcomes" (Booker T. Washington).[1339]

Success, Suffering and

Lorne Sanny, when president of the Navigators, had the following to say, "If you are suffering without succeeding, then someone will succeed *after* you. . . . If you are succeeding without suffering, then someone suffered *before* you."[1340]

Success, Testing in

If you want to determine whether or not an air tank of the kind divers need is usable, you test it. Of course you do not test it when it is empty. No, you test it by subjecting it to pressure. And the pressure used in such a test is far beyond what would be considered normal. Only under intense pressure can hidden flaws be exposed.

Under the pressures of prosperity and success, we are tested severely. Praise detects the crack of pride, wealth reveals the flaw of selfishness, and learning discovers the leak of unbelief.[1341]

Suffering

A Christian is like a tea bag—not much good until it has gone through hot water.[1342]

"If God had told me some time ago that he was about to make me happy as I could be in this world, and then had told me that he should begin by crippling me in arm or limb, and removing me from all my usual sources of enjoyment, I should have thought it a very strange mode of accomplishing his purpose. And yet, how is his wisdom manifest even in this! For if you should see a man shut up in a closed room, idolizing a set of lamps and rejoicing in their light, and you wished to make him truly happy, you would begin by blowing out all his lamps, and then throwing open the shutter to let in the light of heaven" (Samuel Rutherford, *Letters of Samuel Rutherford*).[1343]

Suffering, Reason for

Suffering can do several things in the life of a believer. First, it can "burn out the dross," or purify us and lead us to greater holiness of life. But it can also "burn in the promises," or lead us to a closer dependence on God and his faithful promises to us. Burn it will—but look also at what the burning is for.[1344]

There are many benefits in knowing a foreign language. One of the chief benefits lies in the increased ability to understand and be understood. If a person knows only one language, he is tempted to think that everything he communicates is understood. However, if forced to translate an idea into another language, he must consider various possible words to use and their shades of meaning as well as all of the other elements of the language. This effort opens up a door, allowing him to communicate with many new people.

Suffering is like knowing a foreign language, since things that one usually takes for granted in a normal flow of life must be thought through in new ways in a time of suffering. For those who have lived with suffering, a door of ministry is opened wide to a world of hurting people.[1345]

The Weaver
My life is but a weaving between my Lord and me,
I cannot choose the colors he worketh steadily.
Oft times he weaveth sorrow and I in foolish pride
Forget he sees the upper and I the underside.
The dark threads are as needful in the weaver's skillful hand
As the threads of gold and silver in the pattern he has planned.
Not till the loom is silent and the shuttle cease to fly
Shall God unroll the canvas and explain the reason why.[1346]

"Men seek an explanation of suffering in cause and effect. They look backward for a connection between prior sin and present suffering. The Bible looks forward in hope and seeks explanations, not so much in origins as in goals. The purpose of suffering is seen, not in its cause, but in its results. The man [in John 9:3] was born blind so that the works of God could be displayed in him" (Francis I. Anderson, *Job* [Downers Grove, Ill: Inter-Varsity, 1976], p. 68).[1347]

The following quotation is from a Christian man who has been an invalid all his life, one of those lonely and obscure people who live in constant pain, who do not know what it means to be able to use their physical body in any way without pain and suffering:

"Loneliness is not a thing of itself, not an evil sent to rob us of the joys of life. Loneliness, loss, pain, sorrow, these are disciplines, God's gifts to drive us to his very heart, to increase our capacity for him, to sharpen our sensitivities and understanding, to temper our spiritual lives so that they may become channels of his mercy to others and so bear fruit for his kingdom. But these disciplines must be seized upon and used, not thwarted. They must not be seen as excuses for living in the shadow of half-lives, but as messengers, however painful, to bring our souls into vital contact with the living God, that our lives may be filled to overflowing with himself in ways that may, perhaps, be impossible to those who know less of life's darkness."[1348]

In the midst of the movie *The Hiding Place,* there is a scene set in the Ravensbruck concentration camp in Germany. Corrie ten Boom and her sister, Betsy, are there, along with ten thousand other women, in horrible, degrading, hideous conditions. They are gathered with some of the women in the barracks in the midst of the beds, cold and hungry and lice-ridden, and Betsy is leading a Bible class. One of the other women calls out derisively from her bunk and mocks their worship of God. They fall into conversation, and this woman says what so frequently is flung at Christians: "If your God is such a good God, why does he allow this kind of suffering?" Dramatically she tears off the bandages and old rags that bind her hands, displaying her broken, mangled fingers and says, "I'm the first violinist of the symphony orchestra. Did your God will this?"

For a moment no one answers. Then Corrie ten Boom steps to the side of her sister and says, "We can't answer that question. All we know is that our God came to this earth, and became one of us, and

365

he suffered with us and was crucified and died. And that he did it for love."[1349]

Suffering, Response to

Several years ago, there was a man going through great physical problems and one of his legs had to be amputated. That did not arrest the course of his disease, and he ultimately died because of it. Just a few days before the man's death, a minister visited him in the hospital, and the patient said something that perfectly expresses what "rejoicing in suffering" means to a Christian: "I never would have chosen one of the trials that I've gone through, but I wouldn't have missed any of them for the world!"

This man had an awareness that his suffering was something of value. He wouldn't have missed it! He wouldn't have chosen it either! That is rejoicing in suffering.[1350]

An unknown author has written these very appropriate words about suffering:

"It is well that we should think, sometimes, of the Upper Room, and of the Last Supper, and of His soul 'exceeding sorrowful unto death'; of Gethsemane, the deep shadow of the olive trees, his loneliness, prayers, and disappointment with his disciples, his bloody sweat; the traitor's kiss, the binding, the blow in the face, the spitting, the buffeting, the mocking, the scourging, the crown of thorns, the smiting; the sorrowful way, and burdensome cross, the exhaustion and collapse; the stripping, the impaling, the jeers of his foes, the flight of his friends; the hours on the cross, the darkness, his being forsaken of God; his thirst, and the end.[1351]

You may explain to a child all the medical reasons why he must have a shot in the arm, but when the nurse gets ready to plunge that needle into his arm, he runs to Mommy. Comfort comes not in always knowing the reason why, but in knowing the comforter.[1352]

It is clear from Scripture that "rejoicing in suffering" is not simply stoicism. It is not simply a grin-and-bear-it attitude of tough-it-out-and-see-how-much-you-can-take, or just-hang-in-there-until-it's-over-and-don't-let-anything-get-you-down, or keep-a-stiff-upper-lip. Many people feel that if they do this, they are obeying God and "rejoicing in suffering." But they are not.[1353]

366

Suicide

Some time ago an article in the paper recorded two deaths. A middle-aged couple died in each other's arms—the result of a suicidal overdose of drugs—because they couldn't face separation by death.

A psychiatry professor at a large university and his wife left a suicide note explaining that the wife was suffering from emphysema and kidney, liver, and heart ailments. Doctors had told her she might live up to five years or die at any time. Their oldest son said, "My father and mother were very much in love with each other. We wondered what my father would do if anything ever happened to Mom." Lewis said his parents often discussed suicide. "This solution was not a bad one," he added.

This couple could not face reality, because they had no hope beyond the present.[1354]

Suspicion

Suspicion enters by the door through which love and trust exit.[1355]

Synoptics, Harmony of

The last week of September 1978, KRLD radio station in Dallas, Texas, one of the most respected and popular stations in the city, reported that Jim Gilliam, the Los Angeles Dodger player and coach, had died of a cerebral hemorrhage. One hour later, KRLD again reported his death, but stated the cause of death was a heart attack, seemingly contradicting the previous account. The next hour, the report gave the complete account, for Jim Gilliam had died of a heart attack as a result of a severe cerebral hemorrhage. Both accounts were true, but it took the third account to put the whole picture together.

There is a lesson here for those who would point out that apparent inconsistencies in the various Gospel accounts' chronology and details cast doubt on the inerrancy of the whole. On the contrary, we need the narration and perspective of all the Gospel writers to put the whole picture together.[1356]

Tact

The new minister's family was presented with a pie baked by a congregational member who was a rather poor cook. The pie was inedible, so the minister's wife reluctantly threw it into the garbage. The

367

preacher was faced with the problem of thanking the baker and at the same time being truthful. After much thought, he sent the following note: "Thank you for being so kind and thoughtful. I can assure you that a pie like yours never lasts long at our house."[1357]

An English Puritan, Quire Bruen, was at a dinner given by the sheriff, and a toast to the prince was proposed. As the cup of wine was passed along the line, they looked to see what the Puritan would do. He said, "You may drink to his health, and I will pray for his health," and so passed the cup.[1358]

Teaching

There is a story about a man who wanted to train his mule. The first thing he did was to pick up a big stick and hit the mule a resounding wallop between the ears. As the mule staggered about, someone said to him, "What is the matter? Why did you do that?" The man said, "To teach a mule, you must first get his attention."

That observation may or may not be true of mules, but there is a good deal of truth in it when applied to humans. Interest must be awakened before learning can occur.[1359]

Teamwork

Bear Bryant, former head football coach at Alabama and one of the greatest football coaches of all time, was once interviewed after it was announced that only one player from his team had been named as an All-American. Bryant was asked if he was disappointed. He answered that he was and then stated that since his goal was always team effort, either all of his team should be All-American or none should be.[1360]

During the 1960 Olympics, defending gold medalist Al Oerter and teammate Rink Babka were expected to take the gold and silver medal in the discus throw. Although Babka was very ill the night before the competition he beat his teammate in the first four throws. On the fifth throw Oerter stepped into the circle, spun around, and threw the discus farther than any other that day. He had snatched victory from defeat and won the gold medal, while Babka took the silver. What no one knew until later was that Babka had noticed and pointed out a flaw in

Oerter's technique during the fourth throw. A small adjustment was all Oerter needed, and it cost Babka the gold medal. Babka was not the winner that year, but no one could call him a loser.[1361]

Television

On the table side by side,
    the Holy Bible and the T.V. Guide.
One is well worn but cherished with pride;
    not the Bible, the T.V. Guide.
One is used daily to help them decide;
    no, it isn't the Bible, it's the T.V. Guide.
As pages are turned, what shall we see?
    It doesn't matter, turn on the T.V.
Confusion reigns; they can't all agree
    on what they should watch on the old T.V.
So, they open the book in which they confide;
    no, not the Bible, the T.V. Guide.
The Word of God is seldom read,
    maybe a verse as they fall into bed.
Exhausted and sleepy, and as tired as can be,
    not from reading the Bible, but from watching T.V.
So then back to the table, side by side,
    the Holy Bible and the T.V. Guide.
No time for prayer, no time for the Word;
    the plan of salvation is seldom heard.
Yet, forgiveness of sins, so full and so free,
    is found in the Bible, not on T.V.[1362]

The Twenty-Third Channel

The T.V. set is my shepherd,
    my spiritual life shall want.
It maketh me to sit down and do nothing for His name's sake
    because it requireth all my time.
It keepeth me from doing my duty as a Christian
    because it presenteth so many good shows I must see.

It restoreth my knowledge of the things of the world.
It keepeth me from the study of God's Word.
It leadeth me in the paths of failing to attend the evening
    worship services and doing nothing in the kingdom of God.

Yea, though I live to be a hundred,
    I shall keep viewing my T.V. as long as it will work,
    for it is my closest companion.

Its sounds and its pictures,
  they comfort me.
It presenteth entertainment before me
  and keepeth me from doing important things with my family.
It fills my head with ideas which differ from those set forth in
  the Word of God.

Surely, no good thing will come of my life,
  because my T.V. offereth me no good time to do the will of God.
Thus, though I dwell in the place of the redeemed
who have been washed in the blood of the lamb,
I will let the souls around me slip into Hell forever.[1363]

Karl Marx said that religion was the opiate of the masses. He could not say such in our day, for it is television that is now both the opiate and pagan religion of the masses. Think about it for a moment.

Television's priests are its celebrities. Its denominations are the networks. Its morality is found in the ratings. Its shrines are the millions of T.V. sets that occupy honored spots in our homes, and its icons are the antennae that reach toward the sky. Its worshipers are found in its millions of regular viewers. And its rituals are the regularly scheduled programs that are habitually attended by its misguided addicts.[1364]

Temptation

One three-year-old's explanation for being in the kitchen atop a chair, eating cookies: "I just climbed up to smell them, and my tooth got caught."[1365]

A pastor warned his handsome new assistant about the dangers of immorality in the ministry. The assistant said that he always did his socializing in a group setting and concluded that "there is safety in numbers." The wise pastor replied, "Yes, that is so, but there is more safety in Exodus!"[1366]

A father had to go on a trip for a few days and instructed his teenage son that the car was not to be used while he was gone. When he returned, his son greeted him and said, "While you were gone, I came very close to breaking my promise to not use the car while you were away. You left the keys, and I carried them for three days, fighting temptation."

370

The father smiled, "Son, there's nothing like temptation to show you what you'll do—if you are given the opportunity!"[1367]

A woodpecker is a very interesting bird. The loud rat-a-tat-tat noise he makes as he drills into trees in search of bugs to eat always attracts attention. The secret of his success is simple. When a woodpecker finds a suitable tree, he begins to drill a hole. If the wood is too hard or no bugs are found, he simply moves over a bit and starts again. Over and over he continues, until he meets with success.

Satan uses temptation in much the same way. He will try one temptation on us and then if not successful will move over a bit and try another. And so he will continue, over and over again, until he finds a soft spot in us that he can use to his advantage.[1368]

Temptation, Protection from

In a supermarket one day, a mother was pushing a shopping cart with a small child in it. As she was not paying attention to where she was going, she turned down an aisle and suddenly realized it was the candy aisle. Immediately she turned completely around and went the other direction. She knew the small child would not be able to handle the situation. In the same way, God protects us from things we can't handle.[1369]

Temptation, Resisting

So often we say "Maybe" to sin instead of "No," leaving the option open for us to say "Yes." This is *not* resisting Satan or the temptations placed before us. We are like the person trying to get rid of a salesman on his doorstep without saying a firm "No" and closing the door. Though we say we are not interested in buying Satan's product—sin— we leave the door ajar and continue to discuss the tempting wares. We leave open the possibility for the devil to make a sale. To resist temptation we must say a firm "No" and shut the door.[1370]

A little girl once said in response to a question about how to deal with temptation: "When Satan comes knocking at the door of my heart, I send Jesus to answer the door. When Satan sees Jesus, he says, 'Oops, I am sorry, I must have the wrong house.' "[1371]

When tempted, learn the lesson of the dog. Anyone who has trained a dog to obey knows this scene. A bit of meat or bread is placed on the floor near the dog and the master says, "No!" which the dog knows means that he must not touch it. The dog will usually take his eyes off the food, because the temptation to disobey would be too great, and instead will fix his eyes on the master's face. That is the lesson of the dog. Always look to the Master's face.[1372]

When you flee temptation, leave no forwarding address.[1373]

Physical pressure is similar to the pressure of temptation in some respects. We can often escape it on our own, but we all have limits.

For example, even the atomic submarines built strongly enough to batter through the ice at the North Pole have a maximum crush depth limit beyond which they may not go with safety. The submarine *Thresher* exceeded that depth some years ago. As the pressure increased, the seawater crushed the sub's heavy steel bulkheads as if they were made of cheap plastic. Searchers found only little pieces of that huge submarine.

Yet there are fish that live at the same depth in which the Thresher was crushed. How can these fish survive? The answer is that they have equal pressure within themselves. Thus it should be for all Christians. In ourselves we are doomed. But, in Christ, there is no temptation beyond our ability to resist.[1374]

Master Greenham, a Puritan divine, was once sought by a woman who was greatly tempted. Upon making inquiries into her way of life, Greenham found that she had little to do, and he told her: "That is the secret of your being so much tempted. Sister, if you are very busy, Satan may tempt you, but he will not easily prevail, and he will soon give up the attempt."

Idle Christians are not tempted of the devil so much as they tempt the devil to tempt them.[1375]

Temptation, Testing and

In the New Testament, the word translated "temptation" *(peirazo)* has two shades of meaning. When used of God's tempting of man, it carries a positive intention. However, when it refers to the temptation of man by Satan or another person, the word implies a desire to bring out one's bad points.

The second idea might be likened to Ralph Nader's taking a G.M. car and running a group of tests on it. The emphasis and aim of this testing would be to bring out the bad traits of the car. However, if G.M. were to run tests on its own car, the motivation would be to point out the good traits.[1376]

When the Union-Pacific railroad was under construction, an elaborate trestle bridge was built over a certain large canyon in the West as part of the plan to connect St. Louis and California. Before it was open for commercial use, the construction engineer wanted to test its strength. He loaded a train with extra cars and equipment to double its normal payload. The train was driven out to the middle of the bridge, where it was to remain for an entire day. One worker complained, "Are you trying to break this bridge?" "No," said the engineer. "I'm trying to prove that the bridge is unbreakable."

So, too, does temptation prove our strength under pressure.[1377]

Ten Commandments

Somebody once figured out that we have thirty-five million laws trying to enforce ten commandments.[1378]

Testing

> *But If Not*
> God is able to deliver
>   From my weariness and pain,
> And he will deliver swiftly
>   If it be for lasting gain;
> But if not—my heart shall sing,
>   Trusting wholly in my King.
>
> God is able to supply me
>   With abundance from his store,
> And he will supply my table
>   Though the wolf be at the door;
> But if not—my heart shall rest
>   In the thought "He knoweth best."

God is able to defend me
  From my foes who throng around,
And he will defend me surely
  When their rage and hate abound;
But if not—I'll bless his name,
  And confess him just the same.

God is able to save dear ones
  From the world and self and sin,
And he will both save and keep them
  In his fold safe gathered in;
But if not—he'll hold my hand,
  Teaching me to understand.[1379]

Testing, Limits of

The large tractor-trailer trucks that travel the highways of the nation are subjected to a load limit. This means that there is a limit as to how much weight each truck is allowed to carry. There is a good reason for establishing such limits. If the trucks were allowed to exceed their weight limit, the roads would eventually fall apart, because a given road is designed to support vehicles only up to a certain weight.

Likewise, God knows how much we can bear when he allows us to be tested. He has assigned a definite "load limit" to each of us and never exceeds it (1 Cor. 10:13).[1380]

Testing, Purpose of

He sat by a furnace of sevenfold heat,
  As he watched by the precious ore;
And closer he bent, with a searching gaze,
  As he heated it more and more.

He knew he had ore that could stand the test;
  And he wanted the finest of gold—
To mold as a crown for the King to wear;
  Set with gems of a price untold.

So he laid our gold in the burning fire,
  Though we fain would have said him nay;
And he watched the dross that we had not seen,
  As it melted and passed away.

And the gold grew brighter, and yet more bright;
  But our eyes were so dim with tears,
We saw but the fire—not the Master's hand—
  And questioned with anxious fears.

Yet our gold shone out with a richer glow,
　As it mirrored a form above
That bent o'er the fire—though unseen by us—
　With looks of ineffable love.

Can we think it pleases his loving heart
　To cause us a moment's pain?
Ah! no, but he saw through the present loss
　The bliss of eternal gain.

So he waited there with a watchful eye,
　With a love that is strong and sure;
And his gold did not suffer a whit more heat,
　Than was needed to make it pure.[1381]

When American Airlines trains their pilots they first seek to prove them by use of a simulator. The simulator is designed to present the pilot with a variety of potential problems so that he will be able to handle any emergency in the future. First the pilot is tested with simple challenges, which eventually build up to catastrophic situations. The pilots are given more difficult problems only after they have mastered the previous ones. The result is that when the pilots have completed their courses, they are prepared to handle any problem that comes their way.

This is similar to God's method of working with us. God teaches us how to handle the problems of life, but never gives us more than we can handle. He teaches us through each situation, so that we can be fully prepared and mature people, ready to handle any challenge in life that might come our way.[1382]

Thankfulness

An evergreen is always green despite the changes in weather around it. It is green in the heat of summer as well as the cold of winter. So also our lives are to be characterized by an enduring thankfulness that is unaffected by the changes around us. When the heat of a pressured week or the deadly cold of pain strikes us, we should stand "ever green," always thankful, regardless of that which surrounds us.[1383]

A little boy was asked by his father to say grace at the table. While the rest of the family waited, the little guy eyed every dish of food his

375

mother had prepared. After the examination, he bowed his head and honestly prayed, "Lord, I don't like the looks of it, but I thank you for it, and I'll eat it anyway. Amen."[1384]

There is an imaginative story told of a day when the sun did not rise. Six o'clock came and there was no sign of dawn. At seven o'clock, there was still no ray of light. At noon, it was as black as midnight. No birds sang and only the hoot of an owl broke the silence. Then came the long black hours of the afternoon. Finally evening arrived but no one slept that night. Some wept, some wrung their hands in anguish. Every church was thronged with people on their knees. Thus they remained the whole night through. After that long night of terror and agony, millions of eager, tear-streaked faces were turned toward the east. When the sky began to grow red and the sun rose, there was a loud shout of joy. Millions of lips said, "Bless the Lord, O my soul!" because the sun had risen after one day of darkness.

The very consistency of God's blessings sometimes seems to dull our gratitude. The wonderful thing about the mercies of God is that they are fresh every morning and new every evening. Let us remember to be constantly thankful to our gracious God.[1385]

Bible commentator Matthew Henry, after being robbed, wrote in his diary the following: "Let me be thankful. First, because I was never robbed before. Second, because although they took my wallet, they did not take my life. Third, because although they took my all, it was not much. Fourth, because it was I who was robbed, not I who robbed."[1386]

Corrie ten Boom in *The Hiding Place* relates an incident that taught her always to be thankful. She and her sister, Betsy, had just been transferred to the worst German prison camp they had seen yet, Ravensbruck. On entering the barracks, they found them extremely over-crowded and flea-infested.

That morning, their Scripture reading in 1 Thessalonians had reminded them to rejoice always, pray constantly, and give thanks in all circumstances. Betsy told Corrie to stop and thank the Lord for every detail of their new living quarters. Corrie at first flatly refused to give thanks for the fleas, but Betsy persisted, and Corrie finally succumbed to her pleadings. During the months spent at that camp, they were surprised to find how openly they could hold Bible study and prayer meetings without guard interference. It was not until several months later that they learned the reason the guards would not enter the barracks was because of the fleas.[1387]

Theology

Karl Barth was once asked to sum up in a few words all he had written in the field of theology. This was his summary: "Jesus loves me, this I know, for the Bible tells me so."[1388]

Time

Time has been called a seamstress specializing in alterations.[1389]

When a young man sits next to a hot stove, a minute seems like an hour. But when a beautiful girl sits next to that young man, an hour seems like a minute.[1390]

When you kill time, remember that it has no resurrection.[1391]

Time, Use of

A study revealed that an average seventy-year-old man has spent twenty-four years sleeping, fourteen years working, eight years in amusements, six years at the dinner table, five years in transportation, four years in conversation, three years in education, and two years in studying and reading.

His other four years were spent in miscellaneous pursuits. Of those four years, he spent forty-five minutes in church on Sundays, and five minutes were devoted to prayer each day. This adds up to a not at all impressive total of five months that he gave to God over the seventy years of his life.

Even if this man had been a faithful churchgoer who attended Sunday school and three one-hour services per week, he would have spent only one year and nine months in church!

If you have a question about the above arithmetic, sit down and figure out how *you* have been using your time. How large a portion of it is for the things related to God? When you finish this exercise, ponder what Jesus said: "What good will it be for a man if he gains the whole world, yet forfeits his soul? . . ." (Matt. 16:26, NIV).[1392]

Tongue

This past year, if someone had paid you ten dollars for every kind word you ever spoke about other people, and also collected five dollars for every unkind word, would you be rich or poor?"[1393]

> I said a very naughty word only the other day.
> It was a truly naughty word I had not meant to say.
> But then, it was not really lost, when from my lips it flew;
> My little brother picked it up, and now he says it too.[1394]

Tongue, Control of

On a windswept hill in an English country churchyard stands a drab, gray slate tombstone. The faint etchings read:

> BENEATH THIS STONE, A LUMP OF CLAY,
> LIES ARABELLA YOUNG,
> WHO, ON THE TWENTY-FOURTH OF MAY,
> BEGAN TO HOLD HER TONGUE.[1395]
> If your lips you would keep from slips,
> Five things observe with care:
> To whom you speak; of whom you speak;
> And how, and when, and where.

William Norris[1396]

Some people are too talkative. They are like the young man who supposedly went to the great Greek philosopher Socrates to learn oratory. On being introduced, he talked so incessantly that Socrates asked for double fees. "Why charge me double?" said the young fellow. "Because," said the orator, "I must teach you two sciences: the one is how to hold your tongue, and the other is how to speak."[1397]

A talkative woman once tried to justify the quickness of her own tongue by saying, "It passes; it is done with quickly." To which the famous evangelist Billy Sunday replied, "So does a shotgun blast."

And such is the action of a quick tongue that it also leaves devastation in its wake.[1398]

A young lady once said to John Wesley, "I think I know what my talent is."

Wesley said, "Tell me."

She replied, "I think it is to speak my mind."

Wesley said, "I do not think God would mind if you bury that talent."[1399]

The ancient philosopher Zeno once said, "We have two ears and one mouth, therefore we should listen twice as much as we speak.[1400]

Tradition

Traditions are often an attempt to either protect us from something that can harm us or keep us in the place where we are most likely to do well. Not all traditions are so characterized, and some are nothing more than outmoded responses to situations that no longer exist. Nevertheless, this old saying remains true: "Never tear down a fence until you find out why it was built."[1401]

"The seven last words" of a dying church are: "We never did it that way before!"[1402]

Nothing is more deadly in a church than an attitude that might be expressed as, "Come weal or woe; our status is quo."[1403]

Trials

There is a story about how birds got their wings. The story goes that birds were first made without wings. Then God made wings, put them in front of the wingless birds, and said to them, "Come, take up these burdens and bear them." The birds hesitated at first, but soon obeyed and picked up the wings in their beaks. Because the wings were heavy, the birds laid them on their shoulders. Then, to their amazement, the wings began to grow and soon had attached themselves to their bodies. The birds quickly discovered how to use these new appendages and were soon soaring through the air. What had once been a heavy burden now became an instrument that enabled the birds to soar and go where they could never go before.

The story is a parable. We are the wingless birds. The duties and tasks

379

that seem like a burden and a trial often become the very means that God uses to lift us up and build godliness in us. God's plan is for our tasks to be our helpers and motivators. To refuse to bend our shoulders to receive a load is to decline a new opportunity for growth.[1404]

There once was an ant who felt imposed upon, overburdened, and overworked. You see, he was instructed to carry a piece of straw across an expanse of concrete. The straw was so long and heavy that he staggered beneath its weight and felt he would not survive. Finally, as the stress of his burden began to overwhelm him and he began to wonder if life itself was worth it, the ant was brought to a halt by a large crack in his path. There was no way of getting across that deep divide, and it was evident that to go around it would be his final undoing. He stood there discouraged. Then suddenly a thought struck him. Carefully laying the straw across the crack in the concrete, he walked over it and safely reached the other side. His heavy load had become a helpful bridge. The burden was also a blessing.[1405]

A man was shopping in a grocery story. His young son followed closely behind, carrying a large basket. The father loaded the basket with one thing after another until another customer began to feel sorry for the boy. She said. "That's a pretty heavy load for a young fellow like you, isn't it?" The boy turned to the woman and said, "Oh, don't worry. My dad knows how much I can carry." In the same way, God knows our limitations and gives to us no burden beyond what we can carry.[1406]

In a man's dream, he had a vision of walking through life on a sandy beach with Jesus by his side. As he looked back at the footprints in the sand, he noticed that at the troublesome spots of his life only one set of footprints marked the sand. The man asked Jesus where the Lord had been during those troublesome times. Jesus replied: "That single set of footprints is mine. Then I was carrying you and your burden."[1407]

Have you ever stopped to examine weeds? They serve as a reminder of judgment, a result of the curse on the ground after the fall of Adam. But if you look closely, you can see signs of mercy in that judgment. Some weeds have gorgeous flowers: tiny blue bells, ruffled purple blooms, and even magnificent displays of gold. In the same way—even in trials or discipline—if we look closely, we can see beautiful signs of God's mercy.[1408]

A customer once asked a shopkeeper, "What makes this set of china so much more expensive than that one over there? They look almost the same." The reply was simple, "The costlier set has had more done to it. You see, it had to be put through the kiln twice because the flowers are on a yellow background. On the less expensive set, they are on a white background. The costly china had to be put through the fire once for the yellow background, and then a second time for the design on it."

So it is in the life of a believer who desires God's best. There will be many times we must go through the kiln with all of its fire and heat until we fully display God's intended design in our life.[1409]

There is a story about a traveler in a logging area who watched with curiosity as a lumberjack occasionally jabbed his sharp hook into a log to separate it from the others floating down a mountain stream. When asked why he did this, the logger replied, "These may all look alike to you, but I can recognize that a few of them are quite different. The ones I let pass are from trees that grew in a valley where they were always protected from the storms. Their grain is rather coarse. The ones I have hooked and kept apart came from high on the mountains. From the time they were small they were beaten by strong winds. This toughens the trees and gives them a fine grain. We save them for choice work. They are too good to be used for ordinary lumber."

Has the grain of your character been finely arranged by the toughening action of life's trials and adversity?[1410]

Someone has said, "A brook would lose its song if God removed the rocks."[1411]

No one enjoys a visit to the dentist, although all enjoy the long-range benefits of the visit. In a similar way, no one enjoys the difficulties of a trial, but all who endure them enjoy the side effects of perseverance, proven character, and hope.[1412]

The richest chords require some black keys.[1413]

Trials, God's Help in

Long ago, in the days of sailing ships, a terrible storm arose and a ship was lost in a deserted area. Only one crewman survived, washed up on a small uninhabited island. In his desperation, the castaway daily prayed to God for help and deliverance from his lonely existence. Each day he looked for a passing ship and saw nothing. Eventually he managed to build a crude hut, in which he stored the few things he had recovered from the wreck and those things he had made to help him.

One day, as the sailor was returning from his daily search for food, he saw a column of smoke. As he ran to it he saw his hut in flames. All was lost. Now not only was he alone, but he had nothing to help him in his struggle for survival. Stunned and nearly overcome with grief and despair, he fell into a deep depression and spent a nearly sleepless night wondering what was to become of him and questioning whether life itself was even worth the effort.

The next morning, he rose early and went down to the sea. There, to his amazement, he saw a ship lying offshore and a small boat rowing toward him. When the once-marooned man met the ship's captain, he asked him how he had known to send help. The captain replied, "Why, we saw your smoke signal yesterday, but by the time we drew close the tide was against us. So we had to wait until now to come and get you."

Do not despair when calamity strikes, for God is always able to bring a blessing out of what seems to be a curse.[1414]

A vine clings to an oak tree and in so doing finds the protection in times of trial that preserves it. If a violent storm should arise and the vine is on the side of the tree away from the wind, the tree serves to protect the vine from the wind, which would otherwise tear it away and rip it into shreds. If the vine is on the exposed side of the tree, the wind serves only to press the vine closer to the tree it already clings to.

In the storms of our life, God will at times set himself between us and the fury of the storm and so protect us from it. At other times, he will expose us to the storm so that its ravages may serve to press us closer to him.[1415]

Some flowers, such as the rose, must be crushed if their full fragrance is to be released. Some fruits, such as the sycamore, must be bruised if they are to attain ripeness and sweetness. Some metals, such as gold, must be heated in the furnace if they are to become pure.

The attaining of godliness—the process of becoming a mature Christian—requires similar special handling. It is often through pain, suffering, trouble, adversity, trials, and even temptation that we develop spiritual discipline and become refined and enriched.[1416]

When a wood sculptor wants to create a work of art, he starts with a log and begins to fashion it with a sharp chisel. He meticulously cuts and shapes that log until finally he has his finished product. The log, which might otherwise have been burned in a fireplace, has become a beautiful masterpiece that can be displayed on the mantle *over* the fireplace.

God's working in our lives may sometimes be painful, yet his ultimate purpose for us is to produce a masterpiece.[1417]

The story is told of two artists who were putting the finishing touches on a painting high on a scaffold in a church. The younger artist stepped back to admire the work and became enraptured with the beauty of what he and his mentor had created. His master saw his pleasure and realized that in the emotion of the moment the young man was continuing to step back, inching toward the edge of the scaffold. In another moment he would plunge to his death. Fearing he would frighten his student by a warning cry, the master artist deliberately splashed paint across the painting. The young man lunged forward in shock and cried out, "What have you done? Why did you do that?" Upon hearing the reason, his anger and confusion melted into tears of joy and thankfulness.

God sometimes uses trials to protect us from ourselves, especially from the naive enthusiasm that could lead us to disaster.[1418]

When the time comes, an eagle stirs up the nest and turns her young ones out into mid-air, compelling them to use their wings. In a similar manner, God allows many a human heart to be disturbed by troubles to bring about an urgent sense of need for the Savior.[1419]

> When God wants to drill a man,
> And thrill a man,
> And skill a man;
> When God wants to mold a man
> To play the noblest part,
>
> When he yearns with all his heart
> To create so great and bold a man
> That all the world shall be amazed,
> Watch his methods, watch his ways—
> How he ruthlessly perfects
> Whom he royally elects.

How he hammers him and hurts him,
And with mighty blows, converts him
Into trial shapes of clay
Which only God understands,
While his tortured heart is crying,
And he lifts beseeching hands.

How he bends but never breaks
When his good he undertakes.
How he uses whom he chooses,
And with every purpose, fuses him,
By every act, induces him
To try his splendor out.
God knows what he's about.[1420]

A young boy carried the cocoon of a moth into his house to watch the fascinating events that would take place when the moth emerged. When the moth finally started to break out of his cocoon, the boy noticed how very hard the moth had to struggle. The process was very slow. In an effort to help, he reached down and widened the opening of the cocoon. Soon the moth was out of its prison. But as the boy watched, the wings remained shriveled. Something was wrong. What the boy had not realized was that the struggle to get out of the cocoon was essential for the moth's muscle system to develop. In a misguided effort to relieve a struggle, the boy had crippled the future of this creature. Trials are necessary for growth.[1421]

The trials of our faith are like God's ironing. When the heat of trials are applied to our lives the wrinkles of spiritual immaturity begin to be smoothed out.[1422]

Bees undergo an interesting process to ensure the healthy development of their young. The queen lays each egg in a six-sided cell, which is filled with enough pollen and honey to feed on until the egg reaches a certain stage of maturity. The top is then sealed with a capsule of wax. When the occupant has exhausted its supply of nourishment, the time has come for the tiny creature to be released from its confinement. But what a wrestling, tussling, and straining it endures to get through the wax seal! The opening is so narrow that in the agony of its exit, the bee rubs off the membrane that encases its wings—so that when it does emerge, it is able to fly.

If an insect were to get into the hive and devour the wax capsules, the young bees could crawl out without any effort or trouble but would be unable to fly. Soon their mature relatives would instinctively proceed to sting them to death.

Christians also need the times of wrestling and straining with trials so that they may be prepared to do God's will for their life.[1423]

It is always good to attend church or Bible study and sit and soak up the truth of God's Word like a sponge. But we must realize that sponges work best when they are squeezed.[1424]

Paul's statement in Romans 8:28 that "all things work together for good" sounds like the ingredients for a cake after they have been mixed together. Some of the ingredients used to make a cake taste good by themselves. Other ingredients, such as alum, baking powder, or flour are not very palatable. Nevertheless, they are essential and must be mixed with the good-tasting ingredients to produce a delicious final product.

God can be trusted to take even the bitter experiences of life and blend them together and make them work together for good. God knows which ingredients are needed, and he knows how to mix them to produce the desired result.[1425]

Wilson Johnson, the founder of Holiday Inn motels, once said, "When I was forty years old I worked in a sawmill. One morning the boss told me I was fired. Depressed and discouraged, I felt like the world had caved in. When I told my wife what had happened, she asked me what I was going to do. I replied, 'I'm going to mortgage our little home and go into the building business.' My first venture was the construction of two small buildings. Within five years I was a multimillionaire! At the time it happened, I didn't understand why I was fired. Later, I saw that it was God's unerring and wondrous plan to get me into the way of his choosing."[1426]

In his Bible, an elderly minister carried a bookmark that was made of silk threads woven into a motto. The back of the bookmark was a tangled web of crossed threads that seemed to be without reason or purpose. When the minister visited a home or hospital room where there was great trouble, sorrow, or death, he would frequently show the bookmark, first presenting the reverse side with all its unintelligible tangle. When the distressed one had examined it intently without finding any meaning to the seeming disorder, the minister would ask him to turn the fabric over. Immediately, against a white silk background, there appeared a phrase in colored threads: "God Is Love." That side made sense; it had order and meaning.

So it is in life. We often experience events that seem to be without explanation or meaning, like a maze of tangled threads. But when we are face to face with Christ and can view our life from eternity, we will see that every detail—good and bad, pleasant and unpleasant—was woven together to show us that indeed "God Is Love."[1427]

Hudson Taylor, founder of the China Inland Mission (now the Overseas Missionary Fellowship), was talking to a young missionary who was about to start work in China. "Look at this," Taylor said and then proceeded to pound his fist on the table. The tea cups jumped, and the tea was spilled. While the startled young man was wondering what was going on, Taylor said, "When you begin your work, you will be buffeted in numerous ways. The trials will be like blows. Remember, these blows will bring out only what is in you."[1428]

At a cross-country steeplechase exhibition, one horse suddenly shied away from a hurdle and ran into a barbed-wire fence. The results were disaster, as the rider was taken by ambulance to a hospital and the bleeding horse remained ensnarled in the wire until the slow process of cutting it away was completed.

The underlying tragedy was seen in the fact that the jump was a low one, which the horse could have easily cleared. Yet the horse apparently took the fence to be an opening in the course and thus an escape from the obstacle.

How we as believers are often like that foolish horse! When faced with difficulties, do we look for the the way out rather than trusting in God's provision? Do we break for the open at the first opportunity, only to find that we have become ensnared and that our present difficulty is far worse than the one we sought to avoid?[1429]

A Malayan boy, after having become a Christian, found himself in the midst of a truly demonic attack in the early weeks of his new Christian walk. Allah had been put behind him and the occult practices that had been woven together with this former Moslem faith had been turned from, but his Christian faith was like a tiny child's first steps.

This boy went through demon activity, which he had experienced before in his life, and his call went forth to God, "Oh, God, help me." However, since there was no immediate, visible change, the boy fell into the trap Satan had set for him. "It isn't working!" was the cry of his heart, and his old reaction pattern came forth: "I'll try this, and this. . . ." And so next, he called, "Allah be praised!" and then used some Arabic words in a "magic" formula handed down for generations.

The young Christian did not yet know that superstitious "crossing your fingers" is not a sign of faith. He was later to learn the joy and freedom of trusting the power of God alone. Faith asks not in unbelief, but in belief without doubting.[1430]

Have you ever seen someone break a mustang? When a three-year-old horse who has never had a saddle on his back first feels a saddle, it must be a frightening experience. Some horses will react with anger, rearing back and trying to get away—even striking out with their forefeet at their trainer. Their nostrils flare, their eyeballs roll, and they panic! Others will just stand there, trembling, shaking like a leaf. They won't move; they're so afraid. They don't know what's happening to them.

Immature Christians respond to trials like wild horses. Some panic and cry out to the Lord, "What's gone wrong?" Others just freeze and do nothing. Mature Christians are like horses who have learned to trust their trainer. They sense what is happening and respond to it by submitting to the hand of their Master, knowing that he will do them no wrong.[1431]

Trials are not to our detriment but add to our growth. For example, consider the kite flyer. He must take in hand the string of his kite and run until the kite lifts up into the heavens. But he will not reach his goal of a flying kite if there is no wind. Every kite flyer knows that wind is necessary for flying kites. But note that kites do not rise *with* the wind but rise against it. So it is with trials. The Christian will not ascend to patience and maturity unless he ascends against trials. Do trials make you soar above, or just plain sore?[1432]

A carpenter hired to help restore an old farmhouse had just finished up a rough first day on the job. A flat tire had made him lose an hour of work, his electric saw quit, and now his ancient pickup refused to start.

As he rode home with a friend, he sat in stony silence. On arriving, as he walked toward the front door, he paused briefly at a small tree, touching the tips of the branches with both hands. Then, opening the door, he underwent an amazing transformation. His tanned face was wreathed in smiles and he hugged his two small children and gave his wife a kiss.

Why the transformation? The tree in his yard was his "trouble tree." He knew he couldn't avoid having troubles on the job, but one thing was for sure—troubles didn't belong in the house with his wife and children. So he just hung his troubles on the tree every night when he came home and, in the morning, picked them up again. The funny thing was that when he came out in the morning to collect his troubles, there weren't nearly as many as he remembered hanging up the night before.[1433]

A lot of Christians have an ejection-seat mentality. As soon as they get into difficulty, they want to pull the ejection cord and zip off into glory, hoping to get away from it all.[1434]

No pharmacist ever weighed out medicine with half as much care and exactness as God weighs out every trial he dispenses. Not one gram too much does he ever permit to be put on us.[1435]

In 1895, Andrew Murray was in England suffering from a terribly painful back, the result of an injury he had incurred years before. One morning while he was eating breakfast in his room, his hostess told him of a woman downstairs who was in great trouble and wanted to know if he had any advice for her. Andrew Murray handed her a paper he had been writing on and said, "Give her this advice I'm writing down for myself. It may be that she'll find it helpful." This is what was written:

> In time of trouble, say, "First, he brought me here. It is by his will I am in this strait place; in that I will rest." Next, "He will keep me here in his love, and give me grace in this trial to behave as his child." Then say, "He will make the trial a blessing, teaching me lessons he intends me to learn, and working in me the grace he means to bestow." And last, say, "In his good time he can bring me out again. How and when, he knows." Therefore, say "I am here (1) by God's appointment, (2) in his keeping, (3) under his training, (4) for his time."[1436]

Trinity

Augustine, while puzzling over the doctrine of the Trinity, was walking along the beach one day when he observed a young boy with a bucket, running back and forth to pour water into a little hole. Augustine asked, "What are you doing?" The boy replied, "I'm trying to put the ocean into this hole." Then Augustine realized that he had been trying to put an infinite God into his finite mind.[1437]

Trustworthiness

A little boy walked down the beach, and as he did, he spied a matronly woman sitting under a beach umbrella on the sand. He walked up to her and asked, "Are you a Christian?"

"Yes."

"Do you read your Bible every day?"

She nodded her head, "Yes."

"Do you pray often?" the boy asked next, and again she answered, "Yes."

With that he asked his final question, "Will you hold my quarter while I go swimming?"[1438]

Truth

Truth does not need updating. There is a story of a man who came to his old friend, a music teacher, and said to him, "What's the good news today?" The old teacher was silent as he stood up and walked across the room, picked up a hammer, and struck a tuning fork. As the note sounded out through the room, he said, "That is A. It is A today; it was A five thousand years ago, and it will be A ten thousand years from now. The soprano upstairs sings off-key, the tenor across the hall flats on his high notes, and the piano downstairs is out of tune." He struck the note again and said, "That is A, my friend, and that's the good news for today."[1439]

The relationship between truth and holiness is similar to that between light and vision. Light cannot create an eye or give a blind eye vision, but it is essential to seeing. Wherever light penetrates, it dissipates darkness and brings everything into view.

In a similar manner, truth cannot regenerate or impart spiritual life, but it is essential to the practice of holiness. Wherever truth penetrates, it dissipates error and reveals everything for what it really is.[1440]

Truth, Response to

You are driving down the highway when you encounter a sign that reads, "Dangerous Curve Ahead." Immediately you are confronted with making a choice. One, you can observe the warning and slow down. Two, you can ignore the warning and maintain your rate of speed. Or, three, you can defy the warning and speed up. Whatever response you exercise, you will not change the truth of the sign. The curve remains dangerous, regardless of whether you acknowledge the fact or not.[1441]

Truth, Suppressed

John Cage, a contemporary American composer, believes that the universe is impersonal by nature and that it originated only through pure chance. In an attempt to live consistently with this personal philosophy, Cage composes all of his music by various means of chance. He uses, among other things, the tossing of coins and the rolling of dice to make sure that no personal element enters into the final product. The result is music that has no form, no structure and, for the most part, no appeal. Though Cage's professional life accurately reflects his belief in a universe that has no order, his personal life does not, for his favorite pastime is mycology, the collecting of mushrooms, and because of the potentially lethal results of picking a wrong mushroom, he cannot approach it on a purely by-chance basis. Concerning that, he states: "I became aware that if I approached mushrooms in the spirit of my chance operations, I would die shortly." John Cage "believes" one thing, but practices another. In doing so, he is an example of the man described in Romans 1:18 who "suppresses the truth of God," for when faced with the certainty of order in the universe, he still clings to his own novel theory. (Cited by Francis Schaeffer, *The God Who Is There* [Downers Grove, Ill: Inter-Varsity, 1968], pp. 72–74.)[1442]

Understanding, Lack of

Some of us are like Christopher Columbus when it comes to our understanding:

He didn't know where he was going.

He didn't know where he was when he got there.

He didn't know where he had been when he returned.[1443]

Urim and Thummim

The story has been told of a young man who was a recent graduate of a theological seminary. Educated beyond his intelligence, he had arrived at the spot where he thought he knew all the answers to all the theological problems and was eager to parade his knowledge. He came to a certain town where lived an elderly Christian layman who had never been to a Bible school or seminary but had taught himself the Word of God under the tutelage of the Holy Spirit. In a very humble way, he had gained a reputation as a man of wise counsel. When the prideful young theologian heard about him, he said, "I'd like to meet that man. I think I could ask him a question or two that he couldn't answer!"

So a meeting was arranged. The first thing the young man said was, "Sir, I hear that you have quite a reputation as a Bible student. I'd like to ask you a question." The old man said, "Well, I don't know if I can answer it, but I'd be glad to try. What is your question?" The young man said, "Tell me, what were the Urim and the Thummim? The old man thought a moment, then said, "Well, sir, I don't know really, and I don't think anyone else does either. We do know the names mean 'lights' and 'perfections' and that these were the instruments by which the high priest could determine the mind of God in specific instances. Beyond that, I don't think I could go. But you know, I've found that if we change just one letter in these words, we have the instrument by which we can know the mind and will of God in our lives."

The young man was a bit puzzled. "What do you mean?" The old man said, "Well, it you change the 'r' in Urim to an 's,' you'll make it 'Usim and Thummim.' An when I want to know the mind of God, I just take the pages of my Bible and I 'Usim and Thummim.' And by that means I can learn whatever I need to know!"[1444]

Vacation

The story is told of four couples who rented a summer house for two months. Each couple in turn took their two-week vacation there and kept the combined thirteen children of the four families with them. One of the couples was bragging about this clever plan to a friend when the friend said, "I don't think two weeks in a cabin with thirteen kids would be much of a vacation."

"You're right," was the reply. "Those two weeks were absolutely terrible. The vacation was the six weeks at home *without* the children."[1445]

Vanity

A Chinese legend tells of a group of cultured elderly gentlemen who met often to exchange wisdom and drink tea. Each host tried to find the finest and most costly varieties of tea so as to create exotic blends that would arouse the admiration of his guests.

When the most venerable and respected of the group entertained, he served his tea with unprecedented ceremony, measuring the leaves from a golden box. The assembled epicures praised this exquisite tea. The host smiled and said, "The tea you have found so delightful is the same tea our peasants drink. I hope that it will be a reminder to us all that the good things in life are not necessarily the rarest or the most costly."[1446]

Virtue

"I do not admire the excess of some one virtue unless I am shown at the same time the excess of the opposite virtue. A man does not prove his greatness by standing at an extremity, but by touching both extremities at once and filling all that lies between them" (Blaise Pascal).[1447]

Vision

A cartoon once showed two Eskimos fishing through holes in the ice. One of the Eskimos had made a hole like you might expect to see, about the size of a manhole cover. The other had dropped his line in an immense hole that seemed to reach to the edge of the horizon, in the shape of a whale![1448]

Vision that looks inward becomes duty.

Vision that looks outward becomes aspiration.

Vision that looks upward becomes faith.[1449]

Vows

In the movie *Mary Poppins*, the two children, Jane and Michael Banks, jumped into bed after their incredible first day with the amazing Mary Poppins. Jane asked, "Mary Poppins, you won't ever leave us, will you?" Michael, full of excitement, looked at his new nanny and added, "Will you stay if we promise to be good?" Mary looked at the two and as she tucked them in replied, "Look, that's a pie-crust promise. Easily made, easily broken![1450]

Warfare

Wilfred Owen, a poet of the World War I period, described in the lines below his attitude after seeing a friend gag in a green field of gas fumes during an enemy gas attack. Owen himself was killed in action a week before the armistice but left a legacy of poems that decried the futility and horror of war.

. . .

If in some smothered dreams, you too could pace
Behind the wagon that we flung him in,
And watch the white eyes writhing in his face.
His hanging face, like a devil's sick of sin;
If you could hear, at every jolt, the blood
Come gargling from the froth-corrupted lungs,
Bitter as the cud
Of vile, incurable sores on innocent tongues—
My friend, you would not tell with such high zest,
To children ardent for some desperate glory,
The old lie: *Dulce et decorum est*
Pro patria mori. *
[* "Sweet and fitting it is to die for one's country," Horace][1451]

Wealth

Hetty Green was possibly America's greatest miser. She died in 1915, leaving an estate valued at over one million dollars, but always ate cold oatmeal because it cost too much to heat it. Her son had to suffer through a leg amputation unnecessarily because Hetty wasted so much time looking for a free clinic that he wasn't examined early enough.

Hetty Green was wealthy, but she chose to live like a pauper. Eccentric? Yes. Crazy? Perhaps, but nobody could prove it. She was so foolish that she hastened her own death when she suffered a stroke by becoming too excited over a discussion about the value of drinking skimmed milk.

We laugh at the foolishness of this eccentric old woman, but the fact is that this is a tragic illustration of many Christians. We have limitless wealth at our disposal, and yet we often choose to live in spiritual poverty.[1452]

The great newspaper publisher of the early part of this century, William Randolph Hearst, was a patron of art and spent a great deal of money collecting art treasures for his collection. The story is told that one day he found a description of an artwork that he felt he must own, so he sent his agent abroad to find it. After months of searching, the agent reported that he had found the treasured object and that it was close to home. Where was it? In Hearst's warehouse, with many other treasures he owned that were still in their crates. The great Hearst had been searching for a treasure he already owned!

Such is the power of wealth that it blinds us to the treasures we already have and focuses us on obtaining more, without appreciating what we have.[1453]

Will of God

God is said to speak to men in "a still, small voice" (1 Kings 19:12), which may partially explain why we find it hard to hear him when he speaks. It's much like receiving a phone call in a house with the T.V. going, the stereo blaring, and a house full of people chatting with one another. To understand the caller, it requires asking the friends to be quiet and turning down the stereo and T.V.

So it is with hearing God. It may well require removing those distractions, those areas of sin that deafen our ears to the voice of the Lord.[1454]

When David Livingstone was asked if he didn't fear that going into Africa was too difficult and too dangerous, he answered, "I am immortal until the will of God for me is accomplished."[1455]

Just before Abraham Lincoln issued the Emancipation Proclamation, a group of ministers urged him to grant immediate freedom to all slaves. "It is my earnest desire to know the will of Providence in this matter," Lincoln wrote. "And if I can learn what it is, I will do it. . . . I suppose it will be granted that I am not to expect a direct revelation; I must study the plain physical facts of the case . . . and learn what appears to be wise and right. The subject is difficult, and good men do not agree."[1456]

"If it were in the will of God, I'd plant an oak tree today, even if Christ were coming tomorrow" (Martin Luther).[1457]

F. B. Meyer was sailing many years ago to England from northern Ireland. He told the story of how it was night and, as the ship entered the harbor, nothing was to be seen but a confusing array of lights. Dr. Meyer wondered how the captain could hope to navigate into the harbor safely at night in such a confusing jumble of lights, and so he asked him. The captain took him up to the bridge and said, "You see, sir, it's really very simple. I'll show you how. Do you see that big light over to the left? And do you see that other big light over there to the right of it? And now, do you see that outstanding light farther still this way? Well now, keep your eyes on those three lights and see what happens." As Dr. Meyer watched, the big outer light on the left gradually moved in until it coincided with the middle one. Then, as the ship turned, the light gradually merged into the third. "There now," said the captain, "all I have to do is to see that those three big lights become one; then I go straight forward."

The point is that the believer also has three lights to guide him into the will of God. When Scripture and conscience are lined up with outward circumstances so that the three become one, we need have no fear. We may go straight ahead. God's will is clear.[1458]

God has his best things for the few
That dare to stand the test.
He has his second choice for those
Who will not have his best.

It is not always open ill
That risks the promised rest.
The better often is the foe
That keeps us from the best.

Give me, O Lord, thy highest choice;
Let others take the rest.
Their good things have no charm for me
For I have got thy best.

A. B. Simpson[1459]

A middle-aged farmer who had been desiring for years to be an evangelist was out working in the field one day when he decided to rest under a tree. As he looked into the sky he saw that the clouds seemed to form into the letters P and C. Immediately he hopped up, sold his farm, and went out to P-reach C-hrist, which he felt was God's leading. Unfortunately, he was a horrible preacher. After one of his sermons a neighbor came forward and whispered in his ear, "Are you sure God wasn't just trying to tell you to P-lant C-orn?"[1460]

"I think I'll be a preacher when I grow up," the small boy confided to his mother.

"It's a wonderful calling," the mother agreed, "but why do you want to be a preacher?"

"Well," resolved the youngster, "I figure I'll have to go to church all my life, anyway, and it's harder to sit than to stand up and holler."[1461]

Wisdom

A man begins cutting his wisdom teeth the first time he bites off more than he can chew.[1462]

A man approached a speaker and said, "You Christians are all brainwashed." The speaker replied, "I think we are all brainwashed to a degree. The important thing is that we Christians choose what we want to wash our brains with."[1463]

One morning the young new president of a bank made an appointment with his predecessor to seek some advice. He began, "Sir, as you well know, I lack a great deal of the qualifications you already have for this job. You have been very successful as president of this bank, and I wondered if you would be kind enough to share with me some of the insights you have gained from your years here that have been the keys to your success."

The older man looked at him with a stare and replied: "Young man, two words: *good decisions*."

The young man responded, "Thank you very much, sir, but how does one come to know which is the good decision?"

"One word, young man: *experience*."

"But how does one get experience?"

"Two words, young man: *bad decisions*."[1464]

William Thomson (later Lord Kelvin) was one of the greatest physicists of nineteenth-century England. When he was away at college, his father wrote to him: "You are young: take care you be not led to what

396

is wrong. A false step now, or the acquiring of an improper habit, might ruin you for life. Frequently look back on your conduct and thence learn wisdom for the future." (Cited in G. K. C. MacDonald, *Faraday, Maxwell, and Kelvin*, 1964.)[1465]

Man's wisdom is not enough. It is limited, partial wisdom. T. S. Eliot put it so beautifully when he said in "The Rock":

> All our knowledge brings us nearer to our ignorance,
> All our ignorance brings us nearer to death,
> But nearness to death no nearer to God.

Then he asks the question that hangs over this whole generation:
> Where is the Life we have lost in living?[1466]

A leading economic expert, Professor Irving Fisher of Yale, had this to say about the bright future of the stock market and the American economy: "Stock prices have reached what looks like a permanently high plateau."

His statement was spoken in early October 1929, just a couple of weeks before the stock market crash that ushered in the Great Depression.[1467]

Witness, by Life

Some years ago, on returning from a business trip, a man brought his wife some souvenirs. Among them was a matchbox that would glow in the dark. After giving it to her, he turned out the light, but the object was not visible. "This must be a joke!" she said. Disappointed, the husband commented, "I've been cheated!" Then his wife noticed some French words on the box. Taking it to a friend who knew the language, she was told that the directions read: "If you want me to shine at night, keep me in the sunlight all day." So she put her gift in a south window. That evening when she turned out the light, the matchbox had a brilliant glow. The surprised husband asked, "What did you do?" "Oh, I found the secret," she said. "Before it can shine in the dark, it must be exposed to the light."

Just as the matchbox, having been exposed to the sun, took on the nature of the sun and began to shine, so Christians should constantly expose themselves to the Son, that they may take on his nature and shine as lights in a dark world.[1468]

In the days before electricity had been harnessed, oil lamps were used for lighting. But to have them work to the maximum, the wicks had to be carefully trimmed to spread the flame evenly, and the globes had to be cleaned so as to be clear and shiny.

Christians are like oil lamps: they need to emit a steady, unobstructed light—the light of Christlike life in them.[1469]

In winter months in the northern states, salt and sand are put on the roads to make driving safer. This mixture eventually becomes plastered on the sides of cars, making them filthy and unattractive. One dirty car looks about the same as another. About the time that everyone is used to the universally grayish color of cars, a warm spell comes along and some energetic person will wash his car. Then the difference is apparent. One clean car makes all the difference in showing how much dirt has accumulated on the other cars!

The believer's lifestyle should be like that one clean car. It should stand out so brightly that in contrast the unbeliever's lifestyle is seen for what it is—murky and marred by the darkness of sin.[1470]

Jim, an elder at a church, was to oversee the evangelism of new people that moved into the area. Sun Lee and his family were Vietnamese refugees who had recently been moved into the area. They had no possessions, knew no one, needed help in every way. Jim began by helping them to get food and then spent much time finding Sun Lee a good job. Jim wanted so much to tell Sun Lee about Jesus Christ, but he didn't know Vietnamese and the refugees knew very little English. Both men sought to learn the other's language so that they could become better friends.

One day, Jim felt that he knew enough now to tell Sun Lee about Jesus. Jim began to explain about God and Jesus to Sun Lee, but the more he talked, the more confusing it seemed to get. Sun Lee would repeat in Vietnamese a little of what Jim said in English. Finally, Jim was so frustrated that he decided to give up trying to communicate until he had learned more Vietnamese. Sun Lee at this point blurted out, "Is your God like you? If he is, I want to know him." Jim explained that Jesus Christ was greater than he was, far greater. Yet Sun Lee wanted to know more about Jesus Christ *if* he was like Jim! Jim had thought for all these months that he was not communicating the gospel. But he was, with the greatest form of communication a person can use—the example of a life filled with Jesus Christ.[1471]

A minister was making a wooden trellis to support a climbing vine. As he was pounding away, he noticed that a little boy was watching him. The youngster didn't say a word, so the preacher kept on working, thinking the lad would leave. But he didn't. Pleased at the thought that his work was being admired, the pastor said, "Well, son, trying to pick up some pointers on gardening?" "No," replied the boy, "I'm just waiting to hear what a preacher says when he hits his thumb with a hammer."[1472]

A Christian's life should stand out to the world as different. We should be like zebras among horses. When our life is indistinguishable from the world's, we are like albino zebras. They really are zebras, their parents are zebras, they know they are zebras on the inside. But to all who see them from the outside they are no different from horses.[1473]

> We are the only Bible
> The careless world will need,
> We are the sinner's gospel,
> We are the scoffer's creed,
> We are the Lord's last message,
> Given in deed and word.
> What if the type is crooked?
> What if the print is blurred?"
>
> *Annie Johnson Flint*

It's not our choice as to whether or not we believers wish to be epistles of Christ. We just are! What is the message others read in *you*?[1474]

When budget cuts sharply curtailed athletic programs at an inner-city high school in Chicago one year, LaSalle Street Church stepped in to help. A staff member of this evangelical inner-city congregation drove the basketball team to their away games in the church van, and the team's athletic banquet was prepared and served at the church. After the season ended, the players attended a Christian ranch in Colorado, where all made commitments to Christ. The living witness of LaSalle Street church members sowed some healthy seeds of faith in the young people which later bore fruit.[1475]

The effect of the Christian life lived out in difficult situations is often quite dramatic and forceful in its impact on the non-Christian.

399

An article that appeared in *Christianity Today* (June 21, 1974), was about Christians in the Soviet Union. A former criminal, Kozlov, later a church leader, wrote of life in a Soviet prison:

> Among the general despair, while prisoners like myself were cursing ourselves, the camp, the authorities; while we opened up our veins or our stomachs, or hanged ourselves; the Christians (often with sentences of 20 to 25 years) did not despair. One could see Christ reflected in their faces. Their pure, upright life, deep faith and devotion to God, their gentleness and their wonderful manliness became a shining example of real life for thousands.[1476]

A Chinese farmer, after having cataracts removed from his eyes, made his way from the Christian compound to the far interior of China. Only a few days elapsed, however, before the missionary doctor looked out of his bamboo window and noticed this formerly blind man holding the front end of a long rope. In single file and holding to the rope behind him several dozen blind Chinese whom the farmer had rounded up and led for miles to the doctor who had worked the "miracle" on his eyes. What a recommendation! Restored sight was cause enough for this man to share what had happened to him with those of like condition. Just so with the gospel of Christ.[1477]

> You are writing a Gospel,
>   A chapter each day,
> By deeds that you do,
>   By words that you say.
>
> Men read what you write,
>   Whether faithless or true,
> Say! What is the gospel
>   According to YOU?[1478]

The story has been told of a missionary to China who was in language school. The very first day of class the teacher entered the room and, without saying a word, walked down every row of students. Finally, still without saying a word, she walked out of the room again. Then she came back and addressed the class.

"Did you notice anything special about me?" she asked. Nobody could think of anything in particular. One student finally raised her hand. "I noticed that you had on a very lovely perfume," she said. The class chuckled. But the teacher said, "That was exactly the point. You see, it will be a long time before any of you will be able to speak Chinese well enough to share the gospel with anyone in China. But even before you are able to do that, you can minister the sweet fragrance of Christ to these people by the quality of your lives. It is your lifestyle, lived out among the Chinese people, that will minister Christ to them long before you are able to say one word to them about personal faith in Jesus."

It is like that with us as well. Though we may not be eloquent speakers, unbelievers we encounter will be ministered to by the Christ-likeness of our daily lives, if indeed we *are* Christ-like.[1479]

Jesus stressed the positive effect we can have on others when he said, "Let your light so shine before men, that they may see your good works and give glory to your Father who is in heaven" (Matt. 5:16, RSV). But if sin dims our testimony so that our "light" is no longer visible, some of those we might have influenced for Christ may drift on in spiritual darkness.

On a dark and stormy night, with waves piling up like mountains on Lake Erie, a boat rocked and plunged near the Cleveland harbor. "Are we on course?" asked the captain, seeing only one beacon from the lighthouse. "Quite sure, sir," replied the officer at the helm. "Where are the lower lights?" "Gone out, sir." "Can we make the harbor?" "We must, or perish!" came the reply. With a steady hand and a stalwart heart, the officer headed the ship toward land.

But, in the darkness, he missed the channel and the vessel was dashed to pieces on the rocks. Many lives were lost in a watery grave. This incident moved Philip P. Bliss to write the familiar hymn, "Let the Lower Lights Be Burning."[1480]

Dr. Charles Weigle, who is probably best known for his song "No One Ever Cared for Me Like Jesus," was once preaching at a Bible conference in Pasadena, California. He spent one afternoon visiting some of the famous rose gardens in that city. When he returned to the Bible conference later that day, a number of people inquired as to how he had enjoyed the lovely gardens. Mystified by their knowledge of his leisure time, he inquired as to how they knew where he had been. The response was, "You have brought the fragrance of the flowers with you."

So, too, can our lives bring "the fragrance of the knowledge of him [Christ] everywhere" (2 Cor. 2:14, NIV).[1481]

A Chinese National, Christiana Tsai, told of her ministry to her family after years of suffering pain through many illnesses. One day, one of her brothers, who had rejected the gospel, assembled the members of the family without them knowing the purpose behind it. He then told them: "I have been to see Christiana many times and wondered how she could endure all this suffering. Now I can see that she has been given some sustaining power and can only explain it as coming from God. So, I have decided there must be a God after all. I have read the Bible and realize that I am a sinner. So here and now I want to tell you that I have accepted Christ as my Savior, asked Him to forgive my sins, and promised to follow Him."

Christiana commented that "the brother who tore up my Bible and persecuted me in the early days at last confessed my Lord. In all, fifty-five of my relatives have become God's children and expressed their faith in Jesus. I have never been to college, or theological seminary, and I am not a Bible teacher; I have only been God's hunting dog." (Cited in Christiana Tsai, *Queen of the Dark Chamber*, p. 184.)[1482]

Witnessing, Inconsistency in

Allowing the encumbrances and sins of the world to clog your life affects your witness in the world in the same way water in the kerosene affects a camping stove. The flame will flutter and sputter, or maybe go out completely. It is useless for light or heat.

Likewise, when our lives are fouled with impurities in our spiritual fuel tank, our light will sputter—until the fuel is again clean.[1483]

When visiting in a remote neighborhood, a pastor stopped at a house and asked the man who lived there to visit his church the next Sunday, mentioning at the same time that the man's neighbor went to that church. On hearing this, the man said he would never go to that church because he wanted nothing to do with a religion that would have a man like his neighbor in it. In fact, he said, his neighbor was the worst neighbor he had ever had.

The pastor, seeing that the man had a piano, asked the man's little girl to play a piece by Beethoven that was lying on the piano. The man said that Beethoven's music was far too advanced for his daughter. But the pastor insisted, and the little girl gave it a try. Needless to say, she almost destroyed the piece.

After the little girl was finished, the pastor said, "Boy, that Beethoven sure wasn't much of a composer, was he?" On hearing this, the man suddenly realized that he, too, had been judging the music of Christian living by the player rather than by the composer.

Let us all try to be good players, but let us not judge the composer by the player.[1484]

Woman, Role of

Here is a paragraph by Ashley Montague from "The Triumph and Tragedy of the American Woman," which appeared in the *Saturday Review*:

> Women have great gifts to bring to the world of men, the qualities of love, compassion and humanity (that is, beauty of spirit). It is the function of woman to humanize, since women are the natural mothers of humanity. Women are by nature endowed with the most important of all adaptive traits, the capacity to love, and this is their principal function to teach men. There can be no more important function. It could be wished that both men and women understood this. Once women know this, they will realize that no man can ever play as important a role in the life of humanity as a mentally healthy woman. And by mental health, I mean the ability to love and the ability to work. Being a good wife, a good mother, in short, a good homemaker is the most important of all occupations in the world. It surely cannot be too often pointed out that the making of human beings is a far more important vocation than the making of anything else, and that in the formative years of a child's life, the mother is best equipped to provide those firm foundations upon which one can subsequently build."[1485]

Words

Karl Marx supposedly said, "Give me twenty-six lead soldiers and I will conquer the world"—meaning the twenty-six letters of the alphabet on a printing press.[1486]

Back in 1675, some nine years after the terrible fire in London, Sir Christopher Wren himself laid the first foundation stone in what was to be his greatest architectural enterprise—the building of St. Paul's Cathedral. It took him thirty-five long years to complete this task, and when it was done he waited breathlessly for the reaction of her majesty, Queen Anne. After being carefully shown through the structure, she summed up her feelings for the architecture in three words: "It is awful; it is amusing; it is artificial."

Imagine how you would feel if words like these were used to describe the work of your life! However, Sir Christopher Wren's biographer said that on hearing these words, he heaved a sigh of relief and bowed gratefully before his sovereign. How could this be? The explanation is simple: In 1710, the word *awful* meant "awe-inspiring," the word *amusing* meant "amazing," and the word *artificial* meant "artistic." What to our ears might sound like a devastating criticism were in that time words of measured praise.

There is no doubt a lesson in that story for those who would quibble over the relative merits of the various Bible versions and translations. Shades of meaning cannot alter what God has revealed in his Word![1487]

Work

Employees in a Detroit business office found the following important notice on the bulletin board: "The management regrets that it has come to their attention that workers dying on the job are failing to fall down. This practice must stop, as it becomes impossible to distinguish between death and the natural movement of the staff. Any employee found dead in an upright position will be dropped from the payroll."[1488]

A student staying in the home of an elderly couple greatly admired their fine antique pendulum clock, which had been handed down from one generation to the next in the husband's family. One day the old man said, "That clock has a message to tell."

Puzzled, the student asked, "What message?" The old man replied, "Look at the pendulum going back and forth, as if to say, 'Slow-down-do-it-right.' But then listen to the electric clock: 'Hurry-up-get-it-done. Who-cares-how-it's-done.' "[1489]

Work, God's

"When God's work is done in God's way for God's glory, it will never lack God's supply. God is not obligated to pay for our selfish schemes. He is obligated to support His ministry" (Hudson Taylor).[1490]

World

One of the ways we can recognize the world is that it loves noise. Why? Probably because it does not want to stop and think.

What would it be like if some kind of solar ray suddenly caused all radios, tape players, stereos, and televisions to stop working? Trembling hands would immediately twirl dials, adjust knobs, and flip switches. Eyes would be dilated with fear of the silence. People would be running the streets in terror.

Marx was wrong. Religion is not the opiate of modern man; incessant sound is. People will listen to anything to avoid silence. Why else do we have so much of long talk shows, round-the-clock news, call-in radio programs? Why? Because sound blocks out the despairing cry of our own souls, as well as the still, small voice of God. Perhaps we would be wise to occasionally take God's hand and journey into the land of silence.[1491]

World

"The world is like a drunken peasant. If you lift him into the saddle on one side, he will fall off on the other side. One can't help him, no matter how one tries. He wants to be the devil's" (Martin Luther).[1492]

Worldiness

How would you feel if your spouse, needing something for the house, went to the next-door neighbor and got some money? Or if your child, needing help, always went to another instead of coming to you? It would break your heart.

This is what we do to God when we go the world's way in trying to meet our own needs. It is as if we are saying, "Lord, you aren't adequate. You don't know the best way for me. I'm going to have to get what I want by myself."[1493]

A Christian should be *in* the world and yet not *of* the world. How can this be? Consider the fish who, though he lives in the salty sea, does not taste salty.[1494]

Imagine that you are in a round tower with slits in the walls used for shooting through with guns. Now imagine that you are whirled around the inner circumference. Would you appreciate the beauties of the surrounding landscape? No. But there are openings in the wall. Yes, but your eyes are set for objects near and do not have the time to adjust to

405

distance as you are whirled past the slits. It would be as if the wall were solid.

So it is with earthly living. The near and earthly wall obstructs the view. An occasional slit is left open, perhaps a Sunday sermon or personal Bible reading. Heaven might be seen through these, but the eye which is set for the earthly cannot adjust itself to higher things during such momentary glimpses. So long has the soul looked upon the world, that when it is turned for a moment heavenward, it feels only a quiver of inarticulate light. Unless you pause and look steadfastly, you will not see or retain any distinct impression of the things which are eternal.

C. H. Spurgeon
Feathers for Arrows (Pasadena, Tex.: Pilgrim Pubs., 1973)[1495]

Worldliness, Witnessing and

There was tremendous public resistance to the introduction of the Susan B. Anthony dollar. This small coin was designed primarily to be a durable and lightweight alternative to the paper dollar. But its size created problems, for it could easily be confused with a quarter. Legally it was worth a dollar, but practically speaking, many people considered it a nuisance because of its indistinguishable size.

The same thing happens when the unbelieving world hears the words of a Christian who cannot be distinguished from the lost society in which he lives. This discounts his claims concerning Christ. It is not a matter of real worth—that is decided by faith—but rather of perceived worth.[1496]

Worry

Worry has been defined as "a small trickle of fear that meanders through the mind until it cuts a channel into which all other thoughts are drained."[1497]

Somebody has said that ulcers are caused not by what you eat, but by what is eating you![1498]

Worriers spend a lot of time shoveling smoke.[1499]

Worry is like a rocking chair; it will give you something to do, but it won't get you anywhere.[1500]

406

A child does not worry all day long whether his house will be there when he gets home from school or whether his parents will have a meal for him that evening. Children do not worry about such things, because they trust their parents. In the same way, we as Christians should trust our heavenly Father to supply what is best for us.[1501]

Death was walking toward a city, and a man stopped Death and asked, "What are you going to do?" Death said, "I'm going to kill ten thousand people." The man said, "That's horrible!" Death said, "That's the way it is; that's what I do."

As the day passed, the man warned everyone he could of Death's plan. At the end of the day he again met Death. He said, "You said you were going to kill ten thousand people, and yet seventy thousand died." Death explained, "*I* killed only ten thousand. Worry and fear killed the others."[1502]

Mickey Rivers, at the time an outfielder for the Texas Rangers professional baseball team, stated his philosophy of life: "Ain't no sense worrying about things you got control over, because if you got control over them, ain't no sense worrying. And there ain't no sense worrying about things you got *no* control over either, because if you got no control over them, ain't no sense worrying." (Reported in *Dallas Morning News*, May 20, 1984.)[1503]

"I could no more worry than I could curse or swear" (John Wesley).[1504]

Worship

After attending church with his father one Sunday morning, before getting into bed that evening a little boy kneeled at his bedside and prayed, "Dear God, we had a good time at church today, but I wish you had been there."[1505]

Many years ago, Thomas K. Beecher once substituted for his famous brother, Henry Ward Beecher, at the Plymouth Church in Brooklyn, New York. Many curiosity seekers had come to hear the renowned Henry Beecher speak. Therefore, when Thomas Beecher appeared in the pulpit instead, some people got up and started for the doors. Sensing that they were disappointed because he was substituting for his brother, Thomas raised his hand for silence and announced, "All those who came here this morning to worship Henry Ward Beecher may withdraw from the church; all who came to worship God may remain."

The example of godly leaders is helpful, but only the Savior is worthy of our worship and devotion.[1506]

Youth

"Youth is such a wonderful thing, it's a shame to waste it on the young" (George Bernard Shaw).[1507]

Zeal

Before the opening day of pheasant season, two city-dwellers who aspired to be hunters bought a bird dog, having heard that such a dog would make for much more enjoyable and profitable hunting. When the big day came, they were up bright and early. They hunted all day, but as dusk began to overtake them, they hadn't fired a single shot. The hunters were exhausted and frustrated over the poor performance of their bird dog. Finally one said, "Okay, Joe, throw him up once more and if he don't fly this time, I'm gonna shoot him!"[1508]

PART TWO

Illustrations for Selected Scriptures

Old Testament

Exodus 16

Start with a basic two-door sedan loaded with luggage for a vacation
trip. Add a father, mother, and three children under the age of ten. Aim
the car at an objective that is 500 miles down the road. After 350 miles
have passed, examine the scene. What is the condition of what has
become a traveling circus? Pretty discouraging?

Now, magnify that situation thousands of times over, move it back
some 3,500 years, eliminate the automobile, and you will begin to
understand Moses' predicament in Exodus 16. The thrill of freedom
and the excitement of the exodus were soon erased by the discomforts
of travel. Gratitude usually gives way to grumbling.[1509]

Job 23:12

Would you cook a meal for yourself even if you didn't feel like
cooking? You probably say, "Yes, food is necessary."

Did you skip your devotions today? If your answer is, "Yes, I was too
tired to study God's Word," then consider the words in Job 23:12,
where Job affirms that God's Word is more precious to him than his
necessary food. It doesn't matter if you don't feel like learning God's
Word. It is necessary to your life as a Christian.[1510]

Psalm 23:1

After a Sunday-school lesson one week, a little girl was heard quoting Psalm 23:1, a familiar Bible verse that many children have memorized. Although the child did not quote it quite right, she had the right
idea when she said, "The Lord is my shepherd; I've got all I want."

The truth we adults so often fail to remember is that God does
provide all our needs, and we are to be content with his provision.[1511]

Elisabeth Elliot has told the story of a toddler who was very ill but had learned to recite the Twenty-third Psalm on her fingers. Starting with her pinkie, she would grab a finger as she said each word of "The Lord is my shepherd." As she said the word *shepherd*, she would clasp her thumb in recognition of the care God has for her.

One morning, after a long and hard fight against her disease, the little girl was found dead with one hand clasped around the other thumb. The Lord *is* her shepherd. He has made her to lie down in green pastures. He has led her to quiet waters. Surely she will dwell in the house of the Lord forever.[1512]

Psalm 23:2

Phillip Keller, once a shepherd himself, in his book *A Shepherd Looks at Psalm 23* (Grand Rapids: Zondervan, 1976), relates that the strange thing about sheep is that because of their very makeup, it is almost impossible for them to be made to lie down unless four requirements are met. First, due to their timidity, they must be free from all fear. Next, because of their sociability, they must be free from friction with others of their kind. Third, they must be free from flies or parasites if they are to relax. Lastly, they will not lie down unless free from hunger. It is only the shepherd who can provide release from all these anxieties. As our Good Shepherd, the Lord meets all these needs for us, so that we can "lie down in green pastures," with our souls restored by his care.[1513]

Psalm 32:8–9

The truth of Psalm 32:8–9 is well illustrated by a horse a certain pastor remembers from the ranch he grew up on. The horse's name was Jim, and he had been used only for riding or racing before the ranch manager bought him. Jim was bought to be used for chasing cattle, to be a workhorse for the livestock. At first, Jim would only run in a straight line and was almost impossible to stop or turn. When the cowboys were herding cattle into the corral and one would try to get away, Jim would start to follow the animal. But, if the animal turned, it would take the rider a hundred yards to turn Jim! As you can imagine, by that time the animal would be long gone in another direction.

Training Jim to work the livestock—to follow on the heels of the cow and calf, to sense when an animal would turn, and to be able to outwit it—was obviously very difficult. Of necessity the cowhands had to place a rougher than usual bit in his mouth as well as wear spurs, but eventually Jim learned to be probably the best cattle horse on the ranch. A rider could shift his weight ever so slightly to one side, and Jim would immediately turn that way.

In the same way, God wants to guide us in a gentle and loving way. Let us not be stubborn, as Jim was—or as a mule can be—so that he can always direct us easily.[1514]

Psalm 48:14

Barbara Youderian, the wife of Roj Youderian who died along with Jim Elliot as they sought to reach the Auca Indians, wrote the following in her diary: "Tonight, the captain told us of his finding four bodies in the river. One had tee-shirt and blue jeans. Roj was the only one who wore them. . . . God gave me this verse two days ago, Psalm 48:14, 'For this God is our God for ever and ever; He will be our Guide even unto death.' As I came face to face with the news of Roj's death, my heart was filled with praise. He was worthy of his home-going. Help me, Lord, to be both mummy and daddy. 'To know wisdom and instruction. . . . ' " (Cited by Elisabeth Elliot, *Through Gates of Splendor*, Old Tappan, N.J.: Revell, 1970 p. 191.)[1515]

Psalm 103:12

There is a definite point that is "north" and another that is "south," the North and South Poles. But there are no such points for "east" and "west." It doesn't matter how far you go to the east; you will never arrive where west begins because *by definition* west is the opposite of east. The two never meet. They never will meet and never could meet because they are defined as opposites. To remove our sins "as far as the east is from the west" is by definition to put them where no one can ever find them. That is the forgiveness God has granted us.[1516]

Proverbs 13:24

"The way to stop violence in America is to stop spanking children," argued psychologist John Valusek. In a 1977 speech to the Utah Association for Mental Health, Valusek declared that parental spanking promotes the thesis that violence against others is acceptable. "Spanking is the first half-inch on the yardstick of violence," said Valusek. "It is followed by hitting, and ultimately by rape, murder and assassination. The modeling behavior that occurs at home sets the stage: I will resort to violence when I don't know what else to do."

413

His logic is airtight, isn't it? Why, just think of it. Feeding a child is the first half-inch on the yardstick of gluttony? Hugging a child is the first half-inch on the yardstick of immorality?

Unfortunately, Mr. Valusek did not realize that there is a qualitative difference between discipline and violence, just as there is between eating and gluttony, hugging and immorality, and all other acceptable human behaviors and their exaggerated extremes. To not see the difference is to surrender a part of our humanity to the machines—and for Christians it means being disobedient to God's will for parents.[1517]

Proverbs 14:23

"Well-done is better than well-said," observed Benjamin Franklin. That's pretty much what is meant by "In all toil there is profit, but mere talk tends only to want" (Prov. 14:23, NIV).[1518]

Proverbs 21:23

"The boneless tongue, so small and weak
Can crush and kill," declared the Greek.
The Persian proverb wisely saith:
"A lengthy tongue, an early death."
Sometimes it takes this form instead:
"Don't let your tongue cut off your head."
While Arab sages this impart:
"The tongue's great storehouse is the heart."
From Hebrew wit the maxim's sprung:
"Though feet should slip, don't let the tongue."
A verse in Scripture crowns the whole:
"Who keeps the tongue doth keep his soul."[1519]

Ecclesiastes

The Book of Ecclesiastes can be compared to pieces of broken glass. Each piece of glass is like one of the aspects of life mentioned by "the Preacher" (probably Solomon) in the book. He sees life as empty, meaningless, confusing—like bits of glass in a pile on a table. But at the end he sees that life can take on meaning, and its pieces can form beautiful and meaningful patterns when seen from the right perspective—like small pieces of colored glass viewed through a kaleidoscope.[1520]

Ecclesiastes 12:1

A man came rushing up to a ferry, breathless after running at a terrific pace, but he got there just as the gateman shut the door in his face.

A bystander remarked, "You didn't run fast enough." The disappointed man answered, "I ran fast enough, but I didn't start on time."

To accomplish the most for God in a lifetime, you must start in early—"in the days of your youth" (Eccles. 12:1, NIV).[1521]

Jeremiah 1

If you have ever been served a warrant, you know how intimidating it is to read these words: "The People of the State of [your state] versus [your name]." That doesn't seem like very fair odds. The whole population of the state against one person—you!

But that is what the prophet Jeremiah had to face. All the people of the land and its kings and priests would be against him. But God said "Don't worry; you shall stand. I will make you a fortified city, an iron pillar and a bronze wall against them. Nothing will shake you, for I'll be with you" (see Jer. 1:18–19).[1522]

Jonah 1:17

Many people find it difficult to take the Book of Jonah seriously because they find it hard to believe that a man could be swallowed by a whale and live to tell the story. The following account of a modern-day man who underwent a similar experience and did live to tell his story may be of help. The following account is taken from the *Princeton Theological Review*, Vol. 25, 1927, p. 636:

> In February 1891, the whaling ship *Star of the East* was in the vicinity of the Falkland Islands and the lookout sighted a large sperm whale three miles away. Two boats were launched and in a short time one of the harpooners was enabled to spear the fish. The second boat attacked the whale, but was upset by a lash of its tail and the men thrown into the sea, one man being drowned, and another, James Bartley, having disappeared, could not be found. The whale was killed and in a few hours was lying by the ship's side and the crew were busy with axes and spades removing the blubber. They worked all day and part of the night. Next morning, they attached some tackle to the stomach which was hoisted on the deck. The sailors were startled by something in it which gave spasmodic signs of

life, and inside was found the missing sailor doubled up and unconscious. He was laid on the deck and treated to a bath of sea water which soon revived him. . . . He remained two weeks a raving lunatic. . . . At the end of the third week he had entirely recovered from the shock and resumed his duties.

Bartley affirms that he would probably have lived inside his house of flesh until he starved, for he lost his senses through fright and not from lack of air. He remembers the sensation of being thrown out of the boat into the sea. . . . He was then encompassed by a great darkness and he felt he was slipping along a smooth passage of some sort that seemed to move and carry him forward. The sensation lasted but a short time and then he realized he had more room. He felt about him and his hands came in contact with a yielding, slimy substance that seemed to shrink from his touch. It finally dawned upon him that he had been swallowed by the whale. . . . He could easily breathe, but the heat was terrible. It was not a scorching, stifling nature, but it seemed to open the pores of his skin and draw out his vitality. . . . His skin was exposed to the action of the gastric juice . . . face, neck and hands were bleached to a deadly whiteness and took on the appearance of parchment . . . (and) never recovered its natural appearance . . . (though otherwise) his health did not seem affected by his terrible experience.[1523]

Malachi 2:17

During the first day of Boy Scout camp, a scoutmaster was called home because of an emergency and was not planning to return until the following day. As he prepared to leave, he gathered his charges together and made Joe, one of the patrol leaders, the acting scoutmaster until he returned. As soon as the scoutmaster was out of sight, the newly appointed leader began to give orders. He had the younger boys set up his tent, sent another after candy, and told the rest to clean up the area, even though it was recreation time. "You can't do that," they said. "Mr. Whitten said it was recreation time!" Joe was not impressed. "I can do whatever I want to. And furthermore, I don't care what Mr. Whitten said, because Mr. Whitten isn't here!" He must have seen the smiles on the Scouts' faces, because he turned around to see Mr. Whitten standing there. He had returned for his car keys, had heard everything, and, needless to say, appointed a new acting leader.

Joe assumed what the priests of Malachi's day assumed, that they could act in any way they chose because the one who guaranteed justice was nowhere to be seen. But both Joe and the priests found out otherwise. The keeper of justice was seeing their deeds and hearing their words and would ultimately set things right.[1524]

New Testament

Matthew 5—7

"If you were to take the sum total of all the authoritative articles ever written by the most qualified of psychologists and psychiatrists on the subject of mental hygiene—if you were to combine them and refine them and cleave out the excess verbiage—if you were to . . . have these unadulterated bits of pure scientific knowledge concisely expressed by the most capable of living poets, you would have an awkward and incomplete summation of the Sermon on the Mount" (James T. Fisher, *A Few Buttons Missing: The Case Book of a Psychiatrist* [N.Y.: Lippincott, 1951]).[1525]

Matthew 5:3–11

J. B. Phillips, in his book *When God Was Man* (Nashville: Abington, 1955), gives this version of the Beatitudes:

Happy are the pushers, for they get on in the world.

Happy are the hard-boiled, for they never let life hurt them.

Happy are they who complain, for they get their own way in the end.

Happy are the blase, for they never worry over their sins.

Happy are the slave drivers, for they get results.

Happy are the knowledgeable men of the world, for they know their way around.

Happy are the troublemakers, for they make people take notice of them.[1526]

Matthew 5:23–24

Young Danny was praying at Mother's knee. "If I should die before I wake . . . If I should die. . . . "

"Go on, go on, Danny," said his mother. "You know the rest of the prayer."

"Wait a minute," interrupted the small boy. Scrambling to his feet, he hurried downstairs. In a short time, he was back. Dropping to his knees once again, he took up the petition where he had left off.

Finally his mother questioned him about the episode and issued a loving rebuke. Danny explained: "Mom, I did think about what I was saying, but I had to stop and put all of Ted's wooden soldiers on their feet. I had turned them on their heads just to see how mad he'd be in the morning. If I should die before I wake, I wouldn't want him to find them like that. Lots of things seem fun if you are gonna keep on living, but you don't want them that way if you should die before you wake."

"You're right, dear," said his mother with a quiver in her voice. She thought of herself and many other grown-ups who should have stopped in the middle of their prayers to undo some wrong against another before proceeding.[1527]

Matthew 6:19–21

There is a story of a wealthy woman who, when she reached heaven, was conducted to a very plain house. She objected. "Well," she was told, "that is the dwelling-place prepared for you."

"Whose is that fine mansion across the way?" she asked.

Her guide replied, "It belongs to your gardener."

"How is it that he has a house so much better than mine?"

"The houses here are prepared from the materials that are sent up. We do not choose them; you do that by your faithfulness while on earth."

This may be a story, but it bears a profound truth about the "treasures" we accumulate.[1528]

Matthew 6:26

Said the Robin to the Sparrow:
"There is one thing I would really like to know,
Why these anxious human beings
Rush about and worry so."

Said the Sparrow to the Robin:
"Friend, I think that it must be
That they have no heavenly Father
Such as cares for you and me."[1529]

Matthew 7:22–23

On the day of judgment, there will be some who claim to be Christians who will be turned away from God's kingdom. They will be like counterfeit money when it reaches the bank. Suppose you are given a counterfeit bill in change at the store. Thinking it is genuine, you use it to pay for some gas. The station owner uses it to pay one of his employees, who uses it to buy groceries. From there it goes to the bank where the teller says, "I'm sorry, but this bill is counterfeit."

The bill may have been used to do a lot of good while it was in circulation, but when it arrived at the bank, it was exposed for what it really was and put out of circulation. A counterfeit Christian may do many good works, but still be rejected at the gates of judgment.[1530]

Matthew 11:29–30

The "yoke" Jesus refers to in Matthew 11:29–30 is well illustrated by the process of training a young bullock to plow. In some parts of the world, the farmer will have the young bullock harnessed to the same yoke as a mature ox. The bullock, dwarfed by the other animal, will not even be pulling any of the weight. It is merely learning to walk in a field under control and with a yoke around its neck; the ox pulls all the weight. It is the same when a believer takes Christ's yoke. As the Christian learns, the yoke is easy and the burden light.[1531]

Mark 12:31

The relationship between the greatest commandment, to love the Lord, and the second commandment, to love your neighbor as yourself, is similar to the relationship between the cue ball and eight ball in a game of billiards. The cue ball represents our relationship to God and the eight ball represents our relationship to men. If we are off center when we shoot the cue ball, we can forget about having the eight ball sink in the corner pocket. This is why to love God is the first and greatest commandment.[1532]

John's Gospel

John's Gospel has often been compared to a pool in which a child could wade safely and an elephant could swim. It is both simple and profound. It is for the beginner in the faith and for the mature Christian.[1533]

John 6:35, 51

During World War II, the Germans forced many twelve- and thirteen-year-old boys into the Junior Gestapo. These boys were treated very harshly and given inhumane jobs to perform. When the war ended, most had lost track of their families and wandered without food or shelter. As part of an aid program to post-war Germany, many of these youths were placed in tent cities. Here doctors and psychologists worked with the boys in an attempt to restore their mental and physical health. They found that many of the boys would awaken in the middle of the night, screaming in terror. One doctor had an idea for handling that fear. After feeding the boys a large meal, he put them to bed with a piece of bread in their hands, which they were told to save until morning. The boys then slept soundly because, after so many years of hunger, they finally had the assurance of food for the next day.

Do you have Jesus as your Savior? If you do, you hold the Bread of Life in your hands and therefore have the assurance that you will not go out of this life in terror and fear.[1534]

John 10:4

During World War I, some Turkish soldiers tried to steal a flock of sheep from a hillside near Jerusalem. The shepherd, who had been sleeping, suddenly awakened to see his sheep being driven off on the other side of the ravine. He could not hope to recapture his flock by force single-handedly, but suddenly he had a thought. Standing up on his side of the ravine, he put his hands to his mouth and gave his own peculiar call, which he used each day to gather his sheep to him. The sheep heard the familiar sound. For a moment they listened and then, hearing it again, they turned and rushed down one side of the ravine and up the other toward their shepherd. It was quite impossible for the soldiers to stop the animals. The shepherd was away with them to a place of safety before the soldiers could make up their minds to pursue them—and all because his sheep knew their master's voice.[1535]

John 13:1–17

When you go to another to wash his feet, or when another comes to wash your feet, be concerned as to the temperature of the water!

Some come with boiling hot water. They are so angry, so upset, so distracted by something that has happened in the past—and so mad about it—that they come to the other person and say, "Here, stick your feet in here!" Nobody wants to have his feet washed with boiling water.

Some go to the other extreme and come with ice water. They are so righteous, so holier-than-thou, so above it all. They come with this frigid, freezing water and want to wash your feet. Nobody wants to have his feet washed with ice water.

Some find a third extreme and come without any water! They try to dry-clean your feet with "a piece of their mind," just scrubbing away harshly. What they say may be true, but there is no water of love, nothing to wash the dirt gently away, but only a rigid insistence on scraping away every imperfection and the skin along with it!

There is another way—that is to come and wash one another's feet in love, in the spirit of servanthood.[1536]

John 13:34–37

The sign that you followed Abraham was circumcision.

The sign that you followed Moses was keeping the Sabbath.

The sign that you followed John the Baptist was that you were baptized.

The sign that you follow Jesus Christ is that you love one another.[1537]

John 14:6

A traveler engaged a guide to take him across a desert area. When the two men arrived at the edge of the desert, the traveler, looking ahead, saw before him trackless sands without a single footprint, path, or marker of any kind. Turning to his guide, he asked in a tone of surprise, "Where is the road?" With a reproving glance, the guide replied, "*I am the road.*"

So, too, is the Lord our way through unfamiliar territory.[1538]

John 15:1–8

The usual practice in viticulture, the care of vines, is for the branches to be pruned back each year in order to cleanse them. A vine produces certain shoots called "sucker shoots," which start to grow where a branch joins the stem. If allowed to continue to grow, they would dissipate the life of the vine through so many branches that the vine would produce little or no fruit and would produce mainly leaves instead. Every vinedresser knows it is important to prune away these little sucker shoots to ensure plentiful fruit. Since the shoots grow right where the branch joins the stem, creating a tight cluster where dirt, leaves, and other debris collect, the pruning is basically a cleansing process.

421

The Father's work in our lives is to find a branch that is beginning to bear fruit, beginning to produce the likeness of Christ, and then to cut it back. He trims off the troublesome shoots, so that we may bear more fruit.[1539]

John 19:30

Michelangelo was a genius. He excelled as a sculptor, designer, painter, and architect. His statues of Moses and David, to name but a few, are widely recognized and appreciated. What many people do not know is that in Florence, Italy, an entire hall is filled with his "unfinished" sculptural works. As great as this artist was, he left much unfinished.

Jesus Christ left no unfinished works.[1540]

Acts 8:1

Acts 8:1 represents an important principle of thermodynamics: "The greater the heat, the greater the expansion."[1541]

Acts 19:2

The story has been told of a group of colonists who left Virginia in the late 1700s and started across the mountains to the land that lay far to the west. As the story goes, they were forced to interrupt their journey for some reason, perhaps fear of Indians, or the death of a horse, or the breakdown of a wagon. For whatever reason, they spent twenty years in the mountains, during which time they saw no other white men.

Finally, another group of travelers made its way through the region and came upon these isolated settlers. Naturally, there was much conversation about the outside world. The travelers asked the mountaineers what they thought about "the Republic" and the policies of "Congress."

The isolated ones answered, "We have not heard anything of a Congress or a Republic." Then they went on to explain that they thought of themselves as loyal subjects of the British king. When told all about the nation's independence and how it came about, they entered into an understanding of their new status, and became "American citizens" in that hour by *knowledge,* as they had been for some time in *fact.*

Even many Christians, as in Paul's day in Ephesus, are not fully knowledgeable about the power of the Holy Spirit (Acts 19:2).[1542]

Romans 6:6

How can sin be rendered powerless, as Paul says in Romans 6:6? Consider the effect of gravity on a book. Gravity would cause an unsupported book to fall, but gravity can be rendered "powerless" against the book by simply placing a table under it. As long as the table is under the book, gravity cannot cause it to fall. Of course gravity has not really lost its power nor is it no longer present. It is just that the table is "stronger" than gravity's effect on the book.

For the Christian, the Holy Spirit is like that table and our sin nature is like gravity's pull. As long as we allow the Holy Spirit to hold us up, which places our dependence on his power to give us victory over sin, our sinful impulses have no power to pull us down.[1543]

Romans 6:12–14

A little girl was learning to ride a bicycle. She did quite well until it was time to stop. The only way she could ever stop was by running into something. She was constantly picking herself out of bushes and off the sidewalk. The problem was that although she knew that the bike had a coaster brake, she wasn't using it.

The question implied in Romans 6:12–14 is: What good is it to be set free from sin by Jesus Christ and have every opportunity of walking in holiness and righteousness if—at the moment of choice—we ignore these things and go right on letting sin rule us?[1544]

Romans 6:16

Well before Paul was born, there had been a Roman law stating that no freeborn man could be enslaved. Therefore, a man could literally sell himself into slavery, collect the proceeds, then have a friend come and attest to his status as a freeborn man, and he would have to be released at once. This caused havoc with the Roman economy, which was well oiled by its slave labor. Therefore, just before Paul's day, a new law was enacted whereby any man who sold himself into slavery could no longer claim free status later. The law could no longer help him. It was therefore clear to Paul's readers in Rome that "to whom you present yourselves as slaves for obedience, his slave you are." (From *Tyndale Bulletin* 32 (1981):87.)[1545]

Romans 8:1–2

This passage tells us that, though the law of sin and death keeps a Christian from living the kind of life God wants him to live, the law of the Spirit of life in Christ Jesus sets us free from the law of sin and death.

In the same way, the law of gravity acts to keep a plane from flying. But when a plane reaches a certain speed, the law of aerodynamics takes over and frees the plane from the effects of gravitational force.[1546]

Romans 8:28

All afternoon a little boy tried to put together his birthday gift from his father, a picture puzzle. Some of the pieces were bright, some dark; some seemed to go together, others seemed to fit nowhere. Finally, frustrated and exhausted and with nothing to show for his efforts, the boy gathered the pieces, put them in the box, and gave it to his dad. "I can't do it," he explained. "You try it."

To his amazement, his father assembled the entire puzzle in a few minutes. "You see," he said, "I knew what the picture was like all the time. I saw the picture in the puzzle, but you saw only the pieces."

Paul tells us here that God causes all things to work together for good. Those "all things" are the pieces. He then tells us *how* they work together for the good—according to God's purpose. That is the picture. Are you perplexed and frustrated over this event or that happening in your life? Do not take the situation out of God's hand and try to work it into your own design. God made the picture your life is composed of, and he will complete it—if you will let him.[1547]

Romans 9:1–5

A man said to a friend, "I hear you dismissed your pastor. What was wrong?" The friend said, "Well, he kept telling us we're all going to hell."

The first man then asked, "What does the new pastor say?" The friend replied, "The new pastor says we're going to hell, too."

"So what's the difference?" asked the first man. "Well," said the friend, "the difference is that when the previous pastor said it, he sounded like he was glad about it; but when the new man says it, he sounds like it is breaking his heart."

That is what Paul is saying in this passage. It is breaking his heart that he has to say harsh things to and about nonbelievers, especially those among his fellow Jews.[1548]

Romans 12:1–2

In a church service one Sunday, the offering plate came to a little girl at the end of a row. She took the plate, put it down on the floor, and stood in it. When the usher asked her what she was doing, she responded, "In Sunday school I learned that I was supposed to give myself to God."

Romans 12:1–2 confirms that she had the right idea.[1549]

1 Corinthians 1:23

The story is told of a small English village that had a tiny chapel whose stone walls were covered by traditional ivy. Over an arch was originally inscribed the words: WE PREACH CHRIST CRUCIFIED. There had been a generation of godly men who did precisely that: they preached Christ crucified.

But times changed. The ivy grew and pretty soon covered the last word. The inscription now read: WE PREACH CHRIST. Other men came and they did preach Christ: Christ the example, Christ the humanitarian, Christ the ideal teacher.

As the years passed, the ivy continued to grow until finally the inscription read: WE PREACH. The generation that came along then did just that: they preached economics, social gospel, book reviews, just about anything.

The story probably isn't literally true, but it does illustrate how man's philosophical detours affect how the gospel is transmitted.[1550]

1 Corinthians 2:14

The natural man may be educated and intellectually sharp, but he cannot receive the wisdom of the Spirit as well as a less knowledgeable, but faith-oriented believer.

It's as if your next-door neighbor bought an expensive big-screen color television set and after it was delivered came over to your house to brag about his new acquisition. While he's bragging he notices his favorite motion picture coming in on your little black-and-white K-Mart T.V. and exclaims: "Oh, no! They've got my favorite movie on and all you've got is that crummy little black-and-white job. I've got to go see it on my color set." So he runs home and turns on his expensive set, only to find out that he can't get the channel he wanted. Why? Well, he didn't give you time to tell him that you had just subscribed to cable television. He may have the better equipment but you're "cable ready" for the best shows.

425

In the same way, the natural man may have a far superior head on his shoulders and lots of book learning, but until he gets on line with the Holy Spirit by coming to Christ through faith, he can never receive what even the most ignorant believer receives all the time.[1551]

1 Corinthians 6:1–8

A Spanish proverb says, "The Jews ruin themselves at their passover; the Moors, at their marriages; and the Christians, in their lawsuits." In 1 Corinthians 6:1–8, Paul decried legal disputes within the early church. What a sad commentary it is that lawsuits among Christians have been so common as to warrant a proverbial generalization.[1552]

1 Corinthians 10:6–11

At the site of Dachau concentration camp near Munich, Germany, is a museum containing relics from the camp, as well as grim photos depicting conditions there during the war years. There is a sign next to the exit that reads: "Those who do not learn from history are condemned to repeat its mistakes."

The same idea was in Paul's mind in this passage. The mistakes the Israelites made were cited by the apostle to serve as a reminder and warning, much as the sign at Dachau was.[1553]

1 Corinthians 13:8–10

The important criterion in determining whether or not a particular spiritual gift will endure is its purpose. The purpose of a mercury vapor light is to illuminate the highway at night. When the sun rises, the highway becomes illuminated by a greater and more perfect light. The mercury vapor light then goes out because it has served its purpose. In a similar way, spiritual gifts—whether knowledge, prophecy, or tongues—will cease to function when a state of perfect spiritual maturity is attained. Their "light" will no longer be required then.[1554]

1 Corinthians 15:58

A goose will sit faithfully on a dozen or so eggs and will not move for anybody or anything. But, after three or four eggs hatch, she becomes so preoccupied with them that she walks away from the remaining eggs. She does not persevere to the end.

In this passage, Paul reminds the Corinthians not to become so preoccupied with nonessentials that they are in danger of not remaining steadfast and immovable in the work of the Lord.[1555]

Galatians 1:6–9

Counterfeit money is lacking in authority—it does not have the backing of the federal government. A good counterfeiter can dupe some people into accepting his copywork as legitimate currency. But eventually, when the fake money is brought before the authorities, it will be found false and sentenced to destruction.

Likewise, a false gospel lacks something very important: the authority of Christ. The preacher of a false gospel may believe it himself and persuade men to accept his message. Nevertheless, in the final analysis, there is no salvation in his gospel. Paul tells us that such a preacher will be apprehended by the courts of heaven and judgment pronounced: "Let him be accursed!" (Gal. 1:6–9).[1556]

Sometimes a counterfeit can be deadly, though the real thing it imitates is harmless or even beneficial. In the Binghamton General Hospital a few decades ago, several babies in the maternity ward died suddenly of unknown causes. It was later determined that, in mixing the babies' formula, salt had been substituted for sugar. Though the resulting mixture looked the same, it caused the death of several infants. The gospel, too, can be counterfeited today, just as it apparently was in Paul's day. Though it may sound similar and be undetected as a fake, it lacks the life-giving power of the real thing and is destructive.[1557]

Galatians 5:14–15

A zookeeper tossed a hot dog into a snake pen. Two snakes immediately began to devour the stick of meat, one on either end. When the two met at the middle, the snake with the larger mouth kept on going and consumed the other! We are reminded in this passage that people are often like these snakes, consuming one another with unkind words when they disagree on an issue.[1558]

Ephesians 1:3

A man who had been a drunkard on Chicago's Skid Row for many years came to a mission one night. He heard the message, ate the meal, and went to bed. That was his last night on earth. He died poverty-stricken and friendless, never to see another day. What he did not know was that he had an inheritance of over four million dollars waiting for him in England. The authorities had searched for him but were unable to find him because he had no address. Here was a man who had all the material wealth he could want, but he lived and died in poverty.

In this sense he was just like many Christians and non-Christians alike, who live in spiritual poverty because they are not fully aware of their wealth in Christ.[1559]

Ephesians 3:19

To be "filled to the measure of all the fullness of God" (Eph. 3:19) is like filling a thimble to its brim with water from the ocean. The thimble is filled with the ocean, but the ocean is not fully in the thimble since the thimbleful of water does not diminish the ocean. Yet, the thimble has the "fullness" of the ocean in the sense that it contains every ingredient that makes up the ocean. All the essential characteristics of the ocean are in the thimble.[1560]

Ephesians 4:11

The need for diversity as the basis of unity in the body of Christ is well illustrated by a jigsaw puzzle. All the parts of the puzzle are of equal importance to the completed puzzle, and without all of the parts the puzzle would be incomplete. However, when building the puzzle, one looks first for the four corner pieces that are foundational to the completion of the rest of the puzzle. So, too, the four gifts mentioned in Ephesians 4:11 are foundational to the completion of the mature body of Christ. When the jigsaw is finished, the four corner pieces are of no more value than the rest of the pieces.[1561]

Ephesians 5:15–16

A driver stopped his car at an intersection and waited for the green signal. When the green light came, he waited further to confirm it. That is, he waited until the light turned green a second time! After that, he waited still further until the green light flashed a third time, before he proceeded on his way. Absurd? Of course. No one would drive like that.

But are there not Christians who live like that driver drove? They are so overcautious that they wait for signs from God, wait to reconfirm the signs, and then wait for an auspicious moment to act. They are waiting almost perpetually and can never redeem the time they wasted or the opportunities they lost.[1562]

Ephesians 5:25

The story is told of a prince and his family who were captured by an enemy king. When brought before the enemy king, the prisoner was asked, "What will you give me if I release you?" "Half of my wealth," was the prince's reply.

"And if I release your children?"

"Everything I possess."

"And if I release your wife?"

"Your Majesty, for her I would give myself," said the prince.

The king was so moved by the prince's devotion to his family that he freed them all. As they returned home, the prince said to his wife, "Wasn't the king a handsome man!" With a look of deep love for her husband, she said to him, "I didn't notice. I could keep my eyes only on the one who was willing to give himself for my sake."[1563]

Philippians 4:7

A person whose cancer has been arrested may say, "I am so thankful to God." That is praise. But a person who is dying of cancer and in pain may calmly say, "Everything is all right. The Lord doesn't make mistakes. I have peace in my heart." That is "the peace that passes all understanding."[1564]

Colossians 3:8–12, 14

The put-on/take-off terminology of Colossians 3 finds a literal parallel in first-century baptismal practice, where candidates approached the ordinance wearing old clothes. These were stripped off as they entered the waters of baptism, and on surfacing they put on new clothes. The old clothes represented the old life, while the new clothes characterized the new sphere of life and its accompanying behavior changes.[1565]

429

Colossians 3:12–17

In the fable "The Emperor's New Clothes, an unscrupulous con artist, seeking royal favor, promises to provide the emperor with an outfit of clothing that would be very special. So delicate and rare would be the fabric that the clothes would be undetectable to the touch. More importantly, they would be invisible to anyone of poor character or inferior ability. When the emperor received the empty hanger on which his new outfit was supposedly displayed, he could hardly admit not seeing the clothes without impugning his own suitability for royal office. So he admired the clothes (as did his advisors), put them on, and strutted proudly around his kingdom—stark naked!

We Christians can fall into the same trap. In the first part of Colossians 3, Paul said to "take off" practices such as fornication, lying, greed, and so forth. But the point is that we are to "put on" new practices to replace the old ones. Have we really donned those positive attitudes and actions of compassion, kindness, humility?

Sometimes the answer is "No." Instead, we parade around showing off our new clothes of righteousness and refusing to admit the truth: that we are really naked. And we walk about, blinded to the fact that the world is snickering behind our backs because they don't want our kind of clothes![1566]

1 Timothy 1:15–16

A few years ago a T.V. commercial showed a car in which a jeweler in the back seat made a precise cut in a diamond as the car was being driven along a rough road. What was to be our reaction to the commercial? We were supposed to think, "Since I will never need to cut a diamond in my car, this car will be more than sufficient."

In the same way, Paul in this passage is an advertisement for the grace of God. When Paul says he is the worst of sinners, we are supposed to think, "I am not as sinful as he is, so the grace of God will be more than sufficient for me."[1567]

2 Timothy 2:12

"What's it like to know you will one day wear the crown of England?" An American news reporter put that question to Prince Charles. Without hesitation, Charles replied, "Rough!" The future king expanded on this by describing the almost unbelievable discipline needed to groom a person for the throne. He had to become fluent in a number of languages, master history, mathematics, and the sciences, become expert in heraldry, diplomacy, and protocol, as well as serve in the military. Almost every waking moment has been devoted to his grooming. "It's still rough," said the potential monarch. "I really don't have a life of my own."

Normally we think of a prince as growing up with a silver spoon in his mouth and a kingdom for his playground. But it makes more sense to realize that an heir has to be groomed for the task ahead of him.

We, too, are destined to reign—with Christ. Now we are being groomed for the task.[1568]

2 Timothy 4:2

"Preach the Word . . ." says Paul in this charge to Timothy. Hugh Thomsen Kerr put the emphasis correctly: "We are not to preach sociology, but salvation; not economics, but evangelism; not reform, but redemption; not culture, but conversion; not progress, but pardon; not a new social order, but a new birth; not revolution, but regeneration; not renovation, but revival; not resuscitation, but resurrection; not a new organization, but a new creation; not democracy, but the Gospel; not civilization, but Christ; we are ambassadors, not diplomats."[1569]

Hebrews 12:10–11

A new worker's first experience in painting a car held many surprises for him. One of those took place after the car's fresh coat of new paint was totally dry. The novice looked with favor on the finished product, only to see his greatly experienced trainer come by and begin to sand the paint with sandpaper. The apprentice was shocked, even angered at what the other man was doing to the finish, so he began to complain. But the supervisor continued to sand. After he had sanded the entire car he took out his buffer and, using a special compound, began to buff the places he had sanded. The result left the student painter shocked, but pleased. For, you see, the sanding made all the paint even and clean, and the buffing brought out a new shine—so bright when compared with the previous shine that it hardly looked like the same color. What appeared to be destroying the paint was in fact bringing out its deepest shine.

Paul tells us in this passage that God's discipline may not be pleasant, but its aim is to brighten our polish and reveal the shine of our righteousness.[1570]

431

James 2:10

The honor code for the U.S. Military Academy at West Point is as follows: "A cadet does not lie, cheat, or steal; nor tolerate anyone who does."

This honor code is so stringent that even one violation at any time during the four years of study, including even the day before graduation, requires automatic expulsion of the guilty party.[1571]

Assume that a ship is anchored at port with an anchor that has 613 links in its chain, representing the 613 commands in the Mosaic Law. If only one link breaks, the ship will be set adrift, so the 612 links that did hold count for nothing if just one is broken.

Or consider your situation if you had fallen over the edge of a very high cliff and were clinging to a chain for dear life. How many links of that chain must break before you would plummet to your death?

The Mosaic Law is the same, according to James 2:10. If you fail in one point, you might as well have blown it all—you're dead either way.[1572]

James 3:4

On May 21, 1941, the "unsinkable" German battleship, the *Bismarck*, was sighted in the North Atlantic. Immediately planes and ships from the Royal British Navy sped to the scene. As the *Bismarck* headed toward the German-controlled French coast where it would be safe from attack, to the astonishment of all the massive battleship suddenly swung around and reentered the area where the British ships were massed in greatest strength. At the same time, she began to steer an erratic zigzag course, which made it much easier for the British to overtake her. You see, a torpedo had damaged her rudder and without its control the "unsinkable" *Bismarck* was sunk. As the rudder controls a ship, so the tongue controls a person.[1573]

1 Peter 3:7

"Weaker" is a comparative term. In this passage, if the wife is "weaker," then the husband is "weak." This observation hits the nail on the head: an arch is a strength built out of two opposing weaknesses. And that is the secret of a strong and lasting marriage.[1574]

432

1 Peter 4:8

In the middle of one of my parents' more memorable disagreements, my father jumped up from the table, grabbed two sheets of paper, and said to my mother, "Let's make a list of everything we don't like about each other." Mom started writing. Dad glowered at her for a few minutes, and then wrote on his paper. She wrote again. He watched her, and every time she stopped, he would start writing again. They finally finished. "Let's exchange complaints," Dad said. They gave each other their lists. "Give mine back," Mom pleaded when she glanced at his sheet. All down the page Dad had written: "I love you, I love you, I love you." [Cited by Robert L. Thornton.][1575]

1 Peter 5:2–4

A farmer pointed out to a friend his thriving crops and healthy livestock. His companion was especially impressed with the beautiful sheep in the pasture. He had seen the same breed before, but never such attractive animals. Curious, he asked the farmer how he had managed to raise such outstanding sheep. The answer was straightforward but profound: "My friend, I just take very good care of the lambs."[1576]

1 John 1:9

There are two ways to keep a diesel truck running. The first is called "trouble-shoot and repair" and involves waiting for a breakdown and *then* trying to fix the problem. It involves so much down-time, however, that most truckers now use the "preventive maintenance" approach, in which problems are anticipated and thus solved before they occur.

It is good to be reminded by 1 John 1:9 that forgiveness is there when we sin. But how much better to maintain such a life of faith and discipline that the breakdown never occurs![1577]

1 John 2:4

A small boy liked to pull out of the cupboard the paper bags that his mother saved. He would then spread them around the kitchen floor and use them as a playing surface for his toy cars. This was permitted on the condition that he collect the bags and put them away when he was finished playing. One day, his mother found the bags all over the kitchen and the boy in the living room where his father was playing the piano. When she told her son to pick up the bags, there was a short silence. Then his small voice said, "But I want to sing 'Jesus Loves Me.' "

His father took the opportunity to point out that it's no good singing God's praises while you're being disobedient. This passage in the First Epistle of John puts the lesson in much stronger language: "The man who says, 'I know him,' but does not do what he commands is a liar, and the truth is not in him" (1 John 2:4, NIV).[1578]

1 John 2:15

"Loving the created world is not wrong as long as our loving God is not diminished. To love the world and fail to love God would be like a bride, who, being given a ring by her bridegroom, loves the ring more than the bridegroom who gave it. Of course, she should love what the bridegroom gave her, but to love the ring and despise him who gave it is to reject the very meaning of the ring as a token of his love. Likewise, men who love creation and not the creator are rejecting the whole meaning of creation. We ought to appreciate the creation and love the creator because of it." (From Augustine, "Homilies on the first Epistle of John.")[1579]

1 John 2:17

In an address to the Wisconsin State Agriculture Society in 1859, Abraham Lincoln illustrated the profound and tempering effect that change can have on us. He told of an Eastern monarch who gave his counselors an assignment to come up with a truth that would apply to all times and situations. After careful consideration, they returned with this sentence: "And this too shall pass away." Said Lincoln, "How chastening in the hour of pride! How consoling in the hour of affliction."

Centuries before, John made the same point—that the world passes away, but he who does the will of God abides forever (1 John 2:17).[1580]

Jude 23

Those we save, says Jude, are as if snatched from the fire. They must be treated as we would treat a hamburger patty that falls into the hot coals. We must reach in quickly to prevent its further contamination, but we must also guard against personal injury.[1581]

Revelation

A janitor would wait patiently each week for a group of seminarians to finish their basketball game. While he waited, he would study his

Bible. One day, as the seminarians were leaving the gym, they noticed the janitor carefully reading the text in his lap. One young man asked which biblical book was the subject of the janitor's study. The old man answered, "The Book of Revelation." The ballplayer was surprised and asked the janitor if he understood the complicated book. "Oh, yes!" the man answered. "I understand it. It means that Jesus is gonna win!"

And that is a most accurate analysis of the Book of Revelation![1582]

Revelation 3:17

One of Aesop's fables is the story of the dog who saw his image reflected in a pool of water beneath his feet. Though he already had a bone, he was jealous of the bone he saw in the "other" dog's mouth. He opened his jaws to snarl and snatch at the bone's reflection—and of course lost his bone when it fell into the water.

How accurately this pictures the "church in Laodicea"! Not satisfied with the promises of God, the church in this wealthy Roman city sought for and acquired earthly power through wealth. But she had in reality become poor, and in the end her wealth would be denied her.[1583]

General Index

Spanking, 350
Speaking, 1299–1300, 1393, 1397
Speech, 1393–1400, 1573
Spiegelberg, Nancy, 1013
Spiritual armor, 340
Spiritual gifts, 1301–1312, 1554, 1561
Spiritual growth, 1313; evidence of, 1314; source of, 1315–1316
Spiritual pride, 1317
Spiritual warfare, 1318–1320
Spirituality, 492, 765–767
Sports, 149, 182
Spurgeon, C. H., 60, 84, 99, 374, 378, 380–381, 406, 558, 695, 878, 885, 1015, 1149, 1163, 1226, 1495
Stallone, Sylvester, 360
Stanton, Edwin, 950
Starr, Bart, 809
Statues, 181
Status, 1087
Stealing, 52, 502
Steamboat, 989
Stedman, Ray, 503, 891, 1115
Stevenson, Adlai, 222
Stevenson, Robert Louis, 96
Stewardship, 28, 543–565, 1093, 1321–1323, 1576
Stockdale, James, 680
Stoicism, 941
Storms, 956
Strategy, 929
Strauss, Johann, 691
Stress, 1324–1325
Strife, 191, 192
Students, 501, 1055, 1316
Study, 75, 888
Submission, 484, 852
Substitution, example of, 1326–1336
Success, 355, 443, 444, 488, 566–568, 976, 1337–1338; measure of, 1339; suffering and, 1340; testing in, 1341
Suffering, 40, 146, 205–207, 347, 349–351, 429–430, 592, 768, 938–940, 1096, 1175, 1340, 1342–1343, 1482, 1512; reason for, 1344–1353
Suicide, 239, 906–907, 1354
Sunday, 1505
Sunday, Billy, 1398
Surrender, 320
Suspicion, 1355

Swimming, 568
Swindoll, Charles, 852
Symbols, 49, 50
Synoptics, harmony of, 1356

Tact, 421, 1357–1358
Talents, 760, 1301, 1399
Talleyrand-Périgord, Charles M. de, 1138
Taxes, 214, 243, 987
Taylor, Hudson, 120, 428, 902, 951, 1428, 1490
Teaching, 115, 223, 433–434, 952, 1359
Team, 762
Teamwork, 387, 1360–1361
Teenagers, 946, 979
Television, 705, 1362–1364
Temper, 15–19, 21
Temptation, 323, 398, 401, 1203, 1287, 1319, 1365–1368; protection from, 1369; resisting, 1370–1375; testing and, 1376–1377
ten Boom, Corrie, 302, 696, 1349, 1387
Ten Commandments, 7, 924, 1378
Tennyson, Lord Alfred, 818
Tertullian, 802
Testimony, 78
Testing, 1341, 1376, 1379; limits of, 1380; purpose of, 1381–1382
Thankfulness, 248, 714, 1383–1387, 1509
Thanksgiving, 317, 1336
Thant, U., 960
Theodicy, 40, 592
Theology, 368, 1388
Thermodynamics, 849
Thief, 502
Thomas à Kempis, 591
Thomas, John Charles, 684
Thoreau, Henry, 214
Thorn, Stan, 100
Thornton, Robert L., 1575
Thummim and Urim, 1444
Tillich, Paul, 281
Time, 571, 1316, 1389–1391; use of, 1392
Tithing, 623
Tombaugh, Clyde, 949
Tongue, 599–606, 1232, 1393–1394, 1519, 1554, 1573; control of, 1395–1400

Torrey, R. A., 714, 1295
Toscanini, Arturo, 1210
Tournier, Paul, 389
Townsend, Cameron, 895
Tozer, A. W., 1128
Trading stamps, 1119
Tradition, 91, 1401–1403
Transformation, 1111
Translations, 78, 1487
Transportation, 92
Trials, 8, 220, 347, 349–351, 394, 395, 453, 641, 782, 938–940, 956–959, 1092, 1096, 1294–1298, 1324, 1342–1353, 1376, 1379, 1404–1408, 1515, 1539, 1547; benefits of, 1409–1413; God's help in, 1414–1428; response to, 1429–1436
Trinity, 1437
Triumph, 159
Truman, Harry, 732, 757
Trust, 1355
Trustworthiness, 593, 1438
Truth, 316, 648, 775, 941, 1439–1440; response to, 1441; suppressed, 1442
Tsai, Christiana, 1482
Tutankhamen, 704
Twain, Mark, 63, 188, 225, 373, 775, 819

U.S.S. Pueblo, 808
Unbelief, 29
Understanding, lack of, 1443
Unity, 193–204
Urim and Thummim, 1444
Ushers, 684
Ustinov, Peter, 937

Vacation, 1445, 1509
Valley of Death, 311
Values, 1088, 1093–1094
Valusek, John, 1517
Van Buren, Martin, 92
Vanity, 1199–1201, 1446
Versions, 1487
Vesuvius, 482
Vice, 525, 526
Victoria, Queen, 151
Vietnam War, 680
Virtues, 274, 1447
Vision, 1448–1449
Volcano, 996, 1267
Voltaire, 29, 51
Vows, 848, 1450

445

Scripture Index